For My Dear Friend
In Sai
Mavis.
Lots of Love & Light
In your wanderings,
Here, there & every where

Sai Ram
Myra

YOUR LIFE
IS
YOUR MESSAGE

Life Before and After
Sathya Sai Baba

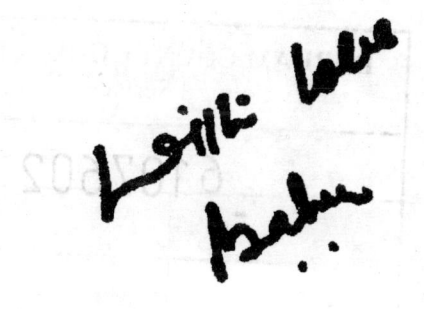

by Charlene Leslie-Chaden
with Syd Chaden

*Title given in interview by Sathya Sai Baba

Copyright © Charlene Leslie-Chaden, 1999

All rights reserved. No part of this book may be reproduced in any form or by any means electronic, photographic or mechanical, including photocopying, recording, taping, or any renewal system, without the written permission of the publisher/author, Charlene Leslie-Chaden, with the exception of brief quotations in literary articles and reviews.

For further informatin, or for additional copies of this book (or the COMPENDIUM) in the USA, please contact:

        Jai Sai Ram
        P.O. Box 900
        Trinidad, Co 81082-0900 USA
        Phone 719 846 -0846
        Fax 719 846 -0847
        E-mail jaisairm@ria.net or jaisairm@rmi.net

Other books by Charlene Leslie-Chaden:
A COMPENDIUM OF THE TEACHINGS OF SATHYA SAI BABA

ISBN 81-86822-86-0

First Edition 1999
Second Edition 2000

Published and Distributed by:
Sai Towers Publishing
23/1142 Vijayalakshmi Colony, Kadugodi
Bangalore 560 067 INDIA
Ph   : (080) 8451648
Fax   : (080) 8451649
E-mail : saitower@vsnl.com
Web : www.saitowers.com

Printed In India on acid-free recycled paper

Printed by:
D. K. Fine Arts Press Pvt. Ltd.
New Delhi 110 052

Table of Contents

Dedication ... v
Introduction ... vi
Acknowledgments ... ix

The Trailer ... 1
My Spiritual Beginnings ... 6
There are No Victims ... 11
Married Life ... 20
My Career, Bob and Robbie ... 24
My Sons ... 27
My Daughter ... 34
Crystal Brook Leslie ... 40
In Retrospect ... 47
Smoking ... 50
Who is Sai Baba? ... 52
Kundalini ... 56
Getting to India ... 58
The Mysterious Phone Calls ... 64
Puttaparthi ... 66
Life on the Ashram ... 72
The Interview ... 79
The Tourists ... 90
Nepal ... 95
Back To 'Reality' ... 102
Becoming Vegetarians ... 103
Trinidad Lake Ranches ... 106
Syd's Near Death Experience ... 108
Our First Miracle at Home ... 110
The Harbinger ... 112
Life After India ... 115
The Moving Experience ... 121
Lessons in Possessions ... 129
Life in the Wilderness ... 131
The Telephone Crucible ... 136
Another Miracle ... 141
Yearning for Baba ... 145

1992 Trip to India	151
Putting the Teachings into Practice	164
Starting a Center	168
1993 India Trip	172
The Ambulance Gurney	173
Getting to Puttaparthi	188
Brindavan 1993	194
Back to Puttaparthi	198
Christmas in Paris	201
Back Home Again	204
First Retreat	207
The COMPENDIUM	211
1994 India Trip	213
The Second Interview	223
Christmas in Puttaparthi	229
The Ring	234
Swami's Workshop	236
The Parel Miracle House	245
Back Home Again	249
Our Center Problems	258
Syd's Birthday Trip	263
Swami's Robe	265
Ian's Second Visit - 1995	269
Vibrations	276
Preparing for 1995 India Trip	278
Trip to India 1995	281
Ladies' Day	286
70th Birthday, November 23, 1995	291
Sending Love	294
After Birthday	297
It's All a Test	301
Another Interview	304
Syd's Illness	310
Christmas 1995	312
Home Again 1996	324
Prayers, Life and Death	326
More Baba Dreams and Leelas	330

Sanjeevini Healing System	335
1996 Jemez Springs Retreat	338
Back to the Book	339
1997 India Trip	341
The Interview and The Compendium	348
Publishing the Compendium	359
Back Home 1997	366
Mother's Death	371
Hennie	375
1998 Trip to India	380
Interview 1998	385
More Life on the Ashram	392
JAI SAI RAM	395
Brindavan 1998	397
Home Again 1998	402
Ian's Visit - Summer of 1998	404
Christmas 1998	407
Facing Death	411
Swami and My Family	416
Goals	419
Bibliography	424

Dedication

I dedicate this book at the Lotus Feet of my
Mother/Father/God,
my Beloved Lord, Bhagavan Sri Sathya Sai Baba,
Who in answer to my fervent prayers,
is leading and guiding me on the path
to the full awareness that
All is God, and that
I AM GOD
too

ॐ

Introduction

This book is the story of my life, before and after finding Bhagavan Sri Sathya Sai Baba. It illustrates how dramatically one's life can change by putting His teachings into practice, along with His guidance, Grace, and His Divine intervention.

While in Puttaparthi during the 70th Birthday celebration in November 1995, I met a lot of people from all walks of life, and from all over the world, and we would often share our 'Baba stories' with each other. A number of people told me I should write a book about my life with Baba and share my experiences with everyone. They also suggested the lessons I learned under Swami's tutelage might be an inspiration to others. It seemed there were signs and messages everywhere telling me the same thing.

Finally, I wrote a letter to Sai Baba asking Him to take the letter from me when He made His walkabouts during 'Darshan', if I should write a book about my life before and after Him. He took the letter. In 1998, I presented Him with an unfinished manuscript during an interview. I was uncertain if I was going in the right direction and was feeling very insecure about whether I should even be writing this book. I desperately needed His help and guidance. He gave me the title for this book, told me to fix it because it was out of balance, and bring it back next time. He did not tell me what was out of balance or what to fix, but I knew He had planted the 'seed', and that I would 'know' after I returned home.

When I began putting my experiences on paper, I had some difficult decisions to make - should I include the suffering I went through? My concern was that some of it may not be pleasant for others to read. I know personally how painful it is for me to hear or read about other people's adversities. Another difficult decision was - should I include the traumatic lessons and experiences I had in the Prashanthi Nilayam Ashram (which translates to Abode of Peace). It is supposed to be a place where one goes to find peace where only devotees of Swami and angels of peace abide, and one would expect that nothing 'bad' could happen there.

I came to the conclusion that it would not be honest of me if I only wrote about the good, when it was both the 'bad' and the 'good' that molded and shaped me into who and where I am today. How can anyone understand how I got from one place to another in the growth process, if they do not know what happened to move me along on the path? Sai Baba says: "People may judge things as good or bad according to their own predilections. But for God all things are the same. In this world nothing will appear bad if one views it from the Divine point of view. Seen from the worldly point of view, there will be differences of good and bad." SS May 1995 P 133 (See Bibliography)

Another point I would like to stress is that everything that has happened to me is a result of my own karma. Unless you have similar karma you will not have the same experiences that I did. Karma is what you create with every thought, word and deed that you think, say and do. Depending upon your motives, it can be good or bad karma. But whatever it is, rest assured that it will come back to you, sometimes tenfold. Payback time can be very difficult, or very rewarding. There are no victims, although we sometimes see ourselves and others in that role. Even the child who is raped and murdered is not a victim. Nor is the infant starving to death in Africa. They are merely working off their karmic debt. I know it sounds cold, but it is Truth. Simply put, what comes around, goes around. This does not mean we should not have compassion for those who suffer; rather that we should help them how and whenever we can. Sai Baba says, "Your heart must melt in compassion when the eye sees another person suffering. That is the sign of a Satvic individual. The Thamasic individual will be indifferent.....The Rajasic man will rush to punish the person who caused the suffering and might even forget to relieve the misery of the person affected!" SSS Vol IX P 191

Karma accumulates from this life and all the lives we have previously experienced. Some 'bad' people have accumulated a lot of good karma and that is why 'good' things happen to 'bad' people, and vice versa. So when you read of my difficult youth, or my negative experiences in the Ashram, please keep in mind that these were my experiences, experiences that I needed to have, to work on and work through, so I could move along on the spiritual path. It took me a lot of years to understand this after being taught otherwise by society.

Some of my experiences were of major importance to the content of this book, while others may seem insignificant to some readers. I feel that there may be lessons to be learned from any of these experiences.

It is my belief that our karma has been accelerated and that we are rushing along on a fast track so that we can move into the Golden Age that Sathya Sai Baba has promised to usher in for us. Knowing that, it may help us to more easily understand and accept the karma in our lives. If we can see and accept every incident or person in our life as a gift from God and an opportunity to work off our karma, then we have come a long way on the road to equanimity and eventually liberation. I found that there is a light at the end of the tunnel if you do your part and follow Sai Baba's teachings. When you surrender and turn your life over to Him, He helps you move along the path with great speed and also helps to ameliorate your karma.

"When devotees surrender their lives to God and obey Him, He takes the full responsibility and cares for his devotees even to the smallest details." CWSSB P 131

In many cases, the reader will see that I have quoted from my journal. I did this because what I wrote while I was going through some experiences more clearly reflected my feelings and thoughts at the time, and I am not the same person I was then. These quotes also help to demonstrate the spiritual growth process I went through.

The reader will also note that quotes from Sai Baba's discourses and writings have been interwoven throughout the text, most of which have been taken from A COMPENDIUM OF THE TEACHINGS OF SATHYA SAI BABA. This was designed to give the reader a better understanding of His teachings as they relate and apply to experiences and lessons in everyday life.

May you all experience Swami's LOVE, Blessings and Grace in every moment of your life.

ॐ

ACKNOWLEDGMENTS

My deepest gratitude goes to my Beloved Lord, Bhagavan Sri Sathya Sai Baba for plucking me out of the hole I had dug myself into and helping me find my way on the path, and for all Your loving guidance. I will be eternally grateful for all the lessons and experiences You have given me, and the many blessings of Your Grace in times of great need, including the many times You saved my life, and lifted me out of the path of danger.

To my beloved and wonderful husband, Syd, my very grateful thanks for everything you have been to me and done for me. I am genuinely grateful for the input you provided for this book, and all the time you spent proofreading the manuscript and the meaningful suggestions and support you gave throughout the process.

To all who have participated in my life and my learning experiences, thank you from the bottom of my heart - without you, I would not have arrived at where I am today.

The Trailer

The Santa Ana winds were beginning to blow in off the desert, bringing in another hot day in the Summer of 1989 in Southern California. I closed the windows in our rented home before it got any warmer inside, and turned on the air-conditioner. My day had been full of packing and putting together several salads and other dishes to take with us on our long 1,100 mile drive to Colorado. Syd, my husband, was picking up our newly purchased 'used' camp trailer from the dealer. The trailer had all the amenities of a home, and although Syd was not much in favor of the idea of owning or towing a trailer, I was looking forward to using it on our trip.

We were building our dream home in the foothills of the beautiful Sangre de Cristo mountain range, about eight miles Southwest of Trinidad, Colorado. Trinidad is a small old mining town near the New Mexico border, and deep in the heart of cattle country. The restaurants in this small town probably had never had a vegetarian come in to eat before, nor did they understand what a vegetarian is, so there was nothing on their menus for us to eat. At an Italian restaurant in the area, we explained that we were vegetarians, and asked for pasta with just plain marinara sauce on it. The waitress said that they were busy in the kitchen and she wasn't sure if the chef would have time to strain out all the meat for us. On another night, we ordered a vegetarian pizza at a pizza house that was part of a major national chain of pizza restaurants. Our mouths were watering with anticipation when our 'Veggie Pizza' arrived, but one bite revealed a sauce made with hamburger hidden beneath the vegetables. We tried a vegetarian sandwich at a local 'sub' shop, and were disgusted to find bits of hamburger in it, which we surmised came off the grill they heated the buns on. The reaction of the people to our requests for vegetarian foods in this community ranged from amusement to hostility, but the thought of compromising our vegetarian diet never occurred to us.

Knowing of our frustration, the man who was overseeing the construction of our home, assured us he knew of a place we could eat safely, so he and his wife escorted us to dinner one evening. We scanned the menu at their favorite restaurant, but there was nothing for us, so we ordered a variety of vegetable dishes the waitress had told us would be safe. We were disappointed to find that the green beans were made with bacon, while another dish had chicken broth in it, and the salad came complete with chopped egg and bacon bits. They consider it good home country cooking. Thus, while in Trinidad, we were reduced to things like snacks, or making sandwiches from our ice chest, or ordering a safe, plain baked potato and salad from the hotel restaurant, all of which got old after a few days.

"It is a fact that plants also have life like animals. But animals are endowed with mind, and nervous systems too while the plants do not possess the same. The animals cry and weep when they are being killed. It is not the case with plants; as such, equating killing of animals and destruction of plants is faulty logic. Further, killing the animals and eating their flesh leads to the creeping or dissemination of the animal qualities and behavior in to the man (meaning that man acquires the beastly qualities by eating animal flesh). Thus follows our acquiring the beastly qualities - tamasic nature - of the buffalos or the sheep. Hence, meat eating should be discarded. Food conditions the nature of the mind. Mind guides the thinking. Thinking results in action.....meat eating leads to beastly actions and the concomitant evil effects." SSAL P 132

Our plan was to have the shell of our home framed out and roofed by a local builder, and then Syd and I would finish the inside ourselves. This would be the fulfillment of a life-long dream that we both had, even long before we met. So whenever we could get away, we would drive or fly to Colorado and put in a week or two working on the house. After several trips, being a practical person, I realized that staying in a hotel was beginning to mount up in expenses that would be put to better use in building our home. And, after the many 'eating out' tragedies, I came up with the idea of buying a camp trailer. In my younger years, I owned a camp trailer in which I used to take my children camping nearly every weekend. There were many fond memories of the joy of waking up in a campground surrounded by Mother Nature's finest, complete with the aroma of pine trees, fresh air, wild animals, and campfires.

Syd, who enjoyed the comfort and privacy of a hotel room, was opposed to buying a trailer from the beginning, but I relentlessly broached the trailer idea at every opportunity. I reminded him that there was a State Park complete with campground just across the lake, and only a few miles' drive from our 36 acre lot, where we would have running water, flush toilets, hot showers and electricity in our trailer, luxuries we did not yet have at our building site. With a kitchen, I could prepare vegetarian breakfasts and light suppers, and we could do sandwiches while we worked. Eventually, Syd wore down and agreed to buy a camp trailer, but he let me know he was still not at all happy about it.

Thus it was that we set out that very warm Friday afternoon with our Chevrolet Suburban towing a 21 foot camp trailer. It had taken all day for Syd to pick up the trailer, because the dealer had insisted on installing a special braking system in the Suburban when he learned we were driving out that afternoon for Colorado. Syd also had to undergo an orientation session with all of the trailer's functions, like emptying the sewage, filling the water tanks, operating the propane refrigerator, heater and stove, etc.. He was not in the best of moods when he arrived home, but he joined me in loading the refrigerator and cupboards in the trailer and then insisted on driving to try out his newly learned skills and procedures.

We entered Interstate 15 in five lanes of extremely heavy traffic, that was moving along at more than 60 miles an hour. It seemed as though everyone else in San Diego County had the same idea - 'Let's get out of town this weekend'. Soon we were going down hill through an area known to be very windy, an area where the wind has overturned large trucks. A strong gust of wind came up and we felt the trailer begin to sway back and forth. Syd started using the special braking system as he had been instructed to do, but the trailer swayed even more as we continued down hill. When we started to gain speed going down hill, Syd tried the car's regular brakes as well, but it was already too late. The trailer had begun to spin, and was now going completely out of control.

The next thing that happened was almost indescribable. Everything suddenly went silent and seemed to be happening in slow motion. When the 21 foot trailer and Suburban began spinning around in all that traffic, we either dematerialized, or we were flying through mid-air, because we incredibly missed hitting any of the vehicles we had been surrounded by. There was no sound of the tires screeching or squealing as we spun around. It all happened either in mid-air, or in another dimension. When we finished our 180° spin, we found ourselves, trailer and all, sitting perfectly parallel to the traffic on the shoulder of the highway, which was just barely wide enough for us. It was as though we had been picked up from the highway, turned around, and set down on the shoulder. We were now facing on-coming traffic, with about a 400 foot, steep drop just inches away from the driver's side of the car and trailer. We sat there in silence for a long time, both of us attempting to recover from the shock and assimilate the inconceivable experience we just had. I felt an unexplainable peace come over me and relaxed into it. Syd seemed to be caught up in the intensity of the moment.

Somehow our nearly 40 foot combined length of Suburban and trailer, completely spun around in five lanes of heavy, fast moving traffic, without hitting any of the other cars and trucks, without the trailer jack-knifing or overturning, without us going over the side of the mountain, and without either of us being hurt. Syd and I both felt the presence of Sai Baba there at the scene. And we agreed that only God could have performed such a miracle! He had demonstrated His Divine Will and saved us from what otherwise would have been a great tragedy.

From that moment on, I was totally and unequivocally convinced that the God that I had been searching for since early childhood was the one we knew as Sai Baba, our spiritual teacher whom we had found in India. Our friends, the Patels, had told me they believed that Sai Baba was God, but it took a major incident such as this to convince me. I can't begin to describe the joy I experienced from this realization, and what it meant to me. My search was over! Our Creator lives on Earth! And He had just saved our lives!

"You will understand me only through my work. That is why sometimes in order to reveal who I am, I show you my 'visiting card'--something you call a miracle. Know the secret of the mystery and carry out the duties I assign you." TOSSSB P 58

All of this new realization was going through my mind, over and over as I sat there, until Syd finally spoke to me. I don't remember what he said, but it brought me back to reality. We discussed what had just happened and then Syd, although still shaken, decided that he should go inside the trailer to see if there was any damage. I continued to sit in the Suburban and ponder this turn of events.

As I sat there in the passenger seat, I noticed that as the traffic was going by, nobody seemed to be looking at us. It was as though we were invisible! There we were, totally out of place, sitting on the shoulder facing the wrong way with oncoming, heavy traffic rushing by us and nobody gave any indication that they were aware of us. I watched as several highway patrol vehicles drove by, and they didn't pay any attention to us either. They were just several feet away, close enough that I could look into their eyes, yet there was no recognition of our odd situation. One might have thought they would come over to see if we were all right, or give us a ticket for parking on the shoulder facing the wrong direction, or ??? It seemed like they were in our illusion, but we weren't in theirs. Could we be in another dimension where we could see everybody else, but they can't see us? Is this how Sai Baba performs these miracles???

Syd eventually returned to the car, still somewhat shaken, and said, "Let's get out of here and go back home!". By then, I had moved over into the driver's seat and told him we might have a long wait. We obviously couldn't move until there was enough of a break in the traffic for all forty feet of us to pull out and make another 180° turn so that we were driving in the same direction as everyone else.

While we waited, Syd described the mess he had just cleaned up in the trailer. Somehow the refrigerator door had come open and all of the food I had prepared had been thrown everywhere in the kitchen area. It seemed a very minor event compared to what could have happened, and I wasn't the least bit upset. If this incident had occurred five years previous, I would have been terribly distraught and angry. But Sai Baba had been helping me to overcome all that inner turbulence since He came into my life.

Within about fifteen minutes, there was a large opening in the traffic, which was another miracle in itself at that time of day. I pulled out into the road, using all five lanes to make my U-Turn, and didn't stop again until late that night, when we were well on our way to Colorado. We sat in silence as I drove across the desert. This wasn't uncommon as we both enjoy the peace of silence. I don't know what Syd was thinking, but I was in a blissful state with this new realization that Sai Baba is God.

We later learned that the special brakes, which were the probable cause of this incident, had not been installed properly. The dealer in California offered to fix them, but once we arrived in Colorado, the trailer was never to return.

My Spiritual Beginnings

For as long as I can remember, I was always in search of God and the meaning of life. There was no religion practiced in my home when I was a child, although my mother's mother was a very devout, religious fundamentalist. But I barely knew her because she lived 2,000 miles away in Southern Illinois until I was about 13, when she and Gramps moved to California to be near us. My mother was their only child. They bought a home several blocks from us and for a few years we saw them often. I had to pass by their home on the way to and from my junior high school, and often went there to have lunch with them. My grandmother would prepare a plate full of things like cottage cheese, sliced tomatoes and cucumbers, potato chips, and a fruit for desert; never with meat. Sometimes she would invite and take me to her Nazarene Church on Sundays. But, she never spoke about her religious beliefs to me.

Unfortunately, Grandma didn't live more than a few years after their move. She spent her last few months in a nursing hospital, her body ridden with cancer. None of the family was with her when she passed on, but her nurses said that just before she left her body, she sat up with a blissful smile on her face and said, "Jesus, you are here!". As far as I know, my mother never had anything to do with religion or spirituality until the last years of her life.

Both of my parents, (mother and stepfather), were very bright and appeared as normal as anybody else to the outsider. After I left home, my mother once took an employment test for the State of California and got the highest score one could possibly get.

During my youth and for as long as I can remember, my mother and stepfather were deeply entrenched in Egyptology, hypnotherapy and most anything to do with the paranormal. Most people saw my stepfather as an average blue collar worker. He worked as an electrician foreman on the night shift for the railroad for 25 years, then for the government until he retired, and I am certain his coworkers never had a clue as to what went on in his private life. He had been offered promotions time and time again, but he would have had to give up his beloved night shift and go to work during the day, which he refused to do.

I can recall when my stepfather called my brother and his wife, and myself and my husband together one night in the early 1960's, so he could tell us about himself. My mother was there with us, and supported the claims he made to us. He said he was not from this planet, and that where he came from, the inhabitants did not experience emotions as we humans do. Falling in love was foreign to them, and something he had to 'learn' how to do. He reminded me of the time he had shown me the second degree burns on the backs and palms of his hands that he had awakened with one morning years ago, when I still lived at home. He now explained that this was a form of punishment from his superiors on his planet for not following their directions when he became emotionally involved with my mother and family.

Once a year, he told us, the beings from his planet who were residing on planet earth, would come together in their natural form up in the mountains for a reunion and replenishment of some sort. This explained his absence each year from the home for a week or two. I asked him what they did during this 'reunion', but he said he could not elaborate further.

My stepfather told us that he had been on the moon, and described to us what it was like up there and how he yearned to return someday. I asked him what his natural form was and if he would please show us what he looked like. He told me it would frighten us too much to see him that way, but he did bring forth a white three foot long 'feathery' looking thing that resembled pampas grass, which he said was part of his natural form.

He explained that he had taken a previous incarnation as one of the pharaohs on Earth and that my mother was his principal wife at that time. I recalled that there were all kinds of reproductions of artifacts in their home symbolizing this period of history.

Several years before the night of his revelation to us, I came into possession of an antique brass plate and my stepfather claimed that he could read the hieroglyphic type symbols on it. He translated it as a poem about the sun rising from the east, casting its glory on all it touched, yielding flowers and other fauna with its power. I asked where he had learned how to read these symbols, and he told me that a very long time ago, an old Indian (from India) had taught him this very ancient language. He never said so, but I understood him to mean this occurred in another life.

He concluded that night by telling us that one of us, (my three step-siblings and I), had been instilled with some special powers, but he refused to elaborate further, suggesting that we would find out someday. He elicited a promise from us that we not share this discussion with anyone so long as he was alive. I tried talking to my brother after that night about his claims, but he refused to discuss it with me, and acted as if he had wiped it from his memory. My stepfather never mentioned it again. When my mother died in 1997, my sister found a letter in her belongings that my stepfather had written before his death in 1983, about what he had told us that night. But he never mentioned which one of the four of us was the one with special powers. My mother had written, "This is the truth!", on the letter and signed her statement. I had completely forgotten all about that night long ago, and the reason I am sharing this with the reader is so that you can understand the unusual background I came from.

My step-father's human family had abandoned their Jewish heritage years before when it was not safe to be a Jew. Thus he was raised without practicing any religion, and claimed that he was an agnostic, which he described as believing in a higher power, but not necessarily that there was "a" God. My mother never made a statement about her religious beliefs, and seemed to adopt my stepfather's beliefs as hers.

But, I knew there was a God somewhere, and never doubted for a moment that I would find Him someday. From the time when I was about five or six or years old, I would ask my friends and neighbors to take me to their different churches as I had a very strong desire to find God and the meaning of life. As a child, I was active in a number of different fundamental churches. I tried them all Each Sunday I would get up early and either go with my friends or alone to one church or another in the neighborhood. When I became active in one of the churches, I occasionally would take one or more of my siblings along, hoping I could get someone else in the family interested in God. I would stay with a church until it became clear they had no answers to my questions.

"Having got this human birth as a result of virtuous deeds done in so many births, if you do not try to obtain the knowledge of the Soul, it is like a persistent scar to this life." Prashanthi April 1971 P 17

I studied the Bible fervently, but rather than finding answers to my questions, my efforts only created more questions. In Sunday School, we often memorized the books of the Bible, and a new Bible verse every week We were given prizes or award certificates for this process. I found that the interpretations of the Bible varied according to the church or minister or the Sunday school teacher, but none of them ever made sense to me. There simply was no logic to their teachings. Nor were any of my questions ever answered: What is the meaning of life? What are we here for? Why are we here for only one life? How can you call a newborn baby a sinner? Where were we before we were born? Why does God let so many bad things happen to good people? Why can only Christians go to Heaven when there are so many people in this world who aren't Christian? Why do different churches teach that theirs is the only church you can attend, and their teachings are the only Truth you should believe if you don't want to go to Hell?

"There is no separate God for different castes, for different religions. It is not broad-mindedness if you go on criticizing some other deity, which is not your chosen one. This is all wrong." DD 1987 P 146

"Let the different Faiths exist, let them flourish and let the glory of God be sung in all the languages and in a variety of tunes. Respect the differences between the Faiths and recognize them as valid as long as they do not extinguish the flame of unity." TEOL P 215

My questions were endless and I was given no logical answers to any of them. And I found that I could not intellectually or spiritually accept that if you just 'believe that Jesus died for your sins', you will be saved from Hell and given eternal life. Something within me knew there was a TRUTH that they were not telling us. I realize today that the teachers in the churches meant well and really believed their teachings, but that they could not share with me what they did not know or understand. I never gave up my search for the TRUTH, but I did put it on the back burner occasionally as my career and family took precedence.

As a young mother, I turned to the church off and on for comfort and support, and to introduce religion into my children's life. I was still in search of answers, but what I found in the churches was an increasing trend toward filling their coffers with donations and their pews with more people to fill the coffers. I got a totally different view from when I was in Sunday School as a child. To me, it was disgusting. The sermons were sometimes boring, and often related to helping the church grow. It appeared to me that Church had become more of a social event every Sunday, rather than the spiritual reunion with God that I was searching for. The women seemed to be more interested in what they were wearing or gossiping about others, than in God. The men were occupied with making business connections, or planning their next golf game. If God was to be found, it wasn't here.

There are No Victims

I was the only issue of my mother and father's marriage. They divorced while I was still a toddler, and my mother immediately remarried, so that the only father I knew or remembered during my youth was my stepfather. I was about ten years old when my mother sat me down and told me that the man I had always called Daddy was really my stepfather, and that I had a real father who had remarried and two more brothers living in Northern California. At that age, it seemed like a story I might have read in a book, like a fairy tale, and since I could not picture them or touch them, they didn't really exist. When I asked when I could meet them, I was told that the possibility of my ever seeing them was very remote. So, I filed them in the back of my mind and went back outside to play.

After their marriage, my mother and stepfather quickly had three children together, a son and two daughters. As I look back on my childhood, I never really felt like I belonged in that household. My mother was a strange person who never learned how to love and was rarely there for us children, physically or emotionally. She never had more than an occasional part time job, but she was always out gallivanting. My stepfather worked nights by choice, I am sure to escape the duties of fatherhood, so we only saw him occasionally on weekends if he chose to stay home.

An appropriate name for me as a child might have been Cinderella, (except for the fact that my stepsisters were pretty and sweet). It was my duty from an early age to get my brother and sisters up in the morning, feed and dress them, make and pack their lunches, comb their hair and get them off to school, while my mother slept in with my father. At night, I was often their babysitter and was responsible to cook dinner for us too. Doing the dishes was always my job, as were most of the chores around the house, 'because I was the oldest'.

When I was young I never felt sorry for myself. I just understood and accepted that this was the way things were and I must have done something to deserve it. Life was just plain difficult for me at home. My classmates made fun of me at school because I was dressed so badly. My mismatched clothes often came from second hand shops, while my sisters were dressed in clothes with well known labels. Because I had had polio when I was a toddler, my mother bought old ladies shoes for me to accommodate my arch supports. I yearned for sandals or saddle oxfords like the other kids wore, but this was my mother's dictate, which I often felt was to punish me for taking up space in the home of her new family.

There was one occasion that my desire to fit in at school got the best of me, so, at nine years old, I stole five dollars from my mother's hiding place and bought a beautiful pair of black patten leather sandals. I made up a story for my family that I was crossing the street when a box fell out of the back of a truck with these beautiful shoes in them. Similar to Pinnochio, my feet grew so fast that I was only able to wear them with comfort for a short while.

Around my thirteenth birthday, my mother bought a lovely new red dress for me in exchange for the money she owed but never paid me for babysitting my siblings every night. I proudly wore it to school the next day. This was the cause of an incident that was forever imprinted on my mind. One of my classmates said to me, "That's a pretty dress, but it's too nice for the likes of you.". A part of me died right there on the spot, but it taught me a good lesson too. As a result of the pain I experienced, it strengthened my resolve to never, ever purposely hurt another individual.

But the worst part of my childhood happened late at night. My stepfather would slip into my bedroom upon returning from his night shift job, often smelling of alcohol. He had been abusing me sexually for a long time, when one night my mother walked into my bedroom, and asked my father, "What in the hell is going on here?". He told her to go back upstairs and then extracted a promise from me to never tell her what was really happening. He somehow made me feel as if I was an active participant, which I never was physically. It was obvious that she knew the dark truth of what was really happening, and I learned to resent her because she never did anything to stop this travesty going on in my childhood. Instead, things deteriorated and she treated me worse than ever before, and seemed to blame me for what was happening to me.

As soon as school let out for the summer after that incident, I ran away from home with my girlfriend who was 15 at the time. We caught a ride with a friend of hers to Las Vegas. I was only 14, but looked older than most my age. I found a job in a restaurant, and things were going fine for me. I never missed home for one minute and never planned to return.

The reason we chose Las Vegas was because my girlfriend had a boyfriend stationed in the Air Force there. We had rented a room with kitchen privileges right across the street from the Las Vegas Police Department. But, things took a drastic turn after several months. My girlfriend got married and then called her parents. She told them where we were, and they contacted my parents. She now had a husband and I am sure the two of them did not want to be saddled with the responsibility of a runaway 14 year old living with them.

Shortly after her marriage, my parents found me and took me back home. On the long drive home, my mother promised to get some therapy to help her become a better mother, but to my knowledge, she never did. They both promised that life would be better for me once we got home, and things were for a short time. But life soon returned to 'normal' with my stepfather's sexual abuse at night, and my mother's emotional and sometimes physical abuse during the day.

When I was 15, I became engaged to be married, and our

wedding was held when I was 16 and just entering my senior year in high school. Because he was in the Coast Guard and stationed in Alameda, we moved there and that is where I finished school. I really loved my new husband, Monty, who was 20 years old at the time of the ceremony, so it was not just to escape from home that I married at such a young age. I never really had a childhood, and part of my reasoning was that if I was going to raise somebody's children, they might as well be my own. And, I really had this terrible, desperate yearning and need to be loved by someone, and I knew that Monty loved me too.

Regarding the question why is a certain person born to certain parents: "Karmic debt is the reason for that. Your actions and samskaras (karmic debts) make you beholden to certain people. You are indebted to them and this debt has to be repaid at sometime or the other. The debt need not be merely financial. It could be that you did something to a certain person or he did something to you. The damage has to be repaired and the debt has to be canceled. If it is left unrepaired or uncanceled in this birth, it has to be set right in the next. This is what is meant by karmic debt. It is the main factor which decides why, where, when and how you will be re-born.

"In the case of a certain person being born to certain parents, Karmic debt can work in three ways - the child has a karmic debt owing towards the parents, the parents have a karmic debt towards the child; or a mutual karmic debt exists between the parents and child which has to be repaid." SSAV P 42

      I never talked to anybody of the sexual abuse I experienced as a child until I was in therapy during my thirties. I had no really close friends when I was young and I don't think I would have told them about this dreadful secret of mine even if I had. There was one junior high school teacher who noticed that things weren't right with me, and when she asked what was wrong, I told her without elaborating that I did not have a normal childhood. She called my mother in for a conference, but my mother assured her it was just my imagination and that I tended to exaggerate.

      When I reached my early twenties, I realized that my mother was not the ideal role model. She was one of the most negative people I have ever known in this life. Unfortunately I had already recognized many of her negative characteristics and traits imprinted in my own personality. I have spent the remainder of my life working on eliminating them.

It was many years before I could forgive my mother for not doing anything to stop the abuse that was going on, and blaming me for it instead. For a long time, I resented her as much as she resented me. After I left home, I realized she never did love me because she continued to carry on her vendetta against me throughout my life. There was a time when I tried my best to be friends with her, but I was continually pulling her knife out of my back. It got to a point where I had to ask myself if I needed this person in my life, and when I was in my forties, I decided the answer was no and stopped all communications with her.

When I look back now, I realize she didn't have a lot of choices in those early days, and I rationalized some reasons why things happened the way they did. If she put the blame on me, then it was not her fault or responsibility. Then she could play the role of 'victim' and my stepfather would give her extra attention to make it up to her, which he did. Or if she chose to see it as just her imagination, maybe it would go away. If she did anything about confronting my stepfather, he might have left her alone with four children to support. My mother was extremely intelligent, but her logic and actions were that of a young teenager, as she never matured emotionally.

Mother never learned how to distinguish truth from fiction, and eventually came to believe her own lies. She became addicted to watching the daily soap operas on television. I can remember visiting her during the day and she would talk about the characters in her soap operas as though they were real people who were experiencing real situations. She would be angry with the 'villains', and feel sorry for the 'victims'. Her life was like a soap opera.

My stepfather was basically considered a good person. He was a kind, compassionate man who was always there to help when his friends or family called out to him. I remember he was often fixing someone's car or rewiring their home in his spare time, or helping them move, or whatever was needed. I recall one time in my childhood when I had a terrible toothache. Most of the teeth in my mouth were rotten by the time I was fourteen years old, and I was deathly afraid of the dentist my mother had chosen for us because he seemed to enjoy inflicting pain on us. Mother had told me it was my choice whether I suffered or went to this dentist. My stepfather found me crying in pain in my bedroom after missing several days of school. After mother told him what she told me, he made an appointment with an oral surgeon and saw to it that I was taken care of painlessly.

In 1978 I quit my job of 18 years and moved to Hawaii to start a new life, taking my 18 year old daughter, Cyndi (a pseudonym), and leaving my parents and family and friends behind. Two years later, my parents followed me to Hawaii, taking up residence in an apartment in the same building I had been living in.

In a fit of bitter and vicious anger, my mother brought the subject of my stepfather's abuse up with me for the first time when I was 42 years old. She was like a deranged maniac in her abusive attack on me, playing the role as though it was from one of her soap operas. She actually accused me of having an affair with her husband when I was a child. She told everyone in the apartment building who would listen to her about what "I did to her", just as though it had happened yesterday. In further retaliation, she attempted to seduce the man I was seeing at the time and told him several outright fabrications about me, hoping to drive a wedge between us. He came to me in tears asking what kind of family I belonged to. I realized at that point that nothing I could do or say would ever change her immature attitude toward life and her malevolence toward me.

Whenever I thought of my mother after that, for years, I initially vacillated between anger and disappointment. After overcoming the emotions of replaying old tapes, I would picture her as a lost child and send her love. I also would say a prayer for her, with the hope that our karma would be finished. When I learned later about karma, I understood that she was in my life to help me work out my karma, as well as hers. In short, I tried everything I could think of to forgive her and put this behind me.

"When you talk of karma in the context of birth and re-birth, you must know that the term karma does not mean only action. When there is an action, there is always a reaction. So, Karma with respect to birth and rebirth refers to the chain of action and reaction.....when I talk of 'reaction', I do not mean the result of action. What I mean is your reaction to the result; the response or the manner in which you receive the fruit of action. It is important for you to understand this because it is not action itself which causes rebirth, but the reaction.....You feel happy and elated when the result is good; you feel unhappy and dejected when the result is bad. These emotional responses set off further desires and impulses which inflate or deflate the ego. This in turn leads to more action, and action results in reaction and thus a never-ending chain of action - reaction - rebirth is produced. The desires and impulses remain with you even after death. They are so strong that you are born into this world again and again in order to fulfill them. As long as desires remain, rebirth is unavoidable." SSAV P 36

My parents returned to the Mainland to close out their affairs once they decided to make Hawaii their permanent home. In a drunken state while attempting to light a welding torch, my stepfather was seriously burned over eighty percent of his body in 1981. It was questionable whether he would survive. I flew back to California to see him and told him I forgave him as he lay there in a semi-comatose state in the hospital's burn unit. I wanted to at the time, but I don't think I really felt forgiveness of this man who had stolen my innocence and my childhood. However, I did not want any karma left with him if he did not survive, and I continued to work on the forgiveness issue within. He understood karma and reincarnation, so I suggested to him that he had to get well so that he could finish his karma with mother in this life, or he would have to come back and do it all over again with her. I knew he heard me because he winced. Theirs had not been a happy marriage with my mother's bitter jealousy, constant whining and immaturity, and manipulating ways, and his alcoholism and many affairs on the side.

Just before I returned to my home in Hawaii, he slipped into a deep coma and remained that way until I stopped to see him on my way to my new life in Alaska six months later. The family had told him I was coming to see him and he came back to consciousness several days before I arrived and had been moved from the burn unit to a rehabilitation unit. He was not the same person anymore and seemed to be very docile, groggy and out of it from his long sleep. He could not move without help as his muscles had deteriorated. But he did seem to recognize me and we chatted briefly in my mother's presence. She would not let me see him alone. It was the last time I saw him alive.

My stepfather had been weaned from his addiction to alcohol while he was in a coma by being tube-fed alcohol in progressively reduced amounts each day until they stopped giving it to him altogether. I don't think he had drawn a sober breath for many years before he was burned. He was extremely inebriated the morning he was trying to light a butane torch with a cigarette lighter and was set on fire when the torch exploded. His lifelong addiction to cigarettes was gone as well when he recovered. He joined the Mormon church and became a very different person from the father we knew as children. According to my sisters, it was as though somebody else inhabited his body. He also made arrangements so that when he died, my mother would be taken care of financially. Several days after he finalized those arrangements, he quietly died with a smile on his face while my mother was out shopping.

Once I understood and realized that it was only due to my own karma that I went through this difficult childhood, I was finally able to reach the point deep within where I could really forgive both my mother and stepfather. This was not easy for me, because for a long time every time I thought of my mother I became filled with deep seated anger, and when I thought of my stepfather, I was filled with resentment for his abuse and use of me. But when I realized that there really are no victims; that everything that happened to me must have been a result of my own actions in another life, I reminded myself of this whenever I would think of my parents or childhood. It was then easy to move into a state of forgiveness. Eventually, I was able to remain in that state of forgiveness and the resentment disappeared. My parents were only instruments to help me get where I am today, and I would not trade my life with Sai Baba, my true Mother and Father, for anything.

"Only a person who has this Kshama (attitude of forgiveness) can be considered to be endowed with sacred love. This cannot be learned from textbooks. Nor can it be acquired from preceptors nor from any one else. It is to be cultivated by oneself in times of difficulties, trials and tribulations that one is forced to meet. Only when we face problems and difficulties that cause grief and misery this quality of forbearance and forgiveness has the scope for taking root. When you are confronted with problems and difficulties you should not get upset, and become victims of depression which is a sign of weakness. In such situation, you should bring tolerance and an attitude of forgiveness into play and should not get agitated giving rise to anger, hatred and revengeful attitude. You are embodiments of strength and not weakness. Therefore, in times of despair, you should be filled with feeling of forbearance and be ready to forgive and forget. This quality of Kshama or forgiveness is the greatest power for a human being. If one loses this quality, he becomes demonic." SS February 1994 P 49

I have met many women, and some men over the years who were sexually abused when they were children, and they were still harboring anger, hate, malevolence, resentment and lots of pain. Holding on to any of these emotions is deadly to the body and only impedes your spiritual growth. It is estimated that one in four girls and one in five boys has been sexually abused in their childhood. This has created a lot of emotional cripples in the world, but it has also provided opportunities for people to learn how to let go and grow spiritually.

Forgiveness is the answer. Love and forgiveness. And accepting the responsibility for one's own karma created in a former life, rather than blaming the abuser, is the key to forgiveness. It helps one to see the abuser as coming into your life to help you work out your karma. **There are no victims.** Everything that happens to a person is the result of something they did in this life or a past life, and it is only an opportunity to work out their karma, which is what one must do to keep from returning to the birth and death cycle.

One of Sai Baba's devotees, Isaac Tigrett, said that he once asked Baba why he had such a miserable and difficult childhood. Swami told him, "To soften your heart!".

Married Life

Not long after Monty and I married, I learned he was an abusive alcoholic. After he was discharged from the Coast Guard, we moved to Oregon where his family lived. My first child, Mark, was born there when I was 18 while his father was out drinking himself senseless in a bar. He was a good man and a very loving person, except when he was drinking. Early in the marriage, I accepted the fact that the man I married was not going to be able to support me and our son, so I found a job when Mark was barely a month old working in an escrow office.

I moved back to California after our second son, Kirk, was born, upon the advice of my dear friend, who was also my mother-in-law. She could see that our marriage was doomed because of her son's alcohol abuse. Her husband had also been an abusive alcoholic, but she stayed with him throughout the nightmare while raising their three sons. He became a 'dry alcoholic' when the boys were in their teens. I believe that since all three of their sons turned out to be alcoholics, she wanted her grandchildren to have a better chance at life. I had no idea when I boarded that bus on December 31, 1959, heading back to California, that I was pregnant for the third time.

Monty returned to California to try and resurrect our marriage when he learned I was pregnant again. He had stopped drinking, and promised to never start up again. We both still loved each other, and with a third child soon to be born, I felt we should give it another try. Most of Monty's drinking bouts were shared with one or both of his brothers in Oregon, and with leaving them behind, I hoped he would leave his drinking behind also. Monty got a job and we began living a normal happy life together.

Unfortunately, our happy reunion was short lived, as his youngest brother moved to California unexpectedly several months later, with his wife and three toddlers. The plan the brothers cooked up was that they would live with us until the brother or his wife could get a job so they could afford to get a place of their own. But the drinking resumed almost immediately, and I reached the end of my rope when

I came home one day and found that Monty had sold our new washer and dryer, and he and his brother had disappeared with the cash from the sale. I had just purchased this set with only a small down payment, and the balance was to be paid on time payments. My boys were both still in diapers and since I was working, it was just too much to try to do the laundry by hand anymore.

Several days later, a phone call revealed what happened to the money he realized from the sale. Monty and his brother called from Reno to ask me to wire them some more money so they could buy gas to get home – they had gambled away all the money, and I was now out a washer and dryer and still had to make the payments for 24 months.

Before I wired them some money, I called my family and told them what had happened and that I wanted to move out. Within an hour, my stepfather and my brother and several uncles arrived and loaded my few possessions in their pickups and moved my boys and me into the basement of my parent's home.

Monty's brother and family eventually moved back to Oregon, and Monty got himself committed to the State Hospital for alcoholism, because when he sobered up, he realized he had a problem. Two days after his committal hearing, I was admitted to the County Hospital in the maternity ward where I gave birth on July 20, 1960, to our daughter, Cyndi (psuedonym). When she was one day old, I was surprised to see my husband walk into my room in the maternity ward with his hands cuffed behind him. He was there to see our new baby. There was a guard standing close by as he greeted our daughter and me. I assumed he was already in the State Hospital, awaiting transfer, which was scheduled to happen that afternoon.

After several weeks in the State Hospital, Monty escaped and came to see me at my parents' home. He joined Alcoholics Anonymous and convinced all of us that he really was going to change this time and give up alcohol forever. When Cyndi was two weeks old, I took a job as a secretary at the Campbell Soup Plant, and Monty found a job as a taxi driver. With two incomes, we were able to rent a nice home of our own and start over.

Things were good for awhile until the demon bottle got a hold on his senses again. After several days of drinking, he lost his job, and came home drunk. For hours that night, he sat in the middle of our bed with an umbrella in one hand and a bottle of whiskey in the other. If I fell asleep, he would poke or hit me with the umbrella to keep me awake. Then when he poured whiskey down Cyndi's throat as she lay in her crib at the foot of our bed, I came unglued. That was the straw that broke the camel's back for me. In a raging tirade, I spent the rest of the night telling him what a miserable good for nothing he was. The next morning he dropped me at work, and then deserted us, taking what little money we had and our old car.

It was like a nightmare that I couldn't awaken from. I was already physically and emotionally exhausted after a night with no sleep. I had waited for two hours after work, but Monty did not pick me up and I had no idea where he was. I had to walk more than five miles home from work in a torrential rainstorm. Our rented home was out in the country, and there was no bus service yet. The last mile of my long walk was after I had picked up the babies (age 3, 2 and 2 months) at the babysitter's home. The babysitter's husband was away for the evening with their car and there were no alternatives. Dear God, I wondered, what terrible thing did I do to deserve this?

Things went from bad to worse when a few days later, I was fired from that secretarial job because I was unable to get back and forth to work without a car. I had assured my boss that I would be in as soon as my husband returned from his trip, but he never did, and the boss's patience ran out. I was so upset, I was unable to eat for days, and when I fed the last of our food to my three children, I had to swallow my pride and tell my parents about my situation. They brought some food to our home, and let me borrow their second car to look for another job.

Regarding people suffering: "They are being tested, but it should not be called so. It is grace. Those who suffer have my grace. Only through suffering will they be persuaded to turn inward and make the inquiry. And without turning inward and making enquiry, they can never escape misery." CWSSB P 110

As a result of all the trials during my younger years, I know that my heart hardened and I never shed a tear for many years. Shutting down my emotions was my way to escape from dealing with the pain. But, I never lost my faith in God, or my belief that things were going to get better someday, somehow. I prayed mightily for a way out of this place I found myself in after Monty left, and was given renewed strength and courage. With God's help, I was able to find a job that would eventually turn into a good career for me.

"When you have bad karma, you have to suffer. However, your Faith in God will mitigate your suffering. I give you a shot of Grace which acts as a drug or a pain-killer. In short, when you have hundred percent faith, God in His Compassion reduces your suffering but He cannot reduce your karmas. Your karmas act as brakes and are binding on you. All the Lord does is to hand out Grace according to your karmas, according to what you deserve. In this way you are bound and the Lord is entirely free.

"But, when you show 100 (sic) percent Confidence in God, He is totally bound to take care of you. No karmas of yours, whether good or bad can stand in the way and act as brakes. When you show such implicit confidence in God and the unshakable belief that 'He will take care of everything for me, so why should I worry?' Then He can never let you down. He has to look after you and take care of everything for you, come what may, and whatever be the circumstances of your karmas." SSAV P 7

"Hundred percent faith means that God will not let you suffer, hundred percent confidence means that God will not let you down. Hundred percent faith plus hundred percent confidence makes for hundred percent devotion or bhakti. It is the highest form of bhakti where the Lord is in a state of golden bondage and the devotee is in a state of supreme serenity and smiling freedom. This is what every devotee has to aim at." SSAV P 7

My Career, Bob and Robbie

When Monty left that day in November 1960, and returned to his family in Oregon, I knew I was never going to be able to rely on anyone else to take care of me and my children. When I landed a job with the State of California, I realized my good fortune and worked hard to build a career which would provide us with a secure life. I took on the role of supermom and became very independent. I vowed that I would never again depend on a man to provide for us, and I didn't. There were times I had to 'moonlight', (take a part time job on the side), but we were never again without money for food or other necessities.

After my divorce in 1961, I met and married a wonderful man from the Boston area, who also worked in the same department for the State of California. Bob was nearly ten years older than me, and seemed to live a very stable life. He did not drink or chase women, and he never once physically abused me. The most important thing was that he was willing to take on the responsibility of helping to raise my children. He had been previously married and had two daughters, but left the East Coast to find a new life in California after his divorce. Life with Bob was good and we settled into what appeared to be a happy family.

I always felt it was my responsibility to provide for my children, so I continued to work. On a whim, I took an IBM programmer aptitude test that was being given to Bob and others in his department. This test was being offered in search of the special kind of intellect and talent the new computer programming jobs would require. I was told that my score on the test was the highest anyone had achieved anywhere in the whole world. My new title was 'Genius'. When I asked how I could go about getting a job in the new computer department, the head of the bureau told me that he could hire me if I were a man. Since I was a woman, he said I needed to have a college degree. That's the way things were in the 60's. My brother several years later took the same IBM test, and he bettered my score by one point. It must have been in our genes.

So, while working full time during the day, for six years I went to college nights working on a business degree with emphasis on programming computers. A counselor in the college called me in after I had taken my SATS. He told me I had the highest score anyone had ever gotten on the SATS, and that I was either a genius or a good test taker.

My fourth child, Robbie was born on March 29, 1966. We named him after his father. When Robbie was two months and eight days old, I found him dead in his crib. This had to be the most devastating experience in my life. The pain of loss of a child was indescribable and only a parent who has experienced this can understand what one goes through at a time like this. The pain was compounded by an incident with my mother.

When the ambulance took our baby away, the police told us we were too distraught to drive to the hospital and that we should call family. Bob called my parents who lived nearby. We sat in the back seat as my stepfather drove, consumed in trepidation that they would tell us at the hospital they were unable to do anything to help our Robbie. I looked up to see my mother staring at me with a big smile on her face. It was not a compassionate smile. I remembered that smile - it was the same one I saw on her face when I was 12 years old and found her drowning a litter of kittens inside a bird cage in the laundry tub. Just as she enjoyed watching them struggle and die, she was enjoying my pain - my own mother! After that, I kept my emotions shut down and swallowed my grief and tears. I was determined not to surrender to the pain. For several years after that, I would have nothing to do with my mother.

Bob and I both returned to church after the funeral, searching for a reason to go on, and for answers as to why something like this can happen to a happy family. We tried several different churches in the neighborhood, but never found the answers or what we were looking for.

When Robbie died, things seemed to be going wrong with Bob.

I knew he loved my children, but he started being too demanding of them, and punished them too severely. There were times he would stand in the street and shout crazy things. Other times, he couldn't seem to keep his thoughts together. He also was having some physical problems, like difficulty keeping his balance, and his eyesight and hearing deteriorated quickly. I knew there was something wrong with Bob, but I had no idea what it was, and he wouldn't go to a doctor. On a visit to see his family in Massachusetts, his oldest brother and sister-in-law recognized there was a serious problem when they witnessed Bob abusing my children, and talked with me about it. They suggested that if things didn't improve, I ought to think about leaving Bob for the sake of the children.

When we returned to California, Bob learned he was about to be fired from his job, so he resigned and started up a gardening business with our savings. He was unable to keep up with that too, and seemed to be going downhill fast, but still would not see a doctor. From his years in the Air Force, he still had a license as an Aircraft and Engineering Mechanic, so he was able to get an overseas job in Guam in that capacity.

After he left for Guam, my children began to tell me some horror stories of how Bob had treated them while I was at work or school. He had picked Cyndi up by the hair and thrown her across the room, tearing out a handful of her hair. Mark told me about the night Bob chased him all over the house with the fireplace poker, threatening to kill him. They said that Bob had threatened them with their life if they dared tell me what he had done.

Bob had been in Guam for about four months when he called to say he was returning home. After what the children told me, I knew I could never let him return to our home, so when I met his plane, I told him I was going to get a divorce, and that he needed to find another place to live. He returned to his family in Massachusetts. After the divorce, his sister-in-law later told me that Bob was recently diagnosed with an advanced case of Multiple Sclerosis and that they had been able to obtain 100% disability from the Veterans Administration for him.

My Sons

Mark was born, November 6, 1957, just 14 months after Monty and I were married. He was a happy, healthy, chubby, blond haired, blue eyed bundle of joy. Oh how he was loved by the both of us and his four grandparents as well. He was the first grandson on both sides, and the first grandchild on my side.

Even though I had to work from the time Mark was a month old, I spent evenings and weekends reading to him. I don't know if that was responsible for his love of knowledge, but I am sure it helped. Mark knew how to read phonetically and do his multiplication tables before he entered school. But, strangely, once in school, Mark did not do as well. He was the smallest in his class, smaller even than the girls. We were told that even though he had the intelligence and kept up with his class academically, he was not emotionally mature enough to move into the second grade with the rest of his class. So we agreed to hold him back. I am not certain whether this did more harm than good, because it placed a stigma on him that never seemed to leave.

As Mark grew up, he tended to stay by himself a lot, rather than playing outside with the neighbourhood children, whereas his sister Cyndi saw everybody as her friend. We later learned that Mark was picked on and taunted by other children. I encouraged him to join the Cub Scouts and I became a Den Mother to help broaden his world and his social skills. When Mark was in the fourth grade, he used his allowance to buy used college textbooks and then taught himself how to do calculus, trigonometry and other difficult math subjects. He also taught himself how to play chess from a book, and became good enough to challenge my brother, who played in chess tournaments, to a game whenever an opportunity presented itself.

My third husband adopted my children soon after we married. At 40, he had never been married, nor had he ever been around children before, as he was an only child with an over-protective mother. He had always wanted children of his own. After we married, I recognized that he did not know how to treat my children, or interact with them, even though he appeared to care dearly about them. One week he would favor one of the children, while ignoring or ridiculing whatever the other one did, while in the following week, he would do the opposite. I tried to help him see how counterproductive this was, but he didn't seem to understand the emotional damage he was doing with the mean-spirited games he was playing with the children.

When the aerospace industry did some serious cutting back, his job of over 20 years went with it, and so, it seems, did his patience. Now he was home all the time with the children, which I first saw as a blessing during the times when they were not in school. Then they started telling me their horror stories whenever we were alone, like his hanging my son's soiled undershorts on the lamppost for all his classmates to see as they walked home. Or tying Mark to a chair in a restaurant because he wouldn't sit up straight. With Cyndi, the issue of her bed wetting was the source of her stepfather's ire and ridicule.

After three years of watching my children go downhill, while unsuccessfully trying every way to make it work, I filed for divorce again. The courts sent us to counseling sessions, which seemed to help for awhile, but nothing ever really changed for the better. So, I became a single parent again with latchkey children, which is one of the most difficult positions for a working mother to be in. When they became too old for a babysitter, as they entered their teenage years, things became more difficult for us. They started smoking cigarettes, and I tried everything in my power to get them to quit, but my efforts were wasted. They both still smoke even today. Next came drugs and alcohol, both of which, I later learned, flowed freely in the upper middle class neighborhood in which we lived. I thought that sending them to the best schools would keep them safe from illicit drugs, when in fact, the drug dealers preyed on these children because they were more apt to have money to spend freely.

Not feeling well, I came home from the office early one day, and found a dozen or more teenagers in my home, who had obviously cut school. They all had been drinking and smoking pot. I called the police, but all the children except mine left in a hurry. The police lectured Mark and Cyndi, and threatened them with detention home if they were found with alcohol or marijuana again, but it didn't seem to make any impression on them.

Soon after that incident, Mark and his friends got into trouble with the law for a misdemeanor theft of a newsstand and Mark was sentenced to the detention center. After a few months in the detention center, he was offered the choice of staying there longer, or getting his GED and joining the Army. He chose the latter option.

With some accumulated vacation, I planned a trip to Japan, and to Korea where he was stationed, to spend some time with Mark. Just days before I was to leave, Mark called from Korea and told me not to come, that he was being discharged and coming home instead, and would explain it all when he arrived. This made no sense to me at all as he still had many months left in the service. But he would not talk about it over the phone, so all I could do was wait for his arrival.

When Mark returned, he was not the same son that we had sent off to the Army. All he would tell us was that he and the Army agreed that he would be better off being a civilian. He sounded as if he had been programmed, as these were not the words my son would have used, and it caused some deep concerns within me. Mark had a hair trigger temper now, and didn't seem to sleep much at all. In fact there were nights when I would hear him moving about the house all night long.

One night, about 2 a.m., our doorbell rang. It was the police, bringing Mark home. They said he was prowling around in a nearby neighborhood and the residents had called them, fearing he was the 'East Area Rapist', who had been victimizing people in our area for the past few years. When the police brought him home a second time a few nights later, they suggested I do whatever I could to keep him at home because some of the neighbors might shoot at him out of the fear that had paralyzed our neighborhood.

While Mark was gone one evening, I searched through the

papers in his duffel bag he had brought home with him from the Army. What I found still didn't make sense - he had been given a General Discharge because he 'Urinated in the Captain's wastebasket'. This did not sound like our Mark at all. I had noticed a long scar across his chest one day as he came out of the bathroom and asked him how that had happened to him. He couldn't remember. I found this very difficult to believe with a scar like that. I had hoped to find the answer to this and many other questions in his papers, but no mention was made of any injury, or anything else, other than the wastebasket incident.

Then a month later on Halloween night, which also happened to be a full moon night, complete with a raging lightning and thunderstorm, Mark slipped out unnoticed. After the trick-or-treaters had come and gone, Mark returned, soaking wet with a wild, distorted look on his face. I told him to go change his clothes as he was dripping on the carpet, but he defiantly took a seat on the family room sofa instead. Then he started saying abusive things to me. I told him not to talk to his mother like that. He said I was not his mother, that his mother was dead. He said the 'voices' were telling him that I was the White Force and he was the Black Force, and that he had to eliminate me. I tried to talk to him about how God would help him if he would just take a moment to ask for help.

He suddenly jumped up off the sofa and attacked, pummeling me with both fists, while screaming and yelling unintelligible words. I fell or was knocked to the floor while trying to escape the pounding blows. I screamed out a plea to God to help me. This was not my son. This was an animal beating and kicking me. Somehow, thank you God, his attention was diverted for a moment, and I managed to get into the next room and lock the door behind me. I called the police, and they arrived within minutes. After a fruitless search of the house, two officers went outside, and found him hiding in the bushes in the backyard. They handcuffed him and brought him through the house to the front door. Mark was yelling abuses as the two officers dragged him through the family room. When they got him to the front door, he turned to me and yelled, "I'll get you for this.....", and then they were gone. The violent look on his face became imprinted on my mind and the words he spat echoed within for a very long time.

In the sudden silence, I collapsed and began to cry hysterically. Two plain clothes officers, who seemed to come out of nowhere, comforted me and stayed with me through the rest of the night. When I think back, I had not noticed them there before Mark left and now I wonder if these were angels sent to help me through this. As we sat at the kitchen table, they explained to me that Mark was without a doubt a paranoid schizophrenic. I had never known anyone with this disease, and really didn't understand much about what to expect. One of the officers told me his brother had been diagnosed as a paranoid schizophrenic several years before after his family went through a similar incident, so he was able to recognize the symptoms in Mark. He told me that as far as he knew, it was incurable, but that the patient could be maintained in a nearly stable condition with drug therapy.

The following day, I called the minister of my church and explained what had happened. I asked her to pray for Mark. She offered the possibility that Mark's body had been taken over by a discarnate spirit while Mark was high on drugs. Mark had shared with me when he first returned home that illicit drugs were very cheap and so easily obtained when he was in Korea, and many of the soldiers resorted to them for recreation, since there was little else to do when off duty. And the Army did nothing to discourage it. Mark's favorite was speed and he confided that he was frequently high on it.

Mark showed up on my doorstep one evening about two months after he was hospitalized. The Halloween incident remained fresh in my mind and I was still terrified of him. He said he had gotten tired of being confined and just walked out of the ward onto the elevator, and came straight home. Somehow, thank you God, I was able to talk him into getting in my car and I drove him back to the hospital. The staff did not seem to be the least concerned about his disappearance. This happened several more times, and I was literally afraid to go home at night for fear of finding him as a raving maniac hiding in the bushes again.

There came a point when a decision had to be made about what to do with Mark. He could not stay in the county hospital forever, and he either had to be committed to the state hospital, or taken back into my home. The first option was out of the question - I could not afford to put him into a controlled board and care situation.

A friend who had been in the military helped me contact the American Legion to see if they could find out what happened in Korea that had turned my son into what he had become. After a lot of research and digging, we learned that while Mark was on guard duty one night in Korea, a North Korean attacked him with a bayonet - this explained the long scar on his chest. Then at close range, Mark shot the North Korean with his high-powered rifle and blew the head off, which landed on Mark. After that incident, Mark went off the deep end, started taking drugs on a larger scale to escape the memories, and was declared no longer fit to serve.

With this information in hand, and with further help from the American Legion, we approached the Army and the Veteran's Administration, and after a lot of form filings, meetings, hearings, inquiries, and time, Mark was granted a Medical Discharge instead of the General Discharge he had been given. He was also declared a 100% disabled veteran, and was transferred by ambulance to the VA hospital in the San Francisco Bay Area.

This whole thing with Mark finalized just as I was in the midst of making a major change in my life. Several years before Mark returned from Korea, I had experienced a life threatening incident that had given me a lot of time to lie there and think about my values and life and where mine was heading. After this soul searching, I surrendered my life to God. Then I made a decision and a vow that I would never let anything or anyone come between me and God and my spiritual growth again. I started going to church again, the Religious Science Church, and was so enthralled with the teachings, that I began their four year course to become a minister myself. I eventually resigned from my job of 18 years, gave almost everything away, and was in the process of moving on to a simpler life in Hawaii with my daughter Cyndi, who had just turned 18.

For the next twenty years of his life, Mark was in and out of the VA hospital so many times we lost count. He had never given up his attachment to hard drugs, which seriously interfered with his medication, and caused him to go off the deep end over and over. He tried it on his own a few times, but always ended up back in the hospital. Mark bounced from one board and care home to another, in between hospital stays, burning his bridges behind himself each time.

After we moved to Colorado, the VA contacted me and asked me to start taking care of Mark's money and finances, since he was incapable of making it on his own. I agreed, even though we lived over 1,000 miles apart.

After a number of suicide attempts, his depression was finally controlled with medication and he received intensive counseling from the VA to keep him going. It was an uphill battle for Mark and he eventually gave up all hard drugs a few years ago. He still resides in a board and care home in California, and he volunteers at the VA hospital and he helps his house mates whenever he can. Since he gave up drugs, he has become the loving and attentive son that I remember from the early days.

I honestly believe that Baba is responsible for the complete turnaround Mark has taken. And what is better is that Mark believes it too!

With regard to my son Kirk, who is 13 months younger than Mark, and 18 months older than Cyndi, it is a rather short story. After Monty and I separated for the seventh and final time, I filed for divorce, and custody of the three babies. Monty returned to California and pleaded with me to give him one of the children - that his life meant nothing anymore without them. He was back living with his parents and assured me the child would get the best of care between himself and his parents, in spite of his addiction to alcohol.

My situation was very unstable financially at the time. I had just gotten a very good job with a promising future, but the pay did not provide enough to cover my rent, food, and child care for three children. There was just enough for child care for two babies. Something had to give or I had to go on welfare, because Monty was not working and never contributed a dime to their support, even though it was ordered by the court. Letting Monty take one of the children for the time being seemed to be the solution; I would have just enough to get by on and I knew his grandparents would give their grandchild a good home. I don't remember how we chose Kirk as the child he should take, but I know now that it was all God's will anyway. By mutual agreement, it turned into a permanent situation and his grandparents gave him all the love and care a child could want, and so did his father, when he was home. Years later, I was told that his father kept his promise and never let Kirk see him drink, and thus he wasn't home very often.

Kirk, who is 40 now, has been married to the same beautiful lady since he was 18, and they have two lovely teenagers. He has an excellent career and takes good care of his family in Oregon.

When my mother left her body in April 1997, I contacted Kirk and Monty to let them know of her demise. During the conversation, Kirk asked me for a copy of the 770 page book I had just put together and published, 'A Compendium of the Teachings of Sathya Sai Baba'. After browsing through it, he e-mailed back that I shouldn't worry about his opinion of the book, because it coincided with his beliefs. Thank You Baba!

My Daughter

When I still lived on the Big Island of Hawaii, I was there with my daughter Cyndi when her first child was born on April 10, 1981. Her husband, Al, called me at work and I left my office right away, arriving at the hospital around 1 p.m., just as her doctor was leaving. He told Al and I that it would probably be much later that night, if not the following morning before Cyndi would be delivering, and that the hospital would call him when it got closer to delivery time.

My son-in-law stepped out for a moment to call his parents to tell them what the doctor had said and while he was gone, Cyndi asked me if there wasn't something that could be done to get this over with sooner. She was very uncomfortable. I could not stand to see my daughter suffer, so I followed my inner guidance, said a prayer, and took both of her hands in mine and filled her with all the spiritual healing energy I could muster. In that moment, I actually felt like a conduit to God.

Cyndi's labor pains started coming at a much faster pace and with greater intensity almost immediately, so while Al stayed with her, I went down the hall to locate a nurse. It was the same nurse that had been there when the doctor talked to us before, and she very reluctantly came back to check Cyndi's dilation. A few minutes later, she came rushing out and said she had to call the doctor and get help to move Cyndi to the delivery room immediately because the baby was on its way. The doctor came running down the hall about fifteen minutes later and I watched as he literally skidded sideways into the swinging doors of the delivery room.

My new grandson, Ian Hanuala, was born less than one hour after my filling Cyndi with the spiritual healing energy, and nobody was more surprised than me! It was a thrilling experience for this new grandmother. Actually I was a grandmother for the first time back in 1977 when my son Kirk and his wife Betty had their first born in Oregon, but the little guy died of SIDS before I ever got to see him. SIDS, or Sudden Instant Death Syndrome, is commonly known as crib death. My fourth child, Robbie was a SIDS death at two months old, in 1966.

On August 1, 1983, Cyndi gave birth to a second son, Sean Kekoa, while I was up at 40,000 feet on my way from my home in Anchorage to Sacramento for my stepfather's funeral. He had left his body on July 27th in his sleep, with a big smile on his face, at the age of 61. While Sean was growing up, I noticed he had many of the same habits, abilities and traits that my step-father had, and I have always wondered if Sean was my stepfather reincarnated.

Three years later, when Cyndi was doing the laundry, she found a receipt for a bouquet of flowers in Al's pocket. The flowers had been purchased the day before, which happened to be their wedding anniversary. When she asked him what happened to the flowers, he admitted they had been purchased for someone else and that he had been having an affair for some time with someone at work. Cyndi was angry and totally devastated when she called me the following day, begging me to help bring her and their two sons back to the Mainland. Syd and I had only just returned from our honeymoon several days before the call.

We agreed to help bring her back to the Mainland. But there was one major problem. Cyndi's husband, Al, was the son of politically prominent and influential parents of Hawaiian heritage. Her mother-in-law had told her many times they would never let her leave the Island with her grandsons, and they had the power to prevent it from happening.

When I lived in Hawaii and co-owned a restaurant, Cyndi's father-in-law told me if anyone ever gave me a hard time, or if I ever needed anyone taken care of, to just let him know. I told him I had always put my faith in God and He took care of things like that for me. I knew this was his way of letting me know of his connections. I had heard only rumors prior to that time.

When my step-father was seriously injured and burned over 80 percent of his body in December 1981, Cyndi and I flew to Sacramento with Ian just days before Christmas to see him, as it was not certain whether he would live. Ian was just eight months old. We boarded the plane at Keahole Airport. When the plane just sat there at the gate with no explanation from the crew, we became concerned whether we would meet our connecting flight in Honolulu. After sitting on the commuter plane for more than an hour, the door finally opened, and in walked Cyndi's in-laws. The locals on the plane exploded in applause! Cyndi's in-laws were very well known. The airline had held the plane up for them to come say goodbye to us and to give Ian, their first and only grandchild, his Christmas gifts. They had been to a holiday party and were more than slightly inebriated. They kissed and hugged the three of us, gave Ian his gifts, debarked the plane, and we took off. This was a simple demonstration of the power this family had.

Thus, getting Cyndi and the children off the Island had to be done in secret. Cyndi knew that Al was going to be out of town on a business trip during a specific time period, so we made reservations and purchased tickets for the day he would leave. We arranged for her to pick up the plane tickets at the counter just before boarding the plane.

It was the night before Thanksgiving as we waited breathlessly at the San Diego airport for their arrival. We had no way of knowing if they were able to board the plane in Kona, and didn't dare call to find out and possibly tip the family off. I was frantic with fear when we did not find them in the terminal where their plane was supposed to arrive. There was some mixup and her plane had debarked at a different terminal than was shown on the monitor. When we learned of the error, we rushed over to the other terminal and there they were, safe and sound.

Cyndi seemed even heavier than she was at our wedding. I reasoned that she must have used food as an antidote for the painful experiences in her marriage. When we first moved to Hawaii, she had been sponsored by the Kona Hilton Hotel in the Miss Hawaii beauty contest. At the time, Cyndi was strikingly beautiful, and closely resembled a famous movie star. Her excessive indulgence in alcohol and food, seemed to have taken a real toll on her physical beauty.

Syd and I helped Cyndi find and rent a home and bought them a houseful of inexpensive furniture and a kitchen full of food. We gave her my old Camaro, and until she could find a job, she applied and was accepted for Aid to Families with Dependent Children. I was delighted to have my grandsons near me and volunteered to take them whenever possible.

Cyndi never did find a job, and I am not certain whether she ever looked for one. She started slimming down nicely and was dating again. About once a month, I would take Cyndi shopping with me at a discount warehouse and load her up with food and staples, and whatever else they needed. But, after a few months, Ian began to complain to me that there never was enough food for them to eat because they always had to share it with their Mom's friends. I was shocked. I knew that Cyndi always had one or more people living with them, but she had assured me that they paid their way and were helping with the rent. I knew that Cyndi had a big heart when it came to her friends or people needing help.

But more than a few times lately, Cyndi came to me with stories about how she had lost her Welfare check, or someone had stolen all the cash from her recently cashed check, or she had loaned out her money to someone in need and they didn't keep their promise to pay her back, and she was unable to make the rent. I knew she wasn't telling me the truth with all her stories, but we didn't want to see the boys out on the street either. So we continued to help her out, paying her rent and buying groceries during her supposed crises.

When her landlord called me to tell me that Cyndi had turned his house into a drug den, with people coming and going all times of day and night and he was evicting her, I was dumbfounded! I had known something was wrong, but had thought it was just poor money management. Apparently, it was much worse than I had imagined. But, there was nothing I could do except to rent a moving van and help rent a new home for them. It wasn't long before she was evicted again for non-payment of rent but she didn't tell me this time until after it had happened.

It was then, when Cyndi was at her lowest, that she told me she was addicted to crack cocaine, and had started taking the drug innocently at a friend's encouragement to help her lose weight. She promised to stop because it was ruining her life. This time the Marshall had physically thrown her and the children out and would not let them take any of their belongings, and she was never able to recover them.

She begged us to help her resettle and promised that she would change her ways, so once again Syd and I helped her start over in a new home. We bought her more furniture, food and this time, clothing for the children.

After helping Cyndi get settled for a third time, I told her that she was on her own now and we were not going to help her again, hoping this would help her to become independent. Nothing else worked; maybe it was time for tough love, which I believe is tougher on the parent than the child. After my tough love lecture, I made many attempts to contact her, but she was either never home, or her house was full of people on drugs and she wouldn't let me in, or she was coming off her high, and that was absolutely the worst time to be around her because she was not just abusive, she would become vicious with me. The children were terrified of her when she was in this condition, and so was I, because I was always her first point of attack, and she was much larger than me.

Regarding sincere devotees who undergo suffering and misfortunes: "If those persons are also sometimes sincere devotees, then sometimes God sends them troubles to test the strength of their devotion. If the devotees realize that the main objective of man is not to be re-born again and again, and if they are striving towards this objective, they will be beset with untold miseries and sufferings as a means of burning away all the karmas of past births. This is all according to the Judgement and Grace of God." SSAV P 47

Cyndi's telephone had long ago been disconnected, so I could not call her before going to visit, and we lived about an hour's drive from her home. Her driver's license had been taken away for reckless driving, but she continued driving anyway. The neighbors had reported her for neglect of the children, and the Child Protective Service investigators did nothing but interview Cyndi, who is a creative fibber. Cyndi loved her children very much, and I am sure this came through to the investigators and contributed to their believing her stories. Sometimes Ian would call me from school because their mother had forgotten to pick them up again, and I would jump in the car and make that long drive across the county to get them. At least I would get to spend some time with them this way.

"Every sadhaka goes through these periods, the so-called 'dark periods'. There are changes going on within you during these periods of which you are not aware. It is the period of maturity and at the end of it, you emerge a stronger and better person.....You are only going through a process of maturing. So do not think that you have fallen in any way.....The end result of this process is spiritual, mental and emotional growth and maturity." SSAV P 16

I threatened to take the children away from Cyndi so they could at least live in a peaceful environment and have regular meals. They never sat down to eat as a family, and nobody ate at the same time, because no meals were prepared to speak of. As young as the boys were, they managed to find ways to feed themselves, if there was something in the cupboards or refrigerator to eat. Often, there wasn't.

Cyndi's neighbors would call me and tell me that she had left the children with them for a few minutes, but it was hours later, or the next morning, and she hadn't returned and there was no food to feed them. Would I come get them? This happened more than a few times. The conditions I would find the children in were appalling. My grandsons were always sick and I worried continuously about them.

"I stir, I knead, I pound, I bake, I drown you in tears. I have come to reform you, to transmute you." TEOL P 232

Crystal Brook Leslie

When we returned from our first trip to see Sai Baba in 1987, I had given Cyndi a book about Sai Baba to read, along with a picture and some Vibhuti. I knew that Cyndi was basically a spiritual person and hoped she too would be inspired by Baba. After asking her several times if she had read it, she finally told me she hadn't and very frankly said she just wasn't interested, but that she was happy for me because I seemed to be very happy these days.

"The Lord is the Sun and when His rays fall upon your heart, unimpeded by the clouds of egoism, the lotus bud blooms and the petals unfold. Remember, only the buds that are ready will bloom, the rest will have to wait patiently." DM P 205

Several months later, I learned that Cyndi was pregnant and would deliver sometime in July 1988. Cyndi told me that when she learned she was pregnant, she stopped drinking and doing any drugs. We got along so well during those few months. It was like having my daughter back. We could talk and share experiences and do things together as a family again. I prayed constantly to Baba to help her to stay that way.

When the day finally arrived, Cyndi called to tell us that her water had broken, but she was having no labor pains yet. Syd and I rushed over to get her and take her to the hospital. Cyndi disappeared with a nurse for a few minutes, and then the nurse came running out into the waiting room with a set of green operating room clothes in her hands. She said Cyndi was a drive-thru delivery and that the doctor was on his way, but probably would not be there in time, and she asked me to help her.

Actually I was delighted to be able to be there during the birth. I hurried into the green pajamas she handed me and rushed in to the delivery room, just as the baby's head came out, which was immediately followed by the rest of my new granddaughter. The nurse laid the baby face down on my daughter's chest, and I suddenly had an inspiration to take the remainder of the Vibhuti out of my purse that I had saved from what Baba had materialized for me. I had always thought Baba had me keep that vibhuti for some good reason, and now I knew what it was. I indicated to Cyndi that I wanted to put it in her baby's tiny mouth, and she nodded approval. Cyndi watched while the nurse was busy at the other end. I wasn't sure whether the nurse would approve. The baby seemed to smack her lips and then looked straight into my eye. I've always read that newborn babies could not see, but the look on her sweet little face said otherwise. She had such a beautiful little face.

About two weeks before the actual delivery, Cyndi went into

what she thought was labor, and after twelve hours in the hospital, she was discharged. But an interesting experience happened while she was in the labor room and hooked up to a variety of machines, one of which displayed the baby's heartbeat. We were talking about what she was going to name her new daughter. Cyndi mentioned several names that she liked, but preferred the name Brooke. When I mentioned the name Crystal, we noticed the heartbeat on the machine went much faster. When I repeated the name of Crystal, the machine again indicated a speedup in the baby's heartbeat.

So we started asking the baby while still in the womb, what she wanted her name to be, and told her to make her heartbeat go faster when she heard the name she wanted. Cyndi suggested Brooke Crystal. Nothing. Then she suggested Crystal Brooke. The heartbeat raced on the machine. We tried a variety of names, some that were ridiculous. But it was only when Crystal Brooke was mentioned, that her heartbeat speeded up, leaving us no doubt that this is what she wanted. Since Cyndi was not married to the baby's father, we went through the same process in choosing the surname. When Cyndi mentioned my maiden name, Leslie, Crystal Brooke let us know that was the name she wanted.

The nurse rubbed my tiny granddaughter down with a dry towel and then put her in an incubator type bed which was slanted downward so that fluids could drain from her mouth. I stayed with Crystal and caressed and talked to her while the nurse continued to tend to Cyndi. When I mentioned to Cyndi that Crystal had the cutest little ears, I noticed the nurse's head pop up and look at the baby from across the room. A few minutes later she came over and started to do what appeared to be a mini-exam of Crystal, at which time the doctor finally arrived. I was ushered out into the waiting room and told that we all could join Cyndi and the baby in about thirty minutes back in the ward.

The nurse returned as promised and took us in to see Cyndi. She offered us a chair, then told us that little Crystal Brooke was a Down's Syndrome baby, and possibly had a heart problem, but until they performed further tests, they couldn't be sure. I guess I went numb at that point. My beautiful granddaughter, whom I had just welcomed into the world, was a Down's Syndrome baby and would never know a normal life! I was heartbroken. The nurse explained that Down's Syndrome was a chromosomal abnormality and happens about once in every 650 births. She assured us it was not caused from taking drugs, which, of course, my daughter had a history of. I knew this came up because Cyndi had apparently asked about it.

Since I was getting this information from a nurse, I began to doubt its accuracy and wondered where the doctor was and why he didn't tell us this terrible news if it was true. I took another look at Crystal's beautiful face and told the nurse I saw no apparent physical features that Down's Syndrome children have, and suggested that maybe she was wrong. I argued that Cyndi was only 28 years old and that I had heard this only happened to older women, as if my argument could reverse the situation. The nurse then opened Crystal's blanket and showed me the straight lines running across the middle of her tiny hands and feet. This, she said, only happened in Down's Syndrome children.

Cyndi, who could see I was upset, told me not to worry, that everything was all right, and she was all right with everything. This brought me back to reality where I recovered from my disbelief, and reluctantly accepted the truth of the situation.

Because her tiny heart had a major defect, Crystal was unable to gain weight, no matter how much she ate, and had to have two open heart surgeries to correct the problems, once before she was a year old and again when she was about 18 months old. She had a difficult time recovering from the first surgery. Syd and I visited her the first night, just after a technician had removed some tubes he had inserted down her nose and throat to suck out the accumulated fluids.

Crystal was very frightened and extremely distressed from the procedure, and I did my best to comfort her. There were so many tubes and lines coming out of her tiny, helpless body that it hurt to look at her. Her eyes pleaded with me to do something, and as we were leaving the hospital and walking to the car, I could feel her trying to will me back to her bedside. It was all I could do to leave her like that. But she survived after nearly three weeks in the Intensive Care Unit, and is now a healthy ten year old. Crystal's facial and body features did change slowly as she grew, leaving no doubt that she is a Down's Syndrome child.

Regarding why some people are born physically handicapped and mentally retarded, Baba says: "In previous births, such people would have been completely amoral, with no standards of right and wrong, of good and bad. Their moral codes would have been very low and they would have engaged in acts of moral degeneracy and decadence. Such people will be re-born with physical and mental afflictions and will suffer in this way for past misdeeds." SSAV P 46

While Cyndi was trying to get her life back together after Crystal's birth, we helped her from time to time with groceries and other necessities. But, Ian called me one day and confided in me that the last few times I had taken his mother shopping, she traded the food for drugs and cigarettes, and they still had nothing to eat. When I talked to Cyndi next, I could barely contain my anger and it was a long time before I saw her or the children again. Ian told me later that he got in serious trouble with his mother for telling me what was going on. Whenever the boys would stay with us, Ian would eat and eat until he was so full he made himself sick. It broke my heart to watch this, because I knew he was trying to get enough to eat so that when he went back home he wouldn't get hungry so soon. Ian was only seven years old and did not understand this would not work.

"Your attitude is the cause of your suffering or happiness. With whatever feeling you see an object, the same is reflected back.....When you see the world through colored glasses, you will see everything in the color of the glasses you are wearing. Whatever happens, you should take it as a gift of God." SS May 1994 P 116

Cyndi left Ian and Sean and Crystal alone for hours at a time, and sometimes all night long. One time, she left them at her friend's apartment while she and her friend went to a party. Long after she said she would return, Ian called me, even though he promised his mother he wouldn't. He was frightened to death because it was a terrible neighborhood, and he was left with two babies besides Sean and his baby sister, Crystal. All of them were crying and there was nothing to feed them, and no clean diapers. This was not long after Crystal's first open heart surgery and she still was on oxygen and still had not completely healed. And Ian didn't even know where he was so I could come help! I stayed on the phone with Ian off and on all night until his mother returned early the next morning.

"Open your heart to pain, for it is God's will, wrought for your own good. It is His plan to dissolve the ego. Welcome it as a challenge. Turn inward and derive the strength to bear it and benefit by it." TEOL P 232

"Why worry when God, in order to make a lovely jewel out of you, heats and melts, cuts and carves, and resolves your dross in the crucible of suffering." TEOL P 232

Just months before we moved to our new home in Colorado, Cyndi was evicted one more time. She arrived at my front door with the children, some clothes and her TV in the back seat. My heart broke when I saw the children stuffed amongst the few things she had been able to salvage. I wanted to bring them into the house and let Cyndi find her own way, but she said, "All of us or none of us!". I knew in my heart that letting Cyndi into my home would be the worst thing I could do. For four years I had been enabling my daughter off and on to continue downhill because the help I had been giving her had only been subsidizing her drug habit. It was time to stop the giving again. I prayed to Baba asking Him what I should do and the answer came immediately. I gave her enough money for a motel and sent them on their way, and went back inside and cried my heart out. Then I surrendered it once again to Baba, and I knew in my heart that He would not let anything bad happen to my grandchildren.

"Come just one step forward, I shall take a hundred towards you. Shed just one tear, I shall wipe a hundred from your eyes." TEOL P 237

Cyndi called me from the motel the next day and told me that her car had run out of gas on the freeway after leaving my home. She said a young couple stopped to see what was wrong. They got some gasoline for Cyndi's car and then took Cyndi and the children out to eat, after which they gave Cyndi some extra money to tide her over for a few days. When Cyndi said she tried to thank them, they told her "Don't thank us, thank Jesus, because He is the one who really helped you tonight!".

I found that with all the challenges going on for me during this nightmare with Cyndi and the grandchildren, that it had become increasingly more difficult and then impossible for me to surrender. I begged Sai Baba to show me what to do, or help me make the right decisions with Cyndi, and sometimes I went so far as to ask Him to intervene, and do whatever it took to turn her around. It seemed that Baba had turned a deaf ear to me and my prayers; like I was in this alone. So I floundered around, making what seemed like more wrong decisions than right ones, until I reached a point of saturation. What I really needed to do was surrender the whole thing to Swami, but I was unable to get even close to the point where I could stop trying to make things happen.

"All the great saints, seers and noble souls have gone through plenty of grief in their lives. Man does not understand the truth that it is only by meeting the challenge of grief one gets the strength to progress upward on the spiritual path. Happiness and grief cannot be separated. You have to treat them equally." Divine Discourse Jan 1, 1998

I was incapable of looking at this situation from a spiritual point of view, or surrendering it, and felt as though I had fallen off the spiritual wagon. I mourned the beautiful spiritual high that I had returned from India with. Nothing seemed to go right for me during this time. Words cannot describe the anguish and torment I went through in worrying over my daughter, and the safety and health of my grandchildren. My heartache was beyond description, and there was no end in sight.

"Man should maintain equanimity in pleasure and pain, loss or gain. Without pain you cannot enjoy pleasure. Sorrow is verily the royal road to joy. Sufferings are the stepping stones that lead man towards virtuous conduct. One should neither be elated by pleasure nor dejected by pain." SS May 1994 P 113

I had not prayed for anything specific, except to help Cyndi see the light, for a long time, but now I prayed almost ceaselessly to Baba to help me find my way back up out of my misery. Finally, in a totally helpless state, it occurred to me that I had to work on surrendering this challenge with my daughter. For the past four years, I had been trying to fix it all by myself, to make things happen the way I wanted them to, forgetting that taking things into my own hands prevented Baba from being able to help me. Sometimes we have to hit bottom before we become capable of surrender, or before we even can become aware that our lack of surrender is the source of the problem. Subsequently, with a lot of help from Baba, I was able to give it all to Him and ask Him to watch over my grandchildren and help my daughter. When I finally surrendered and committed them to His hands, I was able to let go of the worrying and the deep sorrow, and get on with my own life.

"I am happiest when someone with a heavy load of misery comes to me, for he is most in need of what I have to give." TEOL P 233

"When devotees surrender their lives to God and obey Him, He takes the full responsibility and cares for his devotees even to the smallest details." CWSSB P 131

I never would have gotten through these terrible years with Cyndi and the grandchildren without my faith in Baba and His guidance, and without Syd's loving support and strength.

In Retrospect

As other parents have done, I have looked back over the years to see where I went wrong in raising my children. I know I instilled in them the correct values, as they do exhibit them even today. The fault apparently lies in my not being there for them when they must have needed me. There were so many things on my agenda that I just didn't have as much time for the children as I should have. Did I need to have such a full agenda? Probably not. Did I have such a full agenda to avoid spending too much time at home just as my parents did? Probably did.

I tried to make it up to the children on weekends by spending most of my spare time with them, and regularly having a family night every Sunday, and spending quality time with them by taking them camping, or to the zoo, the carnival, the movies, church and temple, or taking them on long driving vacation trips all around the United States. We managed to visit every state in the Continental United States before they were grown up.

Everybody remarked when they were young what beautiful, well behaved children they were, and they truly were. Something happened when adolescence set in though, which is probably when they needed me the most, and I was there the least.

"Above all, realize that children are precious treasures. Yours is the great task of rearing them to become devoted servants of God and sincere spiritual aspirants." SSS VOL II Chap 34

"Children have unselfish love; they are innocent onlookers; they observe the action of the elders and they learn their lessons from the home much earlier than from school. So, parents have to be very careful in their behavior with the children and between themselves.....The child should grow with the mother for the first five years of life. Many children do not know what the Prema (love) of the mother is like. The mother should not hand over her responsibility during those years to some one else and be called simply 'Mummy' as if she is some doll with which the child likes to play. Now the children of rich and educated parents are severely handicapped. They are deprived of the care and love of parents. They are handed over to the care of servants and nannies and they grow up in their company and learn their vocabulary and habits and styles of thought. This is very undesirable." SSS VOL II, Chap 34 P 204-205

If only I had found Baba when I was raising my children; what a difference He would have made! I have watched some of the mothers with their children at the Sai Baba retreats and the Ashrams, and I feel they are truly blessed to be raising their children with Sai Baba's teachings. My mother could not teach me what she herself did not know how to do - to love, because her mother could not love her; and I could not teach my children how to love either because I had not learned how.

I was 44 years old when I met Syd, and he was the first person I ever felt truly loved me **and** never wanted to hurt me or take advantage of me. It was only after Sai Baba came into my life that I began to learn how to really love others, without expectations, and with His help I am making great strides in this area.

"In this worldly life love is manifesting in several forms such as the love between mother and son, husband and wife, and between relatives. This love based on physical relationships arises out of selfish motives and self-interest. But the love of the Divine is devoid of any trace of self-interest. It is love for the sake of love alone. This is called Bhakthi or devotion. One characteristic of this love is to give and not to receive. Secondly, love knows no fear. Thirdly it is only for love's sake and not for selfish motive. All these three angles of love jointly connote surrender. When one revels in this attitude of surrender one experiences the bliss of the Divine. For this, the prime requisite is 'Kshama' (Forgiveness)." SS February 1994 P 49

"The love which is offered to Him should be free from desires. Before you love God, you should love yourself. After loving yourself, you should love the society, then the entire world should be loved. If your love is not selfless, you cannot love the world. If you cannot love the world, you can never love the Paramatma.....Where there is love, there is no room for hatred. Where there is hatred, there is love automatically. There are only two things: love and hatred. Hatred will enable your ego to grow. Love confers on you compassion and grace." DD 1987 P 133

And Baba has been helping me learn how to love by sending people into my life who are very difficult to love, some so full of self-hatred that they feel nobody can love them. These people, who remind me of my younger self, have been real challenges for me, but I have been amazed that sometimes these are the easiest to love. It is the people who have been the closest to me who are the real tests of my being able to love unconditionally.

Regarding people with unlovable natures: "First, you should understand that though the exterior may be harsh, rough and prickly, the interior is sweet. A jack fruit or a pineapple is prickly outside but sweet inside.....the outer forms vary but the inner core of all mankind is the same, saturated with the sweetness of love and divinity. It is up to you to try and see beneath the external appearance and reach below the surface." SSAV P 28

During an interview with Sai Baba in February 1996, Swami told me "You worry about your family all the time. Don't worry. They are not yours, they are Mine, and I will take care of them. I will help.".

Smoking

When I was 13 years old, a friend offered me a cigarette on the way home from school one day. In those days, it was cool to smoke and emulate the rich and famous movie stars. It wasn't long before I was hooked on cigarettes. When my stepfather learned I was smoking, he began leaving packages or cartons of cigarettes on my dresser after his nightly visits to my bedroom. So, in spite of the fact I never had spending money as a child, I had all the cigarettes I needed. They became my best friend.

I quit smoking several times, once for over two years in the early '60's. Bob and I had been playing cards with our neighbors for hours one night, and we were all steady smoking. I started choking on the accumulated cigarette smoke and could not catch my breath. It frightened me terribly because I thought I was going to die before I would get some air in my lungs. The next day, I gave them up. But, several years later, when situations in my life became too much for me, I renewed my relationship with my best friend, and in no time was back up to two packs a day.

The next time I quit smoking was in the late '60's. This time it was because I kept getting bronchitis all the time and the doctor suggested I should quit if I did not want to get emphysema. But after some more stressful situations in my life several years later, I weakened and took a cigarette from a friend at a party one night. That was all it took.

The third time I quit was in the mid 70's; I had turned my life to God and was trying to get rid of everything in my life that was harmful to my body. Within two years of no cigarettes I had accumulated an extra twenty five pounds. It was on a flight back to the Mainland from Hawaii in the Summer of 1978 that I was offered a cigarette by a handsome San Francisco restauranteur I met on the plane. I thought, why not? Well, the weight went back down, but the addiction took over again.

By the time I was in my 40's, I was up to three packages of cigarettes a day. I started and ended my day with a cigarette, and used every event as another excuse for a smoke. It became such that my life revolved around my next cigarette. And I hated it because my life was being controlled by something other than myself. It was no longer 'smart' to be smoking anything. People stayed their distance, and sometimes that was good. People complained about the smoke, and I began to feel ashamed of my habit.

I had been wanting to quit this disgusting, debilitating habit for good, but every time I attempted to quit, something stressful would come along and I would turn to my best friend, in spite of the fact my health was suffering. Eventually, I began praying to God for help in quitting because of a vow I had made while on my honeymoon with Syd in 1986. Syd did not smoke and I watched him suffer silently while sitting in the smoking section on an overseas flight with me so I could indulge my habit. I watched him struggle to breathe in our stateroom during our Honeymoon cruise in the Greek Islands. I watched him become deathly ill on our Honeymoon in Egypt with a respiratory infection. I vowed then and there to give up my best friend and prayed to God for His help in kicking the habit every time I would light up a cigarette.

Then a friend told me about a program called 'In Control' that she had taken to help her quit. She used to smoke as much or more than I did, and I knew if it helped her to quit, it would work for me too. This turned out to be the answer to my prayers. On the second day of the program, January 29, 1987, I took a puff on my last cigarette and with the help of God, I have had the strength to maintain that resolve. At that time, I changed my best friend to God! And twelve years later, I know that I will never smoke another cigarette in my life.

How blessed the children are who are living with parents who are devotees of Sathya Sai Baba and are practicing His teachings. They will probably never be influenced by their peers to take up nasty habits like smoking as I was.

"When we feed the mind and the spirit properly, life will be more purposeful. For example, smoking has become fashionable today. In tobacco there is a dangerous poison, nicotine. The nicotine poison will leave spots in the nose of a person who smokes. While smoking, carbon dioxide is produced. The carbon dioxide gas will not only damage the lungs, but get into the heart causing heart disease and cancer.....And it follows that smoking is responsible for heart attacks and lung cancer. When the lungs and nerves are not healthy, it is difficult to control diseases, and the body degenerates; asthma and other diseases will follow.

"Three-fourths of the human body is ruined because of smoking; one-fourth of the body is ruined due to drinking." SSN Spring 1995 P 15

"If you do not smoke, you escape a number of illnesses that follow that passionate practice." SSS Vol I Chap 28 P 176

"Let Me tell you one thing: Of course, I can bear anything for your sake; I have come to save you and guide you. But somehow, I cannot tolerate the smell of tobacco, of bidis and cigarettes. Can you not postpone the disgusting practice for an hour and come to me without that insufferable smell? Besides, I have laid down certain disciplines and codes of conduct for you here. I would ask you to study the list and practice them not only within this compound, but in your own places, wherever you happen to live." SSS VOL II Chap 31 P 184

Who is Sai Baba?

During my single days, I co-owned a metaphysical book store in Southern California. We sponsored and hosted workshops, seminars and classes in several rooms off to the side of the merchandise area in the old Victorian house we leased. I published a monthly newsletter which included a calendar showing what events were upcoming.

Several devotees of Sathya Sai Baba approached us to hold an *'Introduction to Sai Baba'* meeting. I had never heard of Sai Baba until that time, and only later recalled that along with many other Eastern philosophical teachers, we carried at least one book on the shelves about Him, probably at a customer's request.

The evening of the *'Introduction to Sai Baba'* workshop arrived and I was scheduled to leave about the time it was to start, as it was my night off. People began arriving an hour or more early for the event, and the store filled up quickly. It was a warm evening with the hot Santa Ana winds blowing, and all the windows and doors of the old Victorian house were open. By the time the meeting started, there were more people than the store and the meeting room and the large front porch could comfortably hold. I was impressed! This was the largest crowd to attend any event we had held or sponsored thus far. 'Who is this Sai Baba?', I wondered, as my fiancé (Syd) and I drove off for a much needed night away.

Several days later one of our regular customers, Chuck, who had attended the Sai Baba workshop came in the store. He announced he had decided to go to India to see Sai Baba, and was applying for a loan at the bank to finance his trip. Chuck said he knew it was up to Sai Baba whether the loan went through or not, because nobody could go see Sai Baba unless he was called to go. I asked him, "Who is this Sai Baba?". Chuck replied, "He is an Avatar and they call him the Miracle Man because he aports things". Not being familiar with these Eastern words, I asked, "What is an avatar, and what does 'aport' mean?"

We were interrupted before Chuck could answer my second question, and I soon forgot about this Miracle Man. At the time I was extremely preoccupied with planning for our wedding that Fall and keeping my busy schedule at the store. As any other bookstore owner can attest, you don't own the bookstore, it owns you.

Shortly after the wedding, Syd and I were visiting some friends, and the subject came up about Syd's pending trip to India. At the time, Syd was the CEO (Chief Executive Officer) of a water purification company headquartered in Santa Barbara which also had another manufacturing plant and research and development facility in San Diego. I met Syd when he hired me to be his Administrative Assistant. This position later evolved into the role of Personnel Manager. Syd had put together an innovative joint venture with a publicly owned company in India and his trip was to finalize this joint venture. Our friends asked if I was going along and I answered, "No, but I sure would like to go!" Truthfully, one minute before that, I had never given it a thought.

Syd, knowing what a culture shock it would be for me asked, "Why would you want to go to India?" Then the words flew out of my mouth - "I want to go see Sai Baba!". My first thought after that response came out of my mouth was **"Who said that???"** It certainly wasn't me. That answer surprised me more than anyone else, because I had never thought of or wanted to go to India, nor did I know enough about this Sai Baba to want to go see Him. And this independent lady thought she had already found her own spiritual path and certainly was not looking for a Guru. Prior to that moment, if I had any choice about traveling, it would have been to Hawaii to see my daughter and grandchildren, or to do some more traveling around Europe. And besides, I had a bookstore to keep running.

Syd went off on his trip to India. This was not his first trip to that far off country. On his many previous trips, he had asked various Indian businessmen if they knew of any ashrams or gurus, and always got the same reply: "No, we don't have anything to do with those places. They are for you crazy Americans.". This trip was different. Everywhere Syd went, he encountered people who knew of Sai Baba, and he was told one story after another about healings, miracles, and trips to Sai Baba's ashrams.

At one business dinner in an old restaurant in New Delhi, Syd heard stories from two people whose family members had gone to see Sai Baba and gotten healed of cancer. Syd noticed a statue sitting on the mantle in the dining room during dinner, and he found himself drawn back to staring at it from time to time. One of the older gentlemen in the group noticed his interest in the statue and told Syd that was Sai Baba. Syd responded with, "That's not Sai Baba. I've seen His picture on the cover of a book and He doesn't look at all like that." The older gentleman assured him, "That is Sai Baba of Shirdi, who is said to be your Sai Baba's previous incarnation." At that point, Ashwin, a man of Indian descent, who worked for and was traveling with Syd, volunteered, "Syd, I have some good friends in Santa Barbara who are long time Sai Baba devotees. Would you like to meet them?". Syd was pleasantly surprised to hear this and responded in the affirmative.

Now, all of this was taking place on the other side of the world without my knowledge; while at the same time there were other forces at work at home that were setting things in motion for the future. After our wedding, it had become increasingly difficult for my bookstore partner and me to work together. Her alcohol problem was affecting our friendship and our business relationship. It continued to deteriorate until we agreed that the only thing we could do was sell the store. Putting this bookstore together had been a longtime dream for me, and I really did not want to give up my 'baby'. So, I decided that if we put it on the market and there was a decent offer from a buyer, then it must be God's Will that we sell the store, rather than try to hold on and continue with attempts to make a go of it as a partnership.

It wasn't long before a buyer materialized, but with only enough cash to buy one of us out. I didn't understand why at the time, but my Inner Voice was telling me it was time to let go of the store. So, we all mutually agreed to sell my half of the store to her, which turned out to be a blessing in disguise for me. A few short months later escrow closed and I was free! For the first time in my adult life, I did not have to get up and go to work! And my wonderful husband suggested that I retire from the working world. After putting in more than 30 years, it didn't take me long to say "Yes!".

We celebrated my new found freedom by my joining Syd on one of his business trips to London, with a side trip via train to Edinburgh, Scotland. I feel very comfortable in London and the United Kingdom, and am drawn to its Royalty for some reason. When we visit there, it is as though I have come home. The British Isles is one of my very favorite places, probably because I know I have had many past lives there.

Kundalini

Being away from the bookstore came to be a welcome relief. The last six months or so in the store, I found myself being so physically drained I could barely make it through the work day. Each morning for the previous twelve years, I had performed a morning ritual. I would first pray and surrender my life and everything in it to God, and then do hatyha yoga exercises, followed by a period of meditation. Thus, when I arrived at the store, I would be in a peaceful state of equanimity.

I always prided myself in the fact that many people who came in the store would comment on what beautiful energy it was filled with. But lately, soon after the first customer came in, I would be totally drained of energy, both physical and mental. It was a new phenomenon for me, as I had always had fairly good staying power. It finally dawned on me that I was being drained by the customers, many of whom had become good friends. The energy drain was especially noticeable after I would give them a good, friendly hug. I had been a hugger for years and really enjoyed the practice. Some people would look like they needed a hug, and I would be the first to volunteer. It always did wonders for them, but now it did terrible things to me.

"Another person's sins would pass to oneself through the touch of that person's skin. It is for that reason that devotees are not allowed to touch the feet of some Swamis. Since one cannot be sure who is bad and who is good, it is best to refrain from touching.....It is not just physical touch wherein lies the danger, but in mental intimacy also; bad influences may flow from one person to the other." CWSSB P 69

I was unable to determine why this was happening at the time, but in retrospect, I have a feeling this energy-draining problem started shortly after I received Shaktipat (awakening the Kundalini) from the Tibetan Lama, Ole Nydahl. His disciples had sponsored the Lama's trip to our area, and had arranged to hold their meeting in our store. The night of their meeting, I was surprised to see so many people arrive for this event. Having no idea what a Tibetan Lama would look like, I scanned the large crowd and found that one person stood out remarkably. He was taller than most there, but there was a brilliant glow about him that caught my eye. One would consider this person a very handsome man with his bright blue eyes and silver hair, and sleek physique. I wondered if this could be him because of the way his aura glowed, but he didn't look at all like the Asian I had expected him to be. I later learned that this Tibetan Lama was from Sweden.

Just before the meeting was over, one of Ole Nydahl's disciples slipped out and told me that their Lama wished to give me Shaktipat. An aged Indian guru had performed Shaktipat on me a decade earlier while visiting my church in Northern California. I never experienced anything remarkable, nor did I see any of the other people in the room with us at the time have any special experiences. So, I was unprepared for what was about to happen.

After my last customer left, I closed up the store and sat on the floor in a lotus position in the meeting room and slipped into a meditative state while I waited for the Lama. Soon I felt Ole Nydahl's peaceful presence and opened my eyes to see him standing before me. He squatted in front of me and quietly applied something to the top of my head where my crown chakra would be. I remember seeing what looked like a small silver box in the hand that went to the top of my head. He then touched the base of my spine with his other hand, which I believe also held something in it. My whole body started to vibrate from head to toe, and was bouncing up and down, uncontrollably. It was not at all unpleasant or frightening, so I just closed my eyes, let go and went with it. This movement felt as though it lasted a very long time, or at least it seemed that way, because my thoughts drifted away as I became one with the experience. Although it was a remarkable incident, on the surface, life seemed to continue as usual with the exception of the energy drain problem.

Getting to India

Syd had arranged for us to meet Ashwin's friends, the Patels, in Santa Barbara. Niranjan and Madhu were delighted to tell us about their beloved Sai Baba. Madhu prepared a wonderful North Indian meal for us, and we stuffed ourselves on a dozen or more delicious dishes she set out before us. We were shown a homemade video of one of their trips to Puttaparthi, and we talked until late at night. They were planning to return to India soon and Niranjan suggested that we come to India several months later during the first week of December, when they would be there to help us. They gave us the name and phone number of their travel agent, and we told them we would think about it. There was no further contact between us before they left for India.

Almost a year previous to our visit with the Patels, Syd had given one year's notice to the water treatment company of his resignation. (I left the company when I moved to San Diego to open the book store). We weren't certain what direction our lives would take at the time. Syd's dream had always been to set up his own international business consulting firm where he could work out of his home, but that was a giant step into the abyss for him. I had been encouraging him to surrender it all to God, and let things happen as He willed it. Syd was not sure about this surrender stuff. It would mean giving up control! That was not something a man of his position, character and background could do easily. Syd was used to making things happen; he was an expert strategist. And this is what he did best. As an international business consultant, that is what he would be doing! Nevertheless, he agreed to take some time and think about it, and his severance pay would give us a nice cushion until the future unfolded the unknown.

Meanwhile, we contacted the travel agent Niranjan had recommended and attempted to make travel arrangements for the first week of December. Not easily done! Everything was booked for months in advance, we were told. But maybe, if we didn't mind getting on a wait-list, we could 'wait' and see what happened. Since we didn't have much choice, we agreed. Just in case the trip worked out, we applied for our visas, got our shots, and did everything else one needs to do to prepare for a long overseas trip. The travel agent was many miles away from our home in Cardiff, and we attempted to keep in touch by telephone, with little success. Each time we called, we were quickly dismissed with "Nothing yet." Finally, a week or so before our hoped for departure date, the travel agent told us two tickets had opened up, but there was one leg of the trip from Singapore to Bombay that was still unavailable.

On the day before we were to leave, we got a call from the travel agent telling us our reservations were confirmed and to bring a Cashier's Check for the full amount and pick up our tickets. He wouldn't accept payment by credit card, for reasons we never fully understood. We rushed to the bank, got the Cashier's Check and some traveler's checks, drove to the travel office in Beverly Hills, waited patiently for two hours for our agent to return from wherever he was, got the tickets, drove back through the Los Angeles freeways during the 'afternoon going home from work traffic', packed into the middle of the night, drove back to the Los Angeles Airport and we were off to India, both exhausted and exhilarated.

Part of the Singapore Airlines travel package that Syd had arranged was a week's stay in Singapore. It gave us a chance to rest and recover from some of the jet lag and to visit the beautiful Island City of Singapore, with a side trip to Malaysia. He had also planned a trip to Kuala Lumpur, but that had to be canceled because of civil unrest at the time.

There are two things that stood out prominently during our visit to Singapore - the sweltering humid heat and the pristine cleanliness of this island city. I had never before experienced such heat and humidity at the same time in my life, not even in the Midwest where I was born. Singapore is almost right on the equator, and the temperature hovered in the 90's with the humidity possibly succeeding it, in spite of the fact it was early December. It was totally debilitating for me and the only time I felt relief was in an air conditioned building or tour bus. We took a walk one day and visited an exquisite orchid garden near our hotel.

While the orchids thrived, we were wilted by the intense heat. On one of the bus tours, we were educated by the tour guide on the birth of Singapore and its struggles to become the great city/country that it is today. We were told that everybody who lives there is given employment based on their education and ability, and a home in one of the high-rises that are seen throughout the Island. Thus there are no street people, or poor people that you find nearly everywhere else in the world.

We arrived in Bombay in the middle of the night and were greeted by indifferent customs agents, after waiting hours for our luggage to show up on the carousel. This was a sharp contrast to the warm and efficient welcome we had experienced in Singapore. I looked around at my fellow travelers and nobody else seemed to be upset about the very long wait for luggage, especially the Indians. Having no experience or knowledge of their culture, I figured they had just resigned themselves to the situation, while I, who had always prided myself on being patient, felt just the opposite. Being the organizer, and efficiency expert type, I could see many ways to improve the immigration/customs process we were put through, and wondered why nothing had been done to correct the situation. At the single 'Nothing to Declare' checkpoint, there was one very long line of travelers that snaked around and around, while there were about a dozen Customs Agents standing at their checkpoints to check declared items, with no arriving passengers in their lines. It made no sense to me at all.

Having been blessed/cursed with being born as a Virgo (in both Western and Vedic Astrology), I tend to look at everything from a critical point of view. We Virgos are usually aware of everything that is going on around us, and very conscious of every detail, especially if something is out of place or not happening as it should, or could be done more efficiently. One of the most difficult things for me to learn in this lifetime has been to stop being so critical and judgmental of everything that isn't perfect, especially when it's myself. We all have our lessons to learn.....

One of Syd's Indian business associates, Mr. D, had waited patiently outside the International Airport terminal to drive us to our hotel. As we left the terminal we were barraged with an onslaught of coolies wanting to haul our excessive luggage to the car, which was parked just a few feet away. If we hadn't been so tired, it might have been comical to watch as we tried desperately to keep track of each piece of our luggage going in different directions to the car. Then everybody wanted to get paid, and stood between us and the car, as though it was being held hostage until we paid the bounty. Of course, they were trained to look at what we had given them as totally inadequate, trying to draw even more rupees out of us.

Even though it was four o'clock in the morning, it was still quite warm. Nothing had prepared me for Bombay. I had seen ghettos before in Tijuana, but nothing like this. It was so warm that all the windows were rolled down in the car. I quickly became aware of the putrid assault to my acute sense of smell. And as we drove through the City, it varied from aged urine to burning garbage, to what I believed to be the acrid stench of bodies being cremated on their funeral pyres near the river. As we drove along the streets, everywhere we looked, there were sleeping bodies lined up one after the other on all the sidewalks. Some slept in makeshift shanties, others were covered with filthy blankets or pieces of cardboard; many were just curled up into fetal positions on the cool concrete.

When we finally arrived at the Taj Mahal Hotel, Mr. D went to check us in while we collapsed on a lounge in the lobby. After what seemed like a very long wait, Mr. D returned to tell us that there had been some mistake in the registration, so our room was not ready, and they were just now having it made up for us.

My romantic Taurus husband had arranged for us to stay in the older part of the Hotel where the rooms are wonderfully decorated in an exquisitely, elegant Victorian fashion. If it hadn't been for the television and telephone, one would have thought he had been transported back in time to the Victorian era with the lavish furniture and the heavy red velvet draperies rising up to the vaulted ceilings. After admiring our beautiful surroundings, we once again collapsed from exhaustion, and lay there with our eyes open, too enervated to sleep, until daybreak when we both finally slipped into a deep slumber.

During my travels in different parts of the United States and other countries around the world, I sensed that each place has a feeling or vibration of its own. For instance, when we visited Egypt, I couldn't get over the oppressive feeling and a sense of fear emanating everywhere we went. Since we went to Greece immediately after leaving Egypt, I felt a great sense of relief to be away from the oppressiveness. Greece had a more laid back feeling, but I did feel some contempt from the people who learned we were Americans. In England, there was the old world feeling of aristocracy in dominance and a sense of organization and rigid structure. Singapore radiated efficiency. In India, I felt two things very strongly - poverty and a sense of spiritual peace.

Shortly after selling the book store, I fulfilled one of my dreams and signed up for several art classes at the local college. I especially enjoyed working in the media of hand-building clay. Always being an entrepreneur at heart, I got a business license, and bought a kiln to fire up the clay jewelry and other art pieces I designed and created. Most of my jewelry was a composite of fired clay blended with crystals and semi-precious stones. When I learned we might be going to India, I managed to locate some addresses of gemstone houses in Bombay and sent off letters announcing my possible arrival. Mr. D's wife volunteered to escort Syd and I to the various dealers on my list.

We entered the office of one of the gemstone purveyors unannounced and I guess they weren't expecting anybody, because there were literally thousands of diamonds of varying sizes and shapes spread out on the large table in front of them. When they saw us, they panicked and scattered the diamonds all over the place in their haste to gather them up, probably thinking we were there to rob them. We were quickly ushered out into the hallway and asked to wait for a few minutes, where we all had a good laugh at what we had just witnessed.

I invested some of the money I received from the sale of the bookstore and purchased a good supply of semi-precious gemstones from that particular gentlemen. They delivered them to our hotel room the following evening after much discussion and negotiation on how and where we would conduct the final transaction.

While being driven through Bombay, I marveled at the different modes of transportation all making their way through the streets at what seemed to be a rapid pace. It was evident the British had left their influence. The city was complete with London busses, and the Indian vehicles have the drivers positioned on the right side. There were also 'roundabouts' at various intersections. In America, we have separate lanes marked to keep the vehicles going in a straight line. Not so in India. Everybody was all over the road and there were no visibly marked lanes. Amazingly, all of the vehicles managed to move along safely in a haphazard fashion, in what I consider very heavy traffic. Miraculously, they passed each other without hitting anyone, but it didn't stop them from continually honking their horns.

There were whole families, including father, mother and two or three children perched proudly on their motor scooter speeding along in all that traffic on those bumpy roads. I said a prayer for each family we passed on a motor scooter, because they seemed so vulnerable without any protection from the giant trucks and the very used, double-decker London busses towering above them. There were carts pulled by oxen the same way it must have been throughout antiquity. I found it amusing that we would see an occasional cow laying in the middle of the road, contentedly chewing her cud and watching the world go by, with traffic moving carefully around her. Very few cars seemed to have air conditioning because every vehicle I looked at had all of the windows rolled down. The exhaust fumes were so bad and the smog so thick, I wondered what the life expectancy of the travelers was, especially the taxi drivers and pedicab drivers who are on the road all day long.

We were very graciously entertained by Mrs. R and several other friends at their exclusive country club our last evening in Bombay.

Her husband was the CEO, (Chief Executive Officer), of the company Syd had previously established the joint venture with and he was out of town. We had similarly entertained them in Santa Barbara when they would come to town. It turned out to be a very disconcerting evening for me. I was not used to drinking, and didn't realize that the reason I never managed to find the bottom of my wine glass was because the efficient staff were continually filling it up while I was busily engaged in conversation. Things were beginning to look fuzzy from my perspective somewhere between the first sip of wine in the cocktail lounge and halfway through dinner, when I managed to spill the remains of my soup bowl all over my white suit. I had finally recovered from my embarrassment and was relishing my steak dinner when the glass of red wine found its way into my lap. Little did I know at the time that this was to be the last steak I would ever eat. I don't even remember if it was a good one or what it tasted like.

The Mysterious Phone Calls

Mr. D, the gentleman who met us at the Bombay Airport told Syd that someone had left word at his office asking that a message be given to Syd Chaden that we were to leave for Bangalore right away. Syd asked Mr. D who had called, and Mr. D told him the man who left the message did not leave his name. So Syd arranged for us to fly to Bangalore the following day.

While still in Bombay, we called the Patels at their residence in Bombay and there was no answer. So, we sent a telegram ahead to the Patels at the Puttaparthi Ashram, Prashanthi Nilayam, announcing our plans and tentative arrival. We learned later that they never received the telegram, nor did the letter we had mailed from the U.S. ever reach them, which would have informed them that we were attempting to make travel arrangements to India, and the possible date of arrival.

We left our hotel so early the next morning to catch our flight to Bangalore that we were unable to have breakfast. It was too early for room service and the hotel restaurant was not yet open. Syd had arranged for us to fly first class on Indian Airlines, while our normal seating was in the coach section. When I asked why, he explained that since Indian Airlines was the only airline carrying passengers in the India interior, not much effort or thought was given to the comfort of the passengers. He was right. I have no idea what the coach section looked like at that time, but the first class section was in dire need of attention. The seats were dirty and uncomfortable and in need of repair, and both of our tray tables were broken, but it didn't matter because there was no meal service anyway. Thus we were very hungry and thirsty by the time we arrived in Bangalore, and looking forward to getting to our hotel.

    It had been arranged by Mr. R for his nephew, who also worked for the same company, to meet us at the Bangalore airport. He was nearly two hours late. As we loaded our luggage in his car, he asked us where we would like to go. I asked if there were somewhere I could use a clean restroom and get a glass of water. He took us to his flat which was nearby while we awaited check-in time at our hotel.

    Shortly after our arrival at his home, the phone rang and after answering, he handed the phone to Syd, saying that the party had asked for him. But the party calling was speaking in some Indian dialect and did not speak English. Syd gave the phone back to our host for a translation. He conversed with the calling party for a few moments and then hung up the phone. He told us that the message was, "You are to go straight to Puttaparthi", and then he most graciously told us to take his car which was already loaded with our luggage. He instructed the driver where to take us, and we were off again.

    Syd's Bangalore business associates had organized a dinner party for us that evening at their club, and our host volunteered to arrange a postponement until we returned to Bangalore. We had no idea how far Puttaparthi was from Bangalore, or we would have asked our driver to take us to a hotel where we could get something to eat before embarking on such a long, hot journey.

    Syd and I at first assumed that the Patels had gotten our

telegram and had arranged for a friend to call us. But, when we had a chance to think about it, there was a big hole in this assumption, because the Patels had no way of knowing how or where or when to call us. They did not know the R's, and when we arrived at Puttaparthi, we learned the Patels had never received our telegram or the letter telling them we were hoping to come to India. Nor did they know anything about the message telling us to go directly to Puttaparthi; nor about the message Mr. D received in Bombay telling us to leave for Bangalore. Later we realized that there was no way anyone connected with the Patels or Sai Baba could have known how or where to call us.

We know now that it was our Lord Bhagavan Sri Sathya Sai Baba calling us home.

Puttaparthi

We drove through the gate at Prashanthi Nilayam that afternoon exhausted, dehydrated and hungry. It had been a long four hour drive on unimproved roads through the beautiful countryside. Our driver was told where to park and Syd found somebody who pointed him towards the Accommodations Office where he disappeared for what seemed like a very long time. I waited in the hot car, with the driver standing nearby. Syd returned once to retrieve my passport, and again nearly an hour later with Niranjan Patel (who just happened to be walking along and ran into Syd), and who was going to show us where our accommodations were located. He asked if we had eaten lunch, and when he learned we hadn't eaten yet that day he directed us to the canteen across the road, and said they might have something left from the afternoon meal.

Syd and I were handed what I later learned was a chapati with dal on two large leaves that had been stitched together. We sat down together at the nearest table. I was looking around for silverware when two men came over to us waving their hands in the air and shouting at us in a language we did not understand. I was suffering from heat exhaustion, hunger and a terrific thirst, and was nearly incoherent myself, so it took a long time for me to comprehend that they wanted me out of there. I was in tears when they ushered me outside and pointed me next door. I had no idea what I had done wrong, but later learned that the men and women had separate canteens. I had unwittingly violated a major rule. The food was tasty, and only mildly seasoned, but this Virgo didn't enjoy eating with her fingers and trying to chase the flies away at the same time.

Later that evening, Syd told me of his experience at the Accommodations Office. While waiting in line, he overheard the official in the office tell the two ladies ahead of him that there were no Western accommodations. They pleaded with the official, explaining that they had been traveling for days to reach the Ashram. The official repeated, "There are no Western accommodations". One of the ladies asked him, "Where can we go; is there anyplace we can stay?". The official repeated, "There are no Western accommodations". The ladies left the office in tears. Syd said his heart went out to them and even though he knew he faced the same scene, he approached the official and asked for accommodations for the two of us. "There are no Western accommodations.", came the monotone reply.

Syd left the Accommodations Office, not knowing what to do next, but determined to find a place to stay. We had noticed there were some small places with signs indicating there were hotels outside the Ashram as we were driven through the streets, but they appeared to be just one room homes or shanties with rooms or beds for rent, and not very appealing to westerners accustomed to comfort and cleanliness. As Syd started to walk back to where I was waiting in the car to give me the bad news, he saw a familiar face. Niranjan Patel was walking toward him with another Indian gentlemen and greeted Syd, "Ah, you have come! Where are you staying?"

After Syd described the incident in the Accommodations Office, Niranjan said something to his companion in their native tongue, and then told Syd to come with them. They entered the Accommodations Office and the gentleman with Niranjan said something to the Accommodations official, who promptly found an apartment for us in one of the round buildings. Only Baba knows why we were given Western accommodations and the girls in line in front of Syd were not.

"Not even an eyelid can open without the Lord's Will. So try to get the Lord's Grace and leave all questions to be answered by Him according to His Fancy." SSS VOL II Chap 18 P 100

At this point i must tell you that I had not read any books about Sai Baba or the Ashram or its rules and policies, so I had no idea what to expect, nor did I have any preconceptions. When we met with the Patels in Santa Barbara, we didn't think to ask questions about what kind of clothes to pack or what to expect in the way of food. The one thing we were told was that the accommodations were austere, (and they were right!). So, we packed everything we thought we might need, including cooking utensils, food, sleeping bags, and a variety of clothing, and when we arrived we were loaded with luggage.

The 'apartment' we were assigned to was one large room with concrete floor and concrete walls, and a concrete bathroom with a western toilet, a small sink and a shower head with cold water only, and one window. It was barren of any furniture. Both the main room and the bathroom had a bare light bulb and one 240 v. electrical outlet. There was a separate room off to the side with a big lock on the door. We were told it was a kitchen, and the 'donor/owner' of the flat stored his supplies and belongings in that area. It wasn't the Taj Mahal, but it was certainly very adequate, and better than camping out, which I had done plenty of in my life before Syd. We later learned that being assigned to an apartment such as this was a great privilege.

We were busy setting up housekeeping when Madhu Patel arrived with a friend and asked if we were ready to go to Darshan. I answered with a question, "What's Darshan?" They looked at each other and then back at us and did the best they could to get us ready for this thing called Darshan. I would much rather have stretched out on that cool concrete floor, but Madhu wouldn't hear of it, and ushered us off down the road to Darshan. She explained to me on the way that afterwards, we would go into the village and arrange for proper clothing, some mattresses, buckets and whatever else we might need for a comfortable stay. All I wanted to do was lay down somewhere, anywhere, and recover from my exhaustion and trauma.

"You have won this human body, this human life, as the reward for many lives spent in acquiring merit. You have won this chance, this unique good fortune of being able to see a holy being, to have the darshan of Sai. Plunging deep into the waters of this tumultuous ocean of time, you have heroically emerged from its depths with the rare pearl in your hands of Sai's grace. Do not allow it to slip from your grasp and fall into the depths again. Hold on firmly to it." SSN Sum 1989 P 1

Both this body and mind were simply too tired to appreciate Darshan. After sitting in line with probably 500 or more ladies in the hot sun on the sand for some time, our line filed into the temple grounds, and again we sat and waited. I think I must have dozed off, because the next thing I remember is Madhu saying to me, "Here He comes!". As I turned toward where she was pointing at the temple, I saw for the first time the One who was responsible for my being there. He was slight of figure, short and His mass of black hair glistened in the sun in contrast with His bright orange gown. I know it seems ridiculous now, but my first thought was Halloween; He is wearing Halloween colors. I have read where people who have seen Baba for the first time have said they knew instantly that He was God. It didn't happen that way for me. I didn't feel anything special, and possibly it was because I was so very tired. My mind drifted back to home and our landlady taking us to the Yogananda Ashram in Encinitas, which was just a few blocks from our home. She had invited us to a big celebration there which was always held on Halloween, and I silently wondered if the colors of Sai Baba had any connection with Halloween or Yogananda.

From our vantage point in the third row, I watched Him walk over to an Indian lady nearby. He waived His right hand with palm down in a circular movement, and then after grabbing at something, I saw Him pour a grey substance from His hand into the awaiting cupped hands of the Indian lady. Madhu whispered something about ash to me, but I didn't understand. He shot a quick glance in my direction as He passed by, and then moved over to the other lady's section. Madhu whispered, "He knows you are here!". Once more, I saw the same movement of His hand, but His body was blocking my view of what He was doing. I continued to watch Him until He entered into the men's section. Then I closed my eyes and just relaxed into the soothing warmth of the sun. For the first time that day, I was at peace.

"Never take lightly the transformation that is taking place as I walk among you. All that My Eyes fall on will be transformed. Always find a quiet corner after My Darshan, where you may enter the stillness and receive the completion of My Blessings. My Energy goes from Me as I pass you. If you proceed to talk with others, immediately the precious energy is dissipated and returns to me unused. Rest assured that whatever My Eyes see becomes vitalized and sent transmuted. You are being changed day by day. Never underestimate what is being accomplished by this act of Darshan. My walking among you is a gift, yearned for by the Gods of Highest Heaven, and here you are receiving this Grace. Be grateful. These blessings you receive will express themselves in due time. But also remember that to whom much is given, from him much will be demanded." LMSL P 101

Madhu and I joined Syd and Niranjan after Darshan and walked out the Ashram gate into the village. The first thing I noticed was the stark contrast between the cleanliness and orderliness of the Ashram grounds and the trash littered roads in the village. The noise level went up about 20 decibels. We walked carefully around the cow dung and other debris that littered the street as we were ushered to a shop that displayed shelving with row after row of brightly colored fabrics. None of the bright colors was suitable for me, but I selected several pieces of the fabric anyway and was carefully measured by their tailor to have Punjabis (an acceptable mode of dress for ladies which are similar to baggy pajamas) made, while Syd was being measured for ready made men's white cotton outfits. Then we chose some cotton filled mattresses and other necessities at another shop. While Niranjan arranged for our purchases to be delivered to our apartment, we returned for a quick rest while awaiting their arrival. It occurred to me later that I had recovered from the exhaustion somewhere between Darshan and our shopping tour, so when Madhu invited us to their apartment for dinner later, we readily agreed.

After a delicious dinner, Madhu passed around some ash and we watched as she put some on her forehead and then ate the remainder from her hand. She motioned for us to do the same. I wasn't sure about this, but both Syd and I followed her suggestion. I didn't find it disagreeable, and it did not have much taste. She gave us a little packet of the ash to keep and told us that it was given to them by Sai Baba Himself.

"What I materialize is a manifestation of Divinity with a potent significance as well as symbolism. It is symbolic of the cosmic, immortal and infinite nature of all forms of God, Atma or the spirit - that is, what is left when everything worldly, transient and changeable has burnt away. I have spoken to you of the imperative of desire less life.....

"In the first place, it is symbolic of the life-death cycle in which everything ultimately reduces itself to ash. For dust thou art, and unto dust shalt thou returneth. Ash or dust is the final condition of things. It cannot undergo any further changes. In the spiritual context it constitutes a warning to the receiver to give up desire, to burn all passions, attachments and temptations, and make one pure in thought, word and deed. It is in order to press home this lesson that I materialize ash for those who come to me with love and devotion. Like other materializations, it also acts as a talisman, healing the sick and giving protection to those who need it. It is the symbol of divinity, quite different from the magician's trickery mentioned to you." Spirit & the Mind P 241-242

"It is named Vibhuti since it endows one with prosperity. Bhasma - ashes, because it burns away all sins; Bhasitam - brightened, because it increases one's spiritual splendor, Ksharam - destruction, since it removes danger, and Raksha - protector, for it is an armor against the machinations of evil spirits. This is how vibhuti is praised in the Brihad Jabala Upanishad." SSSun Part 1 P 139

Niranjan explained the significance of the materialization of ash that Syd and I both witnessed during Darshan, and then launched into one of his favorite pastimes - telling stories about Baba. We listened attentively as he shared one story after another about the miracles Sai Baba had performed. We enjoyed his stories immensely, and although we were open to such possibilities, we both remained skeptical.

Life on the Ashram

The following morning we attended the required Orientation Session where we learned about the Ashram and its policies and rules, and also heard some more Baba stories. We were happy to hear that no smoking was allowed on the Ashram grounds and that silence should be maintained whenever possible. It didn't surprise us that no meat or eggs were permitted inside the Ashram, and we figured we could live without either during our brief stay. I was delighted to learn there was a bookstore and planned to visit it at my first opportunity, as I had yet to read anything about Sai Baba and realized I had much to learn. I wanted to read everything about Him and His teachings that I could get my hands on, as that is the best manner in which I assimilate information, and learn about a new subject. Once we completed the Orientation process, our passports were returned to us, and we were now legal residents of Prashanthi Nilayam for the duration of our visit.

Madhu attempted to introduce me to a variety of the Ashram ceremonies and Hindu rituals, including walking around and around the large statue of an elephant God, called Ganesh; and arriving at four in the morning to sit in the temple to listen to the morning chants. I tried doing these rituals several times each, but without understanding the significance of them or what benefit would be derived from them, I found it challenging to continue.

Madhu was not fluent enough in English to explain why people participated in these rituals, and I must admit that I never asked her for an explanation. She encouraged me to continue going to the bhajan sessions, but both Syd I had difficulty with that also. Sitting in a semi-lotus position for long periods of time was not comfortable for either of us, and we both suffered as a result. Also, having come from a Western musical background, (I used to sing on stage), it was unnerving for me to sit there while all around were singing in a language I didn't understand and in a music scale with so many different notes that I could not follow. I also felt awkward and embarrassed, (both products of a demanding ego), in not being able to participate while all around me seemed to be enjoying the singing and clapping their hands.

"I do not need songs glorifying God which like gramophone records, reproduce songs and strings of God's names without any feeling or yearning while singing. Hours of shouting do not count; a moment of concentrated prayer from the heart is enough, to melt and move God." BTBOS P 329

It wasn't just the music and long periods in cramped positions that discouraged us from participating in bhajans. We were not accustomed to the exhausting heat and because of my history of sunstrokes, I felt I had to measure my time in the sun carefully. The long walks back and forth from our apartment to the Darshan area took its toll on me. It had only been ten months since I had quit a thirty-year smoking habit, and my lung capacity and physical strength had not yet returned.

My days were filled with getting up very early to shower to be ready for the pre-dawn Darshan lineup. Then a long walk back to the apartment after Darshan to fix and eat breakfast. (The Western Canteen was not available in those days). Then another long walk to the village to buy fresh vegetables to cook for dinner and supper. I was exhausted from having to walk in the heat of the sun and had to take several short rests every day. We found that the bakery in the Ashram served Pizza on Wednesdays and Sundays, which nicely supplemented the simple meals I prepared on a little Bunsen burner in our room. Madhu invited us to dine with them several times. She said she was very concerned whether we were eating right because she knew we were not going to the canteen, but we assured her we were doing just fine.

On our third day at the Ashram, I was sitting in the first row, and when Baba came along, He looked deeply into my eyes for what seemed like an eternity. I felt as though my soul's history had been exposed. When He came close to me, I squeaked out "Swami?", and held up my letter to Him which asked for His help with my spiritual growth. He took my letter and stopped right in front of me to take letters from others. Suddenly, there were bodies flying all around me grabbing at His feet, and I was being pushed and shoved back and forth. *"How disgusting!"*, I thought. *"I could never do that!"*. When He walked away, I scooped up some of the sand that He had stood on, as I had seen other ladies do, and carefully put it in a plastic bag I carried in my purse.

"As Baba looks at people, he sees the past, the present moment, the future and everywhere in every direction." CWSSB P 73

Madhu had been watching me from her position somewhere behind me, and said later, "How come you didn't touch Swami's Feet? When He stands in front of you like that, He is offering His feet for you to touch!". I had actually thought that the reason He stood in front of me was because He knew His feet might be safer from everyone grabbing at them. She seemed disappointed in me, and I had no answer for her. She would never understand my disgust with such a tradition. Madhu also mentioned that I should not have taken the sand because it costs the Ashram money to have more hauled in to replace what all the devotees take. Somehow, I felt at the time that the sand had special energies in it and I knew in my heart I was taking it with Swami's blessings. We have it to this day on a tray with a small collection of rocks and seashells I also brought home from the Ashram.

"The idea behind bowing one's head at the feet of Bhagavan is that thereby sacred thoughts enter the devotee's mind. This means that when one comes in contact with Bhagavan's feet, the sacred impulses from them flow to the devotee. When the devotee's head touches the Lord's feet, the Lord's divine energy flows towards him. This implies that you should keep contact with only pure objects and keep away from impure objects.....

"But what happens when you come into contact with divine fire? All your bad thoughts and bad actions are reduced to ashes. This is the sanctity attached to the performance of padnamaskar (prostrating at the Feet of the Lord)." SS May 1992 P 97

Madhu watched over us like a mother hen, and offered advice when she felt it was needed, and we were grateful for her caring attention. When she came upon Syd and I strolling along the Ashram grounds holding hands, she was shocked. She explained to me later that men and women don't normally walk together, and it wasn't until then that we realized we had never seen her and Niranjan together outside their Ashram apartment. She also explained that holding hands was forbidden. We were still newlyweds and found this difficult to understand, but we were careful after that to obey the rules.

On our fourth day at the Ashram, I awoke from having my first 'Baba Dream'. I wrote in my journal:

"I dreamed that I was walking with Swami and others, and watching Him heal and help people. When we came to Michelle, who lives here at the Ashram, I instantly knew her to be 'Michok' from another life. When we met her several days previous, I felt I had known her in a past life. As I awoke from the dream, I wondered why Baba had taken me to Michelle. Perhaps it was to confirm my belief about past lives?".

"What you see and feel in a dream has some basis in what you have seen and felt in the waking state; so, too, what you see and feel in the present life has as its basis what you have seen and felt in other lives, previous lives." SSS Vol. IV P 3

"Whenever I appear in a dream, it is to communicate something to the individual; it is not a mere dream as it is generally known. It is a real appearance." Sathya Sai Baba, quoted from TSI by Sudha Aditya, P 64

The Patels had introduced Syd and I to Michelle and her husband Richard, who taught photography at Baba's University at the time. Michelle went to India from New York during the hippie period and was one of the very fortunate members of the 'Gopi Brigade', a group of young lady devotees who were able to spend a lot of time with Baba. After some time Baba arranged and performed a wedding for her and Richard. As I recall, He had also named and blessed their babies, who were already in Swami's school by the time we were there. I instantly liked Michelle and found her to be a gifted and humorous story teller. And her multi-talented husband treated us to a delicious cake he baked. I would have loved to have spent more time getting to know this couple and hearing more of their stories of life with Baba and what it was like living on the Ashram, but time was at a premium.

Also on that same day I wrote in my journal:
"Our 4th day here and so much has been happening it seems like a

week or more already. We have not missed a single Darshan and I have felt Swami's eyes almost every time.....Syd and I both know that He knows we are here. He has made eye contact with Syd also. We have been tested with bugs, mosquitoes, heat, noise, crowds, line jumpers, odors, sore and bleeding bare feet, you name it! My belief system has been tested as well. Whatever the reason, I still don't know why we were called here. Hopefully, Swami will grant us an interview and will tell us why. Niranjan Patel arranged a meeting with himself and Syd and the former Editor of some Indian newspaper this morning, so I had some free time. I read and then had a good, long, long cry. Why? I don't know, except to release, and release I did. I couldn't find any feeling behind the tears, but I felt absolutely wonderful after shedding them.".

"No one can come to Puttaparthi unless I call him. I call those who are ready to see Me. Of course, there are different levels of readiness." LG

"Tests and obstacles are the sign of God's grace, not His anger." SSS VOL IX Chap 14 P 82

One afternoon, I was heating some water to make a cup-of-soup for Syd and I, when I suddenly had a funny feeling I was doing something wrong. While eating the soup, it dawned on me that there was chicken broth in it. Since there was no actual meat in the soup, I didn't think there was anything wrong with consuming it. Afterward, I felt Baba mentally chewing me out from a distance, and then I experienced this incredible sense of shame for breaking Baba's rules, even though nobody else would ever know. My conscience kept nagging at me (with Baba's help I am sure) about the soup until I shared what was going on with Syd. Together we looked through the rest of our food supply from home and found two more packets of cup-of-soup with chicken broth in them. We quickly threw them out, even though our food supply was growing short. This was my first experience in which I was aware of Baba communicating with me as my Higher Self or Inner Voice.

"In spiritual endeavors there can be no stability and no concentration when meat is eaten. As the food, so is the mind. If one partakes of meat, one will have animal thoughts. For example, if the mutton of sheep is eaten, you must ask yourself 'What is the quality of the

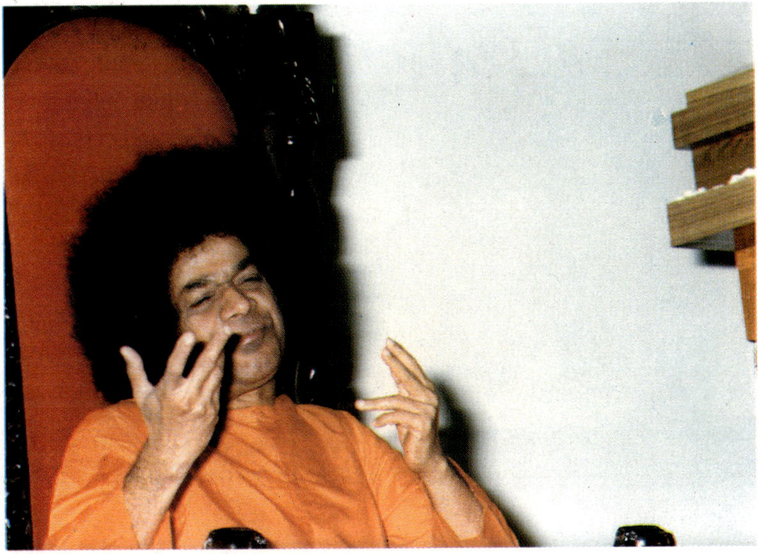

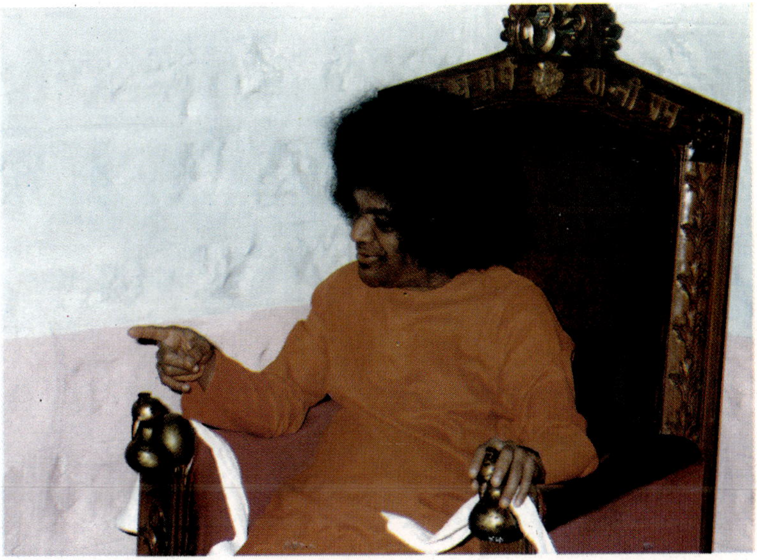

sheep?' They only follow, follow, follow. If you eat mutton, you lose discrimination. If you eat pork, you will develop the quality of the pig, i.e., arrogance. These things not only damage our thoughts, but they amount to violence. It is a sin to kill the animal. You may reply that an animal was killed by the butcher. That is incorrect; it is only because you are eating them that the animals are being killed. If you stop eating animals, then no one will butcher them to sell in the market. Thus, sin is committed by the one who eats as well as the one who kills. Because of this incorrect type of food, we lose human qualities and acquire animal qualities." SSN Spring 1995 P 16

The Patels arranged for us to visit with Baba's official photographer, who was a friend of theirs and was a permanent resident on the Ashram. We were shown a large variety of pictures and portraits, and selected only two. In one picture, Baba is looking directly at the observer, and His eyes seem to follow you wherever you go. The other picture is of Swami standing in front of the Mandir (temple), with a full landscape view of this exquisite structure. After we returned home, I regretted not buying more of the beautiful portraits of Swami, but reminded myself that at the time of the purchase, we did not really consider ourselves 'devotees', nor did we have an inkling of what the future would hold.

Syd and I are both great lovers of animals and when we heard about Sai Geeta, Sai Baba's elephant, we left the Ashram one afternoon and walked through the village and up the road to see her. Her keeper invited us into the compound and gave us food to offer to her. Having never been that close to such a large animal, I was taken aback as she quickly lumbered up to me to take the treats from my hand. Sai Geeta was twice my height, and I wasn't sure how dexterous this gentle giant would be at the speed with which she was approaching me. She seemed delighted to have company and we felt overwhelmed with the love that was pouring out of this beautiful giant animal, especially when she reached up with her trunk and gently caressed my cheek.

When it was Syd's turn to feed Sai Geeta, I noticed a litter of puppies playing off to the side and couldn't resist picking up and playing with each one, while their mother kept a careful eye on me. There was also a camel in the compound, but he was braying loudly and not in the best of moods, so at Syd's insistence, we kept our distance. Otherwise, I would have walked up to the camel to attempt to sooth him. Syd had spent a lot of time in the Middle East on business, and his previous experiences with ill-behaved camels left him wary of the species, even if it was a Sai Baba camel.

After leaving the compound, we walked up to the Administration Building to meet the college boy with whom the Patels had arranged to take us on a tour of the building. We were shown a collection of gifts that had been given to Sai Baba from various foreign dignitaries. I particularly remember a telephone, which I believe was made of gold, that was given to Baba by the Queen of England, and another gift from Prince Charles and Princess Diana. There was a very large, and exquisite temple made of gold and silver, a gift from the King of Nepal. What impressed me was not the gifts from these and other dignitaries and heads of state from around the world, but the fact that they even knew about Sai Baba!

Back in the United States, Sai Baba seems to have been a very well kept secret. We were told that Baba has said one of His greatest miracles is keeping Himself out of the USA's news media. I have since heard that Time Magazine, 20-20 and other major USA networks and media have gone to India and attempted to interview Sai Baba, but He has avoided them altogether, while in the rest of the world, things are much different. There have been many occasions where He has come up in the news in other countries; and documentary videos about His life and miracles have been shown on television; and some radio programs are devoted to His teachings. Several years after our first trip to India I saw Him once here in the U.S. on television. It was a documentary about phenomena in India which briefly showed Sai Baba as a guru. It also featured some men who reposed on beds of nails, and men who go into an altered state of mind where they can survive for long periods of time in airless chambers. I was appalled that our Baba was identified with oddities for the curious such as these.

One morning while waiting in the Darshan lines, it occurred to me that I had not had one single thought about what was going on back home since we had arrived at Puttaparthi. I tried to picture our home or a room in it, and could not even remember what house we lived in or how to get there. I nearly panicked as I wondered where did my memories go? It was a very strange experience, and I really had to struggle to concentrate enough to remember our home in Cardiff by the Sea. It took a long time, but slowly the details returned, with great effort. Later I asked Syd if he had thought about home at all, and he realized he hadn't given it any thought either until I mentioned it, and then he experienced the same difficulties. *"What was going on here?",* we wondered together. Try as I might, I couldn't conjure up any feelings for family or home or the outside world. It was like the rest of the world didn't exist for us anymore, and whatever was going on out there didn't matter to us either. We were at peace, and that is what mattered.

The Interview

Throughout our stay at the Ashram, the Patels emphasized the interview. Each day they assured us we would get an interview with Sai Baba, and as the end of our stay was rapidly approaching, Madhu suggested several times that I pray to Swami to give us an interview before we left. My response to her was, "I have surrendered it all up to God, and if Swami is supposed to give us an interview, He will give us one!" She probably got frustrated with me, but that was the way I truly felt. Surrendering anything I might desire to the Will of God had been my way of dealing with life for a long time. This way I was never disappointed with what came into my life, and things always worked out better than I could have imagined or arranged.

"When you have surrendered yourself completely to God and become God's child, you don't have to tell God what you want. He will give even more than you have asked for. But it is only by love that He is your dearest. Do sadhana (spiritual practice) and there is a closeness to God; then you don't have to tell Him that you want this or that. Because you are like a little child, He will come and give you more than even what you ask for." CWSSB, P 6

I had long before given up praying for anything, other than for help with my spiritual growth, or help in dealing with challenges. God had taught me a great lesson in the '70's when He gave me something I thought I wanted. I had intensely prayed for this particular thing, and used other techniques to bring it about, like visualization and affirmations, that I had learned while involved with the Religious Science Church. By the time this thing I had prayed for came into my life, I no longer wanted it, and it became a big burden for me, and no matter what I did, I couldn't get it out of my life. From then on, I decided I would let God make the decision as to what was best or right for me.

Finally, it was Wednesday, and we were due to leave Friday morning. Even I was beginning to get caught up in the 'Ashram Virus' of wanting to have an interview. So, as Sai Baba walked out of the Mandir, I said a little prayer that if it was His will, we sure would like to have an interview, just in case it would help. He stopped and chatted with a few European women, and as soon as He moved on, they got up and went to sit on the veranda outside the interview room. *"Lucky Ladies!",* I thought. He walked past the section where I was sitting, taking letters and then moved over to the men's side. I saw an Indian gentleman get up and wave excitedly to his wife. A young boy accompanied him to the veranda, and his wife who was sitting near me, moved rather nonchalantly toward the ladies' side of the veranda, as if this were an every day occurrence.

Just as Swami was about finished giving Darshan, I saw a man come flying up out of the men's side and land in a crouched position on his hands and knees, as though he was shot from a cannon. I couldn't believe my eyes when he stood up - It was Syd!!!!! And he was walking slowly toward the veranda waving his hat and scanning the ladies' section. I quickly grabbed up my purse and cushion and moved to the ladies side of the veranda just as Swami arrived to usher us into the interview room.

Later, Syd described to me and the Patels the process he went through to get the interview. Here it is in his own words:

The Stupid Letter

"We had been at the ashram five days and my desire for an interview with Sai Baba had grown progressively, until it consumed my thoughts. My efforts to persuade myself that it was all right if we did not get an interview were effective for only short periods of time. Thus it was that on the evening of the sixth day at the ashram, I wrote 'The Letter' to Swami.

"Perhaps I should call it 'the stupid letter', rather than just 'the letter', because it was undoubtedly the stupidest letter that Swami has ever received. In it, I pointed out to Swami that we had been at the ashram for six days, and that he not only had ignored our prayers for an interview, he ignored our presence during Darshan. The letter read:

"It is said that all who come here, come because you have called them. If that is so, then why did you call us? To ignore us?"

"On the morning of our 6th day at the Ashram, I stuffed the letter into a pocket of my whites, and went to Darshan. I was seated in the second row. Swami came walking up and stopped almost in front of where I was seated. The men seated in front of me were touching Swami's feet, and those on each side of me and behind me were thrusting letters toward Swami.

"Swami stood there looking at me. I overcame the paralysis that seemed to affect me whenever Swami was near, and began looking in my pockets for the letter that I had written. Of course, the object of the letter was to request Swami to grant us an interview, and, with Swami standing there looking at me, I could have asked for an interview, but it never occurred to me to do that. That would have required logical thought, which I seemed incapable of. Instead, I searched every pocket for the letter so that I could give it to Him. But, I couldn't find it! Finally, Swami began to move on, and I called to Him, 'Swami! Swami! Please wait!'

"Swami stopped, and stood there, patiently waiting. Desperately, I searched every pocket again, and finally, I found the letter. It was in the left pocket of my trousers, and I had been sitting on it.

"I pulled the letter from my pocket and thrust it toward Swami.

"Swami reached for the letter, and as His fingers touched it, He looked at me and laughed. He didn't have to say anything. His look and laugh told me everything. It was, indeed, a stupid letter.

"Swami moved on, and as I sat there, it dawned on me that I had missed an opportunity to ask Him for an interview while I clearly had His attention, and that if I had any chance for an interview, my stupid letter had probably eliminated it. My spirits plunged.

Sit There!
"At the next morning Darshan, my row was the next to last called, and I was seated far in back of the Mandir courtyard. There was no chance to ask Swami for an interview.

"At afternoon Darshan, my row was the last called. Niranjan Patel had sat with me in line, and so, we walked into the courtyard together. The rows of men were about ten deep, wherever I looked, except at the far end near the special area for the sick and incapacitated. Swami rarely walked all the way to the end of the aisle there, and so, few men chose to sit there. There were only five rows toward the end of the aisle, and Niranjan and I decided to sit there.

"There, almost at the end of the aisle, I saw a gentlemen that Niranjan had introduced me to previously. He was seated in the back row, with no one on either side of him. I pointed him out to Niranjan, and we walked over and sat down next to him.

"He greeted me, and then asked me how much longer we would be staying at the Ashram. I told him that we were leaving Friday, after morning Darshan. Then, he asked if we had had an interview with Swami, and I said that we had not. 'Have you asked Swami for an interview?', he asked. I told him that I had written a letter to Swami, and that I had prayed to Swami, but that I had not asked Swami directly at Darshan. At that point, he motioned me to be silent, because Swami had entered the courtyard and had begun giving Darshan.

"As Swami reached the point where he would start down the aisle leading to the area in which we were seated, Niranjan's friend tapped me on the shoulder and pointed to the row in front of us, and said 'Sit there.'

"'But, there isn't enough room', I said. He reached out and tapped the shoulders of two men in front of me, and spoke to them (not in English, and so I did not understand what he was saying). They each moved away from each other, to make room for me.

"'Sit there!', Niranjan's friend said to me. And so I wedged myself into the space between the two men, and Niranjan's friend pushed me from behind to help me.

"I was now in the fourth row. Swami was coming down the aisle towards us, stopping to talk to devotees and take letters.

"Niranjan's friend reached past me and tapped the shoulder of the man seated in front of me, and spoke to him. He and the man seated next to him moved away from each other, to make a space for me. 'Sit there!', Niranjan's friend said to me. And so, I wedged myself into the space that they had made, with the help of the men around me, who pushed me from behind.

"I was now in the third row. Swami had stopped a short distance away, and was talking to a devotee.

"Niranjan's friend called to the men sitting in front of me, who did their best to make room for me. However, they were already jammed together, and they were able to make only a small space. I tried, but I could not move into that new space. And so, the men around me lifted and pushed me, until I was in the second row, but with only my right buttock and right foot on the ground. The rest of me was in the lap of the man seated to my left, and I was leaning on the man to my right. I had to hold my knees with my arms to keep from falling over backwards.

"I was still struggling to get myself in an upright position when Swami walked up in front of me. 'Ask Swami for an interview', Niranjan's friend called to me.

"'Swami, can I please have an interview?', I asked.

"Swami did not answer. He did not even look at me. He walked past me and then stopped to take a letter from a man close by.

"'Ask Him again!', Niranjan's friend called to me.

"I knew that this would be my last chance, and so, I bellowed out, as loudly as I could, *'Swami, can I please have an interview. Please Swami!'* Everyone around me turned and looked at me. More importantly, Swami turned and looked at me. After a long moment, He took a step back toward where I was seated.

"'How many are you?', He asked.

"'Just my wife and I, Swami', I said.

"Swami motioned me toward the Mandir, and moved on down the aisle.

"I was ecstatic. Everyone around me was congratulating me and telling me how happy they were for me. In the midst of all of that joyous feeling, I tried to get up, but I could not get any leverage to raise myself to stand. After several failed attempts, the men around me took hold of my arms and legs and launched me upwards. I was catapulted over the row of men in front of me, into the aisle, where stumbling and nearly falling, I finally managed to stand.

"A Seva Dal pointed to the Mandir veranda, and told me to go there to wait for the interview. But first, I had to be sure that Char knew that we were going to have an interview with Swami, and so, I stood there waving my arms toward the ladies section. When I saw Char get up, I went up on the veranda to wait. As I sat there, waves of emotion swept through me. I didn't know what was going to happen, but whatever it was, I knew that it was wonderful."

Back to Charlene:

Since I had never before been in the Interview Room, I had no idea what the seating procedures were, but it was evident that the other ladies did, because I got a few elbows in the ribs and elsewhere as they elbowed me out of the way and maneuvered themselves to the front of the room next to Baba's throne. I was pushed to the far corner in the back. The first thing Baba did was materialize vibhuti for each lady and put it in our hands. I put a little on my forehead and a little in my mouth as Madhu had shown us, and stowed the remainder in a plastic bag I carried in my purse.

Fortunately, it was a small room and I could still see what Swami was doing when He materialized a wristwatch for the young Indian boy at His feet. He moved His hand in a circular motion and then with His palm up I saw the watch materialize from one end of the watchband to the other on His palm, in a flash of light. *"Did I really see what I think I saw?"* He started to hand the watch to the boy, but as if in afterthought, He glanced up at the clock on the wall and set the time on the watch. As He fastened the leather strap of the watch to the boy's wrist, Baba recited: "W, A, T, C, H. Watch. W is for Watch your Words; A is for Watch your Actions; T is for Watch your Thoughts; C is for Watch your Character; H is for Watch your Heart. Remember this when you look at the time.". Swami then escorted the boy and his parents into the inner interview room for a private audience.

When they returned, one of the men with the British group asked Swami if He would help them put together a healing center in one of the British Isles where he lived. He handed Swami something and told Him it was a healing stone. Swami looked at it and said, "This is not a healing stone. I will make you a healing stone." Baba moved His hand in the now familiar way and out of the thin air popped a dark elliptic-shaped stone, about the size of a large chicken egg. "Here, this is a healing stone.", Baba said as He handed it to the Brit. Baba then asked the Brit, "Where is your wife?". The Brit answered, pointing to a lady in the group, "She's right there, Swami.".

Baba glanced in the direction the Brit pointed. "That is not your wife! That is your friend! I asked you where is your wife?", Swami retorted while looking him directly in the eye.

The Brit shamefully looked down at his feet and said, "She is in England with our son, Swami. We are getting a divorce.". Then he quickly added, "But my girlfriend and I plan to get married, and we want you to marry us Swami!".

Baba said with feigned disgust, shaking His head from side to side, "Divorce, divorce, always divorce. Nobody stays married these days. Marriage is sacred and binds the two for life. If there are problems, it is your duty to work them out. Divorce is not good.". I am sure the Brit is not the only one this message was intended for, as both Syd and I were previously married. The Brit asked Swami again to marry he and his girlfriend, but Baba simply ignored the request, as though it was never spoken.

Swami then stood up and ushered all of the Europeans into the inner room and indicated that Syd and I should also go in. Once again I was outmaneuvered and was pushed to the rear corner of the inner room. But I didn't really mind. I was just so grateful to be there. Since there were only a few men, Syd was fortunate to sit right at Baba's Feet.

Baba started a mini-discourse with, "God is all around you and within you. God is in all of you. You are in God. All are in God....." This really got Syd's attention because Sai Baba repeated almost verbatim what Syd recited each and every morning to center himself and elevate his awareness, in preparation for meditation. To put it mildly, Syd was blown away. He explained later that he really was not impressed with the manifestations he had witnessed Baba doing, and they only tended to get in the way of how and what he thought of Baba. But, there is no way that Sai Baba could have known Syd's morning recitation unless he was...... At this point Syd could not put into words who he thought Sai Baba really was.

As Swami spoke, I took every word down in shorthand in my notebook. He continued with:

"Animals are better than human beings because they do everything for a reason and in season, and there is no reason for what human beings do or season.....Possessions, cars, houses, money mean nothing. It is what is in your mind and in your heart that means everything.....The principle cause of the problems in the world is that children do not respect their parents. Parents give the children everything and the children just take it and don't care. And that is wrong. Treat everybody as if it was yourself because you are all One.....

"God is Love. You are all part of God. God is in all of you. You are a brotherhood, a complete brother-hood in God. You are all One. There are no bad people..... The diversity of religions is not real. There is only one religion, and only one God. It is that Unity of All.

"See no evil; see only Good. Hear no evil; hear only Good. Think no evil; think only Good. Speak no evil; speak only Good. Act no evil; act only Good. Do no evil; do only Good. And that is the path to God....."

After the mini-discourse, Swami looked Syd directly in the eye and asked him, "What are your problems?". Syd thought about this for a minute and I watched as a big glow suddenly came over his face when he realized he really had no problems. He just shrugged to Swami, as if to say, *"I don't have any problems."*. Swami nodded to Syd, who felt that Swami's nod and look meant, "You see, you only thought you had problems!". Syd said later that if he had been asked that question outside an hour before the interview, he could have put together a long list of problems, but sitting at Baba's feet, all the things he would have considered as problems no longer seemed important and they were not worth mentioning. Syd later said, "When you are thinking about or talking to God, how can you have any problems?".

Swami moved onto another couple, and addressed the wife with, "Your husband is a good man. Why do you always pick at him? He works hard and provides you with a good home." . You could tell which man was her husband because he had a smirk on his face and was nodding 'yes', and getting all swelled up by what Baba was saying to his wife. Then Swami addressed him with, "And you. Why do you ignore your wife? She takes good care of you and the children and your home.....". The husband seemed to cave in, and the prideful stance he had previously taken transformed to a state of shame and dejection with his head now hanging low, while his wife literally beamed with joy.

Baba then asked another lady in the group, "Why are you always arguing and fighting with your husband? He is a good man and takes good care of you." The lady languished with the realization that Baba was aware of her conduct. But then Swami moved on to her husband and pointed out some of his faults as well.

Baba admonished each of the couples in the room in a similar manner, except Syd and I, pointing out the faults in each of their relationships. Syd and I were virtual newlyweds and had never had an argument, nor any kind of marital problems, and always treated each other with respect, so we were both feeling pretty smug.

Then Swami turned once again to Syd. "Where is your wife?". Syd pointed towards me and Swami leaned to one side and looked directly at me as I waved to let Him know which one was me, in case He didn't know. He said, "Ahhhhhh, Such beauty! So Blessed!". My heart swelled!

As we were being ushered back into the outer interview room I moved next to Syd and whispered to him that he had forgotten to ask Baba why He called us here. Syd loudly snarled some answer at me, drawing everyone's attention our way. He had never spoken to me in this manner before and I was deeply abashed. So much for the smug feeling! Swami managed to arrange that little scene to show us we weren't perfect either!

Baba then brought out His red plastic shopping bag full of Vibhuti packages and proceeded to hand them out to the ladies. When I saw each lady modestly holding up only one hand to receive the packages, I remembered something my former Religious Science minister had once said, "Why go to the well with a thimble if you can take a bathtub?". So I held up both hands, and Swami put the few packages He was holding into my hands, looked me in the eye and grabbed another handful and gave them to me.

When Baba moved to the men's side of the room, He stepped on Syd's foot. Syd grabbed Swami's leg and held on with both hands because he thought Baba might lose His balance and fall. Baba continued to stand on Syd's foot for quite some time, while He handed out Vibhuti packets to each of the men, and while carrying on a conversation with several of them. The Patels later told us that Swami knew exactly what He was doing when He stood on Syd's foot, and that He was probably absorbing Syd's karma or saving him from some future calamity, or both. Syd later said that Swami's skin was very cool and soft.

As Baba ushered us out the door, Syd said to Him, "Swami, we leave Friday morning. Can we come back?" Swami just said, "So blessed. So happy! So blessed. So happy!" I had the strongest feeling that Baba was blessing us with happiness with those words.

Friday morning arrived and after our last Darshan, we hurried to our room to pack and be ready when the car arrived. We gave the remainder of our food, cooking supplies, and our sleeping bags to the Patels and asked them to give them to anyone who could use them, as they were now only excess baggage to haul around, and we still had a lot of places to visit. The Patels had tried to talk us into foregoing the rest of our planned travels around India, and instead spend more time absorbing and learning about Swami at the Ashram. But, Syd was ready to leave, and so was I. At least we thought we were.

When our car approached the Ashram gate, I turned and looked back at the temple and suddenly burst into uncontrollable sobbing, which was totally out of character. It felt as though I was being torn from the womb against my will. I suddenly realized that the comfort of love and peace we had grown accustomed to inside the Ashram was something I had never felt anywhere before in my life, and I wasn't sure I wanted to leave it after all. The look on Syd's face told me he was having a similar experience. But we both knew the time had come and we steeled ourselves for what lay ahead. The contrast of the noise and the filth in the village streets was a sudden ugly reminder of what the outside world was like.

Something indescribable had happened to us during our ten day stay at Sai Baba's Ashram. It was so subtle, and so gradual a change, that I was unaware of its full impact until after we returned home. Those ten days changed our lives forever. Things would never be the same again for either of us. My attitude about material things, my demeanor, my outlook toward life and the world around me, my inner peace, everything felt and looked different.

The Tourists

Our journey from Puttaparthi began with a terrifying ride all the way to Bangalore. Unlike the chauffeur driven car we went to the Ashram in, we were now at the mercy of an Indian taxi driver. The mostly unimproved road was really only wide enough for one vehicle and some of the trucks and busses heading toward us at a rapid speed were wider than the road itself. The way the driver seemed to wait until the last minute to move aside when another vehicle was approaching reminded me of my younger days when the boys would play 'chicken' with their cars on the country roads. Whoever moved aside first was the 'chicken', and sometimes neither lived to tell about it.

I was filled with fear and found that hiding my eyes did little to shut out the drama that was going on. Then a sudden flash of inspiration (*Thank You Baba*) came to me and I knew the best thing for me to do was to close my eyes and chant the Gayatri Mantra for each bead on the sandalwood bead japamala I had purchased at the Ashram shop. (I had memorized an English translation of the Mantra that I found in a book years before and had chanted it every day since finding the book, especially for protection when I was out in public). By the time I reached the 108th bead on the mala, my serenity returned and I felt very high spiritually, and something in me knew there was no longer a need to fear. Wow! I was then able to completely relax and enjoy the scenery the remainder of the four hour trip. The driver had not changed his driving, it was me who changed inside.

"Gayatri will protect your body, make your intellect shine and improve your power of speech." SS June 1995 P 166

Once I was able to enjoy the trip, I became aware of the beauty of all the colorful trucks, or lorries as they are called in India, that passed by. Each was different from any other, but all were gayly decorated in bright colors. Most of the trucks had an altar created on the dashboard, using pictures and icons of various deities they worshiped, and each was garlanded with flowers.

Occasionally there were people working alongside the road. There were times that we would pass over what appeared to be sugar cane stalks laying right in the middle of the road, with some of the villagers sitting nearby watching us drive over them. When we queried the driver, he explained that when the people harvested the sugar cane, they often put it on the road for the trucks and cars to crush for them. A simple, yet effective method of harvesting the sugar.

We came upon a row of women breaking up rocks into gravel with what appeared to be hammers, laboriously hitting one rock at a time. The fruits of their work lay in piles of varying sizes of gravel, accumulating behind them. We were told this gravel would be used to build and repair the road. Later we found where a truck was slowly dumping sand on the road as it moved along. There were about four women walking behind the truck, each carrying a large coffee can of water, in which they would dip their hands and then sprinkle the water onto the sand and gravel on the road.

Syd and I marveled at the arduous yet effective methods the Indians seemed to be using in the construction of their roads. We talked about how much easier their work would be if they had the same equipment our construction crews have in the USA. After giving it some thought, we later agreed that the equipment would put most of them out of work, while their method probably kept everyone from the nearby villages employed and independent.

We arrived safely at our hotel in Bangalore, checked in, had a light supper of tomato soup and salad in our room and went to bed early.

We took breakfast from the buffet table the next morning. Syd selected his traditional breakfast of bacon and eggs, while I chose fruit, toast and cereal. The thought of meat or eggs seemed to turn my stomach after ten days of doing without either. Although most of the meals I had eaten in my life were focused around the meat entree, I never ate much meat, because I preferred the vegetables and grain dishes. Syd seemed to have difficulty eating the bacon and eggs, and later experienced a mild stomach problem.

Once in Bangalore, we were entertained at the dinner party that Syd's Bangalore business associates had arranged, and then postponed until our return. It was a pleasant evening, and we noticed that nobody asked about our trip to see Sai Baba, and we did not feel right in mentioning it.

Our stay in Bangalore was extended as all flights to our next destination, New Delhi, were canceled because of a strike. So, we signed up for a day-long tour arranged by our hotel; a trip to Mysore, which turned out to be a nightmare.

The 'first class, deluxe, air conditioned tour bus' provided by the hotel left before dawn the next morning with Syd and I as its only passengers. We wondered why they would use such a large bus for such a long trip with only two tourists aboard. The driver motioned that we should sit in the front of the bus, right behind him. We weren't two blocks from the hotel when the driver pulled over and took on a few Indian locals who obviously were not tourists. Then a few blocks further, he stopped and picked up a few more. The driver continued stopping and picking up local passengers and dropping some off as we went along. Each time we noticed his palm was greased with what was probably rupees. At times, every seat on the bus and the entire aisle was full of unauthorized passengers.

Most of the local Indian passengers were smoking and I have been dreadfully allergic to smoke of any kind since I quit smoking. I wondered if this was instant karma? We were seated directly in front of the TV which was over our head. The volume was on full blast, probably so that those at the back of the now full bus could also hear, although nobody seemed to be paying attention to the television. It was an Indian movie in some dialect, which was obviously not playing for the two tourists (us) on board.

The driver did not understand a word of English, thus we were unable to communicate to him that the TV was too loud without drawing his attention away from the road. As the day wore on, it was sweltering and we discovered there was no air conditioning in the bus. Rather, there were tiny fans above each window, but ours was not operating, so we opened the window adjacent to our seat. It was late afternoon by the time we arrived in Mysore and my head was splitting because of the noise and not having eaten since very early that morning. After a very quick lunch, we were taken to see various sights in the vicinity.

The driver acted as though he was trying to impress us or scare us to death with showing us how fast he could drive up and down the curved mountain roads. There were times I was certain we were going to plunge off the road and down the side of the mountain in that large bus. Drenched in fear, I had completely forgotten about the safety and comfort I had found in chanting the Gayatri Mantra. On the drive back to Bangalore, the same picking up and dropping off of local passengers started up again. This continued until we arrived back at our hotel after midnight, more than six hours later than the scheduled tour should have ended. We were both exhausted and hungry because we had no supper, and both of us now had splitting headaches. It did little good to complain to the hotel staff, who listened with deaf ears and seemed to sluff the whole incident off as our imagination. This was a five star hotel and we expected better of them.

Somewhere along the way to Mysore, I recalled the Patels telling us when trying to persuade us to extend our stay at the ashram, "Swami says when you travel to India to see Him, that is all you should do. You should not go traveling around visiting tourist sights and temples.". Sometime later I read the same thing in one of the Baba books, and the statement went further to imply that if you extend your trip and become a tourist, it will not necessarily be a pleasant experience. Being a seasoned traveler, whose life's dream was to see all of the world and spend some time in each country, I was disappointed.

Our next destination, New Delhi, did not seem much different from Bombay. We spent a few days there visiting more of Syd's former business associates. The wife of one of them, Mrs. S, took us on a shopping trip. We had been told that Nepal, our next stop, could be cold this time of the year and that we would need warmer clothing. Mrs. S was a very interesting woman, a professor of law at the university, and although subdued, she very graciously shared her wisdom and explained a lot about their culture to us.

As I recall, she said that her husband was the number one son in the family, and thus had many responsibilities, but also many perks. There may be three or four generations of the same family living under the same roof. The sons and their wives continued to live with the son's parents and family, while the daughters, when they married, moved into the home of their new husband and his family. The wives were subjected to the whims and desires of their mothers-in-law, often to the point of cruelty and abuse. Thus, many of the wives worked outside the home, where they had some sense of achievement, identity, and self-esteem.

The subject of our trip to see Sai Baba came up and Mrs. S told me they did not believe in Sai Baba because they are of the Brahmin Caste, which is considered the 'highest' caste, and that Sai Baba denounces the caste system. If they followed Baba, she felt they could no longer claim or maintain their prestigious position in society, among other things.

"There is only one caste, the caste of Humanity, there is only one religion, the religion of Love.....Names and forms are different naturally; but they are all aspects of the ONE. Love must bind all believers together; not only believers but non-believers too must be loved and served as His images." SSS VOL XI Chap 39 P 225

We spent one full day taking a side trip to Agra to see and experience the beautiful Taj Mahal. This time we hired a car and driver. As we walked up the long pathway to the spectacular Taj Mahal, a man called us over to the side where he was perched on a raised partition, along with his gayly dressed pet monkey. With his left hand, he handed me a packet of food to feed the monkey, while holding out his right hand for a fee. The monkey took a while to get interested in the food, probably because we were not the first suckers to accept the call that day. But, with my love for animals, this was a unique experience for me, and I thoroughly enjoyed playing and talking with the monkey. Syd snapped a few photos of this scene for our album.

There is no adequate way to describe the majestic Taj Mahal; one has to see it to appreciate its beauty and wonder. Made of carved alabaster, there are countless gemstones inlaid in intricate patterns in its walls, ceilings and floors. Our enjoyment of this Wonder of the World, and its breathtaking beauty was marred by some of the other 'visitors'. We were only there for a minute before I sensed and became acutely aware of the dozen or so pickpockets milling around through the crowd of tourists, sizing us up, and looking for an opportunity to move in on us. I pointed out these well dressed thieves with their folded newspapers in hand to Syd, and he kept his hand on his back pocket where his bulging wallet was installed. Then, as I stood behind Syd facing the thieves, I let them know I was aware of them. They kept their distance for awhile, and soon moved on to other less aware victims. This awareness of others' motives and thoughts is one of the gifts of being an empath.

Later that night back at our hotel in New Delhi, we packed up and were ready for our next adventure.

Nepal

We arrived at the Nepali airport in Kathmandu, and after collecting our luggage, entered into the customs area. The customs agent checking us through must have been new because he made a very thorough search of everything in our luggage, while the other travelers' luggage was being given just a quick once-over. He found the large volume of semi-precious gemstones I had purchased in Bombay, and became extremely excited. Our customs agent called his supervisor over, probably expecting to get a big pat on the back for catching some smugglers.

We had checked with U.S. Customs before leaving home, and knew that the gemstones were a legal transport from India to Nepal, and all the way home to the USA. But we were beginning to grow concerned because we were in a third-world country neither of us had been to before, and one never knows what will happen. After showing the boss his 'find', the boss gave him a 'so what?' look and dismissed the issue, returning to his office. This did not seem to be good enough for the now embarrassed agent, and he searched through our luggage again, this time with a passion. He found a tennis ball, which I use to massage my sore feet with every morning by rolling the ball under my foot. It helps to soothe my feet which are somewhat crippled from early childhood polio. He informed us he would have to keep the ball because it was not allowed. I started to protest, but Syd wisely said, "Let him have the damn ball and let's just get out of here!".

The scene in customs left us drained and disoriented. We stepped outside the terminal to get a breath of fresh air and then find a taxi to take us to the Oberoi Hotel, our next home for awhile. A very kind and dignified elderly gentlemen approached us, obviously a Hindu because of the red dot on his forehead. In perfect British English, he said he was 'sent' to take us to the Oberoi. How he picked us out of the crowd of tourists and knew who we were and where our destination was, and who sent him still remains a (*Thank You Baba*) mystery. But after the disruptive scene in Customs, we were very grateful for his appearance and gracious assistance. He and his driver loaded our luggage into the back of their white Mercedes Benz and delivered us to our hotel.

During the drive, we learned he was not in anyway affiliated with the hotel. He offered his services as a tour escort, including the car and driver, for our seven days in Nepal at an affordable price. Syd gratefully accepted the offer, which seemed to take care of all our needs and wants during our stay. Our new tour escort told us he was a retired military officer from the Indian Army, and he performed this service to augment his retirement compensation. He knew all about Sai Baba, and respected Baba as a great spiritual teacher.

I took a number of pictures of the breathtaking view of the snow-capped Himalayas from our hotel room window. We also had a good view of the neat and orderly village surrounding our hotel, a sharp contrast to many of the villages we had seen throughout our travels in India. We felt safe leaving the hotel and walking around in the village and talking to the residents and shopkeepers when we had some free time. There were a variety of vegetarian dishes on the hotel dining room menu, for which we were grateful. Syd had given up trying to eat meat while we were traveling, and the thought of eating flesh still made me nauseous.

Our escort picked us up early the next morning for a tour of several villages and an ancient temple. We were treated to so many memorable sights of life in Nepal and its countryside. There was a very large farm that grew a variety of healing herbs that were shipped to many countries around the world for use in Ayurvedic, homeopathic and other remedies. We were told that this farm was the exclusive grower of some of the herbs, meaning they were not grown commercially anywhere else in the world. He took us shopping at a village marketplace where we found an assortment of affordable gifts to take home for Christmas presents. We climbed what seemed like hundreds of stairs to the top of an ancient temple where we had a bird's eye view of the surrounding villages for miles around. We also visited a Tibetan village where many Tibetan refugees lived who had escaped and left their homes behind when China invaded their homeland.

We spent several days just touring around Kathmandu where we visited a mattress factory, another factory where doors and window shutters were being hand carved as they had been doing since antiquity, and a number of temples and stupas, both Hindu and Buddhist.

Our tour guide took us to one very old building and we waited in the courtyard while he made arrangements with someone for a young girl to come to the window above us. When she appeared in the window, her mannerisms were defiant, and we could tell she was very tired of having to go through this ritual whenever someone demanded her appearance. Had we known what we were doing there, we would have told our guide it was not important to us to see her. As she stood at the window, he told us that she was a young virgin chosen as a goddess of some sort, and was worshiped and admired by the locals. The girl was dressed elaborately and her face was painted with brightly colored makeup, mostly red and blue. She would remain in that status until her body experienced its first menses, and then another young girl would be chosen to take her place. Our tour guide explained that this ritual had been going on in this same building in Nepal for centuries. My heart went out to the little girl and I sent her LOVE.

As we walked with our guide down the street in Kathmandu one morning, we came upon a goat sitting on the curb as though he was waiting for a green light. Syd sat next to him and as he chatted with the animal, I snapped a picture, which we have labeled 'two old goats' in our album. Our tour escort must have thought we were balmy and he pretended not to notice our play.

We were driven up into the Himalayas to witness a sunset from the 'top of the world' our last day in Nepal. For some unexplainable reason, I was crippled with a terrifying panic that we were going to go over the side of the mountain as our driver made his way up the steep narrow road. The Mercedes we were riding in completely filled the road at times. When I looked over the side of the mountain, vertigo and nausea rose up within me. It had been a long time since I had experienced vertigo. In 1965 while pregnant, I fainted and fell backwards, cracking my skull behind the left ear on a concrete floor, and vertigo had lingered on for more than a decade, only returning occasionally when I would get very tired.

Since I had never experienced this kind of fear before, I could not understand where it came from, and wondered if maybe in a past life I had lived in Nepal and fallen over the side of a mountain. I huddled next to Syd and buried my face in his comforting chest most of the way up the mountain. Occasionally I would raise up and look around when I felt we were driving on a straight stretch, or when Syd would tell me it was safe to look. After observing my state of mind, our escort suggested that I should find a yoga teacher and start working with the Kundalini, especially in the muladhara (base) chakra, to help overcome this fear. He also suggested that I take Chawanprash on a daily basis to build up my chi and my stamina. Chawanprash is a combination of Ayurvedic herbs, and comes in pill form and in a jar, the contents of which look like a combination of blended mashed fruits and herbs. He found a chemist who dispensed these jars and I purchased two to take home.

On the long drive up the mountain there were hundreds of women walking up the steep slope carrying cow dung (obviously for fertilizer) in large baskets suspended from their brows by straps, and there were hundreds of women going down the mountain carrying recently harvested sweet potatoes and other root vegetables in similar baskets. They were dressed in the same brightly colored garments we had seen in an article on Nepal in the National Geographic magazine. It was like a step back in time. I wondered where the men were and what their role was.

We stopped to have our picture taken by our escort with a group of colorfully dressed children walking up the mountain. The older children were carrying babies on their backs in slings. To show our appreciation, Syd and I gave them each a coin. When we returned to the car, the driver lashed out at our escort in their native tongue. Sensing it was about what we had done, I asked our guide if we had violated a rule or something. He told me the driver was incensed because when tourists give money to children, it encourages them to become beggars. I humbly apologized for my ignorance and vowed never to do it again. In retrospect, the act of giving money to the children was totally out of character for me, and I felt as though I were acting out a part in a play written by someone else, rather than being myself. It was like I knew it was something I was supposed to do, not something I really felt I wanted to do. Perhaps there was a lesson in it for all of us involved. Poverty was evident in Nepal, but we were never harassed by professional beggars as we were in India.

"Serve patients in the hospitals by purchasing medicines or providing clothes, but do not give them money. If you give them money, they turn into beggars." SS May 1996 P 121

"......begging for the sake of work which is inherently good is an insult to human nature; the man who asks and the man who is asked, both are demeaned." SSS VOL 5 Chap 33 P 168

    It was beginning to get late when we finally arrived at the top of the mountain. The icy December wind blowing toward us across the snow made it bitterly cold. There was a tiny cabin off to the side that served tea and snacks and the four of us huddled inside sipping a strong brew of what I believe was 'yak' tea while awaiting the promised sunset. We had insisted that the driver join us, and he very awkwardly accepted the invitation. In all other stops we had made, he had waited in the car for us, but we felt it was just too cold up there for anyone, at what was probably close to 20,000 feet elevation.

    Just minutes before the sun was to go down, the wind blew even stronger and brought in some very large clouds that completely covered us. The clouds blocked any hope of seeing a sunset, so we made the long, slow drive downward to our hotel.

    We arose very early the next morning to pack and catch our flight to Singapore. We hadn't given any thought to the meals on the plane, and were served some kind of beef dish with vegetables and noodles soaked in the beef gravy. Syd ate a little of the meat and all the rest of the meal, and I just ate the pasta and vegetables. Within an hour, I had terrible stomach cramps, which I intuitively knew came from eating the gravy soaked noodles. I am sure there was nothing wrong with the gravy, other than it had beef drippings in it, and I should have known better because it felt offensive when I was eating it.

    We spent a few more days in Singapore resting up and then flew home via a short stop in the Tokyo airport where we changed planes. While on the last leg of our flight home, I did my morning meditation ritual, beginning with surrendering everything to God, as I had been ritually doing for about ten or twelve years. I would start with releasing everything in my life that was important to me, including Syd, my children, grandchildren, our home, income, bills, challenges, etc., listing all of the good and bad in my life and releasing them up to God, until I felt a peaceful freedom from concern about everything in my life. Then I would be able to genuinely say to God, "I surrender everything to You God. Put me wherever You want me to be, show me where You want me to go and what You want me to do and say, and please help me to be the best person I can be." The peace derived from this surrender process would stay with me until something would come along to push one of my buttons.

After our visit to Sai Baba, this all changed. There was a different feeling this time when I went through this process on the plane. I could feel the state of surrender even before I began the releasing process. And, it seemed as though the peace was fortified and sustaining. As time passed, I realized that now the peace stayed with me most of the time, and a lot of the buttons that previously tormented me were no longer there! It didn't take long for me to recognize that Sai Baba had gifted me, (*Thank You Baba!*), with the ability to *really* surrender and experience the peace that 'passeth all understanding'. For a long while after this, it took a major-league incident to pry me from my peaceful existence, and that was only when there were some heavy lessons I needed to learn. But, as some of these old buttons returned to haunt me, I realized that what I had experienced was probably Baba's Grace. Perhaps this happened to show me how it can feel if I do not react when my buttons are being pushed, and to remind me that with a little effort on my part, they would go away forever, and many of them have.

"When devotees surrender their lives to God and obey Him, He takes the full responsibility and cares for his devotees even to the smallest details." CWSSB P 131

"Surrender to God means to leave everything to His will and is the highest form of Divine Love." TOSSSB P 75

Back To 'Reality'

During our layover in the Tokyo airport, we ran into a former colleague in the terminal. He told us he was still with the water purification company we both used to work for in Santa Barbara. We learned he was on the same flight as us, but sitting in First Class section. I gave him a big hug, we chatted for awhile, and he brought us up to date on the latest happenings with our old firm. As we returned to our plane, he said he wasn't feeling well, and must have picked up a bug somewhere during his travels in the Orient. Our immune systems probably had been worn down from the jet lag that was setting in, because several days later, Syd and I both awoke at home with a high fever and other discomforting symptoms, and were very ill throughout the next two weeks with an Asian type flu.

As soon as we started feeling better, we set out on another trip into the Southwest on yet another search to find the place where we would build our dream home and eventually retire to. This time we covered the entire state of Arizona without finding any property we felt right about, and finally resigned ourselves that Arizona was not where we belonged. Our criteria included mountains, water and views, and it was difficult to find all three in the same place that was affordable.

At my suggestion, we continued East into New Mexico and stopped in Socorro and picked up the major New Mexico newspaper. Syd looked for property ads around the Taos area, our next planned destination, while I browsed through the New Mexico magazine, provided by the hotel. In the back of the magazine, I found a tiny two line ad which read "35 acre lots in Southern Colorado from $25,000", with a toll free number.

At any other time, I would have passed over that ad, because since childhood, I had viewed Colorado as a place with terrible winters. My aunt had lived on a ranch in the 40's and early 50's outside Denver, and wrote us letters describing how they had to tie a rope from the back door to the barn so they would not lose their way in the blizzards while trying to get to the livestock in the barn to feed them and milk the cows.

This was not my idea of a great place to live. I had been there and done that for two years in Alaska. But now my inner voice was practically screaming at me to have Syd call the toll free number in this ad. So I showed Syd the ad, but he didn't seem at all interested. He was focused on Taos. As my Inner Voice nagged at me, I nagged at Syd, until he relented and made the call.

While I watched and listened, I could tell Syd was really getting interested as he spoke with the salesman. I heard trees, mountains and lake, and knew there was a strong possibility with this Colorado property. While waiting for him to finish the call, I recalled a trip I made to Honolulu in 1983 and visited my friend Ruth.....

Becoming Vegetarians

After I had moved to Alaska, I returned to Hawaii to visit Cyndi and Ian on the Big Island, and Ruth in Honolulu on the Island of Oahu. Ruth took me to a psychic called Miranda, who predicted that one day I would live in Colorado, and become a vegetarian, and an artist. I told this psychic she was wrong in all three areas.

But was she? So much has happened since that prediction. Since we returned from India the previous month, we had given up beef and pork, and I could no longer tolerate eggs. The only meat we still ate was an occasional chicken or turkey. Syd never did eat fish, but I occasionally liked a little whitefish. And the last few times I had prepared chicken, I was only able to eat a few bites before I felt like gagging. This was becoming a problem, because all of my cooking talents were based around meat dishes as the entree. It looked as though I was going to have to learn how to cook all over again. I started simply with ethnic dishes like taco salads with beans, or pasta and marinara sauce, or a stir fry substituting cashews or tofu for meat, or just a variety of vegetable dishes. With the help of several books on food combining and how to become a vegetarian, it wasn't long before I mastered cooking a variety of vegetarian dishes and we had completely eliminated all meat and eggs from our diet.

Becoming a vegetarian was not a conscious choice, but one of necessity, and we know it was all Baba's doing (*Thank You Baba!*). It was a gradual process which lasted just a few months in which we simultaneously lost our taste for and ability to eat meat and eggs. After India, the thought of putting a bite of egg in my mouth made me gag, while Syd was experiencing the same feeling with the poultry we had been reduced to. Then Syd lost his taste for eggs, and I could no longer tolerate meat of any kind. The Patels told us later that Baba said in an interview that, "Eggs should not be eaten because they cause doubts and confusion". I can testify to that - since I have given up eating eggs in any way, shape or form, my faith and trust in Sai Baba to take care of us and provide for us is unshakable. Why anyone would want to eat something that would deny them of this strength is difficult to understand.

Several months after our trip to Colorado, I purchased some fried chicken for a family picnic with our daughters and grandchildren, since I was no longer able to cook it. The chicken smelled so good that I had to try a piece. After a few bites, I began to gag on the meat in my mouth and spit it out. That night, I felt deathly ill while my system tried to digest the few bites I had eaten, and what now felt like poison. I have never had the desire to eat meat or eggs since.

Syd and I are very careful now about what we eat, and if we are unaware that something we are served has meat or egg in it, we soon find out because it acts like poison and we have had some terrible stomach aches. Thus, we rarely eat out and I cook most everything from scratch. We have found that most restaurants do not understand vegetarians. Even many of the Chinese restaurants put chicken broth in their veggie dishes. We have become great label readers too. I was really surprised to find so many food products made with meat by-products in them, like yogurt and sour cream with gelatin, or ice cream made with eggs, cheese with rennet, tortillas and refried beans with lard, crackers made with lard, and marshmallows with gelatin, ad nauseam. One thing I have noticed since we became vegetarians is that we rarely experience many negative emotions like fear and anger and greed. Our health has also improved tremendously on all three levels - physical, mental and spiritual.

"Today, anyone who believes they are devotees of God should give up eating meat. Why? Meat eating promotes animal qualities. It has been well said that the food one consumes determines one's thoughts. You develop cruelty when you eat the flesh of cruel animals. Not only this, but how cruel it is to kill other living things that are sustained by the same five elements as human beings. So people who want to be devotees of God must give up eating meat completely. How can you call yourselves devotees of Sai, or Rama, or Krishna, when you kill animals? Those people are real demons. Such people never get the grace of God. So whoever they are, whether Indians or from other countries, they should follow Swami's command: Give up eating meat, now!" SSN Spring 1995 P 33

As for becoming an artist like Miranda predicted, when I sold my half of the bookstore, I enrolled in some art classes at the local college, including hand building with clay, painting with oils, acrylics, charcoal, pen etchings, etc., something I had never had time for before when I was working. I started designing and creating clay and gemstone jewelry and other hand built clay pieces. Our art class held an open house, and a famous artist bought one of my first southwestern wall hangings made from fired clay and crystals. Nobody was more surprised than me! I guess this made me an artist. So far, Miranda was right about my becoming a vegetarian and artist.

Several days before visiting the psychic Miranda, Ruth took me to another psychic called Nancy whose prophecy was accurate in every detail. It was on April 21, 1983. Nancy told me that I was about to grow leaps and bounds spiritually and that I would meet my number one soulmate before two years was up. Syd and I met in September 1984, and Syd's birthday is April 21st. She described Syd down to the last detail of his businesses, travels, looks, personality, character and his strengths. Nancy even described our wedding, the wedding cake and said that there would be a waterfall or something like a waterfall where the ceremony would take place.

When Syd and I planned our wedding, we hunted all over

Southern California for a place with a waterfall, but found none that was available for a wedding. So, we chose a beautiful place called The Atlantis, which was situated on a beach in the San Diego Bay, and had a tram that went right next door to the Marine Park in San Diego. Just before the wedding began, they turned on a lovely waterfall that we had not known even existed! The waterfall was part of the 300,000 gallon ocean type aquarium that ran the length of the ballroom, and circled around to the outside entrance and back through to where our wedding ceremony took place on the beach, and then back again. And the cake was like none I had ever seen - two of my girlfriends had arranged for it to be made and kept it secret until the wedding day. There were tiny waterfalls, and crystals glued together with tumbled rose quartz pieces helping to decorate this magnificent cake that sat in five different sections, each of which was multi-layered at different levels. And it tasted great too! It was worthy of being on the cover of a bridal magazine. Spectacular!

After meeting with the Psychic Nancy, I dreamed of Syd that night. We were working in a company that had a manufacturing plant, and I was handing him the announcement about the upcoming Christmas office party across a counter. When our fingers touched, sparks flew out and lit up the Universe and I got the most exciting, exhilarating feeling from it. Syd then said to me, "Wait for me - I will be there!", and the dream ended. Now I even knew what he looked like!

Trinidad Lake Ranches

Syd hung up the phone and told me the real estate salesman would arrange and pay for us to stay the following night at the Holiday Inn in Trinidad Colorado, where he would meet us the next morning to show us the property Syd had called about. But first there was Taos. We entered the outskirts of Taos that afternoon and immediately came to a dead stop. Traffic was backed up for miles. It was ski season and there was fresh powder on the ground. One look at the traffic jam and we knew Taos was not for us after all. We had enough of traffic congestion in California, and that was one reason we were leaving that once beautiful state. We pulled over into a parking lot to turn around and I noticed a combination rock and book shop, which just happened to combine our two favorite places to shop. We spent the rest of the afternoon browsing and purchasing some beautiful stones and books, until traffic cleared so we could continue northward into Colorado.

It was beginning to snow when we left Taos, and continued to get heavier until we got out of the high mountains of the Sangre de Cristo range. It was dark and very late by the time we arrived at the hotel just over the Colorado border, so we went right to bed. I awoke the next morning just before daybreak, looked out the window, and called out to Syd to wake up and come feast his eyes on the view. There was the most breathtaking panorama I had ever seen. The Sangre de Cristo mountain range was covered with snow and the sunrise was casting a bright pink hue on the snow. We were later told that Sangre de Cristo means the blood of Christ, and that name was given by the Spaniards when they came to the area centuries before and witnessed the same sight we were now looking at. It was picture post-card perfect, and we knew we were in the right place. Later I realized the mountains closely resembled the view we had of the Himalayas from our hotel room in Kathmandu.

'Mo', our salesman, arrived at 10 a.m. and took us into the foothills southwest of the Holiday Inn to show us the property. We were ready and waiting, and all bundled up for cold weather with our thermal underwear and heavy jackets that we had purchased when we learned we were going to be looking at property in Colorado. It was February 4th, and we assumed it would be bitterly cold outside. After a half hour of trudging around the different properties, we were overheated from too many clothes. The nights may get cold in Southern Colorado, but nobody needs thermal underwear during the day. We have lived here more than eight years now and have never worn the thermals since.

We looked at several lots in the newly developed Trinidad Lake Ranches, and then told Mo we were ready to go back to the hotel. He said he had other pieces of property in another area if we didn't like this one, thinking we were unhappy with what he had showed us. Syd told him we just wanted to put a down payment on the last 36 acre lot we had looked at. Syd and I had communicated telepathically that **This is it!**, but Mo had no way of knowing that. Never before in my life have I made such a quick decision - it wasn't really a decision - It was just a matter of knowing it was right because my Inner Voice said so. Syd too! Before we left on our trip, both Syd and I, independent of each other, had prayed to Baba to help us find the right property, and there is no doubt in our minds that He was responsible for leading us here.

We left Colorado early the next morning and started planning and designing our home on our long drive back to California.

Syd's Near Death Experience

Syd had a very interesting experience which frightened the life out of me. Several 'psychics' had previously told me our time together would be short because Syd would pass on after a few years of marriage. But they really did not need to tell me that, because I already 'knew' it. I have asked him to share his experience:

It was about two months after Char and I had returned from our first trip to see Sai Baba.

I had awakened in the night, with a strange, very unsettled feeling. I couldn't lay still, and so, I got up and walked around awhile. I tried to read, but couldn't. After an hour, or so, I thought about going back to bed. I sat on the side of the bed, and decided to lay down again, and as I did, I suddenly began to spin. I resisted, at first, but then was totally overcome and the spinning was faster and faster. There was an extremely loud buzzing sound. I seemed to be going somewhere, but couldn't see anything.

Suddenly, the spinning and buzzing stopped, and I was with my mother, who had passed away thirteen years before. It was totally dark, and I couldn't see her, or anything else, but she was there, and I was with her.

"Where have you been?", she asked. "I've been waiting for you."

"I've been to see Sai Baba.", I answered.

I immediately began to spin again, and the buzzing was there again, and then, I seemed to slam into my body, on the bed. I was still spinning, but my body wasn't, and when I entered it, my body and I had difficulty in getting together. My body lurched around, as I spun. I turned onto my stomach and grabbed the edge of the mattress and the side of the bed, and fought to hold myself steady. Gradually, the spinning and the buzzing subsided. I laid there, raised up on my elbows.

My bouncing around had awakened Char. "What's the matter?", she asked. "Are you all right?".

I told her that I was OK, and that she should go back to sleep.

I laid awake the rest of the night, thinking about the experience. I was certain that I hadn't been asleep when it had occurred. The robe that I had put on, and things that I had touched, moved, or looked at, were as I remembered. There was no doubt in my mind that I had been with my mother. I had heard her voice, in sound, or in thought, or in spirit, and the feeling that went with that was unmistakable to me.

Where had I gone? Where had I been with my mother? What did it mean?

Later that morning I told Char what had happened. She was frightened and upset by it. She felt that I had undergone a 'near death experience'.

We decided to phone the Patels and tell them about my experience. Niranjan immediately said that when Baba had stood with His foot on mine during our interview, He had been taking on or changing my karma. He suggested that the night that I had the experience of being with my mother was when I was supposed to leave my body, but Baba had changed that. He indicated that as soon as I mentioned Baba's name to my mother, Baba appeared and brought me back to life. And so, it was Baba's blessing.

Our First Miracle at Home

When Syd and I were married, we both had very little in the way of material possessions. I had given all my possessions away except my collection of books and my sewing machine before moving to Hawaii in 1978, and Syd had given everything to his wife when they divorced eight years later. It was a relief to no longer be burdened by 'things'. I even gave up my three-piece business suits, high heels, pantyhose, bras and wearing wigs! All of these 'things' had helped to create the illusion of the role I played as a career woman, and no longer reflected the real person inside of me.

Syd's mother had passed away nine years before we met. When his mother died, Syd went through an intensive period of soul-searching and rethinking of his life, its purpose, and where he was headed. One of his conclusions was that he should end his unhappy marriage of sixteen years, but he was concerned about his wife and his daughter Leslie. He did not want his daughter to be brought up in a broken home, and he felt that his wife was incapable of supporting herself. And so, he decided that he would wait until his daughter was grown and had left home to be on her own, and until he had sufficient means to assure that his wife would be able to live independently for the rest of her days without requiring his involvement.

In 1984 Syd's daughter left home to attend college. She was twenty-one, and said that she would not live with her parents any longer. And, in 1984, the majority owner of the company that Syd managed decided to sell the company to a major Fortune 500 company. Syd was already fairly well off, financially, and the addition of his share of the purchase price would provide what he considered to be sufficient means to comfortably support his wife for the rest of her life.

The terms of the purchase agreement for the company required that Syd stay on for a minimum of one year, before he received his share of the purchase price. The day after the one year had expired, Syd informed his wife that he wanted a divorce, told her that he was going to give her all that he owned, and that she could file for the divorce, if she preferred. When she declined to do that, Syd filed for the divorce. He gave her everything except his clothes, a used car, and $5,000 cash. He helped her to sell off their ranch and moved her into a condominium of her choice, then left with a clear conscience. And so, he considered himself to be free, not just legally, but of any further obligation.

I arrived on the scene in 1984, just as his daughter left for college. Since we have come to know Sai Baba, we are convinced that He brought us together to find Him, and then to live out our lives helping each other to grow spiritually under His care and guidance.

"Everything that is not 'you' is an object; it is luggage for the journey; the less of it, the more comfortable the journey!" SSS VOL VII Chap 10 P 42

"Aspirants for mental peace have also to reduce the luggage they have to care for; the more the luggage, the greater the bother. Objective possessions and subjective desires, both are handicaps in the race for realization. A house cluttered with lumber will be dark, dusty and without free movement of fresh air, it will be stuffy and suffocating. The human body too is a house; do not allow it to be cluttered with curios, trinkets, trash and superfluous furnishings. Let the breeze of holiness blow as it wills through it; let not the darkness of blind ignorance desecrate it. Life is a bridge over the sea of change; pass over it but do not build a house on it." SSS VOL VII Chap 21 P 109

During the few years Syd and I had shared together before our trip to India, we purchased furniture, appliances, a piano, and many other 'things', which filled the void that we both previously created. After we arrived home from India, Syd felt that we should take pictures of all our belongings so we could validate any potential insurance claim in the future. I hadn't believed in having any insurance (besides my faith in God) for years, but I went along with his wishes. God was my insurance, and He had been taking very good care of me since I had surrendered my life to Him.

"The grace of God is like insurance. It will help you in your time of need without any limit." Sathya Sai Baba

After the film was developed, I casually glanced through the pictures before taking them to the safe deposit box, and couldn't believe my eyes. The picture of Sai Baba standing in front of the Mandir (temple) hung over the piano, and in the photograph of that picture, there was a bright golden glow around Baba that was not to be found in the picture we brought home from India! I had the negative blown up into an 8 x 10 photograph, and there was definitely a bright golden, helix-shaped aura totally surrounding the perimeter of Sai Baba, that was not a phenomena of the film or the camera. We were overjoyed! Syd and I agreed it was Sai Baba's way of showing us that He came home with us and was always with us. Of course we showed the two pictures to everybody who came to our home, but nobody was really interested in our big miracle except us.

The Harbinger

While we were staying at the Ashram in December, I purchased and mailed out Christmas cards with pictures of Sai Baba on them to all of our friends and relatives, and wrote a message in each one telling them of the miracles we had witnessed, and the interview we had. I returned home with great enthusiasm and shared with everybody who would listen, the miracles and wonders of Sai Baba. In fact, every opportunity I had, I would slip in something about Baba in a conversation. People would listen, or pretend to, but rarely did I get a response, or even a question. There were a lot of strange looks, like maybe we had lost our minds or gotten involved in a cult or something worse.

To some of my friends I sent a picture of Baba and a packet of Vibhuti, which I told them was holy ash given to us by Sai Baba, with instructions on how to use it. One friend in the San Francisco Bay Area said she had heard rumors that Sai Baba was the Anti-Christ. I never mentioned Him again to her.

I called up some old friends to have lunch and share my stories about Sai Baba. Only one was interested, and she asked many questions about our trip and Sai Baba. In trying to respond to her questions, I realized that I didn't really know much about Him after all, just what we had observed during our visit. This pushed me to spend more time reading some of the books I had purchased at the Ashram so I would be better prepared next time. Most of the books however, were a difficult read for a neophyte, with so many Sanskrit words and grammatical and spelling errors in them, and trying to interpret British English with its unfamiliar terminology. In my previous attempts to read several of the books during the India trip, I gave up before I got very far into them, and I did the same after another attempt once we returned home.

When we attended a family wedding in Sacramento the following Summer, my very skeptical brother asked, "So who is this Indian magician you went to see?". I had difficulty responding to that. I turned to Syd with a pleading look for him to jump in and respond to my brother's question. He gave me a look that said, 'Not on your life!'. My two sisters made it clear they didn't want to hear anything about Sai Baba. So we dropped the subject with family.

Here I had found what I believed to be the answer to everybody's prayers, problems and needs, and *nobody* wanted to hear about Him. I craved for somebody to just ask a question about Him. No takers. I thought of writing letters to the editors of newspapers, or writing to the television networks to tell them about Sai Baba, hoping I might stir up some interest. But somehow Baba restrained this overly enthusiastic devotee from doing that.

Later, I found Sam Sandweiss' book, *The Holy Man and the Psychiatrist,* and read that he and nearly everybody else who goes to see Sai Baba comes back with the same idea of shouting it from the mountain tops and telling the world about Baba, only to find that nobody wants to hear it. Well, at least I wasn't alone there. So, it was just Syd and I sharing our thoughts about Baba with each other.

There was one bright spot in all of these attempts to share our joy of finding Sai Baba. We made a trip to Santa Barbara to visit some old friends, and just before we left we felt inclined to call one of the Indian gentlemen who used to work with us at the water purification company. We thought he might like to hear about our experiences with Sai Baba. Ken told us he was not a Sai Baba devotee, but knew of Him, and that members of his family in Bombay were Shirdi Sai Baba devotees.

Ken and his wife Bharti came to our hotel room just as we were packing to leave and we shared a few Baba stories and gave them some of the Vibhuti Baba had given us. We were dumbfounded when both of them broke into tears and hugged us. They acted as if we were giving them a sack of gold. Perhaps we were.....

Ken and I used to have many spiritual and philosophical discussions when it was slow at the office. He shared his Eastern thoughts and I shared my Western thoughts, and we often found we reached a common ground of beliefs somewhere in the middle.

On another trip to Santa Barbara about a month later, we had dinner with Ken, Bharti, and their three beautiful daughters. The waitress seemed confused with what must have been a strange scene to her, with Syd and I ordering vegetarian dishes and this westernized Indian family all ordering meat based dishes. We had some more interesting conversations with them about Sai Baba and the good old days at the office.

Some time later Ken called to tell us he had since had a number of Baba dreams and shared one in particular with us. Baba came to him in the dream and told him to move from Santa Barbara to Dallas. Ken told Baba in the dream that he did not want to move and that there was nothing for him in Dallas. The next morning, Ken told Bharti about the dream, but then they both forgot about it. A short time later, Baba came to him in another dream and told him again to move to Dallas. Ken ignored the advice again. So, Baba came to him in a third dream and asked Ken if he wanted to be happy. Ken responded positively. Baba said, "If you want to be happy, then move to Dallas!".

This time, Ken made plans for he and Bharti to go to Dallas and see what, if anything, was there for them. Remarkably, or miraculously, he interviewed for a job that had more prestige and more pay than he had ever hoped for, and was hired! They also found the home of their dreams and purchased it, and there was a wonderful Sai Baba Center to welcome them into their fold. So Ken and Bharti and their three beautiful daughters pulled up stakes and moved to Dallas.

We later learned that the company that had purchased the company we had all worked for was moving all of the Santa Barbara facilities and people to San Diego so that all of the company's facilities would be in the same area. This meant that Ken would have had to either leave Santa Barbara or the company anyway.

Our next few months were occupied with us designing our new home and getting our designs ready to have formal plans drawn up, so that we could go out to bid for someone to frame out our dream home. Our first design was in a pyramid style, but Baba put someone in our path who told us he had lived in a pyramid style home, and the energies drove him crazy. He said that he was comfortable there so long as he only spent a few hours a day. But on a permanent basis, he would not recommend it. We changed our plans to an octagonal design, but realized after a while it was not practical for the building site we had chosen. So we prayed to Baba to guide us, and we arrived at what has become a very practical and comfortable design, perfect for the site and location. It's a three story rectangular shape with a prow in the middle and three decks, two in front and one in back. The bottom story is a finished daylight basement and garage. Our design was to achieve beauty and comfort, to compliment the surrounding area, and to be cost effective as well.

Life After India

When we set out on our trip to India in 1987, we had no idea where our next income would come from. Syd had completed the year he agreed to put in during the transition of ownership to the new owners of the water purification company, and was free to start up his consulting firm, which he did upon our return to the U.S.. After putting the word out to former business colleagues, the owner of a company in Torrance called seeking Syd's assistance with a number of projects. They agreed upon a contract that would require Syd to put in about two weeks a month, and Syd was now in business. The only problem was that Syd had to spend most of the time in their office, which meant a long drive from our home in Cardiff by the Sea on the San Diego Freeway back and forth each day. Syd did not mind that drive and used it as a time to sort through business problems and dwell on spiritual teachings. It was his alone time which he has always treasured.

Life settled into a routine for Syd, but my challenges seemed to begin. To anybody else, they may have seemed inconsequential, but to me they were big ones. It took me a while to figure out what was going on within me, but when I finally did, it was the beginning of a long road upward. My problems were just beginning with my daughter, but there were other calls from my soul as well, for growth.

When I sold my half of the bookstore, I felt I'd lost my identity. I had worked since I was 14 years old, with only a few months off here and there. I was tired of working and grateful that I no longer had to get up in the morning to go to a job. But, when I worked, I had a title, a responsibility, an income, I was independent, and I was somebody! Now I was nobody - just a housewife! My self esteem hit bottom again, and I was so low that I couldn't even identify with the label of artist, which is the only thing I did outside of the housewife thing.

"Without self-confidence no achievement is possible. If you have confidence in your strength and skill, you can draw upon the inner springs of courage and raise yourself to a higher level of joy and peace. For confidence in yourselves arises through the Atma, which is your inner Reality. The Atma is peace, It is joy, It is strength, It is wisdom. So, it is from the Atma that you draw all these equipments for spiritual progress." SSS VOL VI Chap 22 P 109

"The proponents of self esteem often quote the slogan, 'if you cannot love yourself, you cannot love anyone else'. One main problem with this is that it tends to put the cart before the horse, for the converse is even more true! As Baba always points out, the best way to develop oneself is through loving others rather than loving oneself, such as by changing selfish behavior." Robert Priddy in the SS May 1996 P 134-135

"Do not think that you are human and that you have to reach the state of Divine. Think rather that you are God, and from that state you have become a human being. As you think this way, all the attributes of God will manifest in you. Know that you have descended from God as human beings and that eventually you will go back to your source." MBAI P 94

As strange as it may seem to others, I felt guilty every time I bought something for myself with Syd's money. It wasn't my money to spend, it was his. He didn't see it this way, but it was a big hangup for me, and try as i might, I could not change my view of the situation. I had always been very independent and made enough salary that I could provide for all my and my children's needs, and I now found it impossible to live off someone else. Fortunately, I still had a small monthly income from the sale of a restaurant I used to own part of in Hawaii, and it still provided some independence. I limited my personal spending and used my own funds for my clothes, gifts and other personal items.

My other challenge was our sex-life. Because of the sexual abuse during my childhood, I was never able to have a satisfying sex life, until I met Syd. He was very patient with me, and as our relationship matured, I finally experienced a healing in this area. When we left for India, we had a very fulfilling intimate relationship. When we returned, it was a different story. Syd hadn't changed. It was me. After years of longing for a good sexual relationship and finally having one, I no longer felt the desire to make love, and I had no way to convey this to my wonderful husband. How could I explain what I couldn't understand myself? Now making love left me totally drained and feeling very static and sometimes angry at the world, and I began to dread it. I couldn't fathom what was happening to me.

After praying to Sai Baba over and over to help me to understand and deal with this new challenge, I found the answer in a book by another Indian guru. He explained that as you grow spiritually, your desires begin to fall away, including the desire to make love. He further explained that sex is one of the most spiritually draining activities one can experience. I tried sharing this new insight with Syd, and showed him what the guru wrote, but he took it personally. He became angry and closed off, and was stuck with the idea that it must have been some inadequacy within himself that turned me off. Silence began to reign in our previously happy, carefree home.

Syd completely misunderstood what I had tried to explain to him - he believed that it was because of *what* I read in a book that I thought I should give up sex. Since he made it abundantly clear that he absolutely would not discuss it again, there was no way I could convince him of the truth. An impenetrable black cloud hovered over him most of the time. He buried himself in his work and put up an invisible brick wall to shut me out of his life. I volunteered to give Syd a divorce, but he wouldn't discuss it. I then surrendered this problem over and over to God, but it kept coming back to haunt me every time Syd would sink into his dark mood. Even when he was in a good mood, I could not fully relax and enjoy the moment because I felt the unspeakable was hovering there waiting to bring in more gloom and doom.

"Books on yoga say that the generative (sexual) energy, if controlled, will be converted into spiritual energy. Therefore the first step in any spiritual practice is celibacy. There is a common proverb in Kannada language that where Rama (God) is present, Kama (lust) is not there and where Kama is present, Rama is not there." TOAR P 78

"For Maya-constituted beings, there are two Maya-gates: the appetite for sex and the appetite of the tongue. These two have to be conquered by every man; so long as they persist, they cause sorrow. All worldly desires are comprehended by these two; so, only those who have mastered these two can be said to have successfully waded through the world. These are the causes of all sins; and sin is the manure on which Maya thrives." PREMA VAHINI, P 72

"Garuda Purana (Ancient Indian Spiritual Texts) advises to restrict (sexual intercourse) only for the purpose of getting good children and not for getting pleasure. This should be considered as a sacred means to invite good embodied Souls to come to their family." TOAR P 29

At the time, my only solace was burying myself in books about Sai Baba and His teachings. I read Jack Hislop's *Conversations with Sathya Sai Baba* over and over, and each time I got a better understanding of Baba's teachings. Hislop asked Baba the same questions I would have asked had I been given the same opportunity. These were some of the questions I had pondered all my life, and here were the answers. Eventually, with the help of Baba's teachings I was able to lift myself above the challenging situation in my home with Syd. As I grew stronger spiritually, the challenge seemed to take on less and less importance for both Syd and I, until the impure vibrations in our home were virtually eliminated.

"Only thoughts of God and intense love for Him bring peace. As worldly thoughts diminish, thoughts of God increase. Normally, the mind desires these worldly things all the time. As the desires are cut out one by one, the peace becomes stronger.....When there are Godly thoughts, there is peace of mind." CWSSB P 22

"God will lead us; He will help us. There is only one requirement - we must ask God for the help; we must attune to His wave-length and be able to hear His answers.....Some people are afraid to ask God for anything; their fear interferes in their prayers. They have built such a fear of the Almighty, they expect Him to punish them. This is not how God works. His way is not of punishment but of love. To overcome the fear of God, talk to Bhagavan Sri Sathya Sai Baba and ask for His help." V.I.K. Sarin, FFWG P 260

It was during this time that I had a very interesting meditation, which seemed to be guided by Sai Baba. I wrote in my journal:

"Had a talk with Syd yesterday regarding sex. He doesn't understand what I tried to explain. I guess he is more locked into the physical world than I thought. Since our talk, I have felt his anger, rejection of me, total indifference, pain, fear, anxiety. This morning I had a good long cry - I felt so depressed about it. But afterward, I strangely had a wonderful meditation in which I participated first as an observer:

While doing my hatha yoga, I felt the separation of Higher and lower selves within me. I first felt the Higher Self consoling the lower self about the problem with Syd: 'Don't worry, it will all work out, etc.,' Then somehow I became my Higher Self and I knew I was that part of my Self that creates the events and situations and people in my life. I knew I could create anything I wanted - success with writing a book, fixing the relationship with Syd, winning the lottery, etc.. So, I started looking at all the things I could change or fix, knowing that at that moment, I could have any one of them. It was during this process that I realized that everything was already perfect as it was and that to change it would just mess it up! There I was - actually 'knowing' I could have anything I wanted, and I chose to keep my life as it was. It was as if I was given a glimpse of the Truth that everything is perfect as it is, that I will evolve at the proper pace.

"Each will come in his own way, at his own pace, according to his inner urge, along the Path God will reveal to him as his own." SS April 1994 P 100

"I will always be waiting for you at the end of the path and I will be watching every step that you take. I am with you, each one of you, every moment of the day, for I reside in your heart. I will always be there to help anyone who turns to Me in true humility and with a pure heart." FFWG P 259

An answer to the problem finally occurred to me several years later when I once again tried to clear the air and discuss the sex thing with Syd. Or, perhaps Baba put the words in my mouth, I don't know which, but I said to Syd, "You know how I used to really enjoy our love life together. Do you remember how Baba took away our desire and ability to eat meat and eggs? Well, I feel like He must have done the same thing with my desire for making love. So, if you want to be upset, be upset with Baba, not me. It was not my choice." I saw the light dawn in Syd's eyes, and for the first time, I believe he understood what had happened to me.

We have been celibate for years now, and I am certain this is one of the major reasons people tell us we have such good vibrations. There is no longer that continuous feeling of 'static agitation' within me that I know comes with having an active sex life. I am very grateful to our Lord Sai Baba for getting us through this difficult stage in our marriage, and for the benefits we have derived from it. The static vibes that sexually active people carry around is no longer there in us, and we are rarely affected by the 'six foes of man':

"Marriage is for the sake of pursuing dharma. It is not for enjoying worldly pleasures.....The same pleasures are experienced by street dogs. Is that happiness?" SS May 1996 P 121

"Prepare yourselves for a celibate and spiritual discipline from the age of fifty; the five senses have to be mastered by the time five decades of your life are over. The conclusion of six decades means that you have conquered the six foes of man: Lust, anger, greed, attachment, pride and hate." SSS VOL VIIB Chap 28 P 203

"The Brahmacharaya (Celibate) stage is an important step for attaining Atmic wisdom." UV P 57

The Moving Experience

Syd and I returned to our home in Cardiff by the Sea late at night from a long one-day journey into Arizona for a trade show. When we opened the garage door with the remote control to put the car in the garage, we saw all of our furniture and other belongings sitting in the garage. We were so tired, I wondered if it were an illusion. I thought maybe we had slipped into a different reality, and said to Syd, "Try closing the garage door, then reopen it to see if it is still there." He did, and all of our furniture was still there. We looked at it again in disbelief.

Our landlady, who lived next door and was a Yogananda devotee, was still in India visiting Mother Teresa. Before she left, she introduced us to the couple who would be watching over things for her in her absence. They too were Yogananda devotees, visiting from Colorado, and it was they and our landlady's son who had moved all of our belongings into the garage. Shortly after we left early that morning, the upstairs toilet apparently cracked and flooded both the second and first floors of our townhouse during our absence.

We spent the next few days in a hotel, and when we learned it would be another two weeks before we could return to our home, we decided that if we were going to stay in a hotel, it might as well be near our property in Colorado, where we could get something accomplished with the building project.

While we were away, we talked about it and decided it was time to move from our rented townhouse in Cardiff. I had been having terrible, blinding headaches while living such a close distance to the sea, and believed it was caused by the cold damp fog that hovered over us until the afternoon every day. Some days, the fog never did lift, and it was very depressing without seeing the sun for days at a time.

We rented a larger home a few miles Northeast in Vista, California. Our new home was far enough inland that it was sunny and considerably drier. Shortly after we moved, we experienced our second Baba miracle.

Every time I would visit a bookstore, I would first check to see if they had any books about Sai Baba, and I would purchase every new book that came out. I found some good pictures of Sai Baba in several of the books that were suitable for framing. I cut an especially nice picture of Baba out of a book and framed it. As soon as I put His picture in my kitchen in Cardiff, I could feel Him there with us all the time, watching over me while I cooked and worked in the kitchen. Each morning, I would say good morning to Baba in that picture and I would get a warm feeling every time I looked at it.

When we moved, one of the first things I did was to put this same picture on the window sill of my new kitchen. Several days later as Syd and I were sitting at the table eating breakfast, the picture of Sai Baba jumped off the window sill into the empty sink! There were no windows open, so no breeze could have knocked it over, and there was no noticeable earth movement to cause it to move from its stationary placement. We both agreed that we could feel the presence of Sai Baba when it fell, and felt He was letting us know that He had moved along with us to our new home. I returned the picture to the window sill where it stayed until we packed it up again for our next move a year later.

We had not planned to move from our Vista home until our home in Trinidad, Colorado was finished and ready for us, but Baba had other plans. Our landlord, who was a single man, announced one day that he was putting the house on the market and moving to Thailand where he had visited the previous year and fallen in love. So we started shopping around again for another temporary home. This time when we searched for a new home, we interviewed the owners to find out if they had any thoughts about selling it out from under us.

We found a beautiful home on an acre of land with lots of fruit trees in a development situated in an isolated area out in the country. The owners assured us they could not sell the home because nobody would buy it in its present condition. Part of the house had settled about four inches from the rest of the house, and they were suing the developer. Actually the settling had created a sunken living room effect and it had been repaired to the point that one would not have seen it as a problem. But, we loved the home and the country setting, so we rented it and moved in.

By now our possessions had multiplied and the moving process became more difficult with so much to pack and haul. When we moved into the Vista home, we hired a moving company to pack and move us, and I will never forget what one of the movers said: "Who is the guy in the picture with the 'fro' and the orange dress? His eyes keep following me wherever I go!" Of course he was talking about Baba's 'Afro' hair, and orange gown. The mover listened intently as I explained that Sai Baba was our spiritual teacher and played a large part in our lives.

The objective of the married couple from the moving company who packed our belongings seemed to be simplicity, not order, and there was something from every room in each box they packed. If it fit, it went in. It took me forever to unpack and find things so I could set up housekeeping, and I vowed to never again let anybody else pack for me. It had been a frivolous thing anyway, but Syd had suggested it in his concern for me, as I was still suffering from those debilitating headaches.

During this move, I felt we should be more conservative. So we hired a rental moving van and packed and moved ourselves, trying to save our resources to put into the home we were building in Colorado. Actually, I packed everything and Syd moved it. One doesn't realize how much 'stuff' one collects until one has to pack it and move it!

Even though we had moved inland, and a considerable distance from the cold moist air, the severe headaches returned every now and then. When they did, I was virtually unable to function. I slept sitting up at night in the recliner because the pressure increased terribly when I lay in bed. The severity of the pain increased during the Full and New Moons. Eventually, I could not take the screaming pain any longer, and my Inner Voice pointed me in the direction of medical assistance, a move that I had been resisting for years. Since neither Syd nor I had much faith in doctors or allopathic medicine, neither of us had been to one in a very long time. So after selecting an emergency clinic from the phone book, Syd drove me to get help, as I was virtually blinded with pain.

While checking my blood pressure, the nurse pointed out it was very high, and after several visits, I was referred to a 'specialist' who confirmed that the headaches were caused by high blood pressure, and I was given medication to control it. I explained to the doctor that I was a vegetarian and meditated and did hathya yoga and exercised every day, didn't drink or smoke, and therefore could not understand why the high blood pressure. He said that it was probably hereditary and sometimes that just happens to people with no explanation. Years later, upon my mother's death, I learned that she too had suffered from high blood pressure. But also, while reading an Ayurvedic manual, I found that when a child is sexually active at an early age, that child is prone to high blood pressure later on. Thus, another legacy from my mother and/or stepfather.

Eight months after our move to the country home, on August 1, 1990, our landlord told us that he had settled out of court with the developer and because of tax purposes, his accountant said he would have to sell the home before Christmas, and we had until then to find another place. Both Syd and I had no doubt in our minds that it was Baba telling us that it was now time to leave California and move to our new home in Colorado.

"The body is the temple of God; in everybody, God is installed, whether the owner of the body recognizes it or not. It is God that inspires you to good acts, that warns you against the bad. Listen to that Voice. Obey that Voice and you will not come to any harm." SSS VOL II, P 28

But the new house wasn't finished and still had no electricity or water or telephone lines to it. Now it seemed like we were heading out to Colorado every time Syd could get time away from work. We sheet rocked most of the second floor, which was the main floor of the house, in one long trip. In another, we rented a trailer and picked up the kitchen cupboards we had special ordered up in Colorado Springs, then installed the lower cupboards. The next trip we picked up the kitchen appliances in Colorado Springs and installed them. During another trip we picked up bathtubs, toilets and sinks for all the bathrooms and kitchen, but only had time to set up the bathroom on the main floor. Things moved along rapidly, and with the grace of Baba, the electricity was turned on quite unexpectedly in late October and the water made its entrance to the house on November 2nd, the day we arrived to put in some more intensive labor. We slept on the floor in our new home that night and I had the following Baba dream:

"Dreamed that Syd and I were at a gathering of some kind and I was looking at a newspaper where I found a large ad, 9 x 12", of two or three different full poses of Sai Baba. I called out to Syd across the room to tell him about it, but he didn't hear me. A lady nearby did and wondered what had excited me so, and I showed her and started to tell her all about Sai Baba. She wanted to go to where she could learn more about Him and I 'knew' at that point it would be the beginning of a Sai Baba Center in our new home. I immediately began planning to have our first meeting (in my dream) in Trinidad, playing the bhajan tapes I had purchased at the Ashram."

All the while we were at home in California, I was praying to Baba to help us get through this move while packing, packing, packing and arranging for our big relocation across country. Several years before, I created what I called my 'Baba Box', a cubed box about 8" in each direction. I covered it with photocopies of pictures of Sai Baba and cut a slot opening in the top. Every time I needed to surrender something, I would write it on a small piece of paper and stuff it in the box, symbolically giving the problem to Baba to take care of. The box was nearly full by the time we set out for Colorado. One day when Syd was in a terrible state of mind, I pointed out his mood to him, because his moods always affect me adversely. (Being an empath, I tend to absorb the feelings, thoughts and emotions of whoever I am with or close to). When Syd realized the state of mind he was in, he volunteered to jump into my Baba Box!

We did this move solely on faith, because we knew the owner of the firm Syd was consulting for would not take our moving 1,100 miles away lightly. He wanted Syd there physically where he could see him and call him in when he felt the need. And here we were moving to a house that had no telephone, and no immediate prospects of getting one, although we had been in contact with the phone company since we purchased the land nearly three years previous.

"Anxiety is removed by faith in the Lord." TOSSSB P 99

"Hundred percent faith means that God will not let you suffer; hundred percent confidence means that God will not let you down. Hundred percent faith plus hundred percent confidence makes for hundred percent devotion or bhakti. It is the highest form of bhakti where the Lord is in a state of golden bondage and the devotee is in a state of supreme serenity and smiling freedom. This is what every devotee has to aim at." SSAV P 7

My son Mark, who lived in a board and care home in the Bay Area, had volunteered to help us with the move. So it was that we bought him an Amtrak train ticket and planned to have him arrive the evening before we picked up the moving van. The schedule said his train would arrive around 11 p.m. We arrived early to find the station empty. Around midnight, we knew something was wrong and finally found somebody who could tell us that there had not been a train connection from Los Angeles to San Diego for a long time because they were repairing damaged tracks, and that Amtrak passengers were being bussed in from Los Angeles. Why they didn't tell us this when we purchased the tickets, I will never know. The busses did not arrive until many hours later, with a tired and angry Mark greeting tired and angry us. This was no way to begin the project that lay ahead of us.

It became obvious early on that this move was definitely to be a lesson in possessions and a test of our ability to cope with obstacles. When the time came to pick up the moving van we rented, an unusual arctic freeze had set in and it rained steadily everyday where we lived in the San Diego area. We had had a drought for years, and uncannily, it ended just as we began to move things into the truck. It was the move from Hell, because everything seemed to go wrong from the moment Mark arrived.

Mark is a six-footer and physically strong. But, he had been on intensive medication since he was diagnosed as a paranoid schizophrenic and manic depressive. I had no idea when he came to help us move that he was also taking street drugs which interfered with his medication. This caused him to become extremely temperamental, and sometimes volatile. And my being an empath did not help, because now I too was becoming temperamental. Try as I might, there was no way to get centered with his frenetic energies and the stress of the move. It seemed like I had fallen off the 'Spiritual Wagon' and Murphy's Law set in. I have since learned that whenever we involve somebody in our plans or someone comes into our home who has bad vibrations and is not spiritual, everything goes awry.

"Nature has many mysteries in its makeup. Man is able to unravel only those that are cognizable through his five senses; he does not realize that there is a vast unknown beyond the purview of the five faulty instruments of perception that he has. For example, from every being and thing, constantly, without intermission, millions of minute particles and millions of vibrations are issuing forth. Certain substances like camphor emanate so much of these that a lump disappears in a few days. The bodies of others affect us by these emanations and we too affect them in the same way. For good or bad, we are interacting in this manner, inescapably. Naturally, the growth of the body is affected, as well as its health and strength, by the contact or company we develop."
SSS VOL IX Chap 26 P 140

It took a full seven days to get the moving van loaded in the freezing rain, since Syd had to do most of the work himself. Then we discovered there was not enough room for everything, so we rented the largest trailer available and loaded it as well. At last, it was time to leave and while driving the van out of the driveway, it was so heavy its rear-end got buried in the pavement at the end of the driveway. We waited hours for the large commercial tow truck to arrive to free up the van. Just as the tow truck was about to leave, we discovered the battery in the Suburban was dead, and needed to be jumped. By the time we got our caravan on the road, it was 10 p.m., so we drove a few hours and checked into a motel East of San Diego.

I was extremely grateful for the time alone on the road in which I could pray and commune with God. My job was to drive the Suburban with the trailer in tow, while Syd drove the moving van with Mark as passenger, towing our large station wagon. Fortunately, Syd was able to put his wall up and shut out most of Mark's energies. We had walkie-talkies in which we communicated back and forth, and they worked so long as we were in sight of one another. Because of the medication Mark was taking, he drank large volumes of fluids, and we had to make pit stops nearly every hour. This was a big deal because it was not always easy to find a place to park with the both of us towing the car and rental trailer, and it became a major source of irritation for all of us.

We had planned to arrive at our new home on December 23rd, but because of the inclement weather from the Arctic Freeze which spanned across the Southwest, we didn't get to Las Vegas, New Mexico until Christmas Eve around midnight. Under normal conditions, we would have reached our home in only two more hours. It was snowing heavily so we had to stop for the night because the Raton Pass at the New Mexico/Colorado border would be too big a challenge to take on as tired as we were. On Christmas morning we felt fortunate to find a restaurant open for breakfast in that small town. We learned there were many other travelers like us who had to stop there for the night because of the weather. After checking out of the motel, we found that our moving van had frozen itself into the ground and we now had to wait for it to thaw out before we could get underway. Apparently the heat of the tires had melted the snow the night before and then froze solid from the sub-zero temperatures.

"No one can predict what calamity will overtake one and at what time. Everything depends on the will of providence; it all happens according to the Divine Plan." SSS VOL X Chap 46 P 234

Our home was a welcome sight on Christmas Day as we drove up the road leading to it. But the challenges weren't over yet. When Syd rounded the bend in our original driveway, the moving van got stuck in the mud. We had to drive the Suburban back to town to call AAA for a tow truck again. But, we were home now, and so grateful to be here. It turned out to be a Merry Christmas after all!

Lessons in Possessions

The 'Move from Hell' became a great lesson in material possessions, and we now needed help to unload and carry our 'things' upstairs. To our great dismay, everything had frozen inside the moving van also, including the can goods which burst and made a terrible mess. Our waveless waterbed also froze, even though we had taken great care to empty all the water. When we attempted to move it in its frozen state, it broke and leaked the remainder of the water inside the house.

"Having been born, man earns and acquires land, riches, materials, grain, articles of comfort and luxury, which he feels will give him happiness and which, therefore, become the objects of his struggle. But, the object of realizing God is forgotten." BTBOS P 140

Shortly after we moved into our new home, I had the following Baba Dream and wrote in my journal:

"Dreamed of Sai Baba again. (Had a short dream about Him during our move to Colorado and didn't record it) We were at some kind of gathering in a large hall, and I walked in with several friends and saw Baba sitting up on the podium (head table) with about six to eight other people. He looked at me and said 'Hello Charlene'. I was amazed He knew my name and He smiled at my surprise. We got a rectangular shaped table close to the head table and I sat where I could see Him. I looked at the other people at my table and none were holding their hands in the 'Namaskar' position in reverence to Baba, but I did so anyway. He came down to me and spoke for some time telling me all kinds of things, but all I can remember is 'Don't worry about anything. I am fully aware of all that is going on (in the world), and I am taking care of almost everything.' The 'almost' bothered me as I awoke at the end of this dream, and as I pondered what He said, I thought He meant that people still have to make their own choices, but He will not let them destroy the world. Sure wish I could remember all the other things He told me, but guess I'm not supposed to consciously."

I was so grateful to Baba for giving me this dream because it reassured me that everything was going to be all right, and that He was there with us and still loved us, in spite of our negative reactions to the adversities we encountered with the move and with Mark.

"The Avatar has to take humanity and put it into a crucible in order to remove the slag and inferior metals that have diminished its real worth." TOSSSB P 127

Back in 1978 when I left California and moved to Hawaii, I gave nearly everything away, but it was not long before I had another houseful of furniture and other possessions in Hawaii. When I left Hawaii, I gave all of my furniture and most of my household goods to my married daughter and put the rest of my things in storage. Shortly after going to work for Syd In 1984 in Santa Barbara, I flew back to Hawaii and emptied out my storage unit. With the exception of my books and clothes, I gave everything away once again.

Syd had also given everything to his ex-wife. When he arrived at the home we would share, all he had was his clothes, an old beat up dresser and $5,000. Their divorce agreement included a stipulation that what he had given her would provide for her the rest of her life, and he therefore would not be responsible for any alimony or future needs she may have. This was his way of starting life with me with a clean slate.

During our first year together, we rented furniture and acquired very few 'things'. Once we were married, though, it was an entirely different story. How we both went from little or nothing to what we have accumulated up to today is unbelievable. It seems like when we gave everything away, independent of each other, we both created a big void, which the good Lord filled right back up! And today, we have accumulated more than we ever had before, individually and collectively. Yet we both agree, we could easily walk away from it all again tomorrow with no regrets, if that is Baba's Will for us. Before Syd and I met, we had both arrived at a point in awareness that 'stuff and things' are not what is important in life. They are nice to have, but one can easily live without them so long as they have God as the foundation in their lives.

"All are gifts of God. You must treat all possessions in that spirit. You must take good care of them as long as you have the responsibility for their proper use and maintenance. That is your duty.

"As long as you live in the world, you have the responsibility to take care of your wife, children and possessions. But you must regard this as an obligation imposed by God. You must not get attached to them as your possessions. Most people in the world, however, are deeply attached to kinsfolk and properties. How lasting are these possessions? You can never know when you may have to leave all of them behind. Hence, the proper attitude for men is to recognize one's duty towards others and consider everything as a gift from God." SS September 1997 P 227

Life in the Wilderness

We quickly settled into a new routine in Colorado. Syd would leave around noon every other Sunday, drive to Albuquerque to catch a flight to Southern California, rent a car and a room, work all week, and then would return home late Friday night. Flights out of Colorado Springs at the time cost more than twice as much as from Albuquerque, so it was worth the extra hour's drive there. This kept our only source of income coming in.

I don't know where we got all the energy, but during our first year, we dug holes and planted ver 400 trees to make up for the ones that were plowed under or cut down when they cut our pad, and put in the road and drive way to our home. We also put in a large organic garden, from which I canned, dehydrated, pickled, jellied. Or froze everything we did not eat or give away to neighbours and friends. And we continued to work on building and finishing the interior of our home.

On March 4, 1991, I had the following Baba Dream and wrote in my journal:
"Dreamed that Sai Baba was going before us and clearing all the obstacles ahead in our path. He was like sweeping and pushing away the 'things' in our way. Don't know who 'us or our' was, but the number 12 was very important. Maybe there were 12 of us. Anyway, in my last remembrance of the dream, He was standing just ahead and to the left of us on this wide road like He was waiting for us, and the number 12 came to mind again. There was much more to the dream, but I can't remember it."

While we still lived in California, I had a series of dreams in which I understood I was being shown what was going to happen to beautiful California. There were earthquakes where the mountains seemed to collapse into themselves, and fires that seemed to consume everything in their path. I witnessed huge tidal waves that rushed in and covered what remained of the mountains, and covered the foothills and the valleys. In the cities, I watched the skyscrapers fall to the ground with people running in every direction, and screaming helplessly. At the end of the last dream, a voice said, "Tell all your friends to get out of California!" And in the dream I ran around and told all of my friends that they had to get out of California. In the dream, nobody wanted to hear it, and I knew that they would be where they are supposed to be when the earth goes through its catastrophes. Nevertheless, I spent the next few days calling all my friends, telling them about my dreams and that I was told to tell them they needed to leave California. Nobody wanted to hear it, just like in the dream.

Shortly after we moved to Colorado, a friend made us aware of the predictions and visions of the coming earth changes recently made public by several modern day prophets whom I had never heard of. Actually, I had 'known' all my life that 'earth changes' would be happening in this lifetime, just as I had known all my life that the Golden Age was coming during this lifetime. I was aware of these things even before I read books outlining what Nostradamus and Edgar Cayce predicted, and the book, "We are the Earthquake Generation", among others. After hearing about the latest predictions, both Syd and I felt the urge to write a letter to Sai Baba asking Him to watch over our new home and us as well.

"Man's inhumanity to man expresses itself in the form of natural catastrophes, like earthquakes.....There will be physical repercussions due to man's growing selfishness. Minor adjustments to the planet, and a certain clear out.....The world is the body of God. There is a cancer in the body and it must be removed." TEOL P 85

Several days after mailing our letters off to India, I had a Baba dream and recorded it in my Dream Journal as follows:

"Dreamed that I was looking at a map of Trinidad Lake Ranches (the Development we live in) and it showed the places where earthquakes and floods had been historically. Lot 50 (our lot) seemed to be okay. During the middle of the dream I saw the damage the floods were doing now and was using a strainer to pick bodies out of the debris. There were people of all ages, limp and dead. I found a bird body also. Funny, but they were all the same size and would fit in my strainer. I couldn't stomach the death anymore and was going to leave it for someone else to clean up. Then toward the end of the dream, we were in a house (ours) with a lot of other people, and Sai Baba appeared. 'Death' came to the door and Sai Baba raised His hands in front of 'Death' and said, 'Go and leave this place. It is an abode of peace and these people are all on the path to God!' And 'Death' departed." Then I awoke, knowing that this was Baba's way of telling us we would be safe here in our new home in Colorado."

In an interview with Sai Baba on December 7, 1995, He asked me where we live and I told Him Colorado. I could see Him picturing our home in His mind and then He told us that Colorado was a very good place to live. He has repeated that Colorado is a very good place to live in two subsequent interviews.

Just before we moved to our new home, I had the following dream. I have wondered since then whether it would turn out to be prophetic:

"Dreamed that I was getting back on the Path to wherever I was going in the mountains and I saw a big bear going up ahead, so I turned and went the other way - down where I ran into a much smaller bear. I first tried to scare him off and it worked for a moment, then he jumped at me and I screamed 'Oh God, please help me, Dear God', and then I shouted *'Sai Baba'* as loud and long as I could and the dream ended. Nothing seemed to stop the bear coming at me until I shouted for Sai Baba!"

Syd and I go for long walks with our dogs nearly every day, and from Spring through Fall, we often hear a bear nearby, as they will grunt to let us know they are around if they hear us. When we hear the grunt, I call out loudly, "Hello Mr. Bear, thank you for letting us know you are there. You stay there and we will stay here". Then Mr. Bear (or Mrs., as the case may be), will grunt again and wander off in another direction. One morning, we rounded a bend in the road, and flushed up a bear feeding on juniper berries just several yards away. He was more frightened than we were and immediately took off through the brush and trees. We have had bears right under our decks, and almost on top of them, but our dogs usually chase them away. There are long claw marks on the side rails of our rear deck where a bear slid down after climbing up in his attempt to escape the dogs that were barking and nipping at his rear.

One night our dogs woke us up barking their 'bear bark', over and over. They have a different bark for every situation. We went out on the deck and in the bright moonlight we watched Nik, our fearless Siberian Husky going nose to nose with a 400 pound black bear. When the bear would lunge and swat its mighty paw at Nik, Nik would back up, and then he would lunge at the bear, and it would retreat. Maggie,

Nik's daughter, was behind the bear and against the house, giving the bear no quarter. Back and forth they went, over and over. Angie, our Chow, was in the garage guarding the dog food. She is no dummy. When the bear heard our voices he finally lumbered off into the night. Bears are more afraid of people than anything else, and unless they feel threatened, they will leave as soon as they know we are there. We all have a healthy respect for each other.

    We believe Mr. Bear was after our dozen or so hummingbird feeders up on the deck, which feeds probably thousands of hummers throughout the Spring and Summer. Some are passing through and some stay throughout the season. We have our own natural wide open aviary because we put an assortment of feed out on the decks every morning for the large variety of birds that come through and/or live here year round. Many of the birds who arrive to feed on our decks are not supposed to be in this area according to the six different bird books we have to identify them with.

    We have had bears in our garden too - they loved our lettuce bed. They regularly check out our compost pile and have torn it apart several times. It is near the garden and the dogs really get a workout on the nights after Syd hauls the fresh kitchen food scraps to the compost pile. Our dogs have treed nearly every bear that has come around. One morning they treed a tiny baby bear in a 30 foot Ponderosa Pine tree right next to our kitchen window. Syd had to go out and physically drag each dog into the house, one at a time, before Mama bear came along looking for baby, otherwise it could have been disastrous.

    We have only seen one mountain lion near the house, and that was when we first moved here. But on two separate occasions, Nik has come home with some very deep gashes on his throat and about his body. The vet said these injuries could only have come from having tangled with a mountain lion or a large bear. Nik seems to be fearless when it comes to defending his 'territory', except for one time when it came to a cow defending her calf. We live on open grazing land, and every couple of years, cattle will make their way to our home. We watched Nik and the other dogs herding the cows away from the house, but one of the cows got concerned when Nik got too close to her calf, and she moo'ed and started to take the offensive, moving toward Nik as if to charge. Nik stopped his advance and his barking, looked around as if to see if it was going to rain or something, turned and walked off as though the cows did not exist. Nik is no dummy either.

When Syd travels, I still go for a walk with the dogs, and sometimes they will tear off chasing a coyote or deer or rabbit or something, and I am left alone, often a long way from home. People have asked me if I am afraid to be alone out here in the wilderness with the bears and cougars and coyotes, etc. I tell them what Baba says:

"I shall be ever with you, wherever you are, guarding you and guiding you. March on; have no fear." SSS VOL IX P 221

"Why fear when I am here? Put all your faith in Me. I shall guide and guard you." SSSun Part I P 99

And I am no dummy either. If I sense there is a bear or some potential danger nearby, I will turn around and return home instead of continuing my walk.

The Telephone Crucible

It became obvious, while we were trying to set up housekeeping the first week in our new home, that we would have to get a cellular telephone, because the only phone company serving our area indicated they had no intentions of installing telephone lines to our area for a very long time, even though we were less than four linear miles from their nearest customer. We learned to our dismay that many folks in rural areas of Colorado had been waiting for phones for as long as ten years.

We checked with the Colorado Public Utility Commission who did their best to discourage us from taking action. They said there were so many claims in ahead of us that it would be a long time, perhaps years, before ours would be processed, let alone be heard. Neither one of us really wanted to get involved in going through a hearing anyway. We later read in the newspaper that there was some collusion between employees of the Colorado PUC and the phone company, and much later an investigation took place.

And the plot thickens.....We purchased a cellular phone for an outrageous price from the only cellular phone company servicing our area. They also charged exorbitant rates for their services. We learned later that this cellular phone company was a funded subsidiary of the telephone company, so it was not in their best interests to put in phones for us! Our monthly cellular bills were often as much as $800, and we used the cellular sparingly. Also, I had to check the bills thoroughly every month. There were so many errors, we had to keep a log of every incoming and outgoing call to keep on top of them. Among the many errors, we were often charged for calls we had not made or received, and we were sometimes charged for two or three telephone calls that their computer said were happening at exactly the same time.

"Patience is all the strength a man needs." On a sign in the Puttaparthi Ashram

A friend, who owned a service station with mini food store in Trinidad, let us put a telephone and fax machine in his office above the store. Since the cellular phone only worked part of the time because of the poor service lines and the hills we were surrounded by, we had to go to town nearly every day that the roads were passable to check for faxes and message. It was important that Syd keep in touch with the company he consulted for in California, as it was our only source of income at the time. For the first four or five years we lived in Colorado, our dirt roads were sometimes impassable because the rain or snow melt turned the roads into deep clay-like mud.

This telephone situation became, for us, a major source of irritation, and a great opportunity for growth. It was one of the most difficult things I had ever encountered to surrender up to Baba. With my Libra rising sign, I had never been able to tolerate things which were unfair, whether it was happening to me or somebody else, and this definitely fell into that category. Having come from the 'civilized' State of California, I found it difficult to believe that this type of thing, this unfairness, was still permitted to happen in the 90's. And Baba never let me relax and forget it for more than a short period of time, because there was always a need to use the telephone, either for business, or to order building materials, or check on a missing order or part, or find out why we suddenly had no water, or make plane reservations, or to see if my pregnant daughter was doing all right, ad nauseam.

Regarding sincere devotees who undergo suffering and misfortunes: "If those persons are also sometimes sincere devotees, then sometimes God sends them troubles to test the strength of their devotion. If the devotees realize that the main objective of man is not to be re-born again and again, and if they are striving towards this objective, they will be beset with untold miseries and sufferings as a means of burning away all the karmas of past births. This is all according to the Judgement and Grace of God." SSAV P 47

  My telephone button got pushed regularly, and while Syd and I expended a great deal of effort, our patience grew very thin. I kept trying to surrender the situation, but found it increasingly difficult. It eventually became apparent to me that the best thing I could do was not associate with my neighbors who had even less patience than we did, because this was nearly always the topic of our discussions, and we seemed to feed each other's anger. This in itself was difficult because we were on the Board of Directors of our Property Owners Association (POA), which meant we were always knee deep in the telephone problem.

  We eventually approached the telephone company as a POA, which was a major hurdle in itself, because the POA met only once a year and then we had to get a two third's majority vote of the attending members to agree to this strategy. After many, many trips and long distance calls, the telephone company finally agreed to lay a minimum of telephone lines to service the seven current residents in the 96 unit development.

  The telephone linemen arrived to install the underground lines without our being aware of it one day, but were turned away by one of the owners who demanded a written plan and installation design before he would allow them to do any installation in 'his development'. He didn't want telephones in the development because he did not want to encourage others to move here. The owner who turned the telephone linemen away led them to believe that he was the developer, and that is why they canceled the installation. Since the allocated supplies had already been reassigned and installed somewhere else by the time we heard about the incident, the phone company could not say if or when they would ever return.

I don't think I have ever seen Syd as angry as he was when he talked to the phone company and they told him they had canceled the installation and reassigned the men, equipment and supplies to another development up North.

"One's anger is one's greatest enemy and one's calmness is one's own protection. One's joy is one's heaven and one's sorrow is one's hell." SSIB 1972 P 237

"A man consumed by anger can never be free from misery. Anger carries with it a blazing fire. Anger is also described as 'Krodhaagni', the fire of anger. As long as one is consumed by the fire, he cannot have happiness. To get freedom from misery, man has to get rid of anger. Anger is also the cause of depravity in man. It ruins him in various ways. It alienates him from his kith and kin. For the decline in human qualities today, pride and anger are primarily responsible." SS August 1995 P 197

It was much, much later that I could see this as Baba's grace working for us. A sense of hopelessness set in and there was nothing left to do but surrender! Some may see it as giving up and that may have played a part in it, but we were actually able to surrender the telephone issue and get on with life. Before that incident, we were constantly working at trying to get the telephone lines installed, and plotting and planning with our neighbors. It consumed our lives. After that incident, there just was no longer any point to it. Syd and I realized we weren't going to have real live telephones in our home until Baba willed it and not a second sooner. So, we just gave it to Baba and let His will prevail!

"For all the confusion and conflict prevailing in the world today, it is the feelings and thoughts of people that are responsible. To take offense when someone criticizes you or to think of retaliation when one does some harm to you is not the right way of reacting to them. Consider whatever good or bad that happens to you as the consequence of your own actions. Do not attribute them to acts of the Divine. God is like a postman. The postman delivers one letter to one address and the people in the house rejoice over the good news contained in it. He delivers another letter at a second house and there is lamentation over the sad news contained in the letter. Is the postman responsible for the joy or the sadness of the recipients of the letters? No. It is the content of the respective letters that is responsible. What you experience by way of joy or grief is a consequence of your own actions. God is only a witness." SS December 1994 P 312

Of course before I could reach the point of being able to surrender, I had to be able to forgive the owner who turned the phone company linemen away from the development.

"Only a person who has this Kshama (attitude of forgiveness) can be considered to be endowed with sacred love.....Therefore, in times of despair, you should be filled with feeling of forbearance and be ready to forgive and forget. This quality of Kshama or forgiveness is the greatest power for a human being. If one loses this quality, he becomes demonic." SS February 1994 P 49

But how does one forgive someone who has deliberately done something that affects your ability to earn income and otherwise live with peace of mind? I struggled with this forgiveness thing, and prayed relentlessly to Baba to help Syd and I get through this. Then one day, Baba answered my prayers and I 'knew' what steps I had to take to rise above this situation. It was to send this 'unlovable' person LOVE. In my angry state of mind, I had never thought of doing that. So, with Baba's help, I concentrated on sending him LOVE constantly, until I was finally able to feel LOVE for him. It was a major step in the healing process.

Since 1976, I had been using a method I developed to send love to people in distress. Whenever I would see someone with their car broken down on the road, or a baby crying in a restaurant or on a plane, or if I saw someone being mean to their child, or if people were having an argument, I would send them love. First I would picture all of this love in my heart, then I would send it from my heart up through the top of my head and into the distressed person's heart. Then I would simply cover and fill them totally with all this love. I witnessed it working every time, if I was still around to see the results. The crying baby would stop crying. The people would stop arguing, etc.. And I would feel better too.

Shortly after we learned the phone company had been here and was turned away, the owner of the company Syd had been consulting for told him his contract would not be renewed and he would call him if he ever needed his services again. Syd had been doing some work for several other firms off and on, but there was nothing forthcoming from there either. Suddenly, we no longer had an income.

Several months after I was finally able to surrender the whole telephone challenge, the phone company arrived unexpectedly to install the underground lines for the entire development! We fell to our knees in tears at the joy of knowing that our Dear Lord's grace was working for us.

"How can you get God's grace without undergoing trials? You know what severe processes gold goes through from the crucible onwards before an ornament is made. There can be no happiness without pain.....Pleasure and pain go together in this world." SS February 1995 P 36

"Like a lighted lamp, God's Grace spreads all round on all who approach Him and love to be near him; but if you interpose a shade which shuts out the light from you, you have only yourself to blame if Grace does not shine.....To get the program right and pleasantly, you have to switch on and tune in the receiver That is an inescapable effort. Individual effort and Divine Grace are both interdependent; without effort, there will be no conferment of Grace; without Grace, there can be no taste in the effort. To win that Grace, you need only have faith and virtue." SS January 1994 P 26

Another Miracle

On my way home from town one day while Syd was still

working in California, it suddenly began to hail as I entered the Development. I drove along as quickly and carefully as I could, because in those days when the clay roads got wet they turned into slick, soupy type mud. It was nearly five miles from the entrance to our home and I wanted to arrive home before the hail turned the roads to slime. I made it to the 'pass' and was heading down the hill above and behind our home when I noticed a large buildup of hail on the road in front of me.

The winding road was already slippery and I had previously slowed down as much as I could, but it was to no avail, as the road was now going downhill. The hail acted like ball bearings and simply rolled my big Mercury Grand Marquis Station Wagon right over the side of the mountain. Amazingly, the car suddenly came to a stop, with its nose pointing almost straight down. I sat there in shock for awhile, wondering why the car had suddenly stopped, when there was nothing in front of it to stop it. As I recovered my senses, I found that I was covered with mail and groceries that had flown forward from the back of my station wagon as the car went over the side.

A sense of great peace came over me and I knew Baba was with me. I heard Him say, **"Wait until it stops hailing and then crawl out of the passenger door and walk home."** I looked at the passenger door which was almost over my head and wondered how I could crawl out of it without jiggling the car enough to send it the rest of the way down the mountain. There weren't any trees or large bushes in front of the car holding it back. In fact there didn't seem to be anything preventing the car from continuing its journey downward. Nevertheless, I waited as Baba had instructed me. The nickel sized hail was making a lot of noise on the roof of the car and I wondered if it would crack the windshield or dent the car. When the hail finally stopped, I sucked in my breath and very slowly and carefully moved up into the passenger seat. Then after several attempts, I was eventually able to get the passenger door open, crawl out and trudge home through the mud, which was about a mile in distance. As soon as I reached the front door, it started hailing again.

I was covered with mud and soaking wet and was shaking by the time I reached the front door. After I cleaned myself off I called Syd in California. As soon as I heard his comforting voice, I broke down and sobbed hysterically. The realization of my very close call hit me as I tried to describe it to him, and I could not stop the flood of emotion. Syd said he would catch the next plane home if I wanted, but I told him no, I could handle it. When I calmed down, he told me to call the AAA towing company and then let him know what happens from there.

The tow truck pulled up in front of my home several hours later. The hail had melted and the roads, although very muddy, were passable with care. I got in the truck with him and his wife, and we drove back to where my car was. As he drove, he said, "I saw the ruts where your car went over the side and crawled down the hill to see what was holding your car there, but I couldn't find anything. No trees, no bushes. I could not see anything that is keeping your car from going on down the hill." I said, "God is holding it!" Neither he nor his wife said another word.

As we rounded the bend, you could just see one of the rear tail lights from the road. If it weren't for the very prominent and deep tire ruts, one would easily pass by without noticing my car there. It took the tow truck driver nearly an hour to extricate my car, and when he did, I signed the claim form, got in my car and very slowly drove it home. We carry large heavy sandbags in the back of our cars to provide ballast so we can better navigate the roads when they are muddy, but this did not help me while driving on the piled up hailstones.

Later, the manager of the development called and said: "Mrs. Chaden, are you all right? I was driving by and saw the tire tracks where your car went over the side of the mountain. I crawled down to see if you were all right, and took a good look around, but I couldn't see what was holding your car there." I gave him the same answer. "God was holding it! And He held it there until the AAA tow truck came and towed me out, and it is home now. Thank you!" And Thank You Baba! There was no physical or rational explanation as to why my car didn't keep going. Only the Grace of my Lord.

"My Grace is proportional to your effort. Try to win grace by reforming your habits, reducing your desires and refining your higher nature. One step makes the next step easier; that is the excellence of spiritual journey. With each step, your strength and confidence increase and you get bigger and bigger installments of grace.....

"Grace is showered on those who seek. Knock and the door shall be opened to you; ask and food will be served; search and the treasure will be yours. The Grace of God cannot be won through the gymnasium of reason, the contortions of Yoga or denials of asceticism. Love alone can win it, Love that needs no requital, Love that knows no bargaining, Love that is unwavering, Love alone can overcome obstacles, however many and mighty.

"My grace is ever with you; it is not something that is given or taken; it is given always. But it is accepted only when the consciousness is aware of its significance. Win the grace of your own sub-conscious, so that it may accept the grace of God, which is ever available." Golden Age, P 228

In June 1991, I had the following Sai Baba dreams and recorded them as follows in my Dream Journal:

"Dreamed I was with Sai Baba and He was teaching a class of children, and I was there to learn how to teach too. After the class, He was very thirsty, and looked in my refrigerator for something sweet - specifically a Pepsi. He pulled out a beer (?) And I took it away from him and found the one Pepsi stashed in the back of the fridge. We were also busy getting rid of some garbage and then I was going to leave with Baba and go on to other classes and places. We were in India, I believe." Since we never have beer in our refrigerator because we don't drink it, and rarely have Pepsi in the house except when a guest would leave one, I don't understand this part of the dream. I did have a later dream in which I was teaching a bunch of people about spiritual values and was telling them they must not pray for things, only for help."

"Dreamed that I was visiting my best friend, or just being with her, and wanted to talk to her, but she was always busy with other people. I took her to dinner thinking we would have time to talk. But while we waited for a table she was moving around talking to other people. When we finally got our table, we sat down and we ordered, then the next thing

I know she was sitting at another table with other people, and I was feeling very left out. As we left the restaurant, it seems I walked down the stairs alone, and there on the ground at the foot of the stairs was a large picture of Sai Baba facing me. Message: Forget friends. All I really want is to merge with God anyway. I knew that the picture was there to remind me that my only true friend is God."

"True love consists of serving the Lord, recognizing the Lord in everyone in the same way. He is the closest and dearest friend. Forgetting such a dear friend, you are taking shelter with others who are not real friends. In this world, it is impossible to recognize true friends. If you have some money with you and if your father is in a good position, everyone comes and says, Halo, Halo. But the moment your pocket is empty and your father has no position, people are not prepared to say even goodbye to you.....That is the type of friends you have today. But God, who is your true friend, at all times He is with you, and He will never leave you at any time at any place. Believe firmly that God alone is your true friend and follow him. This is the right royal path to reach the Lord." DD 1987 P 136

Ken, the Indian gentlemen who used to work with us in Santa Barbara, called Syd from Dallas not long after Syd's contract in California expired to tell Syd about his latest Baba dream. In his new position as Vice President for a company in Dallas, he had encountered a number of challenges that he needed help with, and he prayed to Sai Baba to help him know what to do. Then he had a dream in which Sai Baba told him to **"Call Syd Chaden"**, who could help him. After sharing the dream, Ken wanted to know if Syd was available to help them out. Thus, Baba never let us go one month without an income. We were profoundly overjoyed and thanked Baba over and over!

"When devotees surrender their lives to God and obey Him, He takes the full responsibility and cares for his devotees even to the smallest details." CWSSB P 131

Yearning for Baba

It is 1992 and it has now been nearly five years since our last trip to India and I am yearning for Sai Baba's Darshan. During these five years, virtually all of our resources, both physical and financial, have been put into building and finishing the interior of our home in the wintertime, and the last two years taking care of our large organic garden the remainder of the year.

Even before springtime, I start my seedlings in the kitchen, then plant them outside as soon as it is possible, using different methods like 'wall of waters' apparatus to protect my plants from the last of the frosts in late April and early May. We live in a rather short growing season at 6,700 feet elevation, but I never let that discourage me from trying to grow anything. Our garden has everything from strawberries and raspberries, to potatoes and greens, to herbs and spices, to snow peas and eggplant, to cauliflower and corn. Actually, I must give Syd the credit here, because I just start the seedlings and plant them. He digs up the soil, waters, weeds and harvests, unless he is traveling on business, then his chores become mine. I have also experimented with hydroponic gardening in the kitchen, and achieved a modicum of success, enough that if we ever had to fall back on this indoor growing method, I would know how to do it. Throughout the growing season, I freeze, can, dehydrate, juice, or make jams out of what we do not eat or share with our neighbors and friends.

There has been no way Syd could get away from his work commitments long enough for us to make another long trip to India, especially with his traveling back and forth to Dallas all the time. His work with Ken and the Dallas company is coming to an end in November, and his other work has decreased. So, once again we have no idea where our next income will come from. But, we are not worried because Baba takes such good care of us. Since we learned to put our complete faith and trust in Baba, we are never lacking or in need, and He hasn't let us down yet.

"Your faith should give you total confidence in Me. You should have the implicit confidence that I will look after you, take care of you and provide for you. You should have the confidence that My Grace is always with you and that I am always watching over you and protecting you. You should have the confidence that I will never let you down, that I am always there beside you, helping you, supporting you, comforting you and carrying you through troubles and hardships. Just as you lean against the wall knowing that it will not collapse, lean on Me and depend upon Me entirely. I will then look after you and take care of everything for you.....if you depend upon Me with complete faith and confidence, I shall provide for your welfare and look after all your needs in this world and in the next." SSAV P 8

My yearning for Baba's Darshan since we moved to Colorado must have been partly responsible for my dreams which I recorded in my journal as follows:

"Dreamed of Sai Baba again. Baba and I and others went to this old building, and then upstairs where we gathered around Swami, and He talked to us. I felt very honored to be among this group. Later that evening, we went to a gathering in a large hall. At some point, Swami told me that something was not good for me. I promised Swami I would either not go to a cinema again or eat the wrong foods. (Syd and I have been to one movie in 15 years). The next day I was asked if I had any other clothes to change into. I said 'no', so I was given a white Tee shirt with some kind of emblem on the front, and I wore it with the same pants. I was taken to the kitchen where I had volunteered to work and stood next to Swami at a double sink where together we prepared the food for the gathering. I received His Darshan for a long time and luxuriated in its warmth as we worked side by side, peeling carrots and preparing the food together. I remember in this old building there was a fallen large tree outside and some of the roots had grown into the building and we had to step over them as we moved around."

"Dreamed that I walked into a room and saw Swami laying down on a cot. His feet to my left and His head to my right. He raised His head and said, 'Don't worry Child, I never sleep!'" (I believe He gave me this dream because I had been praying to Him because of the dreadful wars and earth changes that have been going on in the world.).

"Dreamed I had died and was standing in a field of wheat (golden brown color) and thinking of all the physical things I could no longer do and was talking to Syd about it when I realized that I had missed the opportunity for enlightenment! I then said pleadingly, 'Please God, give me another chance, Please Baba give me another chance' over and over until my dream ended and I awoke, still in this body.".

"Dreamed that we were in India to see Sai Baba and He gave us a big baby (but He didn't want us to see Him giving it ???). He went into a room in the middle and had pictures taken of Himself with the baby. Niranjan and Madhu Patel were involved in bringing the picture and message to us so we would have proof it was from Sai Baba. Then He gave us a new vehicle and it was parked on a corner up and to the left and we had to go collect it. We were taking a long route to get there and I was afraid it would get stolen so I mentioned this to Syd. I awoke before we got to the vehicle, but remembered at the end of the dream that we had already gotten to the vehicle in the past and had inspected it."

"Dreamed that we were with Sai Baba. He invited me to sit next to Him for a long time, about one half hour to get His Darshan. He gave me a bag of what I thought was Vibhuti, but it turned out to be some pills, dark gray, about 3/8" in diameter, various greys, just like the ones I threw away because I couldn't remember what they were, (kelp or herbal diuretics?). We had been invited in for an interview, but I told Syd to go in alone. Cyndi, my daughter, asked me why and I told her I would get to go too later, and this would give us two separate interviews. Then, we went off to the right somewhere, Sai Baba and me, but I can't remember where or what for. When we were sitting, I was on Sai Baba's right, right next to Him. I don't think He said anything directly to me at that time, but He let me be with Him for a very long time soaking up His Darshan. A lot more happened, but can't remember what it was."

"Dreamed that I was going somewhere and was jauntily jumping very, very high (like 20 to 30 feet up in the air) with each step and making great strides. Then I came to a bad neighborhood and saw some threatening characters. I had several hundred dollars in my purse, I recalled. So I started chanting 'God is taking care of me' over and over, but they came after my purse anyway. Then I called out to Sai Baba and rearranged the ending of the dream (during the dream), so they didn't hurt or rape me and the dream ended."

When my longtime friend Ruth called to wish me a Happy Birthday on September 19, 1992, my 53rd, she told me she was planning to go see Sai Baba before the year was out. After our first trip to India in 1987, I sent her His picture and some Vibhuti. Then she and several friends came to visit us in Colorado for the first time in the Summer of 1992, and we showed them several Baba videos. After watching the videos, Ruth said she knew that Sai Baba was God, and when she returned to Northern California, she started going to various Sai Baba center meetings and events.

After talking to Ruth the day before, I started thinking about how wonderful it would be to go to see Baba again. So, I suggested to Syd that since his contract with Ken and the Dallas company was about to end, that we should take what was left of our savings and make another trip to India while we still could, and before he got too busy working again. It had been five years since our previous trip, and I felt the need to reestablish our link to Swami in person. Perhaps Baba could give us some guidance as to what we should do next. Syd agreed and we started looking at dates and making plans to go.

On my way home from running errands in town that afternoon, I was driving on our mountain dirt roads singing bhajans and was blissed out about our pending trip to India. Suddenly I felt something burst or explode inside my skull. There was a popping noise inside my head as it happened, but I felt no pain, just surprise and wonder at what was going on inside my head. I continued driving, and then became aware of something warm moving slowly downward inside my head from the crown area. My vision began to blur, and then dimmed, until everything went dark, and I realized all at once that I was blind. As the darkness set in, I remember yelling out, "No, Baba!", while simultaneously and impulsively slamming on my brakes, just before I lost consciousness. The feeling I had when I yelled "No, Baba", was that I was telling Him I was not ready to leave yet.

When I regained consciousness, my first awareness was that I still could not see anything and I wondered if I would be blind forever. I felt no fear at all. I was strangely at peace. I replayed the events of what I could remember had happened just before I lost consciousness, and the rest of it slowly came back to me. Then I wondered if I was still alive. I pinched my arm to see if I was still in the body and found that

I was. I reached out in front of me and felt the steering wheel and knew that I was still sitting in the car. I sat there for a while, pondering on what to do next. I realized there wasn't much I could do. So I decided to just stay in the car and wait until someone came driving along. Then it occurred to me that I might have a very long wait, because at the time only two families lived out in our end of the development who were likely to pass by. As I went through this reasoning process, I finally remembered that Syd was home this week and would come looking for me if I was gone more than a reasonable length of time.

After a while, I felt that same warmth inside my skull, and realized this time it was beginning to rise upward and seemed to be returning to the spot where it originated at the top of my head. Very slowly, my vision returned, first just a faint hint of light, then blurred and then gradually it became clearer. Finally, it was as though nothing had happened to it.

I sat there for a few minutes and assessed the situation. I had no recollection of what happened after I lost consciousness, or where I went or was, or for how long. My car was sitting along the side of the dirt road with the engine off and set in the 'Park' position. I had no memory of turning the engine off or shifting into 'Park'. My last recall was when I slammed on the brakes and cried out to Sai Baba. Then I knew, it could only have been Sai Baba who not only saved my life, but reversed what was probably an aneurysm, giving me back my sight. Sobs broke the silence as tears poured out of my eyes when the realization struck me of how much He must love me to have given me so much. I tried to think of what I might have done to be worthy of all this Grace, but could not come up with anything. I sat there for some time in wonderment as I pondered the situation, and cherished this moment of God's Grace. After thanking Sai Baba for helping me through this, I started the car and slowly returned home. It was hours later before I could talk about it and share it with Syd.

That night I dreamed again of Sai Baba, but couldn't remember anything about the dream except that there was a road involved.

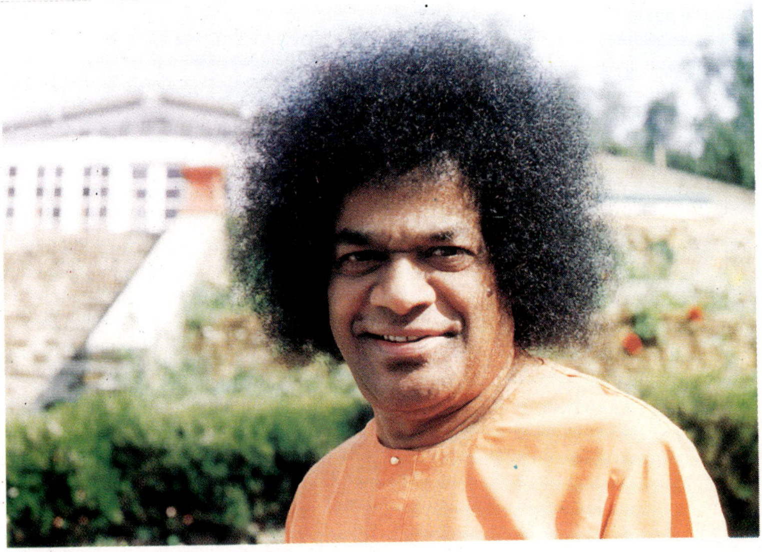

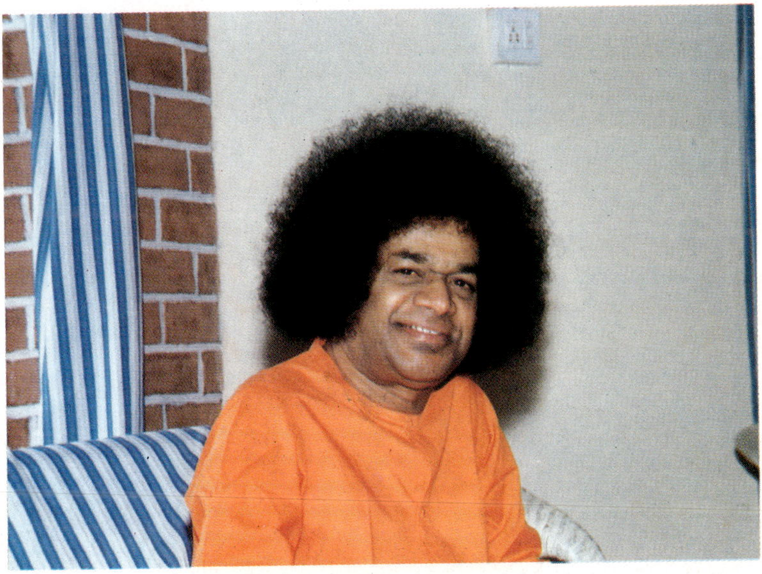

1992 Trip to India

While busy planning our second trip to India, it occurred to us that we would be leaving our home in a vulnerable state. Our home is in a rather secluded area and at the time, we had only one neighbor who passed by it occasionally. Although we have more than a 180° view of the Sangre de Cristos mountain range and the twin Spanish Peaks, we cannot see any homes from ours, except the ones that are in the valley about ten miles West of us. Since there was and still is very little traffic, it would be simple for someone to break into our home without being noticed.

Early in 1990, while the construction crew was still working on the house, it was broken into over the weekend. One of the two generators we had purchased for the use of the crew and for our auxiliary energy system after we moved here, was stolen, along with a few other things. We believed it to be an 'inside job' because they knew exactly how to get in, as there was no forced entry, and the generator they stole was the one that was in the best condition. When construction began on our home, we hung a picture of Sai Baba in a glycine envelope on a tree next to the building site. The man we had hired to oversee and take care of our building project told us the workers called Baba 'The Old Man', and that they said the picture sometimes made them nervous. When the house was broken into, the picture was found afterward in several pieces around the grounds.

Shortly after we moved into our home, one of our neighbors had their home broken into while they made a trip to town for groceries. There were some valuables taken, but what the thieves were really after was the collection of guns. Apparently, somebody knew their comings and goings, and possessions. When we became devotees of Sai Baba, Syd gave away the guns he used to own. We have had people tell us we are crazy not to have a gun for protection out here in the middle of nowhere, but to us, guns and God just don't go together. You either put your faith and trust in God or in your gun. When you have God taking care of you, you don't need any other protection. If you feel that your gun will protect you, than God can not step in and interfere with your karma.

"When you have full faith, God will surely help you and make you fearless. People who have faith in God will never be let down. But those who have no faith suffer. You need not search for God. It is God who is searching for a real devotee." SS July 1994 P 178

"You must have full faith in God, who is the universal sustainer. He is the protector, but not the punisher. The punishment you get is the consequence of your own actions." SS December 1993 P 315

Before we left for India, we took reasonable precautions and set up some lamps on timers and a radio that would go on and off occasionally, and put the house in Baba's hands. Our major concern was with leaving our pets behind. The only outdoor kennel in the area was over 30 miles away, and the pens were small. But there was inside shelter, although unheated, for their food and water and for them to get out of the weather. We attempted to locate a house sitter, but couldn't find anyone who fit our criteria - non-smoker, vegetarian (we permit no meat in our home except dry dog food in the basement), trustworthy, clean, and caring, and they had to love and care for our three large dogs. Unable to locate anyone who we would feel comfortable with staying in our home and who we could trust, we put the dogs in the kennel and left our home untended, but in the hands of Baba. This was an opportunity for the both of us to test our faith and trust once again.

"In all effort, if you trust in a Higher Power which is ready to come to your aid, your work is made easy. This comes from true devotion and reliance upon God, the source of all Power." TOSSSB P 141

We flew out of Colorado Springs to San Francisco on November 30th, where we were joined by Ruth, and her two friends, Vincent and Nino, and were off to Puttaparthi, via Hong Kong, Singapore and Madras.

When we boarded the plane from Singapore to Madras, a lovely lady who appeared to be somewhat nervous sat in the seat next to me. Before we took off she asked me where we were going. When I told her Puttaparthi, she instantly knew we were going to see Baba and said with great excitement that she was also going there and had been praying to Baba to seat her next to one of His devotees. She introduced herself as Mavora from New Zealand, and confided that she had always had a fear of flying and was so grateful that Baba had answered her prayer, as it lessened her fear.

I immediately felt there must be a past life connection because Mavora seemed very familiar to me. I learned that she too was an astrologer and a vegetarian and with that for a beginning, we had much to share. We chatted throughout the flight and became instant friends and have remained good friends since then. We have connected in Puttaparthi on two separate trips since that trip in 1992, and remain in touch through letters and the Internet. She is like a long lost sister to me and I treasure her friendship.

We arrived in Madras late at night and hired a taxi to take us to a hotel. It was pouring down rain, and the taxi driver was driving through the streets with his lights off. His windshield wipers weren't working either. We knew the lights worked, because he would turn them on every now and then to let an approaching vehicle know he was there. Occasionally, he would stick his right hand out the window and wipe the rain off the windshield with a cloth. If that didn't work, he would stick his head out the window while driving down the road to see where he was going. Welcome to India! A test of our faith, Swami?

We left Madras on the early flight the following morning, December 3rd, and arrived in Bangalore where we were met by Suleman, who said he was there to help us get to Brindavan where Baba would be staying until at least December 5th, when it was predicted that Baba would return to Puttaparthi. Suleman owns a taxi service that mostly caters to Sai Baba devotees. We were thrilled to be going to Brindavan, because we had heard and read so much about Baba's Ashram there. Mavora joined us in one of the two taxis of Suleman's that it took to carry our luggage and the six of us.

When we arrived at Brindavan, Syd took our passports and left us outside while he went to see about accommodations. He returned some time later with an unhappy report that there were no family accommodations. Mavora had just come back from the accommodations office to get her luggage, and said 'Let me see what I can do'. She returned in a few minutes with the news that there was a dorm room that just had three ladies vacate their space, and if Ruth and I hurried, we would be able to stay there with her and the room's other two tenants. Syd wasn't happy about being separated, but told me to go ahead with Mavora. He checked further and found there was room for himself, Vincent and Nino in the men's dorm also. It took awhile to sort through our luggage, because I had packed with the thought in mind that Syd and I would be sharing accommodations. But, we were finally settled, and hurried off to line up for darshan.

Darshan of our Lord was combined with bhajans that first afternoon, and our row sat so far back that I only got a few brief glimpses of my Beloved Baba. Tears flowed at the joy of being in His presence and feeling His Love so strongly. I wrote in my journal the following day:

Brindavan, Friday December 4, 1992

At Darshan this morning, we were the first line chosen and I got to sit in the third row. Baba threw candy and I caught a piece from His last toss. I ate it right away and immediately felt renewed. Ruth said she made eye contact with Baba. Once again my tears flowed. So hard to believe I am finally here! Baba was all smiles today, unlike His usual stern looks I recalled from Puttaparthi. Just as we were leaving on a shopping excursion into Bangalore after Darshan, we ran into Niranjan and Madhu Patel near the Ashram gate. Niranjan said they had been very worried about us, and whether we were able to find accommodations. They were very happy to see us and relieved that we were able to stay inside the Ashram, as they were staying outside in the home of friends.

Niranjan shared a few recent 'Baba stories' with us, the most memorable of which was the story about their friends in New Jersey who had their car stolen recently. On the dash board of their car was a statue of Ganesha that Sai Baba had materialized for them. When they discovered the car was missing, they prayed to Baba to help them get it back with Ganesha still intact. The car was missing for a few days, when several black men appeared at their door one evening. They admitted to stealing the car, and asked, "Who is that dude with the orange dress? He suddenly appeared in the car out of nowhere and told us to return it to you. Then he shows up in our home a couple of times and tells us again to return the car. He said he won't leave us be until we bring the car back. Who is this guy?"

Niranjan said his friends told the thieves who Baba was and invited them to come to a Center meeting if they wanted to learn more about Him. They came, and are still coming to the meetings, and their lives have been changed forever. Niranjan finished the story by telling us that Baba has said that if He has given something to one of His devotees, and it is taken from them, He will see to it that it is returned to them.

We went into Bangalore in two cars - Mavora rode with Syd and I, while Ruth, Nino and Vincent went in a different direction with the other car. I purchased two meters of silk, two shirts, a blouse and a bed cover which I plan to sew into a suit or something. When we returned, I stretched out on my bed on the floor to catch a little rest, and had just laid down when I heard a thud. A baby monkey had reached in the window through the bars and stole one of the German girl's lotus blossoms from the windowsill inside. He was still sitting there outside the window, and was eating the flower, while watching to see what I would do. I frightened him off, and rearranged the vase in a safer position on the sill. I had just fallen asleep when the little monkey returned to steal some more and knocked it over, this time spilling all the water out onto her bed.

Saturday, December 5, 1992

Arose early for the ceremony - Baba was dedicating the new meeting hall, the Sai Ramesh Hall, where everybody congregates for Darshan and Bhajans. There are very large crowds today. I am told it is because it is the weekend and many devotees come from Bangalore and surrounding areas. The lady from Holland in our dorm was very sick all last night. She must have gotten up a dozen times. The German lady returned late at night after the lights were out, and found that her bed was soaked from where the monkey had spilled her vase. It took her a long time to rearrange her bedding and get settled in. We didn't get much sleep.

After the ceremony, the Seva Dals passed out pictures of Baba along with prasad, (usually sweets blessed by Baba), neither of which I got. I was stuck in the center of a mob of about a thousand ladies screaming and pushing each other, trying to get some prasad from the Seva Dals who were nearest to us and who were refusing to distribute anything until a single line was formed. There was no room to form a line with that mob and everybody was yelling and pushing. It was a standoff. A real undisciplined mess! I finally found my way out of the mob and retreated to our peaceful room, trying to shake off all that negative energy I had absorbed. It left me very rattled and shaken.

Rumors flew regarding Baba's departure for Puttaparthi. Syd finally found Niranjan, who confirmed that Baba was definitely leaving, so we left early by car, thanks to Suleman. Mavora rode with us again. The car Ruth was in had an inexperienced driver who took a wrong turn and also got a ticket. The fine was Rs. 100, which Vincent paid on the spot. It took a very long time for Syd to get through the line at the Accommodations Office at Prasanthi Nilayam. Mavora came back from Accommodations before the others and said she was staying in the Ladies Shed. As I had been assigned to stay with all of our luggage, I was in misery with a full bladder by the time she returned, so she took me into the Ladies Shed to use the bathroom, while keeping an eye on our luggage for me.

When Syd returned, he said we were assigned three squares in the Family Shed. We hired several boys to carry our luggage to the shed, and Syd sent me on ahead with them and the first load, while he stayed with the rest of our luggage. When I entered the shed, there were children running around, screaming at the tops of their lungs. The nearly empty shed was dirty, and noisy and there was no privacy, whereas I had noticed the shed Mavora was in was clean and quiet, and there was some semblance of privacy, with saris and sheets draped across ropes to separate the assigned plots. I had never seen the inside of a shed before today, and I knew that Syd would not last long under the conditions in the family shed, and when he is miserable, I become miserable. Once he saw the conditions for himself, he agreed we should try to see what there might be outside.

Syd set out to find a hotel room and came back an hour later in a taxi to get me and the luggage. At last, we had a place to rest - in the Sri Sathya Sai Towers, just outside the main gate at Rs. 500 per day. It was a lovely room with a bed, table and chairs, electricity, a ceiling fan and a private western bathroom with hot water.

Puttaparthi, Sunday, December 6th

Having no idea what time Darshan started, I was late, arriving at 6:30 a.m. and got in the line that waits to go in until all the queued lines are seated inside first. Sat in the back row and had a fair Darshan. Later, had breakfast back at the vegetarian restaurant in our hotel with Ruth, Nino and Vincent - a delicious tomato cheese sandwich and tea. We met for lunch at the Eastern Canteen, but I was not feeling well and could not eat. I returned to the hotel for a long nap and seemed to recover - it felt like it was a heat stroke coming on.

I'm sitting here waiting for Swami to give Darshan. Am in the fourth row on the West corner, but will have a good view. I was first in line, but the lady next to me drew Row 11, which turned out to be the number for both our lines. Things have really changed since 1987. The sand is gone, replaced with rough cement. The Mandir grounds are larger, and so are the crowds.

Baba came out and looked me straight in the eye!!! He was passing by and just for a minute, He turned and stared straight into my eyes! His eyes seemed to change - they grew much larger and with an indescribable intensity that seemed to consume me. They glowed like embers, as though I was looking straight down into a volcano. It was very dreamlike. I felt He was showing me a part of Himself that few people had ever seen. Oh, but this special blessing He gave me did my heart Good! He knows I am here. I had not been feeling well before Darshan, but this special blessing seems to have brought me back up again. Just prior to His coming out, I was praying - asking for help to rid myself of the confusion I have been surrounded with and have absorbed from the crowds, and to help me develop better spiritual practices.

Monday, December 7th

What a very special Darshan this morning. I ended up in the fourth row, but in the South corner. When Baba came out He raised His hand (as He does when it seems that He is lifting up our consciousness), and I saw a cloud of white arise from His hand, all sparkly and misty, then vapor like. I got a beautiful rush from it. I had written my letter to Him earlier this morning but never got a chance to give it to Him. Finally felt moved to sit down and write Him. The crowds are multiplying each Darshan. Ruth came by our hotel room and we chatted for an hour, then we went shopping for pictures of Baba, while Syd was getting money exchanged in a very long line.

At afternoon Darshan, I was in the second line chosen and then got in the second row. Baba never looked at me but took my and Rebecca's letters. I was moved to 'tears of bliss' once again. Swami's Love is so strong today. Then at afternoon Bhajans, we were told to sit and wait by the road across from the Poornachandra Auditorium, from which Baba emerged. He came by and looked through the rows of people and directly into my eyes again! I was about four rows back on a raised level with a perfect view! All of this Grace! - I feel so blessed! Vincent joined us for dinner - pizza (from the restaurant downstairs) in our room. I only ate a little - still not feeling too well.

Tuesday, December 8th-13th

I was in line #2, but got in the third row at Darshan. Baba never looked my way - He chose ladies on either side of me for interviews. I went and copied today's Message for the Day, then ran into Syd - he was absolutely glowing with bliss, and holding three large packages of vibhuti to his heart. He had gotten in the first row and Baba came along and blessed the vibhuti for him. The people around him told him how blessed and lucky he was. I am so happy for him.

I tried to shop after Darshan, but began to feel terribly ill, so I came back to the room to lay down. Got sicker and sicker, vomiting, dry heaves, diarrhea, fever, chills, four wool blankets and still couldn't get warm. Later, I drifted in and out of consciousness. Don't remember much. Poor Syd - he went through so much to get me into the hospital. I wasn't conscious most of the time, couldn't stand up or walk - never so sick in all my life. On top of the virus I must have gotten from that lady in our Brindavan Dorm, I also had a kidney and liver infection, and possibly an allergic reaction to the pills that were supposed to protect me from getting malaria. The back pain was terrible. The doctors never did agree upon a single diagnosis. I remember coming back to 'life' and looking up to see this beautiful tall, white haired Indian lady. My first thought when I saw her was that she was an angel, and I asked her if she was. She smiled and told me she was Doctor Kamala, that I was in the hospital and she assured me I would be okay and that to trust that I was in Baba's Hands now. Then I felt a needle in my hip and drifted away again.

The next time I came into awareness, I opened my eyes and there was a large picture of Baba hanging over my bed looking down on me. It was so comforting. I knew He was taking care of me, and I told Him if He wanted to take me home with Him, I was ready any time. Syd came frequently to see me and bring me water and coconut water, which is all I could take. He told me they chased him away all the time. I was in a ladies ward with several European ladies who both had Hepatitis.

Syd was told that he needed to find an attendant for me, as the hospital does not provide for any of the patient's personal needs other than medication and the bed, and he couldn't do it because he was a man. He located Ruth and brought her to the hospital, but it turned out she was also sick, and she slept most of that day and night in the empty bed across from mine. The only toilet was a dirty, smelly hole in the floor, and neither of us could handle that. I wasn't strong enough to get out of bed alone, much less squat over a hole. Ruth left the next morning.

Mavora came to visit after Ruth left, and put some of Baba's vibhuti in my coconut and had me drink it down. I started feeling better almost immediately. She suggested I get out of the hospital as fast as I could, or I might wind up with the Hepatitis my roommates had, and Lord knows what else. She suggested that I would get better care in my hotel room with Syd. I had to agree with her. When Syd arrived later, I asked him to get me out of there, and he was more than happy to do so. The doctor gave him a prescription for more antibiotics and Syd arranged for a taxi back to the hotel. I knew this was Baba's Will.

It was taking a long time for me to heal and my diet was still restricted to coconut water as that was all I could keep down. Syd took me back to the hospital one more time where I spent most of the day hooked up to an I.V. to rehydrate this body. We were scheduled to leave for home on the 14th and I needed to be well enough to travel. What bothered me the most was that I did not have the strength to be able to get up and go to Darshan, which was the **only** reason I was there. Mavora located a Homeopathic Doctor and then told Syd how to find him. The doctor prepared some packets of tiny pills, and gave Syd dietary instructions for me. His wife prepared some 'beaten rice' for my first meal. He instructed Syd to buy some "Liv 52" Ayurvedic pills in the Ashram Shops, or from a chemist outside. For 15 days, I was not to have any fats (butter, cream, nuts, oils of any kind), or sweets, and very little protein. Was told to restrict my diet to coconut water, beaten rice, and later try some unripened bananas and then vegetables.

The day after I started taking the homeopathic pills and restricted diet, I felt much stronger and healthier. I gave up taking the antibiotics as they didn't seem to be doing any good and I had the feeling they were impeding the healing process. I insisted on walking to Darshan, which Syd was not too sure about, and got in the line for sick people. It seems that we stood there for a very long time before we were finally permitted to go inside the Mandir grounds. By then, I was beginning to feel very wobbly and sat in the first place I could find, which was on a concrete step next to a blond haired lady.

A Seva Dal rushed over and said I couldn't sit there, and pointed me to the farthest corner from where Baba can be seen, and a long walk from where we were. I told her I only needed to sit for a moment as I was just out of the hospital and still quite weak. Then I impulsively asked her what made the blond lady next to me more special than me that she could sit there and I couldn't. She couldn't answer that, but got very frustrated with me and gruffly asked if I wanted a wheelchair. It was obvious she wanted me out of there, now! And if I didn't move soon, it could get physical. I wasn't trying to give her a hard time, I was just very weak and still not thinking clearly. Later I learned I had sat down in the VIP section next to the wife of a very wealthy USA devotee. As I recall, back in 1987 there was no VIP section, and this special seating was all new to me.

Years later, in 1998, I visited an Ayurvedic Doctor in New Mexico who told me that my body was telling him that I had had Hepatitis and that it was basically the root problem with my health. In retrospect, it has been since 1992 that I have had so many problems with digestion, as I can no longer tolerate a long list of foods that I used to eat regularly.

Monday, December 14, 1992

Am sitting in the Bangalore Airport awaiting flight to Madras. Stayed overnight in the Gateway Hotel. On the drive from Puttaparthi last night, I had a long dialogue with Baba in my head. I left with feelings of remorse and discontent, knowing we should not have stayed outside the Ashram. That wonderful feeling we had last time (in 1987) just wasn't there anymore.

Baba told me, **"You sacrificed being near Me for your physical comfort! When you are ready to sacrifice your physical comfort to be near Me, you can return."** I asked Him about my health and He said, **"Follow the advice of your doctor"**. Which doctor? **"The homeopathic one!"**. And so I am. He also said that all would be okay when we return home; that the puppies are okay, as is the house. I suddenly felt relieved during this conversation, knowing Baba will be with us and protect us on our journey home. I asked about starting a Center in our home. **"You are not ready to start a Center. You will know when the time is right. You need to start a regular devotional program in your home now - bhajans, meditation....."**

While Ruth and Nino stayed on in India, Vincent left with Syd and I, and we parted company in Singapore. He was returning to his home in San Francisco, and we were flying to Los Angeles where we would catch a flight back to Kona, Hawaii to spend a few days visiting my daughter and grandchildren. Just before Cyndi moved back to Hawaii in 1991, she gave birth to Marlena Gabrielle Leslie, who was now 16 months old, and, this would be the first time I would meet my new granddaughter.

Amazingly, my strength had fully returned and I was literally running through the airports with Syd, after having been so ill in India. When I returned home, I started building a homeopathic pharma-copeia as I had become an absolute believer in this alternative healing method.

On December 7, 1992, while we were still in Puttaparthi, our neighbor's cats had kittens. She knew that we had talked about getting a cat because of the mouse problem we were having, and asked if we wanted to take one when we returned from our trip. We did not know we had a mouse problem until we put my car in the shop to find out why it was having to labor so hard to make it up the mountain to our home.

We got a very strange call from the owner of the automobile repair shop that afternoon. He asked if our dogs seemed to be losing weight. Not knowing what he was getting at, I took a look at our three dogs lounging in the sun outside and told him they appeared as healthy and full-bodied as ever. He then told me that they had found several nests that some mice had made in the car, but that was not what was causing the sluggishness. The mechanics had also found, extracted and weighed, over 40 pounds of dog food that the mice had stashed away in the air intake of my big Mercury station wagon. The following week when Syd went to the barber shop to get his haircut, they asked him how his car was running, and how his dogs were. Everyone had a good laugh. In this small town, the word gets out very quickly. What was peculiar to us is that we only know a few people in town. But we later learned that a lot of people knew who we were because we were some of the first 'outsiders' to buy property and build here during the beginning of the 'boom' days in the late 1980's when developers started carving up 'their' forest land into 35 acre lots.

Several weeks after we returned from India, I was sitting in the living room enjoying the peace and silence of our home one evening, when two names suddenly popped into my head, Pasha and Tigre. "Where did that come from and who are they?", I wondered. Then as if in answer to my question, I had a vision of two small kittens, one orange and one white.

Some time later, I remembered that our neighbor had offered us a kitten from her anticipated litter before we left on our trip. It seemed like years before, and I had forgotten all about the kittens, because so much happens to one when they go to spend some time with Sai Baba. I had never seen her cats so I had no idea what the kittens would look like. Syd and I talked it over after I told him about my vision and the two names, and agreed to take a look at her kittens. We called her the next day and she invited us to come right over. Sure enough, just as in my vision, there were several orange kittens and several white ones. As we sat there watching these tiny balls of fur crawl around, playfully swatting at each other, two of them pounced over to where I was sitting; one white one with blueberry eyes, and one orange one. Pasha and Tigre. Our family had suddenly increased by two.

The kittens were almost six weeks old when we brought them home. Syd was concerned whether our three large dogs would accept the kittens or try to hurt them. He needn't have worried, because Angie, our chow/husky mix, adopted them as her own. She tried to nurse them, and gently cleaned them on a regular basis, watching over them and protecting them on their first venture outdoors. Her thick fur protected her from their sharp teeth and claws. Today, Pasha hangs out and often sleeps curled up with Nik, our Siberian Husky. They both are white with blue eyes. Tigre hangs out with Angie, whose fur is exactly the same color as Tigre's. As the cats grew, they earned their keep by taking care of the mouse problem.

Putting the Teachings into Practice

Before I became ill during the 1992 trip to India, I was able to purchase some books by and about Sai Baba, and tapes, and pictures of Him as well, in the Ashram and the outside shops. When we arrived home, I hung pictures of Baba in every room and on nearly every wall in our home. The pictures helped to remind us of His omnipresence and seemed to make a difference in the way our home felt. We both could feel Baba's energy in those pictures, and they did help us keep focused on Him.

We had some friends visit who had just adopted two infants the years before. The mother, Mrs. A, was standing in my kitchen talking to me while holding her 16 month old daughter against her chest, so that the baby was facing in the opposite direction. Suddenly, little Paulette got very excited and cried out, "Baba, Baba", and was pointing at a picture of Sai Baba sitting in the dining room. Over and over again, she would point at the picture and say, "Baba, Baba!". Paulette's adopted parents are strict Catholics, (her new father studied to be a Jesuit Priest for 15 years), and have had no contact with Sai Baba at all, so there is no way she could have learned about Baba from them and this was her first visit to our home. We could only assume that this little girl must have known Baba in her past life.

Determined to learn all I could about Baba's teachings, I dove into the books like a starving animal in a feeding frenzy. There were few books about Sai Baba on the open market in the United States at the time. Most general bookstores didn't carry Sai Baba books. The nearest bookstore that would carry a book about Sai Baba was a three hour drive North of our home. We had never been to a Sai Baba center meeting or retreat, and had no idea there were now so many books about Him. I wanted to absorb all of His teachings as quickly as I possibly could so I would know how to conduct my life in accordance with those teachings. My main objective was to achieve liberation in this lifetime, but I also wanted to have the answers to the scores of questions racing through my mind, and for the questions my friends and family had posed about Him in case they ever asked me again.

"It is the practice of that which one reads that imparts strength just as food does when digested, and exercise does to promote health." TOSSSB P 64

My life seemed to change significantly as I read and began to put into practice the teachings of our Lord. I was totally immersed in Baba, as I read, breathed, slept, ate, drank, thought, sang, and lived Him without cessation.

"You may ask, why should any one seek good company, do good deeds and direct his mind towards good thoughts? You are listening to Me and what do you get when you so listen? You agree that I am giving you Bliss, is it not? Well, what do you give Me in return? Give Me the Practice of what I am telling you; practice what I teach, that is enough. That is all I ask." BTBOS P 141

In one of the books, I read that Baba says we should chant the Gayatri Mantra three times a day, once in the morning while bathing, once mid-day preferably before taking your meal, and before retiring at night. I searched through the tapes I had purchased at the Ashram for one with the Gayatri Mantra in Sanskrit, because until then, I only knew how to chant a rough English translation of the Gayatri. I took the tape on which Baba chanted the Gayatri three times prior to His discourse on the Mantra, and recorded Him chanting it over and over on a blank tape, so that we could sing along with Him until we had it down correctly. I read somewhere that the proper enunciation and the tune were vitally important to achieve the full effect of the power within the Mantra, and I was determined to perfect it. I have since shared many copies of this tape with others who also wanted to learn it.

"The sage Viswamithra devised the Gayathri mantra as a fine drug for the spiritual aspirant; he is also to be revered for the drug awakens your buddhi (intellect) and confers upon you wisdom, detachment, and discrimination - the three distinguishing marks of humans, elevating them far above other animals.....This Gayathri has the subtle power of removing evil tendencies and implanting virtuous habits.....The Gayathri promotes the acquisition of Daivisakthi - Divine Power. Gayathri means 'that which saves when repeated'!" SSS VOL IV Chap 44 P 278

When I read that food should be offered to God before partaking of it, I knew we should be doing it, but I only casually mentioned it to Syd and took no further action. Then one day while meditating, I got a very strong message from my Inner Voice that it is the woman of the house who is responsible for making any spiritual changes in the household, like saying grace, so I knew it was my duty to start this practice. I wasn't certain what to say or how to go about it, as we had never blessed the food in our family when I was growing up, except for an occasional holiday, nor had I ever been around anybody who did it on a regular basis.

When I still failed to make an attempt at offering the food to Baba, I heard that little Voice Within again telling me that it was my duty to get it started. I knew it was Baba talking to me this time. So, I told Syd that Baba said we needed to start blessing the food before we ate each meal. We were clumsy and felt pretty awkward the first few attempts, but we never fail to offer our food to God before we eat anymore, even in restaurants. We eventually learned to chant the Food Prayer, the Brahmaparnam, and always sing it at home.

It was not surprising to learn that other people's vibrations go into the food when it is prepared, because there have been times when I have had some weird feelings and thoughts after dining in a restaurant. I have entered a restaurant in a very good state of mind, and left bitterly angry or deeply depressed, for no other reason than having absorbed the vibrations of whoever participated in preparing the meal I ate. Actually, I have become so sensitive that I feel and absorb the vibrations of the person who was previously sitting where I have just taken a seat. We rarely eat out anymore, and only do so if we are traveling, but we always offer our food to God before eating it no matter where we are. There have been times when people have come up to us in restaurants to tell us how delighted they are to see that some people still pray over their food.

"In one of the jails of this state, there was once a very pure soul devoted to spiritual ideals, carefully practicing sadhana; he had advanced very far in meditation and single mindedness. One day, however, when he sat for meditation, he felt very savage emotions surging up in him and was shocked to find that he could not, in spite of a tremendous struggle, suppress the hateful and murderous thoughts that took hold of him. He was rocked in agony and his Guru too was upset at the turn of events. The Guru probed into the history of the disciple rather deeply but could not find any valid reason for the tragedy. At last, he found that a certain fanatic murderer had acted as the cook in the jail kitchen the day previous to the calamity and his hateful homicidal thoughts had pervaded the food cooked by him, which the sadhaka had consumed.

"There are subtle invisible thought-forms that can pass from one person to another by such means. Here, one has to be very careful about food, especially where one is proceeding Godward." SSS VOL II Chap 15 P 77

"We should partake food with a Sathwic (pure) mind. Our ancestors recommended the offering of food to God before partaking. Food so partaken becomes **'Prasad'** (consecrated offering). Prayer cleanses the food of the three impurities; caused by the absence of cleanliness of the vessel, cleanliness of the food stuff, and cleanliness in the process of cooking. It is necessary to get rid of these three impurities to purify the food; for, pure food goes into the making of a pure mind. It is not possible to ensure the purity of the cooking process, since we do not know what thoughts rage in the mind of the man who prepares the food. Similarly, we cannot ensure cleanliness of the food ingredients as we do not know whether it was acquired in a righteous way by the seller who had sold it to us. Hence, it is essential on our part to offer food to God in the form of prayer, so that these three impurities do not afflict our mind.....

"The food thus offered to God is digested by 'Vaishvanara' in the digestive system. Since God exists in the form of fire as Vaishvanara, He digests the food along with impurities. So, man will not be affected even if the impurities enter the food." SSIB 1993 P 86

After our return from the 1992 India trip, I had a number of dreams in which I was all over the world, Thailand, Columbia, India, United States, etc., helping people with various things, some of whom were Baba devotees. In another dream I was with a large group of people and we were learning how to love.

Shortly after we returned, Syd got a call from Mr. R, the CEO of the Indian company Syd had put together a joint venture with seven years previous. Would Syd be interested in doing some consulting work for them which would probably require some travel to India? We danced with joy! When we left for India, we did not have a clue as to where our next income would come from and had surrendered it up to Baba. Our Beloved Baba had not only provided us with a new income, He was also providing the means for another opportunity to come see Him!

On April 1st in 1993, Mr. R called again and offered Syd a Business Class ticket to India or two economy tickets, with all expenses paid, plus fees for Syd during the week he was to lecture to their staff in Bombay. We would not be leaving until November, but we were overjoyed to know we were going to see our Lord for certain this year.

Starting a Center

Vincent had put his apartment building up for sale when he returned to California in 1992, and it sold within a very short period of time. Vincent was living in that building when the big 1989 quake occurred in the Bay Area that collapsed parts of the freeway and killed a lot of people. His apartment building had experienced some major damage also. He had decided it was time to leave California after being nearly frightened to death in that earthquake. Vincent had fallen in love with the little town of Trinidad when he visited us with Ruth the previous year. So he made several more trips back to Trinidad, bought a larger apartment building, and returned to California to close out his life in San Francisco. Vincent arrived in Trinidad one afternoon shortly after that in a moving van with his longtime friend Jon. Syd helped them unload the van into one of the apartments, and there were now three Sai Baba devotees in Trinidad.

Vincent wanted to start a Sai Baba Center or study group right away, but because of what Baba had told me during my ride from Puttaparthi to Bangalore, I was uncertain whether we were ready. How could we teach or share what we did not know or practice? And judging from the books I was reading, we had so much to learn. Then Syd read a copy of Jon Roof's *Pathway to God*, and suggested this would be the perfect book for a study group. So I ordered six more copies of the book from the Tustin Book Center and we put an ad in the paper that said: "Sai Baba Study Group meets Thursday Evenings", and gave a phone number to call. In a short period of time, there were a number of people in this tiny community expressing interest, so we had our first meeting. There were five people in attendance.

For the next year our number of attendees ranged from four to a dozen. We had some very captivating discussions, and a variety of Truth seekers with interesting backgrounds attend our meetings. Some attended only one meeting, while others stayed until they got what they were looking for. Our core study circle settled into five people. Vincent started another group which met on Wednesday nights, for the people who were only interested in things metaphysical and not specifically in Sai Baba's teachings. His group became more like a support group, and continues to this day.

Ruth and Nino stayed a full two months in India, spending most of the time with Baba, but did some sightseeing around the country when Baba traveled to Bombay and Madras. Upon their return to California, Ruth started making plans to move to Trinidad also, and she and Nino arrived in the Summer of 1993 and rented one of Vincent's apartments. Thus our core Sai Baba Study Group was increased by two and we were now seven.

"A study circle does not mean only just reading and discussing and taking information into the head, but also putting into practice what is learned. If knowledge is stored in the mind, it causes confusion and confusion leads to blowing of the fuse.....For instance, if you go on eating all the 24 hours, it will result in indigestion. This will lead to disease. What is eaten should be digested and then only you should eat again. In the same way, you should listen (eat) in the Study Circle and put into practice what you have learned.....

"In the Study Circle, whatever we listen to and assimilate in the mind should be distributed to others. In that way we show gratitude for what we have received. We should not listen and keep it with us only for our benefit. Whatever we hear and practice should also be distributed to society at large." SS April 1985 P 99

After a year of meetings, the possibility of our Sai Baba Study Group becoming a Center was explored, and everybody in the core group agreed that they wanted to become an official Sai Baba Center. I called the Tustin Book Store, as they were the only connection with the Sai Organization that I knew of, and I had only recently learned of them. I was put in touch with the Regional Director of our Region and was eventually sent a copy of the Guidelines. We submitted our application to the Regional Director, which was later officially approved. The group appointed me as their President.

Of the variety of Baba dreams I had this year, the following stood out the most in my memory because of later incidents:

"Dreamed that I saw Sai Baba coming out of a doorway into a corridor to give Darshan. It was like He was coming out of the Poornachandra Auditorium, but I couldn't understand why He would be coming from there instead of from the doorway of the Interview Room in the Mandir, like He had during our previous two visits. Anyway, I rushed over to Him and asked Him for padnamaskar. He said yes, but only for a second and only on one foot. So, I fell down and lightly brushed His left foot, and got a real good touch of His right foot. Then I sat back on my knees and started sobbing with joy and He touched my Third Eye with His thumb while touching the top of my head with His hand. I felt so fully blessed. The dream continued on, but I was abruptly awakened by our dogs howling back at a pack of coyotes, and can't remember the rest of the dream." Although not relevant, it was interesting to note that on the day of this dream, India had the 6.5 earthquake that killed thousands."

"Dreamed that I had come to a turning point and realized that Sai Baba was standing there above me, waiting for me. He pointed me in the right direction, and I moved in that direction. Sai Baba was all dressed in white."

"Dreamed that there was a forest fire near our house and possibly heading in our direction. Then I remembered that Sai Baba would protect us from any harm."

I hadn't been back to California since leaving there in 1990, and we had many friends and family still living there, so Syd and I returned for one week to see them once again. We spent a few days with the Patels in Santa Barbara, and it was a memorable experience. Madhu was concerned about my problem with high blood pressure, and gave me some rudruksha beads that had been blessed by Swami. She instructed me to wear one around my neck and to soak one of the beads in water which I should drink and replenish every day. She also gave me a small and very beautiful Ganesha pendant, which I continue to wear on a chain around my neck.

We slept in a guest room in the Patels' beautiful home that Baba had appeared in to other guests of theirs just the previous month. His energy was still there and we slept soundly surrounded by it. In fact, their home was so peaceful and full of Baba's energy that I found it difficult to stay awake the first two days. It was very much like the energy in our own home, perhaps even better. I had spent the previous days visiting with some old friends whose vibrations were not the best and I was totally drained by the time we arrived at the Patels' home. Actually, we found the vibrations in the whole State of California to be very difficult and static, while the Patels' home was like an oasis of spiritual energy. Either California had changed, or we had.

The Patels sing bhajans every night in their home and although it was awkward for us, we immensely enjoyed our attempts to sing with them, as they do only Sanskrit bhajans. I told Syd later that I would very much like to do bhajans in our home because it left me with such a good feeling. But we both knew this would be a challenge since we had never really participated in bhajans before, and I only knew a few English ones I had learned from several tapes purchased from the Tustin Bookstore.

Our new Center which started as a study group did not do bhajans, and we could not generate any interest among our members. We tried playing one of the tapes with Baba singing bhajans, and singing along with Him, but the words and music were just too difficult for the newcomers to follow. And the English bhajan tape didn't inspire anyone to want to continue either. Rather than have anyone leave the Center, we decided not to try bhajans again for awhile, at least until the new members understood more of His teachings. This decision seemed to relieve the tension that had been growing during the Center meetings.

"Those who sing bhajans get what can be called 'double promotion', for they derive joy and distribute joy! Life today is filled with sorrow, it is beset with fear and despair. The only time you can forget these thoughts and strengthen yourself to meet the hard times is when you contact the source of all strength, God. You cannot get that peace and joy while you bend under the burden of daily life.....spend that time with God who can make your shoulders strong and your burden light. You will relish the bhajana as you make it a daily function, like eating and sleeping. You eat twice a day for the upkeep of the body; should you not do bhajana at least once for the upkeep of the mind?" SSS Vol X P 82

1993 India Trip

Finally it was time to leave for India again. We had been anticipating this trip since April when Mr. R, the CEO of the India company, asked Syd to come to India in November and present a management training course to some of his staff. His company had agreed to pay for both of our tickets. I was really looking forward to this trip, as my trip the previous year had been such a disappointment because I saw so little of Swami due to the illness.

The following is from my journal:
November 23, 1993

Up at 4 a.m., awake since 3:30. Took the dogs to the kennels and the cats to the Vet where we knew they would be safe, and then back home again to finish packing, load the car and go. Finally on the road at 10:18 a.m. We decided (Syd got the message from Baba) to drive to Colorado Springs and see if we could leave a day early and get a flight to Dallas from there, because if we continued with our plan to take off from Denver, it could be the end of the trip for us. We had changed the departure airport from Colorado Springs to Denver a month ago so that we could attend the Sai Baba Birthday Celebration in Denver the night before we were to leave for India. Now, the storm of the year had arrived and promised to stick around for several days. Some flights were canceled and others delayed, and we may not have made our connection in Atlanta to Frankfurt.

The ticket agent, Fergie, was not very happy with us when we told him our plight, and made it abundantly clear that we were really asking too much. We arrived at the ticket counter at 1:05 p.m., and he told us after checking in his computer that the only plane they had available was scheduled to leave for Dallas in one half hour, at 1:38 p.m., today. Nothing later, nothing tomorrow. It was the **only** flight that would get us to an airport where we could catch a plane to Frankfurt, so we could make our connecting flight to Bombay the following day. It was a big deal getting us re-ticketed, but Fergie stayed with it and told Syd to go get our luggage and park the car, and then to go to the gate with our carry-ons, while I waited for the tickets. At 1:35 p.m., Fergie handed me the tickets and then called the gate while I ran as fast as I could to get on the plane. It was Baba's miracle!

Syd had a major learning experience with surrendering to Swami, which was also a part of this ticketing experience and this trip to India. I have asked him to share it in his own words:

The Ambulance Gurney

The following events primarily concern an ambulance gurney, but their real significance has to do with the meaning of surrender.

Before we knew Sai Baba, if I was having trouble resolving a problem, Char used to tell me to "Let go and let God!". After our first visit to Puttaparthi, she would say, "Surrender it to Baba". But, I didn't feel comfortable with either of those. I viewed the options of doing things myself or giving them to God to take care of as the only options available. I felt that God, Sai Baba, expected me to do my best to solve my problems, and not to just dump them on Him. Char and I debated the matter of surrender many times, but I just couldn't accept the idea. My experience with the ambulance gurney changed all that. I learned the meaning of surrender, and I accepted it and began putting it into practice.

In October 1992 Char and I made our second trip to see Sai Baba. At Brindavan, Char had been housed with three other ladies, two of whom had been quite ill. After a week at Brindavan, Baba returned to Prasanthi Nilayam, and we followed. Char had apparently contracted whatever illness her Brindavan roommates had been suffering from, and she became ill shortly after our arrival at Puttaparthi. Her condition rapidly worsened. She had a very high fever, and she began to lapse into periods of unconsciousness.

A doctor from the U.S.A. who was serving at the newly opened Super Speciality Hospital helped make arrangements for Char to be examined at the General Hospital at the Ashram. She had to be carried to a taxi to be driven to the hospital. There, the head nurse told me to bring her in. But, Char was unconscious, and so I asked for a wheelchair or a gurney. After awhile, two small men appeared, carrying a long, very dirty canvas stretcher. When they put it on the pavement and unfolded it, a cloud of dust arose. But, that was not the time to fuss over cleanliness. We lifted Char out of the taxi, and laid her on the stretcher, and the men carried her into the hospital.

Inside the hospital, Dr. Kamala examined Char, and told the administrator to have her taken upstairs to a hospital ward immediately. The two men began to carry the stretcher, with Char on it, up the stairway, but could not negotiate the turn in the stairway because the stretcher was too long. The stretcher had no straps to keep a patient from falling off. The men tried to lift the stretcher over the stairway railing, and in the process, Char rolled off the stretcher and fell onto the stairs. She was unconscious, and so, was unaware of her fall, which, fortunately, didn't injure her.

Since Char was off the stretcher, the men were able to lift the stretcher over the railing to the next set of stairs. We then put Char back on the stretcher, and they carried her upstairs and into the ward. There, they lifted the stretcher to bed height, and rolled her onto a bed.

After Char had been treated by Dr. Kamala, I asked the doctor if the hospital had an ambulance-type gurney, which would have made the process of getting an unconscious or immobile patient into the hospital and up the stairs a great deal easier. An ambulance gurney is a narrow bed with wheels, onto which a patient can be strapped. The legs of the bed can be folded, to permit the gurney to rest at ground level, so that a patient can be moved onto it. Handles at each end permit the gurney to be lifted or carried like a stretcher. And, the legs of the gurney can be extended to normal bed height, to wheel a patient about in a hospital.

Ambulances are generally equipped with gurneys, to facilitate moving a patient from the ground into the ambulance, and then, from the ambulance into the hospital. And so, that is what I had in mind when I asked Dr. Kamala if the hospital had a gurney.

Initially, Dr. Kamala and I had to resolve a difference in terminology. Dr. Kamala was not familiar with the term "gurney". When I described what a gurney was, she said, "Oh, you mean a trolley". But, I knew a "trolley" as a streetcar that was powered by overhead electric lines, not as a gurney. Once we had resolved the terminology, it was clear that the hospital did not have a gurney. It was equally clear that the hospital badly needed one, and so, I resolved that I would provide the hospital with a gurney, and told Dr. Kamala that. She took me to the head doctor, who said that he did not have the authority to approve my giving the hospital a "trolley". When I asked who did have the authority, he said that he didn't know, and that maybe only Baba had the authority. I thought that was he was being facetious, at the time, but I ultimately learned that he was right. Only Baba had the authority.

Through Baba's grace, Char recovered, and we returned to the U.S.A..

Once home, and after recovering from jet lag, I addressed the matter of the gurney. I didn't know what a gurney cost, or how I might get one to Puttaparthi. We had spent all of our available cash on the trip to India. We didn't know when or if we might be able to go to India again. I had lost my principal consulting clients after we relocated from California to Colorado, and so, we didn't know where our income would be coming from, either. Nevertheless, I was determined to get a gurney to the General Hospital at the Ashram.

Char told me to ask Baba for help, and I did.

And so it was that the phone rang. The call was from India. It was the president of a company, headquartered in Bombay, that I had dealt with some years before when I was managing an international business. He wanted to know if I was available to provide consulting assistance to his company, in setting up a joint venture with a major (Fortune 500) U.S. company. I was. He flew to the U.S., and after our meeting with the proposed joint venture partner, I invited him to spend the weekend at our home in Colorado. While there, he asked me if I could come to India in December of that year (1993) to give management training to his senior employees. I said that I could. He said that his company would pay a business class fare for me, or, if Char came with me, the company would pay for two coach class fares.

And so, suddenly, we were going back to India. We hadn't planned it, we hadn't arranged it, we hadn't even contemplated it, but we had hoped and prayed for it. And, we were going.

I asked my new Indian client to look for a gurney for me in India, that I could take to the General Hospital. They were unable to locate one. They told me that, if I was going to bring one to India, I should get a letter from the hospital requesting it, which would enable me to avoid having to pay a very high customs duty. And so, I wrote the hospital, but never received a reply.

I began a search in the U.S. for a gurney. I learned that there are only a few manufacturers of such equipment, and they schedule their production runs on the basis of the quantity that they have orders for. As a result, it could be another year before a new gurney became available to me. I also learned that a new gurney was quite expensive. One of the hospital equipment distributors that I had contacted suggested that I try to locate a renovated gurney. Many hospitals regularly return their used equipment to the manufacturers for renovation. Some of the renovated equipment is sold through distributors, but some is donated to service organizations, to be given to needy hospitals that can't afford to purchase equipment. I spent many hours of many days on the phone, trying to locate an available gurney, but to no avail. Several equipment dealers were also trying to locate a gurney for me, but, one by one, they phoned to tell me that there were none available.

Everything that I had tried had failed, and I didn't know what to do next, and so, I said to Swami, "Baba, I would like to take a gurney to the hospital at Puttaparthi, but I don't seem to be able to work it out. If You would like me take a gurney to the hospital, You will have to arrange it, because I can't."

Baba let me wallow in my despair for several weeks, before the phone call came from a distributor in Texas. "Mr. Chaden, are you still looking for a gurney?" he asked. "I was on the phone with an associate, and he mentioned that he was going to acquire a renovated gurney. I told him that I had been contacted by someone who wanted to give a gurney to a hospital in India. He said that he would be willing to make it available to you. And so, if you want it, I'll let you know as soon as he gets it."

I was overjoyed. I thanked him profusely, and, of course, I thanked Baba.

About two weeks later, he phoned and said that his associate had the gurney. I asked him how I might get it, and he said, "You're in Colorado, aren't you?". I said that I was, but that was a long ways from Houston, where his facility was located. He responded, "The gurney isn't here in Texas. My associate's business is in Denver, Colorado. You can pick it up there." More of Baba's doing.

I telephoned his associate. He asked me why I wanted to give a gurney to a hospital in India, and I briefly told him the story. When I finished, he said that he would let me have the gurney for what it cost him, a relatively low cost. That solved the problem of my having the funds to pay for it.

And so, I began to consider how I would get the gurney to Puttaparthi. I had seen people at airports checking in bicycles in "bicycle boxes" as luggage, and the thought occurred to me that I could put the gurney in one of those boxes, and take it as personal luggage. Returning from a business trip, I picked up a "bicycle box " at the airport, and took it home. I hadn't picked up the gurney yet, and so, I didn't know its dimensions, or how much it weighed. I phoned the business in Denver that had the gurney, and asked them. The gurney weighed about three times the weight of a bicycle, and would only fit in the bicycle box if it was partially dismantled. Then I phoned the airlines to ask if I could take the gurney, in a bicycle box, as personal luggage. The answer was, uniformly, "No.".

The Indian company was going to prepay our tickets, and so, we had to choose an airline and select the flights that we would take. At the time that we did so, I asked the airline representative if we could arrange to take the gurney. He said that neither he, nor his supervisor, had the authority to approve that. He suggested that I contact the Vice President-Marketing at the airline headquarters. I did that, and again, received an emphatic "No.".

I concluded that I would have to find another way to send the gurney, and I began to contact air freight companies. The freight costs that they quoted were several times the cost of the gurney, and we didn't have the money at the time.

And so, I again told Baba that if He wanted me to bring the gurney to the hospital at the Ashram, He would have to arrange it, because I couldn't.

This time, Baba responded almost immediately. The phone rang, and it was a special representative of the airline. He said that he was calling to tell me that they had received the authorization to issue our prepaid tickets, and that I could pick them up at the nearest airport, which was at Colorado Springs. He mentioned it wasn't customary to telephone people when their prepaid ticket authorizations were received. The notices were usually mailed, but for some reason, he felt that he should call.

Then, he asked, "Is there anything else that I can do for you, Mr. Chaden?".

I told him about the gurney. First, he suggested that I contact the airline customer service office, but I had already done that and received a negative response. Then, he suggested that I contact the Vice-President Marketing, but I had already done that, too, and received a negative response. Then he said that he would think about it and see what he could do, and that he would get back in touch with me.

He phoned that same afternoon: "Mr. Chaden, your primary service airport is Colorado Springs. The Marketing Manager at Colorado Springs is responsible for taking care of whatever service problems may arise. He has a certain amount of discretion in what he can do. I think that he can help you. Call him."

He gave me the name and telephone number, and I called. The Marketing Manager wasn't in, and so I left a message on his answering machine. I didn't hear from him, and so I phoned the next day, and the day after that, and the day after that, leaving messages each time. I began to get discouraged, and I told Baba that I would accept whatever He decided.

The phone rang, and the Marketing Manager was on. He apologized for the delay in getting back to me. He had been in a series of meetings. He had received a call from the airline employee who had called me about the prepaid tickets, and he knew about the gurney and my desire to take it with me as personal luggage, and my flight itinerary. He told me that it was all taken care of, and that the computer record for my reservations stated that I was authorized to take a hospital bed in a bicycle box as personal luggage on the flight to India. He wished me a good trip. I thanked him profusely, and, of course, I thanked Sai Baba.

I picked up the gurney in Denver. It required quite a bit of dismantling in order to fit into the bicycle box. I put the loose pieces in plastic bags, and taped them to the gurney frame. I wrapped the entire gurney in blankets, and secured them with tape. Then, I crammed it all into the bicycle box. The bicycle box bulged out in several places, but I taped it shut.

Several weeks before we were scheduled to leave for India, Char learned that a Sai Baba birthday celebration was going to be held in Denver on Baba's birthday. And so, we changed our flight reservations to depart from Denver the day after Baba's birthday, stopping in Dallas, Texas, and then flying to Frankfurt, Germany. On the morning of Baba's birthday, we took our two cats to the veterinary doctor to be boarded while we were away, and then took our three large dogs to a kennel, about thirty miles from our home. We then returned home, loaded our Suburban with our luggage and the gurney, and started out for Denver.

Denver is about a four to five hour drive from our home, depending upon traffic and weather conditions. Colorado Springs is on the way to Denver, about a two to three hour drive. As we drove toward Colorado Springs, we could see heavy clouds gathering over the Sangre de Cristo mountains. We tuned in the weather report on our radio, and heard that a very heavy storm had unexpectedly hit Denver, with snow expected to fall for several days. In those days, it was not uncommon for the Denver airport to close for days at a time, when heavy snowstorms occurred.

We began chanting the Gayatri Mantra, and I heard Baba say, **"Go to Colorado Springs"**. I told Char that, and she said, "But I was hoping to go to Baba's birthday celebration." By the time that we approached the Colorado Springs area, we could see that it was snowing to the north and over the mountains to the west. We drove to the airport, and parked in the temporary parking zone. Inside, we approached the counter, and explained our situation to the airline representative. We had reservations to fly out of Denver the next day, but it looked as if the Denver Airport might be closed because of weather. We had to get a flight to Dallas, so that we could connect with our flight to Frankfurt the next morning.

The airline representative listened to our story, and then told us that the next flight to Dallas was scheduled to depart at 1:38 PM. It was 1:05 PM. He said there was no way that he could change international flight tickets in time for us to get on that flight, and Colorado Springs Airport was expected to close within an hour because of the approaching storm.

Char and I both said our prayers to Baba, and Char said to the airline representative, "Please, sir, won't you try?". He began to shake his head and say "no", and then stopped, and then said to me, "You had better bring your luggage in, in case I can get you on the flight.". When I came back with the luggage, he had one phone hooked onto his shoulder, was holding another phone in his hand, and was typing on his computer keyboard with the other hand. His eyes widened when he saw the bicycle box, and he looked at the computer monitor, and said, "It says here that you are authorized to carry a hospital bed as personal luggage." He shook his head and went on with his efforts to get us on the flight.

Then, he said to me, "You had better take the carry-on luggage and go through security, because it's getting close to flight time. If I can get this done, your wife can bring the tickets and the boarding passes." And so, I went to the gate, and told the attendant that we were being ticketed for the flight, and that my wife would be along in a few minutes. But, at 1:35 PM they announced the final call for the flight, and at 1:38 they closed the doors to the jet way. Char had not arrived with the tickets and boarding passes. The attendant said that they could not hold the plane because they had to take off before weather closed the airport. I prayed to Baba.

I asked the attendant to phone the ticket counter, and she did. They said that Char was on the way, and so, she phoned the plane and opened the door to the jet way. Char came running along, we got on the plane and into our seats, and within minutes, took off, chanting the Gayatri Mantra. They told us later that we were the last flight to get out of Colorado Springs before the airport closed.

Once in the air, it occurred to me that I had last seen our luggage and the gurney sitting at the ticket counter. There were baggage tags stapled to our ticket folder, but there hadn't been time to load the luggage after Char had received the tickets and boarding passes, and the airline attendant had said that it would not be loaded unless and until he had been able to confirm us on the flight. And so, I worried over the luggage and gurney all the way to Dallas. Char wasn't worried about the luggage and gurney, but she kept saying, "I wanted so much to go to the Sai Baba birthday celebration." We took turns reassuring each other, saying that whatever happened was Baba's will.

In Dallas, we waited anxiously for about 45 minutes, and then, our luggage appeared. A half hour later the gurney was brought out. We asked if we could check the gurney at the airport, and were told that we could not. I phoned a hotel near the airport, reserved a room, and asked to be picked up.

We arrived in Dallas and checked into the Holiday Inn North. We decided to call our friend Ken to see if he and his family would like to join us for dinner that evening. Ken's daughter Umi answered and took a message. Then, Bharti, Ken's wife, called us when she got home from work and told us to eat now, as they would be by later to pick us up and take us to the Birthday Celebration at their Sai Baba Center. We had never attended any other Center meetings or a Baba Birthday Celebration, or any other event having to do with Sai Baba, and had really been looking forward to the Denver celebration. Now we would be able to celebrate with our dear friends, the Pandyas. Baba's wonderful leela - A birthday gift to us on His Birthday!

The Celebration was held in their regular meeting hall, and most of the attendees were Indian. The altar was very beautiful and most elaborate. Traffic in Dallas was very heavy, and we were late getting to the Celebration. They were already singing bhajans when we arrived. Both Ken and his daughters were signed up to lead bhajans, and they missed out because they took the time to drive far across the city to pick us up. We had no idea they sacrificed this special event just to pick us up until later. After bhajans, they showed a film made in India with a message from the ancient scriptures, which was very fast paced and we found difficult to follow, but enjoyed just being there anyway.

After the video, Vibhuti was passed around, and everyone was given prasad as they left the building - a full Indian dinner to go, complete with our favorite - laddu - a delightful sweet. What a wonderful treat! Ken drove us to their beautiful home where we ate together. Their large and luxurious home has a wonderful altar which is actually built into the wall, with doors to secure it away. Vibhuti and kum kum appeared to be manifesting on the altar, and especially on one picture of Baba. After some delightful chai tea, Ken returned us to our hotel and we fell into bed and slept in the next morning.

The following morning, Char was suffering from terrible back pain, so she did some yoga stretches on the hotel room floor. She had fallen on the ice in the driveway yesterday while trying to put Maggie in the car to drive to the kennels. Maggie is the daughter of Nik and Angie.

The hotel van had been large enough to hold us, our luggage and the gurney, but the hotel baggage check room wasn't large enough to hold the gurney. And so, it sat in the lobby of the hotel until we left. At the airport, we checked our luggage and the gurney in, and flew on to Frankfurt. We had a long wait for our flight to Bombay, but finally, were on our way.

When we arrived in Bombay, at about 1:30 in the morning, we retrieved our luggage fairly quickly, but there was no sign of the gurney. It was almost an hour before the gurney was brought in. The bicycle box was torn in several places, and the gurney frame protruded through. One of the bags of parts was hanging outside the box.

The customs agent asked for our documents for the gurney. I showed him my receipt for the purchase, and explained that we had brought the gurney to give to a hospital. He asked if I had a letter of request from the hospital, and I said that I didn't. He said that the customs duty would be 300% of the purchase price. I said that was ridiculous, and asked to speak to his supervisor. After a half hour of arguing with his supervisor, and his supervisor's supervisor, their asking duty had been reduced to 100% of the purchase price. I was very tired, very frustrated, and was getting angry. In that mood, I demanded to see the highest ranking official of customs. After a long wait, he appeared, and after listening to my tirade, said that $100 was the smallest amount that he could accept. I gave him the $100, got a receipt, and we went on through customs.

Several officers of the Indian company had been waiting to meet us, since 1 o'clock in the morning. It was now 3 o'clock. I had faxed them that I was bringing a very large package, and asked that they have a van with a roof rack pick us up. But, they didn't have a van with a roof rack, they had a little car with a roof rack, that could hold four passengers. It could not hold all of us, and the luggage, and the gurney. And so, they hired a taxi, and put all of the luggage in the taxi, and one of the officers of the Indian company accompanied it. We put the gurney on the roof of the little car, rolled down the windows, and we held the gurney on the roof while we drove through the streets of Bombay to the hotel.

The gurney would not fit in the baggage checkroom of the hotel, and so we left it in the lobby. Char went on to Puttaparthi, and I stayed in Bombay to give the training course. The company sent a truck to the hotel for the gurney, and took it to one of their warehouses. There, I removed the various parts from the remnants of the bicycle box, and assembled the gurney. Remarkably, all of the parts were there. I then disassembled the gurney, and repacked it. The people at the warehouse gave me a set of tools, which I included in the package.

I contacted Indian Airlines, the domestic air service, to make arrangements to ship the gurney. Both their passenger and airfreight services refused to accept it, because its size and weight exceeded their limits. The Indian company offered to send it to Bangalore on one of their trucks, and to ship it from there to Puttaparthi. They estimated that it would take three or four days to reach Puttaparthi, which would have put its arrival there on the day before I was scheduled to arrive.

I was feeling very confident about getting the gurney to Puttaparthi, and relished the thought of the prospect of delivering it to the hospital. But, Baba would ensure that I learned my lesson of surrender.

I flew to Bangalore, and found Char waiting for me at the Airport. She had been in Brindavan since Swami moved there several days before. Before leaving Puttaparthi, Char had been checking with the General Hospital, and the gurney had not arrived. When Swami returned to Prasanthi Nilayam, we followed. Then I began checking daily with the hospital for the next week, without any sign of the gurney. I thought that, since the gurney was addressed to the hospital, it might have been mistakenly delivered to the Super Speciality Hospital, and asked Dr. Kamala to phone there. Dr. Kamala clearly had her doubts about what I had said about the gurney, and took me in to see the head doctor. "This man", she said, "claims to have shipped a trolley from Bombay to the hospital ten days ago, but it hasn't arrived. He thinks that it might have been delivered to the Super Speciality Hospital by mistake, and would like us to check."

The head doctor phoned the Super Speciality Hospital. They had not received the gurney.

I telephoned the company in Bombay, and told them that the gurney had not arrived, and asked them to check on its status. They confirmed that it had been shipped, and that it had arrived in Bangalore, and had then been sent on to Puttaparthi. They had received no word after that, and said that they would inquire.

The next day I phoned the company, and they said that they had learned that the truck, on which the gurney was being transported from Bangalore to Puttaparthi, had broken down somewhere along the way. The gurney had been transferred to another truck, which was supposed to deliver it to Puttaparthi. They didn't know the company, or the number of the truck, or the name of the driver. That had occurred a week before.

There were only three days remaining before we were scheduled to depart, and I didn't know where the gurney was, or who had it. But, I understood what had happened. Baba was showing me that if He wanted something to happen, it would, and if He didn't, it wouldn't, and it didn't really matter what I wanted. It didn't even matter what I did. What mattered was that I surrendered the results of my actions to Him. And so, I told Baba that I accepted His will, whatever it might be.

I checked with the hospital the next morning, and the gurney hadn't arrived. But, that afternoon, when I went in to check, the gurney was sitting in the Emergency Ward reception area. The packaging hung in pieces on the frame of the gurney. The bags of parts were sitting separately on the floor. The tools that the warehouse in Bombay had given to me were gone. I thanked Baba for having delivered the gurney, and asked His help in assembling it.

I sought out Dr. Kamala. She introduced me to two young men, who, she said, would help me assemble the trolley. They borrowed some tools, and we began to assemble the gurney. Dr. Kamala supervised. The gurney did not go together as easily as it had in Bombay, but we eventually had it completed. When we had finished, the two young men took turns pushing each other on the gurney around the Emergency Ward. Then, they took Dr. Kamala for a celebration ride. They were laughing, and happy.

I watched their celebration, and then turned to a large picture of Baba that hung on the wall. I was immensely grateful to Baba for having used me to get the gurney there. I thanked Him, and surrendered to Him, and went off to tell Char the news.

Back to Charlene:

I was able to sleep some on the flight to Frankfurt. While I was standing in line to use the bathroom on the plane, the man who had been sitting in front of us told me he was on his way to Moscow, via Vienna. He then asked where we were going and why. I told him about Syd's work and also about Sai Baba. He asked many questions, so I showed him some of the Baba books I carried with me. After a lengthy conversation, I told him I believed Baba was the second coming and the Messiah everyone has been waiting for.

My Inner Guidance told me to give him the book *Embodiment of Love* which I had already read. He shared with me that he was a Baptist and a farmer from Minnesota whose church sent him to help build a church in Russia. He intimated that he wasn't sure why they had chosen him because he had not been very active in the church, but he had been in the construction industry. I could tell He was genuinely interested in Baba by the questions he asked, and I felt like I was a vehicle for Baba somehow. I will always wonder whether he ever was drawn by Sai Baba to Puttaparthi. Perhaps I will see him there someday.

Bombay, November 26, 1993

We arrived in Bombay at 1 a.m. It was an hour after our luggage came in on the carousel before the gurney finally arrived. Syd spent a lot of time being shuffled from one official to another regarding how to get the gurney through customs. Unbelievable! It seemed like many hours had elapsed before we finally got checked into a room at the Centaur Hotel, in Juhu Beach.

We were exhausted and hungry, so we unpacked a few things and then tried to heat some water for a cup of soup, but we must have blown a fuse because the lights went out. After calling the front desk, we eventually got repacked and moved (with the help of several candles) down the hall to another room where we ate a granola bar and fell asleep sometime after 5 a.m. We slept all day until somebody from the company called at 3:30 p.m., to remind us to meet them at 5:30 for dinner downstairs with several other business associates from the firm

Syd consults for.

I dreamed that we were with Sai Baba at the Ashram, but never actually saw Him. In the dream, I knew that I was dreaming.

Syd is not feeling too well tonight - his sinuses are draining continuously. He's very quiet and suffering with head pain, very hot with fever, and is going to sleep sitting up. Lots of fireworks going off all evening long; firecrackers, shooting stars, etc. Outside the hotel, on the streets below I watched some horse drawn carts, which were very gayly decorated, trolling along empty. A camel cart, also elaborately decorated, slowly made its way through the intersection. Very large camel! There was an election today which threatens the position of the current Prime Minister. Ballots are now being counted. It's 11:25 p.m. and I can still hear what sounds like cherry bombs exploding below on the streets. We checked with the Indian Airlines office in the hotel today about a flight to Puttaparthi, and they (like the people at Customs) acted like they never heard of Sai Baba or Puttaparthi. They said it must be some private airline that goes there. We know they have had flights there for more than a year.

November 27, 1993
Syd has been sick all day. We had breakfast downstairs and then he went back to bed until 8 p.m. I was able to get him some antibiotics from the chemist in the hotel's shopping arcade. His fever finally broke late tonight. Fortunately, it is the weekend and he doesn't have to meet with anybody.

November 28, 1993
Mr. L., the Manager of Industrial Relations of the firm Syd consults for escorted me around Bombay today. He volunteered to take me wherever I wanted to go. Mr. L is a devout Catholic and says his family was from Goa where the Padres from Portugal converted a lot of Indians many years before. Even his last name is Portugese, though he is undeniably of Indian descent. My first request was to go to the Dharmakshetra, Sai Baba's Ashram in Bombay. My second was to a shop where I could pick up some nice Punjabis to take to

Puttaparthi. We stopped first at the shop, which was on the way to the Ashram.

I spent over an hour in the Ashram bookstore, picking up books and tapes I had never seen before. I wonder why the bookstores in the three main Ashrams, Puttaparthi, Brindavan and Dharmakshetra don't carry the same things? Mr. L. seemed very interested in looking around the Ashram and perused a number of Sai Baba books in the store too. He is a very kind and friendly person and he seems so familiar that I feel I must have known him in another life. I suddenly started feeling very sick in the bookstore and asked him to return me to my hotel room. Now I'm starting to feel feverish and full of some kind of infection, probably the same thing Syd has come down with. It seems that whenever we leave the pure air of our Colorado mountain home, and get on a plane, we are very susceptible to whatever germs are floating around in the very used air we are forced to breathe on the airplane.

December 1, 1993
I've been ill for two and one half days now also, with a viral infection and have slept most of the time. Mr. L arranged for a doctor to come to the hotel room yesterday. He gave me a shot in 'the bum', and medicine plus prescriptions. I've developed a terrible cough and phlegm has filled all my air passages, so much this morning when I was coughing, that I thought I'd never get air into my lungs again. Scary!

Dreamed that I called on Sai Baba to help me know what to say to some boys who had caused me trouble. The perfect words came out (in the dream) spontaneously and I thanked Baba and the problem was solved.

Getting to Puttaparthi

From my journal:
Puttaparthi, Sunday, December 5, 1993
Yesterday was a total exercise in futility. Neither Syd nor I slept well the night before. He was so sad and depressed and concerned

about my traveling to Puttaparthi alone and I felt his feelings all night. Then we got up at 4 a.m., hurriedly bathed and dressed and repacked so that we would be ready for the porter to take my bags downstairs to the lobby at 9 a.m.. The hotel bus leaves at 9:30, which will get us to the airport at 10 a.m.. We checked my luggage in for the flight to Bangalore, and then we sit in the smoke filled terminal and wait until my plane leaves at 11:40. Syd insists on staying with me until my plane takes off. I am grateful for this, but I know he should be working at the office.

While waiting for my flight, a group of Muslims gathered across from us in their long white gowns with their wives in gayly colored gowns, which cover them from head to toe. A little old man is apparently doing his seva, by efficiently serving coffee and canapes to one and all in their group. He is serving them in full china dishes with white linen napkins that he brought forth from his portable stainless steel, mini-canteen on wheels. After much waiting, we begin to see a lot of security people gather around us and we watch and wait some more.

Soon a group of men in long white gowns come sailing through surrounded by even more security, and in the center of this group is the reason for their concern - an Ayatollah or leader of some kind - whatever - as he is getting a lot of security and a lot of attention. Someone makes the leader aware of the crowd of Muslims across from us, who have been waiting all this time, apparently just to see him, and he waves his arms and says a few words as the crowd of security moves him on. Then another bunch of white-gowned Muslims arrive with a very large box, eight feet high, four feet wide, two feet deep. No way can they get it in the elevator after much shifting and moving efforts. After much more waiting, a band of Indian maintenance people show up and they muscle the monster into Security, and then out towards the plane to Hyderabad. Then all the white gowns disappear and the row of seats quickly fills with smoking Indians again.

My flight is finally announced and they are telling us to go through Security. So I kiss Syd goodbye at the door to Security, and then I disappear downward on the escalator and into the boarding area. It is so cold in this airport that people are shivering uncontrollably. There was a sign upstairs announcing they had just had a new air conditioning system installed and boy are they overdoing it! I buy a Nescafe (coffee from powder) to warm up my insides and can feel Syd watching me. I look up and see him standing at the upper level looking down on me through the room sized window. Time passes very slowly and my flight is still not boarding. Some people are getting very agitated. I wonder what is happening. Soon, I see that they have sent a little man down with his radio and people gather around him and soon there is yelling and shouting. I am unable to hear what he is telling them for all the shouting. I can see this little man is just letting the complaints fall on deaf ears. It sounds and looks for all the world like the beginning of a riot, but after more Security arrives, it disperses.

The monitor shows the plane to Bangalore will leave now at 1:40 p.m, two hours late. After much waiting, and a similar frightening mob scene as before, the departure time is changed to 2:40. But 2:40 comes and still nothing happens. Then a large crowd gathers at the window and a horrible blaze and thick black smoke is rising up into the sky across the runway about a mile from the airport. We watch a tall building become engulfed as the thick toxic smoke and flames spread onward. Just what Bombay needs to add to its TERRIBLE SMOG PROBLEM. Probably major loss of life this old Indian lady next to me speculates. I agree.

I look up to Syd again and he motions me to bring my bags and return upstairs and I do. I am by now both starving and frozen and get in the snack bar food line. I'm told by someone I must go get in line to get another boarding pass. So I get in another line and Syd stays to get something for us to eat. By now it is after 3 p.m., and I tell the airline people that I just want to cancel today's trip, retrieve my luggage and try going again tomorrow. My flight is to Bangalore and I would no longer be able to get there in time to catch a taxi to Puttaparthi anyway. Another hour passes while this is taken care of, during which Syd finds me in their office and gives me a dry 'cheese' sandwich, (two pieces of white bread with a piece of cheese between), which I eagerly eat. It was all they had left at the snack bar.

      Syd explained to me later the reason the plane never took off. He was watching the action from upstairs. A gasoline tanker ran into something and ruptured its tank and the fuel spilled all around the plane we were supposed to be boarding. Syd said there seemed to be much debate as to what to do. Finally they moved the plane away from the spill area and let it sit there for awhile, but they didn't move it entirely out of the fuel on the ground, and the plane still has fuel on it too. So they make an attempt to clean it off. Things were moving so slowly, Syd said, that there was no way the plane would take off today. For the reader, the gasoline spill was in no way connected with the fire on the other side of the airport. Syd will escort me to the airport again tomorrow.

Puttaparthi, Monday, December 6, 1993
      Very tired. Disoriented. Got bounced to bits on the long drive here from Bangalore yesterday. Went from roasting to freezing, fever to chills, in the car on the way here. Still feeling the effects of the viral infection Syd and I caught on the plane. Feeling better today now that I'm here with Baba. I was assigned to the Ladies' Shed. My two allotted squares are in the center row, a lady from the Midwest on one side and vacant on the other. Two very sweet girls with guitars from Australia behind me. It took me a long time to fill my air mattress with the foot pump I brought and some lady angrily yelled out from across the way that I had better finish that before the lights go out at 9 p.m. The vibrations here were nerve shattering last night and I got little sleep because of the static, in spite of how tired I was from the day long journey.

      The Midwest lady says she is leaving tomorrow as she 'doesn't know what she is doing here'. It is her first time and she finds it all too austere. She smokes, I think and seems very agitated, and the closest smoking area is a long way to the outside. I try to help her relax and give it some more thought but she says her mind is definitely made up, and she will stay in a hotel in Bangalore or wherever necessary, except here, until she can get a flight home. She gives me a bundle of letters and asks if I will give them to Baba - they are from her center. "Be happy to help!", I tell her. I have a bundle from home to offer to Him anyway. On the other side of Midwest lady is a lady from Holland - seems very sweet and friendly. It is her first time here too.

Nothing is the same at Darshan. Both times today Baba came from the Poornachandra Hall and passed us up altogether. I have been choosing seats on the aisle where he used to come out of the Interview Room to give Darshan. This explains what happened in my 'Padnamaskar' dream when He came from the Poornachandra Hall to give Darshan, instead of from His quarters in the Mandir. I ask and learn that Baba now has a small apartment above the Poornachandra Hall - it has to do with the attempt on His life earlier this year. But the security is really overdone, I think. Didn't Baba say nothing will prevent Him from fulfilling His mission? But, He also said that soon the government would send armed guards to protect Him, which would place Him even at a farther distance physically from His Devotees.

Can't take our bags into Darshan anymore, or our water bottles. They now have a security gate and the Seva Dals feel you up, or pat you down, whatever, and use one of those detector instruments on you. Sorta takes the joy out of Darshan. Wonder what it will be like at Whitefield?? Swami seemed so much more relaxed there (last year), and so was the security and Seva Dals.

I was surprised to learn that the Western Canteen is open. I had a great lunch. (It has never been open when I was here before). They actually had a garden salad with cabbage instead of lettuce, but very good. Missed bhajans today, once because of Orientation, during which I learned a lot about the Ashram and its new policies. Still can't talk or sing without coughing from that viral infection. Went to see Dr. Kamala at the Puttaparthi hospital next to the Ashram today - She was not there, but I told a lady who seemed to be in charge, that the trolley (gurney) is being shipped from Bombay and should be arriving any minute. The lady was concerned whether it would go the Super Specialty Hospital. I assured her my husband would go get it from there if it did. Syd had given me this duty to notify them the gurney was coming because he was afraid it might arrive from Bombay before he did and they wouldn't know what to do with it.

Sign in Western Canteen:

"God gave you the time, space, cause, material, idea, skill, chance and fortune. Why should you feel as if you are the Doer?" Baba

Wednesday December 8, 1993

Yesterday was another busy and difficult day. Went to see Dr. Kamala again and she is still sick and not at work. Probably has the same thing I had. It sounds like we are in the middle of a T.B. ward both in the shed and at Darshan, with all the hacking and coughing. I finally, after much asking for help, was able to talk to the Hospital Administrator who spoke little English, so everything had to be translated. He said, "So what does she want with Dr. Kamala". I explained about the gurney while he was busy examining patients and the doctor next to him was doing the same while translating for me. I felt badly that their attention was being drawn away from the patients they were examining to talk to me.

Yesterday I went to a taxi company outside and tried to arrange a car for going to Brindavan tomorrow. The agent tells me that Baba is not leaving until Thursday morning. So upon his advice, I reserve the car for Thursday at 9:30 a.m.. In the Canteen where I have been doing seva, they told us it would be today and I found out they were right. I knew the guy at the taxi company was putting me off, but I accept it as Baba's Will. Baba left this morning while I was busy peeling and chopping potatoes, carrots, tomatoes, and garlic. Very rewarding seva.

This afternoon, Utta from near Frankfurt arrived to take the space left by K.C. lady. It is her first time to see Baba. On the other side of her is Hennie from Holland. She will share the taxi to Whitefield with me tomorrow. All day a hornet, big and red, was busy building a nest on my little brown bag. It finally left long after I covered up the bag and waved it away.

Last night, I finally felt moved to write my letter to Baba. This morning, it was as though I knew all I had to do was write the letter and Baba responded to it because after I wrote it, I felt so much better and clearer at Darshan. There was so much confusion in the shed and the Ashram when I arrived. It was extremely difficult for me to think clearly. At Darshan, Baba looked my way and I'm not sure if He looked at me or not, because I never 'felt' eye contact. While standing as near to me as He could, He said, "Very happy, Very happy!" And I suddenly felt Very Happy and so full of Bliss that I could have floated all the way back home! I knew His comment was directed at me and it was the best gift He could have given me at that point! I felt so blessed. I already was happy, but I knew and felt this was a different kind of happiness He was blessing me with. Thank you my Beloved Lord!

"Man has to understand that he is the cause of his own happiness or misery and that all that he seeks or loves are not for their sake, but for his own sake. Hence, he has to understand his own true nature. Realizing the ephemerality of all worldly objects, man should recognize that enduring happiness can be got only by developing love for God."
SS December 1993 P 331

Brindavan 1993

From my Journal:
Brindavan, Monday December 13, 1993

Arrived in Brindavan very late last Thursday night after a terrible day trying to get here and being treated very badly by the people at the taxi company. Our car had been reserved since Tuesday morning for leaving at 9:30 a.m. on Thursday and they kept us waiting all day Thursday. I was back and forth on the very long, hot and exhausting walk from the shed to their office several times, and each time he told me the car was coming and to go back to the shed and wait. It never did come. At noon I went and sat in their office (with Hennie) and told him this time I was staying there until our car arrived. I still have not regained my strength after being so ill, and was just too exhausted to make that long walk back to the sheds again anyway.

Later, I saw him take a Rs. 100 bribe from an Indian, and I

knew it was for the car we had been waiting for and I lost it and yelled at him that I saw him take a bribe and that I was going to tell Suleman about it. Where did all this anger come from? This was not me. I was so filled with anger, I was shaking. He told me to go back and wait at the shed again. I yelled at him again that I was not leaving there until it was in the car I had reserved. More anger. I couldn't believe this was coming out of me. I had to go outside on their porch and clear my head so I could overcome the space I had gotten myself into.

"Anger is debilitating in its effect. The nerves become weak; blood is rendered warmer; its composition changes. A simple burst of fury consumes the strength gained from food during three months! Anger drastically reduces one's stamina." SSS VOL XI Chap 32 P 181

It seems that my greatest tests come when I am here in India with Baba. It is so out of character for me to get angry about anything back home, because I know and accept at home that everything that happens is God's Will for me. My life is so peaceful at home and my challenges are so rare there. I never get sick like this at home either. And now I have flunked another test! Are you having me come here to bring out all this buried stuff Baba?

"There are isolation hospitals where patients suffering from chronic infectious diseases are treated and cured. The ashrams in the forest are such hospitals where people who want to be cured of the infection of samsara (worldly desires), can undergo the treatment and come out free in order to serve other patients." SSS VOL IV Chap 38 P 234

"When suffering comes in waves, one behind the other, be glad that the shore is near; bear them bravely; do not like cowards throw the blame on some outside power or develop dislike for the Lord.....Welcome the test, because thereafter you are awarded the certificate. It is to measure your progress that tests are imposed. So do not flinch in the face of grief. The Lord bestows a favor when He decides to test you, for He is impressed by your achievement and wants to put upon it the seal of His approval. Rise up to the demands of the test, that is the way to please the Lord." SSS VOL II Chap 28 P 165

"Tests and obstacles are the sign of God's grace, not His anger." SSS VOL IX Chap 14 P 82

"Everything is the Will of God. For every small act, God's command is the cause. Without His Will, not a blade of grass can move. Good and bad are projections of your feelings, but in the eyes of God, everything is the same." Divine Discourse, Nov. 17, 1996

But our reward (from Baba of course) for being kept waiting was a lovely apartment in the guest house for donors, across from the Eastern Canteen. Frankly I didn't feel worthy of it and was still rather embarrassed for my outbursts in front of the ever patient Hennie. There was nothing available inside the Ashram by the time we got there long after dark that night, and we were very fortunate to be given any room to sleep in. Utta, who joined us in the car, and Hennie and I seem to do well together and look after each other.

On Saturday I got an excellent seat at Darshan and Bhajans in the second section, second row. Swami looked me in the eye as He passed His eyes along the crowd. After Darshan, I cried and cried, like a real cleansing. Something very subtle happens to you when He looks you in the eye.

"Never take lightly the transformation that is taking place as I walk among you. All that My Eyes fall on will be transformed. Always find a quiet corner after My Darshan, where you may enter the stillness and receive the completion of My Blessings. My Energy goes from Me as I pass you. If you proceed to talk with others, immediately the precious energy is dissipated and returns to me unused. Rest assured that whatever My Eyes see becomes vitalized and sent transmuted. You are being changed day by day. Never underestimate what is being accomplished by this act of Darshan. My walking among you is a gift, yearned for by the Gods of Highest Heaven, and here you are receiving this Grace. Be grateful. These blessings you receive will express themselves in due time. But also remember that to whom much is given, from him much will be demanded." LMSL P 101

Then on Sunday, yesterday afternoon, I was again in the very back, but could see Swami quite clearly and at one point He appeared to be a royal blue color on face and hands. Could have been my imagination, but I don't think so. Anyway, I cried and cried again afterward. So much releasing! I don't remember ever being so emotional before. Are you bringing this up from inside me too Baba?

"Cry so that you can digest the joy of knowing God; cry and shed tears of joy; the tear glands have been allotted to you, not for weeping helplessly before others with hands extended for alms, but to shed tears of joy, of thankfulness at the Feet of the Lord." SSS VOL II Chap 31 P 187

The food in the Brindavan Western Canteen is very good, but must be one half hour early in line to have a choice of what to eat. One night they only had cream of cauliflower by the time I reached the serving counter. It was excellent, but would have liked a variety.

This morning after breakfast, I found Syd peeling potatoes - his seva. He is staying in the men's dorm on the Ashram - said he didn't mind. He met 'Chris' from Cypress at the airport in Bombay on his way to Bangalore, and they became instant friends. Chris used to be Chief of Police on Cypress and Baba came to him in his dreams repeatedly for several years until Chris found his way to India. He had been in a hotel bookstore while at a convention in a major European city, and a book with Swami's picture on the cover had fallen off the shelf and gotten his attention. That was how he discovered that the man in his dreams was Sai Baba! We heard all his other wonderful Baba stories about how Baba changed his life forever during our drive to Whitefield. I had hired a car to pick Syd up at the airport in Bangalore so he would know where I was staying. As far as he knew, I was still in the sheds at Puttaparthi.

This morning at Darshan, I was again in the second row, second section and Baba looked me directly in the eye and refused to take my new letter. I knew immediately that I had to rewrite it and I knew what I had to ask for - 'To help me to always love everyone as God does', instead of asking for a robe for our new Center. It's like He told me what to write and what to ask for in that one glance.

This afternoon at Darshan, I was in the front row of the very back section after being in line 19, the last row called. Baba came all the way to the back, where He hasn't gone since I have been here, and took my rewritten letter @ 4:05 p.m. And all the other letters too! I cried, "Thank You Swami", and He walked on, only looking at the letters

He took from me, not at me. Lovely Darshan. Afterward, I knelt and put my face to the space on the ground where He stood in front of me while taking my letters. It felt so special.

Tonight, still Monday, we got a taxi and went to Hennie's favorite vegetarian restaurant at 50 Residency Rd, called Konark Vegetarian Restaurant. It is the same place Syd and I ate lunch at last year with Mavora. It is owned and operated by Baba Devotees. Excellent! Hennie was so concerned whether we would like it after she suggested it.

Back to Puttaparthi

From my Journal:
Puttaparthi, December 15, 1993

Arrived back at Puttaparthi yesterday a.m. after another ride in a van with Hennie, Utta and Chris from Cypress. The feeling here in the Ashram is not good. The Seva Dals in the sheds treated Syd and me very badly. They would not give us a corner space in the empty family shed, although we were the first to arrive from Brindavan, because 'they needed to be allotted consecutively'. But a few minutes later, all the corners were all given to Indians. Not Fair! Each time the Seva Dals put an Indian family in the corner, I would question them about it. One time they said someone in the family was ill and they needed their privacy. Another time they said he was a doctor, as if that made him any more special than anybody else. I can feel their resentment toward us because we are from the USA. Syd and I settled into a space in the shed under a window, determined to stay inside the Ashram, after what Baba told me last year about sacrificing our comfort for Him.

The feeling here just is not the same as at Brindavan. I am doing my best to remember that it must be our karma that is causing us to be treated like this.

"Your own bad thoughts and actions are the cause of your misery. As you sow, so shall you reap. The seed determines the fruit. When man cherishes bad thoughts, bad results haunt him. When he has good thoughts, the results are also good. Those who do not recognize this fact go about blaming God. They lament: 'Oh God! Why are you inflicting these miseries on me? Why are you denying me peace of mind?' God is the Eternal Witness. He is the dispenser of the fruits of actions. He gives you according to your deserts. He is in no way responsible for your grief or happiness." SS August 1995 P 198

After getting very upset with Seva Dals, I found the following sign staring at me in the Western Canteen:
Bear all and do nothing
Hear all and say nothing
Give all and take nothing
Serve all and be nothing.
"Baba"

The greeting on this sign is something I can only hope to aspire to in the future. Right now I am still reeling from the unfairness of everything that has happened to us this past week. Oh Baba, I need your help with rising above this seemingly impossible situation.

"Ask me, when you need any help. Extend your hand only for Grace from God. Ask Grace as a right, not in a groveling style. Ask, as child asks the father; feel that God is nearest and dearest.....Grace is showered on those who seek. Knock, and the door shall be opened; ask, and food will be served; search, and the treasure, will be yours.....

"Like a lighted lamp, God's Grace spreads all round on all who approach Him and love to be near him; but if you interpose a shade which shuts out the light from you, you have only yourself to blame if Grace does not shine.....To get the program right and pleasantly, you have to switch on and tune in the receiver That is an inescapable effort. Individual effort and Divine Grace are both interdependent; without effort, there will be no conferment of Grace; without Grace, there can be no taste in the effort. To win that Grace, you need only have faith and virtue." SS January 1994 P 26

December 17, 1993
Stayed in the family shed for one night and two days. The fires where they burn the rubbish was right outside our window, which could not be closed, and the smoke was making us both very ill. We are still full of phlegm from the viral infection and we both coughed all night

long. And the swarms of mosquitos were eating us alive too, in spite of our mosquito nets. Getting worse instead of better, so we pleaded with Swami (on the Inner) to let us move to a hotel, and together, we agreed that if we found a room, we would look upon it as His Will.

Syd went outside and found us a room at Sathya Sai Towers again. I really wanted to stay inside, especially after what Baba said last year, but this year I felt we were moving with His blessings. We stayed with the smoke longer than we should have because it aggravated our physical condition so much.

December 18, 1993
Getting depressed. Leaving Puttaparthi already on Sunday 12/20 at 9 a.m.. Almost as far away as I can be this morning in Darshan. We were late to breakfast. Syd has been angry and uptight since he arrived. His moods affect me terribly. The gurney finally arrived yesterday from Bombay and he had trouble putting it together, but finally succeeded. Syd has been talking with MH regarding bringing other medical and hospital equipment from the large hospital in Galveston, Texas to donate to the General Hospital via help from the Rotary Club there. But nobody will cooperate or get involved or help with Syd's efforts.

Here is all this free, completely renovated, very expensive medical equipment and everybody is afraid to have anything to do with it. Syd had to write a letter yesterday to the Medical Administrator, as nobody at the small Puttaparthi hospital felt authorized to write one. The purpose of the letter was to open the tightly locked doors to putting this free equipment to use where it was so sorely needed in the small Puttaparthi hospital.

Syd made several fruitless attempts to get the project considered, then surrendered it to Baba. Long after we returned home, we received a letter from the Administrator of the new Super Specialty Hospital, indignantly informing us that they do not want or need, nor will they accept used equipment. We were not trying to donate the equipment to the new hospital which currently serves only heart and kidney transplant patients, it was intended for the ill-equipped, little village hospital that services the sick at the Ashram. Some time after that, a letter was issued by the Sai Organization saying that devotees are not to send medical equipment to the Ashram. Syd's view was that it clearly was Baba's Will that he take the gurney to the hospital, regardless of what any organization official might say, and if he had lessons to learn from it, he certainly accomplished that.

I spent the last two days doing seva again in the Western Canteen kitchen and one day before we moved from here to Brindavan where life was much more joyous. Utta, Hennie and I had such a lovely apartment there, complete with private bath.

December 21, 1993
Arrived in Bombay yesterday and finally got to our hotel at 8 p.m. Our plane was very late. We left our hotel room in Puttaparthi at 8:45 a.m. and finally arrived at Mr. D's home in Bombay at 9:10 p.m. - was supposed to get there for dinner at 7:30 p.m. And the flight took only an hour. Very delicious dinner. All vegetarian. All our old friends in Bombay were there.

Christmas in Paris

From my Journal:
Paris, December 23, 1993
Dreamed that someone told me there was something big going on in Florida, like the Lord had come again, so I packed up my car with only the essentials and started saying goodbye to everybody - friends, family, dogs, and kept trying to leave but each time I was slowed down or prevented from leaving. Then I kept trying to take people with me - Syd, my sisters, friends, etc., one at a time and things kept happening to slow me down. I knew if I drove it would only take me three days to get there, then only two days if I had help driving. I also sorta knew once I got there I would probably never return, although I was telling everyone I would see them in a few days. (I think the point of the dream is that I should stop worrying about everyone and everything else, and just get busy on my own spiritual growth, and quit trying to

help everybody move along on their path, so there is nothing else to hold me back. It seems that I can't really help them anyway - they have to want to.)

Back at home, I had been guilty of attempting to get all my old friends interested in Sai Baba. After this dream, I finally realized that my efforts have been in vain, and I am being held back by the depletion of spiritual energy as a result of my efforts.

"Each will come in his own way, at his own pace, according to his inner urge, along the Path God will reveal to him as his own." SS April 1994 P 100

We arrived in Paris yesterday and are staying at the Holiday Inn. Hopefully it won't rain again today and we can get around. We walked the nearby streets for an hour or more last night trying to find a place for dinner and ended up eating next door to our hotel at the Italian Restaurant. Spaghetti was delicious - so was the French bread. Got a headache from the house wine - only one glass, as usual. I thought European wines would not have the preservatives that causes the headaches - am I supposed to stop, even though I only have an occasional glass of wine? **"Yes!",** comes the answer.

Paris, Christmas Day, 1993

Spent the last two days exploring the Louvre' - one of my lifelong dreams fulfilled. Thank you Syd and Baba. Have had several dreams about Sai Baba with lots of messages, but none with Him in it physically that I can remember.

Christmas in Paris is not at all what I expected. The streets and sidewalks are empty, as are the cars in the very efficient underground railway. The only sign of people are the few gathering in the pubs where we looked to see if there was anything we could eat. No last minute shoppers scurrying about like at home. There are no Christmas decorations anywhere to be seen on the streets, or in the shop windows or restaurants. The only sign we have found of Christmas here is the small decorated tree in the lobby of our hotel. The lack of commercialism here is refreshing. I guess most of the Parisians are home celebrating Christmas with their families.

Even the Louvre' is closed on Christmas Day, so we take the underground across town and walk through the old cemetery where some very famous people are buried. Syd had stayed at a nearby hotel while here on business several years back and found this place fascinating. I come across one tomb that gives me the chills and stirs an ancient memory deep within me. It is a Jewish woman who died just before World War II and not long before I was born - Madeline Kahn is the name on the tombstone. Could I have known her, or could it have been a past life of mine? Syd leaves me there and moves on to another section. I try to tune in and see if there is a message for me, but nothing comes.

While walking from the underground to the cemetery, we see an Indian Restaurant and the sign says it will be open at noon for dinner. We finish our cemetery tour, and walk back to the Indian Restaurant just as they are opening up for business. After a while, we notice that we are the only people in the restaurant, other than a staff of four or five. What a wonderful Christmas feast with a delightful variety of Indian dishes they prepare for us! They lock the door behind us as we leave, and hang out the 'Closed' sign. And we were so worried whether we would be able to find a vegetarian meal today with everything else closed except the smoke filled pubs. Thank you Baba! Only You could have arranged this beautiful meal for us

Back Home Again

After we were home from our trip to India and Paris for about two months, I awoke one morning feeling very despondent over having lost that good and wonderful feeling I came back with. Every time I have talked or listened to someone on the phone, I could feel the bliss slowly drifting away, especially when I spoke with family or not-so-spiritual old friends. I feel like I am mourning the spiritually high self I came home with, Who got lost or buried somewhere in all those telephone conversations. It seems that I have become even more sensitive to other people's vibrations now than I ever have been. I understand that we return to the Lotus Feet to get our batteries recharged. Is this inability to handle other people's energies what happens to us after we have been to India and gotten our energies lifted up? I found that Baba has much to say to us about talking:

"Excessive talking must also be avoided as it is a waste of energy. When one gets weak due to wastage of energy, he is prone to get angry and develop hatred. You must, therefore, use the God-given energy for good purposes. Energy is a divine gift. By curtailing unnecessary talk and keeping silent, you can conserve energy. 'Talk less and work more' is the golden rule to be adopted." SS May 1994 P 118

"You have to practice speaking sweetly and softly and avoid unnecessary connections and relationships with all and sundry. The easiest Sadhana is to reflect on God with love that is expanding and embracing one and all. It is the only way to realize the Divine." SS May 1994 P 120

"When the control of speech and control of the mind have been achieved, the state of supreme silence is easily realized. " SS March 1994 P 58

"Unnecessary talk should be avoided as this results in waste of energy and reduction of memory power." SS August 1994 P 213

From my Journal:
While meditating this morning, the thought came to me, 'This too shall pass' - the same advice I have given others in the past when they were going through difficult times. Also got the strong feeling I

should start doing bhajans alone tonight, if necessary. I have mentioned doing bhajans at home to Syd several times since we were at the Patels, but he hasn't seemed at all interested. He hardly ever answers me when I talk about something he is not interested in. So, tonight I put the tape on and started singing bhajans alone, and Syd came and joined me after all. Thank you Baba! What a wonderful feeling it left us with. Syd was actually glowing afterward.

"The wealth derived from singing God's name, and meditation, is the influence of the higher energies in nature on one's life. These not only cleanse the external body but also purify the inner tendencies." TOSSSB P 13

Later that night after doing bhajans, I had a dream that left a very strong message that I should 'keep the door closed' to non-spiritual people. The following night, we had several friends over for dinner and they brought a guest who was not spiritual, and who immediately hugged me. After swearing off hugging people anymore, I got myself into a situation where I could do nothing to avoid getting hugged, and absorbed a lot of junk. When will I ever learn?

"Another persons's sins pass to oneself through the touch of that person's skin." CWSSB P 69

I've had many dreams about Sai Baba lately, but none that He appeared in. In several of the dreams (which seemed very real), I was visiting old friends and some family members and telling them about Sai Baba and His miracles and His mission on earth. There was one very interesting dream that I felt (in the dream) was a reward from Baba for doing bhajans in our home every night:

"Dreamed that we had been to see Sai Baba again at Brindavan. Then we were all standing around joking and I said I was so high I could probably make Vibhuti and I held out my hand and moved it like Baba does and the Vibhuti started coming out of my hand through my fingers, just like it does with Baba. I said, 'Look, I can make ash too'.

Syd's Wedding Ring

Syd had another major lesson in possessions and surrender, and I asked him to put this experience into his own words for the book:

The last frost of the winter had, hopefully, come and gone, and it was time to prepare the beds in the vegetable garden for planting. There was little soil for planting, and if one dug down three or four inches, one would hit rock. It was clear why they were called "The Rocky Mountains". And so, I had built twenty-three raised beds, four feet by eight feet, and five feet by ten feet, and about a foot high. I filled each of the beds with approximately one-third pine and juniper mulch, one third silt and clay, and one third peat moss and compost.

Each year I dig up the soil, add more compost and mix it in. This year, to prevent the gophers, who showed up last year, from coming into the beds from under the frames, I removed the soil and laid small gauge chicken wire in the bottom of each of the beds.

I spent the better part of a day filling the beds, and then, in late afternoon, I began to mix the soil in one of the beds, adding water as I worked. I worked with bare hands, and as the sun dropped behind the mountain crest, I began to feel the cold. And so, I quit for the day, and went back to the house.

I was washing the mud off my hands when I noticed that my wedding band was gone. I knew instantly what had happened. My fingers had shrunk in the wet cold soil, which acted as a lubricant, and the ring had slipped off. But, had that happened while I was working the soil in the bed, or somewhere else? My hands were cold, and numb, and I wouldn't have felt the ring slip off.

I went back to the garden with a flashlight, examining the ground as I went, and spent about an hour looking for the ring in and around the bed, before I gave it up for the night.

I was very upset at the loss of the ring, and was awake most of the night thinking about it. I decided that I would have to go through the soil in the bed, handful by handful, until I found the ring.

Early the next morning I returned to the garden, and laid out a tarpaulin next to the bed I last worked in. Then, I made a frame of mesh fencing. My idea was to take every bit of soil out of the bed, and work it through the mesh onto the tarpaulin, a handful at a time. I estimated that it would take me all day, or perhaps longer, to do. Finally, I was ready to start.

Before I started, I prayed to Baba to help me find the ring. And then, I knelt next to the bed and began.

I had worked for less than an hour, praying to Baba all the while, when I heard Him say, **"Go to the other side of the bed."** And so, I got up and walked around to the other side of the bed. As I stood there, wondering what I should do, or where I should look, my attention was drawn to a spot outside of the bed, next to where I was standing. As I looked down, I saw a small raised circle begin to form in the soil. I bent, and when I touched the soil, I saw the gleam of gold.

I brushed the soil aside, and spent a long moment looking at my wedding band, before I picked it up and put it on my finger. I was dumbfounded, awed, and most of all, very grateful to Baba for having given me back the ring. I thanked Him for His love and Grace, and went back to the house to tell Char.

First Retreat

My friend, Ruth joined me on my trip to my first Sai Baba Retreat, which was in Prescott, Arizona. It was a two day drive for us, although we could have made it in one day if I had driven all day long with only short stops to eat, like I used to do when I was younger. Two other friends, Sharon and Keith from Las Vegas, Nevada, would be flying in and meeting us there. Ruth, Sharon and I slept in a dorm type room with a number of other women, and sleep was very hard to come by. The energies were just so full of confusion in that large room, and I probably slept a total of one hour the first night.

While getting dressed in the bathhouse after my shower the next morning, I noticed that the rudruksha bead Madhu had given me, and that I had worn around my neck ever since, was no longer on the chain. I searched everywhere, in the shower, my bedding, my clothing, under the bed, but could not find it. "Okay, Baba", I said, "If the bead has disappeared because I have been healed of high blood pressure, I accept and release it up to You. If You want me to have it back, then please help me to find it."

"Surrender to God means to leave everything to His will and is the highest form of Divine Love." TOSSSB P 75

It was a wonderful retreat and the speakers were so inspiring. I especially enjoyed hearing from Sam Sandweiss and his wife, and also Faith Penn who are all long time devotees of Sai Baba. For the first time, I was able to sing English bhajans with a large group and the energies that arose during the music program were so very uplifting. Never before had I participated with such a large group in meditation. And I really was happy to hear the Suprabhatam being sung in English so I could understand the meaning and purpose of this ritual. One of the handouts was the English translation of the Suprabhatam and I plan to learn it when I get home. All that singing about the glory of God lifted up the energies of the large crowd, and it was much easier for me to fall asleep the second night, although it was a short night by the time everyone got settled in.

Being able to participate in Nagarsankirtan, the singing of bhajans first thing in the morning while walking around the grounds of the retreat, was an exhilarating experience. And the daily bhajans have been so inspiring. I have learned new songs and bhajans, and would love to be able to include them in our bhajans at home. The bonfire on our last night of the retreat was very special and the energies from the devotional singing while walking and Shiva dancing around the large bonfire were just incredible. We all hoped it would never end. I was so full of Baba I could hardly sleep that last night.

I was very surprised to see some of the food they served at this Retreat. The first night, we were served a salad with the dressing already mixed in. It was a mayonnaise based dressing, and of course the basic ingredient in mayonnaise is eggs. Thinking that perhaps it was a yogurt dressing, we ate it anyway. The three of us were up and down to the bathroom and sick to our stomachs all night long. They also served scrambled eggs for breakfast. And one evening they served baked potatoes with butter and sour cream. When I checked in the kitchen, I learned that the sour cream had gelatin in it, a product rendered from the body of an animal. And the last night of the retreat, marshmallows were passed out to all the children for roasting. The basic ingredient of marshmallows is gelatin, which is rendered from the body of a dead animal! I wondered if the ones who prepared the menus were aware of Baba's teachings regarding vegetarianism. Everything I read in the discourses Swami has given was directing His devotees to give up eating meat. And eggs are never served in the Ashram. They told us during Orientation at the Ashram that Swami had said, "No eggs in My house!"

This was the first Sai Organization function I ever attended, and it was also the first for the three friends of mine who I had invited to come. I had been coaching them about Swami's teachings regarding the importance of vegetarianism, and was really embarrassed to see that other devotees and those who organized the retreat did not follow Swami's directives. One of my friends questioned whether strict vegetarianism was really important after all, and probably wondered if I was making much ado about nothing. After I returned home, I wrote a letter to the Regional Director about the food that was served, but never received a response.

On the last morning of the retreat, we were getting packed up before breakfast. I sat down on the edge of my bed for a moment, as did Ruth and Sharon on their beds nearby. We were chatting and suddenly from over my head and behind me, my rudruksha bead came flying through the air, landed on my lap and bounced to the floor in front of me. All three of us said almost simultaneously, "Where did that come from?". Since there was a wall behind my back, and nobody else in the room at the time, we knew it could have only come from Baba. Thank you my Beloved Lord for this special treat, and for arranging this drama so that my friends could be a witness to it!

I reached for the container that held my Baba watch and Baba ring that I had purchased at Puttaparthi and Brindavan the year before, but it was no longer where I had placed it on the box beside the bed. I searched everywhere for it, including carefully unpacking and repacking each piece of luggage. The container was a hot pink color and could not possibly be missed. This was a real test, because I had grown somewhat 'attached' to these items. The watch had a picture of Sai Baba on it and the ring was a small silver one with Baba's head in slight relief. It was the only ring like it I had ever seen and I knew I would never be able to replace it.

"Nothing in the world is yours and you are just a trustee for the wealth which belongs to the Divine. Developing the feeling of 'mine' and 'thine' people get attached to the unreal and the transient and forget the eternal." SS July 1995 P 185

In the hope that someone had seen or found the container, I asked that an announcement be made during breakfast, and our Regional Director asked if anyone had seen it to please let me know. I had done all I could do to locate it, and finally surrendered it to Baba after that. I said to Him, "If somebody else needed the watch and ring more than me, I accept that Baba. Your will be done!" Then Ruth and I packed our belongings in my car, said our goodbyes to everyone and drove off.

We arrived in Albuquerque late that evening, had dinner and checked into a motel. The next morning I opened my little brown bag, and right there on top of everything, where I could not possibly have missed it the day before, was my hot pink container with the ring and watch still in it! There was simply no way I could have overlooked the bright pink container during my search, because everything else in this suitcase was white or blue. Oh Baba, You are so very good to me! Thank you!

"Besides being spontaneous tokens of my love, my so called miracles are to plant the seed of faith in the minds of unbelievers and to foster humanity and veneration towards a Higher Power." DG P 75

Perhaps I had grown too attached to the rudruksha bead and the watch and ring, and Baba decided I needed a little test about attachments to things. Or, perhaps these were Baba's leelas, and He was just having a little fun with me.

The COMPENDIUM

Our Center's Study Circle had used and gone through Jon Roof's book, "Pathways to God" three times. This book provoked a lot of healthy discussions, just as it was designed to do. But, after the third go around, we agreed it was time to try another book. There weren't really any other books addressing Baba's teachings that were designed for study groups at the time. Syd said he had gotten a lot out of the book, "Voice of the Avatar", and so we all agreed to try it for our Study Circle. It was awkward to use in our first attempts, but we decided to order it anyway so that everybody would have a copy to read and work from. Then we learned it was out of print, and I agreed to ask Swami what we should do next.

The next day, while sitting at my computer answering some correspondence, I heard Swami say, **"Put together a book of My teachings"**. Wow! I had been praying for a way to serve mankind, and I knew immediately that here was the answer. Since we live in such a remote location, seva projects were hard to come by, outside of feeding the birds. We had approached the Meals on Wheels people in town to see if we could prepare and deliver meals on the weekends, because we heard there were no deliveries to these poor people then. We were told that we would have to follow the Federal guidelines; which meant we would have to prepare and serve meat. None of us felt we could do that, as we were all vegetarians. Everywhere we turned in the tiny town of Trinidad, we were told, "There are too many volunteer organizations here already." The Salvation Army put on a Christmas Dinner recently for indigents. There were 45 volunteers, enough food to feed three hundred people, and only thirty showed up to eat.

Ruth and I started a project where we made small quilts for the children who, for one reason or another, were taken from their homes and put in foster care, or in a safe place with their mothers. Because of other commitments, neither of us could produce enough to make a difference. No matter how much time and effort we put forth, it still took days to finish one quilt.

Every seva project we attempted failed before it got off the ground. Now Swami had given me one that I would really enjoy participating in. But, I didn't know where to begin, so I asked Swami to guide me as I formatted a page on my computer. Then He planted a seed idea in my mind. Fortunately, I have always been an avid reader, and our library is full of every book I could find about or by Swami. As I would read a book, I would highlight the important points, not knowing this was going to come in handy later on. Thus, it was easy for me to simply go back through all my books, and type in what had been highlighted.

The book of His teachings began to take shape as the months went on. In my first attempt, I decided to put together a textbook with questions and answers for a study circle. After several months, I felt Swami required something different. So I chose about a dozen topics that Swami speaks about all the time. I attempted to categorize everything I entered into those topics, such as Love, Health, Education, Service, etc.. I began to see this was too limiting, and branched out into other topics. Soon, there were hundreds of different subjects Swami had addressed, and the book grew and grew. There were times that a page would disappear from my computer, while other times, it might be a group of pages sent into oblivion. I just assumed that I must have entered something Swami did not want in the book. At first, this was very alarming and I did not respond well to these incidents. Eventually, I learned to surrender and accept these episodes as His Will. Most of the time, I would ask Him to help when I sat down at the computer, and then I could feel Him working through me as "I" selected what would go into the book.

One time, during a period of great frustration, the whole book disappeared from the memory bank of my computer when my hard drive crashed. Fortunately, I had just printed out the several hundred pages of entries, so that I could retype them. I began on an old 386 computer, and before I was finished with the book, I had actually worn out two more computers. They simply could not handle the volume of work I was giving them.

An amazing thing began to happen to me as I worked on the book. I realized that I always came away from the computer absolutely filled with Swami and His teachings. As I typed, His words became imprinted on my mind and in my heart. Each time I sat down at the computer, it was a joyous occasion for me. I worked day and night and almost began to resent things that would interfere with my being able to have time to work on the book.

I am certain I must have annoyed all my friends and Syd, because at every opportunity, I was spouting what Baba said about this or that, as if I was now an authority on His teachings. It was like I had an answer (from Baba's teachings) for everything. But the best thing for me was that in every aspect of my life, I attempted to apply Swami's teachings. And I grew and grew some more.

1994 India Trip

On August 16th, Syd received a fax from the Indian firm he consults for telling him to come to India later that year. We made reservations to leave on November 23rd, Sai Baba's 69th birthday. Since I was going to be using frequent flyer miles, the choices were few as to the dates I could fly, and this was the best date available. We did not want to be there anyway on Baba's birthday because of the crowds, which we were told were multiplying each year.

On each of our previous trips to see Sai Baba, we had only stayed several weeks with Him, and I knew in my heart that a longer stay would be much more meaningful and beneficial. It had always seemed like we had just arrived when it was time to turn around and go home. Syd felt he should get back home sooner because of business commitments, and also because we really did not like leaving the pets for such a long time.

So Syd arranged his return to Colorado on December 16th, and this time, I was staying on into January. It would be my first Christmas with Swami and I was really looking forward to participating in the celebration. Syd said he didn't mind spending Christmas alone on the other side of the world. Since we had no children at home, celebrating Christmas in the American way had become almost uneventful for us. Some years we didn't even put up a tree. But, Syd agreed to my extended trip only if I stayed in the Sai Towers Hotel where he could communicate with me by fax or phone on a regular basis.

While we were busy making preparations for our journey, I had several dreams about Sai Baba:

"Dreamed that I was looking into Sai Baba's eyes and they changed very dramatically. First they got larger and larger, and then darker and so intense they were almost frightening. Was He looking into my soul again like He did in 1992?"

"Dreamed that I was at some gathering sitting on the grass and Sai Baba came out of a nearby building and walked over to me. He looked me in the eye and gave me a great big smile. I don't think it was in India. He was also involved in other events in that dream, but I can't remember what they were."

"Dreamed that a neighbor was having trouble with an animal that kept attacking her home and I noticed that it had two arms and a head like a man, and pointed out to her that it was not a demon animal, but a demon man. Then I was on the ocean and the demon was in the only vessel. I had to get him out of it so I could get in it or I would drown. My only weapon was a small pair of wire cutters and I struck at it a few times, but it had a larger weapon and went to strike back at me. I called out *"BABA, Please help me!"* and threw the pliers at it and miraculously, the demon fell off the vessel and I climbed in and watched it drift away with a look of astonished anger in its eyes. I wondered why it didn't throw the tools back at me, but it didn't. It just focused on watching me while drifting away. Then I realized it was because Sai Baba was standing beside me."

I have had a number of dreams throughout my years with Baba

in which I was in danger in one way or another, and have always remembered to call out to Baba for help, and He has always been there for me. Since we became celibate, several of my dreams have had to do with someone or something trying to arouse me sexually while I am sleeping. I have always remembered to call out to Baba in my sleep to help me get out of this situation, and the dream ends immediately after I call on Him. It amazes me that even when I am asleep and dreaming, that I am totally conscious or aware that He is my savior and protector.

"I shall be ever with you, wherever you are, guarding you and guiding you. March on; have no fear." SSS VOL IX P 221

After the unexpected weather change when we set out on our trip to India last year, we decided to leave a day early on November 22nd, and spend the night in a hotel near the Colorado Springs airport, rather than take a chance and miss our first flight due to poor driving conditions.

Putting the animals in the kennels is always so traumatic, both for them and for us. So as we set off on our journey we have the cats crying and mewing unhappily in their carrier, and the three dogs crying and whimpering throughout the long drive to the kennels. Our first stop is at the Vet's where the cats are installed in their cages. Then we head North to the kennels with the dogs. Sometimes they get physically ill and vomit, so our luggage and everything else in the back of the Suburban is covered with tarps. This time Maggie wrapped her paws around my legs once we got her inside the fenced area at the kennels, and literally cried. The frenetic, pleading look in her eyes was almost more than I could bear. Syd was having his challenges with Nik as well. Angie was being a good sport about it all, as usual. Donna, the lady who owns the kennels tells us that they are always just fine as soon as we are out of sight. Still, they make it very difficult for us and really tug at our heartstrings.

As we drove away from the kennels, I could tell by the vibrations in the car that Syd was very disturbed about the whole thing and had gotten himself into a terrible mood. I reminded him that those three dogs and two cats have the best possible life with 35 unfenced acres all their very own to live life as it should be for a pet, whereas most pets live inside apartments in the city, or their domain is confined to a small fenced area. Some never get loose from their chained up existence. That didn't make him feel any better, but it did help me to shake it off. So I put a tape of Baba singing bhajans in the tape deck and started singing bhajans with Baba, and after awhile, Syd joined in too. Soon, his mood improved and then we were finally able to enjoy the trip.

Our first flight is to Dallas, where we join a friend who I shall call Abigal (pseudonym), and who will be traveling with us to Puttaparthi. Abigal was one of my best customers in my bookstore in Southern California, and we had kept in touch over the years. However, I had never spent much time with her, as we had always lived in different parts of the country after we both left California. Mostly, we just talked on the phone. She had expressed a desire to join us on our trip to India, as she said she wanted to see Sai Baba.

During the flight to Frankfurt, our main meal was noodles and vegetables in a sauce. We discovered after eating it that the noodles must have been made with eggs, or the sauce had a meat broth base, because Syd and I now have a sick stomach. It is like we have been fed poison, because the human body is not designed to eat these things.

As I look back, I remember when my children were infants and toddlers, and I was introducing new foods to them. It never occurred to me that the meat and eggs in those baby food jars that I was feeding them were what was causing them to cry all night with stomach problems. I feel so bad about what I did to them and almost wish I could do it over again. Oh the lessons we learn.....

When the flight attendant offered us yogurt and croissants for breakfast the following morning, we discover the yogurt is made with gelatin and the croissants are brushed with eggs. But, we are still suffering too much from the ill effects of last night's meal to eat anything anyway. We always order 'pure vegetarian' or 'vegan' meals, which means no meat, eggs or dairy, but some of the airlines just don't understand what a vegetarian is. We do take dairy in our diet at home, but there is no category on flights between the USA and Europe such as lacto vegetarian. We never eat eggs, in accordance with Swami's teachings. The Patels told us they once asked Swami about eating eggs, and He said, "Eggs are (like) the American's white potato. Not good! Eating eggs causes doubts and confusion!". How can anyone surrender and maintain their faith and trust in God (Swami) if they are full of doubts and confusion from what they eat?

After waiting an extraordinary amount of time for one of Abigal's bags, it finally arrived on the carousel in Bombay, long after everyone had already located their baggage and gotten in line at Customs. As we pushed our luggage carts to the end of the 'green zone', where there is nothing to declare for customs, an official waves us over to the red zone to have our luggage x-rayed, something which had never happened to us before.

We finally arrived at the Taj President Hotel in Bombay in the early morning of Friday, November 26th, and retired to our separate rooms. After eating a few crackers, we fall into bed. Syd had a meeting that afternoon, and Abigal and I were given a car and driver, from the company Syd consults for, to take us anywhere we wanted. Abigal wanted to go shopping, so we visited a few shops and purchased some shawls and punjabis for Puttaparthi. I dozed in a chair as I waited while Abigal exhausted a rug salesman showing her every rug in his shop, and he had hundreds of them.

On Saturday, the three of us went to the Prince of Wales Museum, wherein are stored many ancient artifacts, including statues of Indian Gods, old coins, cooking vessels, clothing apparel, etc. What a wonderful experience. I have always loved looking at articles from antiquity.

We learned that the operators of all modes of transportation in Bombay would be going on strike Monday, so we stayed in the hotel and rested. I had many dreams while staying in that hotel:

"Dreamed that in a past life here in Bombay, I was attacked and stabbed over and over in the face with a big knife. I knew I was being shown a past life in the dream, and I experienced no fear or anger in it."

"Dreamed that this hotel - the Taj President, was bouncing up and down in an earthquake and I looked outside and all the other buildings were swaying and moving up and down too, then the whole city and my hotel building seemed to collapse into itself and I awoke."

I had the feeling I was being given a vision of the future in the last dream, and wanted to get out of Bombay as soon as possible. But it was not meant to be. Syd had to work every day.

On Sunday morning, I awoke to discover that my right hip had gone out again. This same thing had happened to me only once before - when Abigal had visited us for a week in August when we planned this trip. Could this be coincidental, I wondered? Her vibrations in our home had virtually destroyed the peace we live in, and I had great difficulty trying to cook or think, or function. It was one mishap after another during her visit. After two days with Abigal in our home, my hip had gone out and I visited the Chiropractor for the next three days with only minor relief. But as soon as she left, the hip was okay again. I learned that while she was here, she was reading Stephen King horror novels at night, and she listened to them on tape during her long drive to our home. Her visit in August was the first time I had ever spent more than an hour or two with her. If not for her desire to go see Sai Baba, and my obligatory feeling that I should take her, I had seriously considered canceling the trip. But as always, Baba's Will prevails. There were some lessons ahead for all of us to learn from.

In Bombay, I must have looked like a cripple or the Hunchback of Notre Dame when I walked because I was so bent over from the pain. There simply was no comfortable position for some parts of this body, whether I was sitting, walking or lying down. After several days of being unable to get around, the hotel masseuse returned from her days off, and after one hour of an Ayurvedic massage, she completely eliminated the problem with my hip. Simply amazing what they can do.

We were graciously entertained one night by Mr. R, the CEO of the Indian firm and his wife at their exclusive club, and they invited Abigal and I to stay with them on our return in January to Bombay while we awaited our flight back to the USA. Syd was going to be returning home several weeks before us.

I was beginning to grow very impatient with being stuck in Bombay, as the **only** reason I had come to India was to sit at the Lotus Feet of my beloved Lord. Finally, on December 3rd, we flew to Puttaparthi, and checked into Sai Towers Hotel. I was just starting to unpack our things when Abigal came knocking on the door. She wanted me to come see her room. "Just look at this!", she said disgusted as she dramatically flung the door open. "I don't have any room to put all my luggage!" She did have a lot of luggage, most of which was overweight. I looked around her room with private bath, and tried to explain to her that if she could see the tiny spaces allotted in the sheds, and the community baths, she would be very happy to have such a nice room. Abigal wasn't going to be happy no matter what I said, so I suggested she hurry and get ready to go to Darshan, and then afterwards, inquire at the desk to see if they had another room. She skipped Darshan instead, and told us when we returned that there would be a larger room being vacated in two days, and she had reserved it.

Abigal went to her first Darshan the next morning with me, and when Sai Baba came walking out, she said, "He's just an old man!". Remembering my own private thoughts at my first sight of Baba, I didn't know how to respond to her comment, so I said nothing. She went to two more Darshans and never returned, claiming she was sick, although most of the time I would find her in the streets or see her in the village shops on my walk back to the hotel. This was difficult for me to understand, that someone would come all the way to the other side of the world to see Sai Baba, and only go to Darshan three times. She refused to go inside the Ashram to eat in the Western Canteen, where the food would be good for someone who is 'ill'. Instead, she preferred the restaurants outside. Finally, I just surrendered her up to Baba, and would take no further responsibility. I have since read that there are some people who go to see Swami and can not handle His energies, or the thought that He is aware of everything about them.

From my journal:
Puttaparthi, December 5, 1994, Monday

This afternoon, I was in Line 2, and when I entered the Mandir grounds, a seva dal grabbed me and put me in the second row. Thank You Baba. Knowing this was an opportunity to get a letter to Baba, I wrote a request: "Baba, Please watch over my children and grandchildren. Bless them with Your Grace and help them wherever You can." I was wondering how I would get Baba's attention with this tiny 2" x 3" piece of paper from my notebook, when somebody passed two letters up to me from the back to offer to Baba. He came along and took my tiny note and the letters. Tears flowed. He threw candy from a tray nearby, and four pieces of candy landed in my lap. I gave one to a little boy sitting next to me, ate one, gave one to Syd and the last one to Abigal when I got back to the hotel. She said she felt better immediately after eating it, but still didn't want to go to Darshan. I wondered what went on between her and Swami that has frightened her away from Him?

Puttaparthi, December 6, 1994, Tuesday Morning

As Swami walked up onto the Veranda, after He finished giving Darshan, He stopped and talked to a man in a wheelchair who was part of a group waiting to go into the Interview Room. From a distance, I watched as Swami slapped the man on each knee, raised His hand and told the man to get up and walk in to the room, and he did, on his own. The crowd applauded and cheered.

Rumors are running amuck that Swami is going to Whitefield tomorrow and everyone is scurrying around packing and arranging transportation, including us.

Brindavan, December 7, 1994

Because Abigal had so much luggage, she hired her own taxi for our journey to Whitefield. Suleman drove her personally in his car, as a favor to us, to the Bangalore Hotel. After we were settled in, we had our driver take us to her hotel so we could take her to dinner at the Konark Restaurant. We learned that she did not register at the Bangalore Hotel. So, we drove to the Gateway Hotel, and then the Rama Hotel, which was where Suleman maintained his offices. But, she was no where to be found. We had the Rama Hotel staff call Suleman's home to find out what happened to them. There was no answer. We are still puzzled over what happened.

We went straight to Darshan in Brindavan, and I sat right next to the entrance where Swami had walked in the previous year. Today, He came in through the door on the stage and went straight to His chair, where He sat throughout the whole time. The college boys were all given an interview. I am told that on certain days, only Bhajans are held and Swami does not give a walkabout Darshan.

Since there are no family accommodations on the Ashram at Brindavan, we took a private room our driver knew of, three miles down past the Eastern Canteen at Rs. 300 a night, with Rs. 600 payable in advance. We had to buy clean sheets, as the ones on the twin beds were filthy. We were told that hot water would arrive in two buckets outside our door at 6 a.m. so we could wash before going to Darshan. The water never arrived and we never saw the owners again. So we kissed our Rs. 600 goodbye, and our friends, Olga and Gilly helped us to find a room where they were staying, right across from the Ashram at a lot less Rupees. Another lesson learned.

But what a wonderful compensation at Darshan. I was the first person in our row and I drew the #1 chit, so I was the first to go in and choose a seat. Swami never came near me, but I had a beautiful Darshan while He was up on the stage after He gave His walk through.

4:26 p.m. - the time when Swami took our letters. I asked Him in my letter to help me to not be so affected by other people's vibrations. He also took letters from me for Ken, Ruth, Nino and Vincent.

Brindavan, December 10, 1994

Just as Swami was leaving the Darshan area, I heard Him say to me in my mind/heart, **"I Love you Child!"** When I heard this, I realized that Baba was revealing to me that it was Him all throughout my life who had been calling me Child, and talking to me as my Inner Voice. Thank You Baba! I was reduced to tears, once again. I used to think of my Inner Voice as my Higher Self, or the part of God within me, and I pictured it over my head when I would communicate with It and surrender to It.

Swami returned to Puttaparthi today, and so did we. We never did find Abigal, and we were told that Suleman was ill in Bombay and had not been back to work.

Puttaparthi, December 14, 1994 Wednesday
Dreamed that I was at a special celebration having to do with Sai Baba. Someone had given me prasad - a special piece of cake to eat.

It seems that as soon as I ask for something this trip, it is granted, whether Swami takes my letter of request or not. Yesterday, I asked Him to help Syd with his desires and anger. Syd was sitting in the first row, his cupped hands filled with packets of vibhuti that he hoped Swami would bless. He was totally absorbed with the bliss of His presence, and did not notice that Swami's hand was resting on the packets of vibhuti in his hands. When he did become aware of Swami's hand, he said, "Thank You, Swami!", and Swami gave him a beautiful loving look and moved on. Swami's touch and look was all Syd needed. He was my glowing, happy, wonderful husband all over again. Then I wrote a letter asking for His help with my diet and my appetite seemed to diminish.

Puttaparthi, December 19, 1994
This afternoon I was in the first row again. About 4 p.m., Swami came along and looked me straight in the eye, something I didn't ask for or expect. He held my eye for a long time, or so it seemed, then took my letter of surrender. As He threw candy from the dish next to me, I took padnamaskar for only a short time, and only

touched His left toes, but with the right hand, I quickly touched His foot through His gown. Shortly after He passed by, I remembered the dream where He came out of the Poornachandra door, and He granted me padnamaskar of the right foot only and for just a short time, and how I had wished for full padnamaskar. I've finally had full padnamaskar, with half during a dream and the other half just now. Swami, your humor never ceases to amaze me.

More Westerners are arriving everyday for the Christmas celebration. I joined the large 600 member choir and we have been practicing two and three times a day for long periods of time. Such beautiful music. I haven't sung Christmas Carols in a choir since my last year in Sacramento in 1977. We have a lot of work ahead if we are going to learn all these songs. I am not familiar with some of them, and the choir director is not using the traditional four part harmony we sang in the USA in the carols I am familiar with, so I have to unlearn the old and relearn the new Alto parts. I notice other Westerners are experiencing the same struggles with the harmony as I am.

We found Suleman in his office and we asked him about Abigal. He told us she was unable to get a flight from Bangalore to Bombay and that is why he drove her to Bombay himself. Suleman explained to us that Abigal had told him she was very ill and he had helped to arrange for her to fly home early on December 9th. She never said a word to us before she left Puttaparthi that day about being so ill and that she had to leave India.

The Second Interview

Puttaparthi, December 22, 1994

Our choir director asked us to forgo Darshan this afternoon so we could practice again. I was the first to protest - "Darshan is my first priority - that is why I am here!". Nearly everyone agreed. The choir director shot daggers at me. I think we were all tired of practicing over and over, every spare minute of the day and night. In my youth, I sang in many a'cappella choirs in school and in the different churches I attended. Invariably, the choir directors were never fully satisfied with our performance no matter how much we practiced. But we always came through with our best performance in the end when it mattered.

In the afternoon, I was in the first row again for Darshan. Before Swami came out, I heard the Voice Within say, **"If a swallow flies over your head, you will get an interview."** This is ridiculous, I thought, and laughed at myself, thinking the ego had somehow imitated my Inner Voice. But then seconds later, I looked up just as a swallow flew over my head, and wondered if I was losing it. Then a minute later, another swallow flew over my head, and another, and later, still another. After the fourth one flew over, I heard the Voice Within again, **"How many times will you doubt Me, My Child?"**. Was Swami playing with my head, I wondered? Then a fifth swallow flew over my head and I knew that was my answer. I was now convinced we were going to get an interview.

There had been no interviews for Americans since August, we were informed by other Americans when we arrived. Rumors abounded that the American people were being punished for some reason or another. No one knew why for certain. Some had heard that Swami has said there was a lack of unity in the USA Sai Organization. Just the day before, several devotees called a meeting and tried to organize all the USA people in an effort to appease Swami. But they were doing so in an arbitrary manner that was causing a lot of disharmony. I attended the meeting with Diane from San Diego, who I had met several days before in the Darshan lines. The organizers were dividing us into groups. They didn't want us in their group, and their motives became obvious by the manner in which they were dictating which people would be in what group. Frankly, we were treated pretty shabbily. So, I stayed with our original group of five, which included Olga and Gilly from Las Vegas, Gilly's daughter Ashley from Toronto, Diane, and myself.

About 4 p.m., Baba came walking along and stopped in front of me to take some letters. I asked if our small group could have an interview. He said, **"How many?"**. "Only 5 Baba". Then came the Magic word that can send one into heavenly orbit: **"GO!"**. My heart could barely contain itself. I quickly jumped up to go to the Veranda, and just as quickly, a Security Seva Dal pulled me down, saying "Wait!", with a tone of disgust in her voice. I quickly realized what she meant - Swami was still only a few feet past me and I needed to wait until He was farther away down the line. Later, people told me I was glowing as I floated up to the Veranda. I looked around the crowd and found the rest of my group standing up wondering whether they were to come with me. I raised my hand and motioned for them to come on up, indicating a group of five. Several of the USA people who were acting as organizers from the day before also rose up to come with me, but they were sent back by the seva dals.

Once inside the Interview Room, I sat at Swami's feet. It had been seven years since my last interview, a long dry spell, and I knew this time it would be very different. Swami moved His hand in an upward motion, I am certain to lift the energies of the people in the room. He made vibhuti for all the women, and I quickly devoured mine. As He continued with the vibhuti for the other women, He brushed the top of my head and then came back to me and tapped the palm of my hand three times with His fingernails lightly digging in. I knew there was something out of the ordinary going on here with this movement, but it will always remain another one of Swami's mysteries.

Behind me, Diane began sobbing. Swami turned to her and said, "Don't cry. This is a time to be happy. Tears of happiness (only)!". She abruptly stopped crying.

Swami sat down and spoke in an Indian dialect to an Indian couple. He materialized a pendant for the woman and a watch for the man, within inches of my eyes. When He took them inside the Inner Room, He left the curtain ajar and I was able to take His Darshan the whole time. I didn't feel I was invading their privacy as the couple was facing Swami with their backs to me and they were speaking in their native tongue.

When our group of five were taken inside the Inner Room,

again sat at Swami's feet. He said to me, "How are you Sir?" I couldn't get my mouth in gear to give Him an answer. Nobody speaks to Swami unless He wills or permits it. The next thing I knew, He had my right hand in both of His and massaged it and held it for a long time looking at my two rings. I have no idea how my hand got into His, or what He said to me prior to that. He must have willed my hand into His.

I pointed to what had been our engagement ring on my ring finger, (A diamond, fire opal and blue sapphire in an unusual gold setting), and said, "From my husband". Then I pointed to the other ring on my index finger and said, "From the shops outside". (The ring was a simple slightly raised bust of Swami in a blend of silver and other metals, which I believe is called pancholi, the same ring that disappeared at the Retreat). Then He asked how long was I here for and I responded, "Until January third, Swami". He told me, "I will change this one before you go", tapping the silver bust ring three times. Other people in the group said He spoke to me of other things before addressing the rings, but none could remember what was said. I don't have any memory of hearing Him say anything else to me. It must have gone into the recesses of my mind somewhere.

Then he addressed the other people in our group, one by one. To Gilly, Baba asked "Where is your wife?", and Gilly pointed to Olga across the room. Baba said some personal things to him and then asked, "What do you do?" Gilly shrugged his shoulders. Baba said, "Loading, unloading, loading, unloading." Gilly went into shock when he heard this, as Baba was obviously letting him know that he really had no secrets. "Monkey mind, monkey mind. You need to work. Depressed. Late at night the mind goes..... then depression. And you fight all the time. Even yesterday."

Then Swami turned Olga, "And you.....you 'nyit', 'nyit', 'nyit!", Baba said as he moved His fingers in a pinching fashion to demonstrate her nit-picking at Gilly. We all giggled. Swami turned back to Gilly and said, "Monkey mind. I will help. I will help you." Then He slapped Gilly's face, patted him on the head and gave him lots of loving attention. This was Gilly's first interview. Baba had been giving

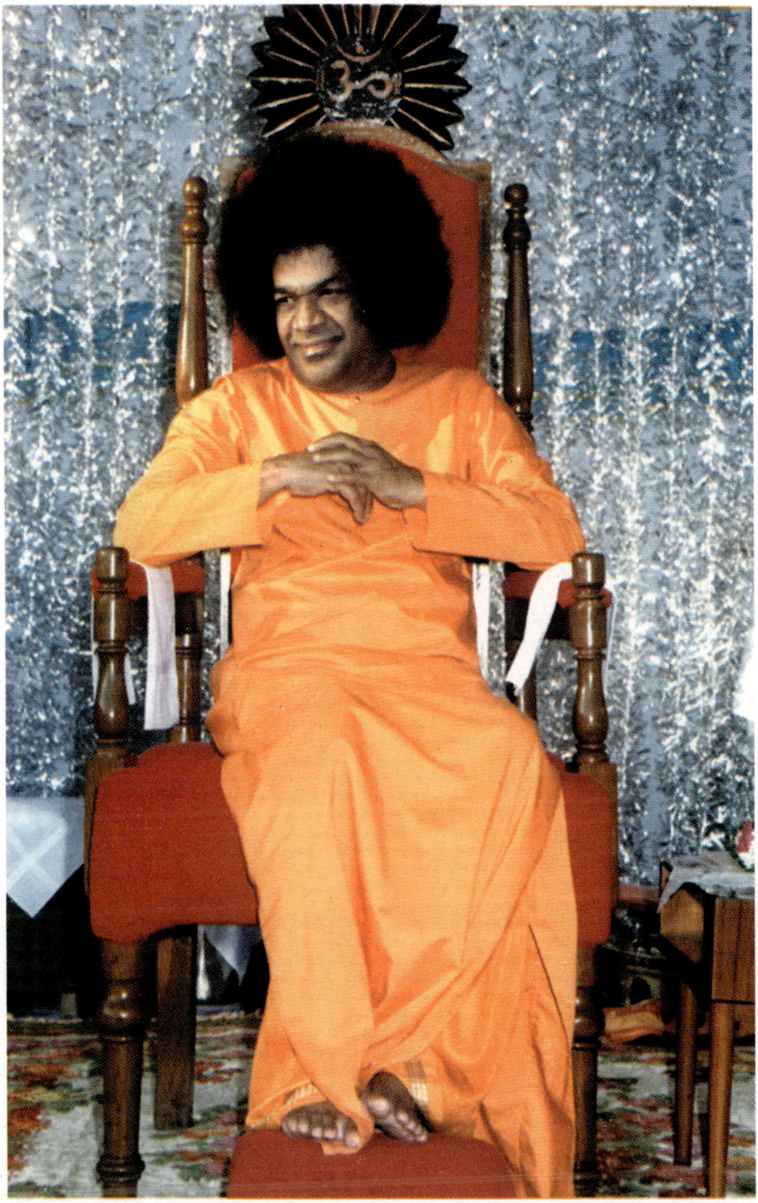

Gilly lots of attention in Darshan with padnamaskar day after day. Gilly had been to India once as a young man and saw Swami one time from a distance outside the fence at Brindavan. Swami briefly spoke to the others in the group and then got up to usher us back into the Interview Room.

I thought of asking Swami for padnamaskar as we sat in the Inner Room, and was too shy to interrupt. But, as we started to get up to move back into the Interview Room, I blurted out "Padnamaskar Swami?". He said, "Outside". I knew at that moment, I should have asked for it while we were in the Inner Room, and I never had another opportunity to take it. We returned to our original seats and Swami disappeared for a moment. The next thing I know, an orange robe came flying through the air, landing perfectly folded in my lap. Then another one landed next to me in Olga's lap in the same condition. How did He do that, I wondered? Nobody saw Him throw the robes to us. Then we heard Him say from behind the curtain, "And they have been worn too!". Later someone explained to me that rumors were going around that the robes He gave away had never been worn by Him, and I guess He wanted to make certain we knew the truth.

While Swami stood there in the Interview Room, an old man broke the silence and told us his story. He said he was 91 years old and that his parents long ago had given him his horoscope showing that he would live to be only 80 years old. On his 80th birthday, Baba called him in for an interview and said he would change his date of death and that he will now live to be 141. He showed us the ring and jeweled pendant that Baba had made for him. Baba nodded, indicating to us that the old man was telling the truth.

Once all the Inner Room interviews were over, Swami sat down in His chair for a moment and chatted with some of the people. I saw someone hand Swami a letter, so I pulled out the two letters that I had carried to Darshan and He took them and put them all in a basket next to His chair. One of my letters asked Swami to take the letter only if I understood Him correctly that I was supposed to put together a book of His teachings. I don't know why I didn't think to ask Swami about the book in person. Yes I do - It must have been His Will that I go on without His verbal approval. It was a test of my trust and faith. The other letter asked Him to please help me to stop being so critical of my fellow man, and to help me think before I speak.

Swami materialized a diamond ring for a man and while everyone was admiring it, I was looking at Swami. Suddenly, a flute began playing outside and at that moment, Swami said, "Ahhhh, Flute!". He laid His head back and appeared to go into a swoon, obviously very taken with the music.

When I left the Interview Room, I headed straight back to my hotel room, holding Swami's robe pressed against my chest, with the vibhuti packets stashed inside the robe. I was so blissed out, I was not even aware of the beggars and vendors in the street who always annoyed me so much. I must have dropped a packet of vibhuti Swami had given me because as soon as I locked the door of my room behind me, the Doorman knocked and handed it to me when I reopened it. Later, I gave him a packet of vibhuti to thank him for being so honest.

I had an appointment for a massage an hour later, and was considering canceling it. After smelling my hands, I never wanted to wash them again - they smelled just like Swami. I just wanted to stay in my room and relive the Interview over and over, and keep that feeling of Bliss that I came away with. As I was pondering what to do, I heard Swami say, **"I will give that smell to you again Child - go on with your life and get the massage."**. What else could I do?

After I explained to the massage lady, Vidya, that I had had an interview with Swami that afternoon, she showed me a pair of tiny Padukas - sandals - that Swami had materialized for another of her clients. Swami had told her client to give the sandals to Vidya, with the message that her hands were His hands helping the people. When I laid down for the massage, the room began spinning and I felt nauseous. I was so dizzy I had to get back up for a few minutes. I wondered if it could have been all the excitement of the day.

The following morning, when I awoke and started to get up, the vertigo returned. Now I began to wonder if maybe Swami had done something to me or perhaps my Kundalini. The vertigo returned even stronger, when I laid down for a short rest before Darshan. The world seemed to be spinning around, starting with the ceiling above me and my stomach followed. It only improved after I sat up for awhile. I 'knew' this time that it was nothing harmful, and that Swami had a hand in it.

Puttaparthi, December 23, 1994

At Darshan this morning, I sat in the third row on the opposite side and made short eye contact with Swami as He came along - the surprised expression on His face said, "Are you still in the front rows?". As He walked by, I could smell that wonderful sweet Jasmine-like aroma radiating from Him. As a matter of fact, it continued on throughout that whole Darshan, even after He had gone through the men's section and was up on the Veranda. And it happened again at nearly every Darshan for the next week or so.

Someone shared the following excerpts with me from Nisargadetta's teachings while waiting in line for Darshan.
1. Don't you understand you are not living?
2. Don't you understand you are being lived?
3. Stand back and watch yourself living.
4. Stand back and watch yourself being lived.
5. All action is God
6. All reaction is man.
7. The first rule for achieving peace is "Mind your own business!".

Christmas in Puttaparthi

Puttaparthi December 1994

You can feel Christmas in the air in Puttaparthi, certainly not the same feeling that one experiences at home. Instead of wishing everyone a Merry Christmas, we are wishing one another a "Holy Christmas". There are no decorations, no trees with lights, no last minute shopping, no gifts and no feasts going on in the Ashram. What one feels is the real Spirit of Christmas here: LOVE!!!

"Christmas in Prashanthi Nilayam is a 'Holi day" and not a "Holiday". Practice whatever you have learned here, even after you go back to your respective countries. Strengthen the feeling that you are the messenger of God and propagate the divine message far and wide. That is your Primary duty. There is no greater service than this. We have been celebrating Christmas every year here. True Christmas is celebrated only in Prashanthi Nilayam, where people of all religions get together (cheers). Generally Hindus celebrate Hindu festivals; Muslims celebrate their festivals; Christians celebrate their festivals so on and forth. It is only in Prashanthi Nilayam that people of all religions - Hindus, Muslims, Christians, Parsis etc., come together to celebrate Christmas (cheers) Prashanthi Nilayam symbolizes the unity of all religions. Elsewhere people drink, eat non-vegetarian food and make merry in the name of Christmas. But Christmas in Prashanthi Nilayam is celebrated in a holy atmosphere." Christmas Discourse 1998

Before Syd left India, I purchased Christmas greeting cards at the Ashram Shops, and wrote individual notes to all my old friends and family about Christmas in India being celebrated with the Lord Himself. Syd was going to mail them once he returned home. He should be home by now, as he returned early to free up the pets from their prison cells, and to take care of his business.

Everyone on my mailing list probably will think we have lost it when they read our card, but while here at the Lord's feet, it is difficult to think otherwise, and I really didn't care what they will think. Maybe we will open some doors for them. Syd and I have never tried to hide our life with Sai Baba. We have pictures of Swami all over our home and we openly wear vibhuti on our foreheads. Syd even wears his vibhuti when he attends board meetings and other events with his business associates. Everyone who knows us, knows about our devotion to Sai Baba.

Wherever we are and whoever we are with, we pray over our food, and when at home we chant the food prayer and the Gayatri Mantra, no matter who is joining us at the table. The CEO of the Indian firm has visited our home a number of times, and the last time he was here, he asked for a tape of the Gayatri Mantra and the food prayer, the former of which he had not chanted since he was given this Mantra during a ceremony when he was a boy 60 years before. We have had house guests who are Sai Baba devotees who have commented to us, "You really do live Swami's teachigs!". They seemed to be surprised, but isn't that what we are supposed to do?

More Westerners have been arriving everyday for the holidays, a very special time in Puttaparthi. Mavora arrived yesterday and we ran into each other at the bakery line. She wants to join the choir and I agree to see if she still can, since it is so close to Christmas.

Some Westerners are learning how to be seva dals to replace the Indian seva dals during Christmas. Some are working with the children for the Christmas Drama. Others are sewing costumes for the children, or building stage sets for the Play. Olga is in charge of makeup this year.

There were two choirs, one for the Play, and the one I sang in, a choir of over 600 people from all parts of the world singing Christmas songs together in a variety of languages. We have been practicing two, three times and now four times a day for up to three hours at a time for the four different events we are to participate in. The first event is Nagarsankirtan, when we will walk around the Ashram singing a variety of Christmas carols before dawn on Christmas morning. The second are the songs we will sing to our Lord Sai Baba on Christmas Morning when he grants predawn Darshan, the third event is when we sing a variety of songs to Swami on Christmas Eve, and for the fourth event are the bhajans we will lead shortly thereafter. One of the songs, 'Sai You are More Precious than Silver', puts me into tears every time we sing it. I can't get past the first line without that sob rising up in my throat. It is such a beautiful song and just says it all. There has been little time for anything but choir practice, and I am absolutely exhausted running back and forth from my hotel room outside, to the shed where we practice.

I finally was able to get through on the telephone to Syd last night to tell him about the interview. He was so happy for me that I could tell he was dropping a few tears as I shared the events of the interview, especially about the robe and the ring. He told me that after he left Puttaparthi, he started praying intensely for Swami to give me an interview. And it worked! I still feel so high from whatever happened when Swami held my hand. Also, I can still smell that beautiful aroma every time Swami gives us Darshan. I hope it lasts forever.....it is so powerful, it sends me into a swoon.

There are so many people here. Somebody said they were told at the Administration Office that a quarter of a million Westerners are staying inside the Ashram for Christmas. Choir practice has been so draining for me. But, all this hard work has paid off. The choir sang beautifully this afternoon, and Swami gave us a wonderful Darshan, after which He passed out prasad - laddu! I ate mine right away, so sweet and so good.

After Darshan, it was time to line up for the 6:30 p.m. Christmas Drama in the Poornachandra Auditorium. My seat was way in the back, and after sitting there for another hour, I just could not sit any longer, and I could not hear anything anyway. So I went and found Vidya, took her to my hotel room and got a massage. I fell asleep right after she left

Puttaparthi, Christmas Day, 1994

Up at 3 a.m. for the 4:30 meeting at the Ganesh Gate for Nagarsankirtan. We sat again until 5:45, then lit our candles and wended our way around the Ashram, into the Mandir grounds, and up to the foot of the balcony to await Swami. All the while we were singing Christmas Carols. Suddenly the silver doors opened and Swami floated out in His white robe. The Choir burst in to song with, "Joy to the World the Lord Has Come, Let Earth Receive Her King!" Swami moved slowly back and forth across the balcony, looking down and blessing all of us. My emotions got the best of me when I realized that this song that I have sung at nearly every Christmas of my life has taken on a new meaning with our Beloved Lord standing right there above us. I could not contain the tears, and reached down for a tissue to wipe my face. When I looked back up, Swami was looking down into my eyes with the sweetest, most beautiful, loving smile on His face. O Swami, I LOVE You sooooo much!

I can remember years ago praying to Swami to help me to learn how to LOVE Him. I had seen the joy and bliss on the face of others who loved Him and I had wanted to have that experience also. He has given it to me this year, and I must say there is no other love like it in my experience. When I think of Him, I just bliss out.....

"Today thousands of people have gathered here. What has brought them together here? Love is the main cause. Without love, few of you would have come from such distant places. How does this love express itself? It is a process of give and take. You have to receive God's love. And you have to offer your love. But both are one and the same love. God's love is reflected in your bodies. That is the meaning of the Gita declaration: 'A fragment of Mine is present in everyone in the cosmos'......Your heart is inherently filled with love. But you are ignoring this plenitude and going after the trivial. Your real sustenance will come from this Divine love and not from other petty pleasures.

"Every cell in the human body is filled with love. It is this microcosmic love that fills the entire cosmos. You have no need to go in search of love elsewhere. It is all within you." SS Dec 1996 P 311

Eventually Swami went back through the silver doors, and we all were seated again in the Mandir grounds, waiting for 7:30 a.m. for His Darshan. This time, Swami appeared in a yellow saffron robe. The crowd went up in cheers at such a beautiful sight of our Lord.

Swami's chair had been placed in front of the Mandir and we received His continuous Darshan throughout the ceremony. The students put on a small play, and one by one, brought in trays of things for Swami to bless. Then Maynard Ferguson, a famous jazz musician, directed the Indian boys' band in several renditions of Christmas songs he had taught them, i.e., 'We Wish You a Merry Christmas' in Polka time.

Baba again passed out prasad and this time I took two, the

extra to take home for Syd. At the time, I was not certain I had done the right thing here, because there have been times since that I was never able to get any prasad when Swami brought it out. I meant no harm, but I now realize that it was wrong, because if everybody did the same thing, there would never be enough for everyone present. Oh, the lessons we have to learn.....

We broke for lunch and then lined up again at 1:45 for the Christmas Program and Baba's Discourse which will follow. Arthur Hillcoat from Australia gave a long uplifting talk, as did five of the lady devotees from the "Messengers of Sai" organization, reporting on their worldwide service activities. These are all former students of Swami, most of whom have married and moved away, but return each Christmas for a reunion.

We were treated to a delightful play put on by deaf children. These children are students from a school for the deaf which is run by the "Messengers of Sai" organization.

The Ring

While sitting and waiting for Swami to come out on Christmas morning to give His 7:30 a.m. Darshan, I heard Him say in my head, **"Look at your ring - it is changing!"**. It had just turned daylight as I held up the ring to get a good look at it. I could see that Swami's head had turned somewhat to the right, whereas before I remembered it as directly facing out.

After our interview three days before, a number of people had looked at this ring that Swami was going to change. Most had the opinion that what He meant was, He was going to call us in for another interview and change it then. I had no feeling that we were going to get another interview before we left.

So, after Darshan, I joined my group and others and showed them the ring again that Swami had promised to change. I felt I needed confirmation that I was not creating this in my mind. They too agreed that Swami's head had turned to the right. What a wonderful Christmas present!

Was able to get through on the phone to Syd again. He told me that Vincent is now home after two days in Kaiser Hospital in Denver and is staying with his friend. Vincent isn't saying so, but it seems that his HIV positive status has gone into the dreaded AIDS Syndrome. When Syd returned home and learned that Vincent was in the hospital up in Denver with pneumonia, he sent Vincent some vibhuti, an OM pendant and picture of Swami, all of which Swami had blessed for Syd.

Syd said he had dinner with Ruth last night at the local Chinese restaurant to celebrate Christmas, and also to share with her the story of my interview. Her live-in boyfriend Nino apparently left to return to California for good on December 22nd.

On the morning of the 26th, I awoke and looked at my ring, and could not believe my eyes. Swami's head seems to have tilted downward, which caused His full head of hair to raise up considerably on the ring. When our group and others gathered together for breakfast after Darshan at the vegetarian restaurant in Sai Towers, I showed them all the ring again, and they all agreed that another change had taken place. Someone asked, "How does it feel waking up to find something like that going on while you slept and how do you like all the attention you are getting because of it?" I didn't know how to answer that. Getting other people's attention has not ever been anything I craved. For anyone familiar with Western or Jyotish Astrology, I have my Virgo Sun conjunct three other planets in Virgo on the cusp of my 12th house or in the 12th in Jyotish, so you know that I would prefer to remain away from the public eye.

When I awoke on the morning of the 27th, the ring had changed again. It appeared this time that the ring has grown as it is much larger than yesterday! Once again, I show it to everybody over breakfast after Darshan, and everyone agrees that it is larger than before.

Swami's Workshop

Puttaparthi, December 28, 1994

When I awoke this morning, the first thing I did was look at the ring after I turned the lights on. There is no visible change today. Has Swami finished with it? He tapped it three times - does that mean it will change only three times, I wondered? It is so beautiful now and the bust of Swami just seems to radiate His Love. When I pressed it to my forehead in the third eye area, I could feel Swami's energy radiating from it. Thank you Swami!

Still feeling tired this morning. Just had a banana for supper last night and awoke at 4 a.m. I was extremely dizzy with vertigo for three days after the interview. Every time I moved, the room or area around me would begin spinning. It is still there from time to time, but not with the same intensity.

While waiting for the lines to go inside the Mandir grounds, the one everybody called the Gestapo seva dal was talking to us. She said that Baba's energy is so much more powerful here at Puttaparthi than at Brindavan where He is more relaxed. I had never looked at it that way before, nor had I noticed any difference in His energy from here to there. She also said that Puttaparthi is Swami's workshop while Brindavan is His playground.

I've been in a blue funk which started on Christmas Day. I was able to pull out of it for awhile yesterday and thought I had left it behind, but this monkey mind went out of control again today. I was in Line 1 in Darshan and watched as soooooo many Indian "VIP's" lined up again to take all the good seats. There must have been hundreds of them. Who are they and where do they all come from, I wondered? What makes them so special? Other people were complaining all around me and I unwisely joined in.

It was Diane who had drawn the Number 1 for our line this time, and there was no place in the first row for her to sit when she got inside, and only a few places left in the second row on both sides of where

Swami walks. This simply is not a fair practice. Being able to be in line one is a great privilege, especially with so many lines because there are so many people here, but it did me no good today. I was only able to get into the third row inside. An Indian lady came and squeezed into the tiny space beside me and then told me to move over. I was already in a very tight space myself and refused to make myself and my space smaller for her.

Then, that 'Voice Within' told me there really was enough room for me to give her another inch or two if I tried, but I didn't budge. When Swami came along, He looked me right in the eye and turned and went to the other side. Having read about it from other people's experiences, I realized and understood that at that moment, I had been put in Swami's workshop. The look He gave me told me that He was snubbing me and the letter I was handing out to Him. He was within reach, but would not take my letter.

Strangely, I was not the least bit upset when Swami looked me in the eye and turned and went the other way - the rejection He implied by His action was itself giving me the instructions I needed from Him on where I needed to go next. I knew deep inside that I needed to take corrective action and in what areas. And, any attention from Swami is Special Attention! Thank you Swami!

During Darshan, I really smelled that wonderful, sweet Jasmine aroma coming from Baba today as He passed by, and again as He walked in front of the open Mandir door when the breeze brought it over to me once more. It is so uplifting, like a healing via aromatherapy. If only there were some way I could capture some of it in a bottle to take home.

When Darshan ended, I was just starting to get up when an Indian woman jumped right over the top of me trying to get into the space in front of me for Bhajans. She knocked me over and I became very angry and called her an animal. I knew she understood what I said, but she only acted as if it were her right and I was the intruder. This made me even angrier and I wanted to strike out at her, like punch her lights out or redesign her face with my fist. As I picked myself and my belongings up and walked away, my head hung down as I realized it had all been a test, and I flunked again.

"Good thoughts can elicit the best from man and help him use all of his energy for his spiritual progress. To harvest good fruit, cultivate good sankalpas (thoughts, intentions). You can easily indulge in bad thoughts and intentions about others, but remember that you have to bear the consequences of such evil thoughts. Nobody can escape the consequences of thoughts and intentions, good or bad.

"For example, one might entertain a desire to injure someone else, and it might fructify as harm to that other person. But it is certain that it will rebound on the person who first welcomed it into his mind, bringing with it a hundredfold harm and injury. A bad thought hurts both the sender and his target." Sathya Sai Baba, quoted from LIAD by Joy Thomas, P 164

  How quickly I went from bliss to rage. What is going on inside of me? Where did all this anger come from? I never act or even feel like this at home or anywhere else. I have never, ever wanted to physically retaliate against anyone for any reason. Is it something that happens to people who come to Puttaparthi? It seems that the worst of me makes itself known when I am here in Puttaparthi. Perhaps the worst in that Indian woman was coming out also? These are feelings and reactions I did not know existed within me. Oh Swami, I am so ashamed. I really need Your help here!

  The following morning, I tripped on an uneven concrete block and fell as I was following my line into the Mandir. I skinned both my knees which was very painful, and got blood all over my Punjabis. I have read where we sometimes receive instant karma from outbursts of anger like I had just had. I recall that I have fallen several times and injured myself in Puttaparthi after other similar incidents of losing my temper. Does 'Bringing someone to their knees!' mean giving them a dash of humility, or what?

  Mavora, my dear friend from New Zealand arrived just before Christmas. She was full of jet lag when we ran into each other at the bakery, as she had just arrived and had not had anything to eat for some time. We arranged to meet for lunch in the Western Canteen. It was so crowded and noisy, we could barely hear each other even though we were sitting in the "Silent Section". Today, we are going shopping outside so that she can pick up some gifts for John, the love of her life, and others back home. She has not left the Ashram since her arrival; prefers to stay inside, but was happy when I agreed to help her find the gifts in the shops outside. It turned out to be a lot of fun for both of us. I really do enjoy her company. We must have been very close in another life.

Puttaparthi, December 12, 1994
After being grateful for Swami's snub yesterday, and working on it part of the night, I realized that when we come to Puttaparthi, we are on a fast karmic track. In other words, we are here to work out some heavy duty karma with Swami where He can help us get through it. The couple in the room above mine were fighting throughout the night, so they must also be faced with their karma.

"True, all those who come to Baba are not cured of their incurable diseases. But their past karmas and the intensity of faith in Swami's healing power are the two major factors for their recovery or otherwise. The omnipresent, omniscient and omnipotent Sai knows the past, present and future of everyone. He is fully aware of the past karmas of each and everyone and intervenes only in cases where the individual has atoned sufficiently for his past sins. There is, however, no doubt that once He steps in, there is no ailment which He cannot cure. He can, and He does, cancel the residue of karmas of those who are sufficiently repentant about their misdeeds and eager to return to the path of love and service of humanity." V.I.K. Sarin, FFWG P 137

"There are three types of karma: past, present and future. Present karma must continue. It is like the carriage behind which is a trail of dust. If the carriage stops, the dust will settle on it. A doubt might be that the carriage cannot forever continue so as to be ahead of its dust. The highway is equivalent to the grace of God. There is a difference between the benefit of grace and the benefit of bhakthi, of devotion. A patient with a pain is given a sedative which dulls the pain. But grace is an operation that does entirely away with karma. Like a medicine which was labeled, 'good until 1968'. If used in 1972, the medicine is entirely ineffective. The body is the bottle, the karma in the body is the medicine. God puts a date on the 'medicine' so it is not effective." CWSSB P 111

Most of that crowd of VIP's are gone today. I got line one again this morning, and sat in the first row between Olga and Ashley. Baba came along and took my letter which I wrote this morning. I was able to take padnamaskar with my left hand on His right foot only for a brief instant. He also looked me in the eye for flash, as He did Olga.

My bladder was full to bursting as I sat through Bhajans. Swami gave an extremely long Darshan during Bhajans because of all the children, and He gave prasad to them - an apple and a laddu. He smelled so sweetly of Jasmine again.

I am still struggling with not losing my temper when I get pushed around and climbed over. It seems to be happening to me on a regular basis now, tempting me to lose my temper again and again. And every time it happens, I end up falling and injuring myself. Three falls so far on this trip already. Is this part of your Divine Design to bring me to my knees Swami? Climbing over this challenge is not easy, and I really do need Your help with this Swami. Baba's snub treatment yesterday was like the Mother telling her child it had overstepped its bounds, and it was the best thing He could have done for me.

Puttaparthi, December 30, 1994

Once again, I am in line one and get to sit in the first row. This is incredible, because there are so many people here for the holidays. I wonder what the odds are of getting in line one so many times? Swami came along and briefly glanced at me. As He came down the aisle, I felt this terrible static all around me from the women's excitement. Up until then, I thought there may be a chance for that second interview. But I was ready for anything. Whatever is Your Will Baba! I am just happy to be here at Your Feet!

While waiting for Swami to come out, I talked with Him internally and asked if I understood Him correctly when He told me to put together the book of His teachings. He said, **"Yes, you do the book**

and bring it here and I will bless.". Oh, if only I could be certain it was Baba and not my ego, because I don't have that feeling of conviction strongly enough, probably because of my ego and lack of belief that I am worthy of such a task. Perhaps it will come. I have been working on the book of His teachings for many months already, but still am uncertain that it was His voice I had heard. I am getting so much and joy and pleasure out of this work, that I know I must continue, if only for my own spiritual growth.

When Swami reached where I was sitting, He stopped and threw candy from the lady's tray next to me. About a dozen pieces fell on me, quickly followed by all of the Indian ladies around me grabbing them off my lap. I was only able to get three pieces for myself. I would have gotten more if I had not reached out and taken padnamaskar. When I did this, I felt instantly chastised by Him, as I really did not have His permission to take it. I felt terrible and apologized in my mind. Baba said through my Inner Voice, **"You are forgiven Child, but don't do it again."**

Mavora and I had lunch together again today - a lovely time. After Darshan, I turned and saw her three rows behind me and offered her my front row seat because I was leaving to get breakfast. She out-maneuvered all the ladies behind me who had set designs on my space when they could see I was about to leave. My feet and legs have been giving me a lot of trouble this year from sitting so much, and there are times when I just can not stay through until bhajans. Even the massages are not helping me enough. My feet seem to go to sleep after only twenty minutes or so, quickly followed by my legs.

Still beating myself up over taking padnamaskar without permission at Darshan, and will not do that again because I get nothing from it but rebuke, which was far worse than being ignored. I did feel His eyes look into mine for a split second, but there was no hint of recognition in His this time. He took in a very large group of people from Turkey for an interview this afternoon. This morning, it was our Choir Director, and a large group of Guatemalans who were blessed with an interview.

Puttaparthi, January 2, 1995

Today is my last full day with Swami, as I leave tomorrow morning for Bombay. I have been carrying a tray full of candy, pictures of Swami, pendants, key chains, rings, and japamalas to Darshan for Swami's blessings the past three times, but have not gotten close enough for Him to bless them. I was in one of the last rows to go inside the Mandir Grounds. I am about eight rows back and realize that my Inner Voice is telling me that I should not take any chances on getting close enough to offer the tray to Him on my last Darshan tomorrow morning. So, I pass a note up to Sasha from the USA who is in the first row, with a request that she present my tray to Swami for His blessing. She readily agrees and I ask the ladies in front of me to pass the tray up to her. When Swami came out to give Darshan, I steadily prayed to Him to please come to our side and bless my tray. My heart jumped for joy as He strolled over and took several hands full of candy from the tray and threw it out to the crowd of women. Thank You Baba for giving me the message to pass up the tray for Your blessing. And, Thank You Swami; You have given me the perfect last day with You, I silently said to Him.

Before I left Puttaparthi, I shared things from the tray with everyone in my group, and with Sasha, and some of the Sai Towers staff. I had looked all over for Mavora, without success so I could share with her too. Then, the morning I was to leave, as I sat in the queue lines, I asked Swami to please help me find her. I happened to turn around a few minutes later just as she took a seat in the queue three rows over from me. I rushed over with my little package of gifts, including a package of vibhuti Swami had given me, and with tears in my eyes, I hugged her goodbye once more. Mavora is very dear to me, dearer than my own sisters, and I never know if or when I will ever see her again. New Zealand is so far away.

While sitting in the Puttaparthi Airport waiting for my direct flight to Bombay, a black lady from South Africa strikes up a conversation with me. She is also on her way home. Having never been to that part of the globe, I asked her what it was like there. As she described it, it sounded a great deal like some of the land in the USA. After a while, she moved into what she really wanted to talk about. She shared with me that the former president of South Africa, de Klerk, had been to see Sai Baba and that Baba has also called Nelson Mandela to Him. She said that Mandela is expected to arrive in Puttaparthi within the week.

I remember talking to Syd about how it could be none other than Swami's doing when we read that de Klerk called for the free elections in which Nelson Mandela later won. I also heard that Raisa Gorbachev had been to see Swami, and am willing to bet that He had a major hand in the Iron Curtain coming down, as well as the Berlin Wall. Nobody but God could have arranged these miracles!

Bombay, January 4, 1995

My plane arrived an hour late in Bombay this afternoon. While on the plane, just as the stewardess was handing a glass of water to me, a boy came running down the aisle and bumped her arm. Guess where the water went - all over me, head to toe! This was probably one of Swami's leelas, because I had been tempted to read an Indian newspaper that had been staring at me out of the pocket in the seat in front of me. The temptation to see what was going on in the world was too much, even though I knew I should not pay attention to it. I even thought I heard Swami telling me to **"Leave it!"** So, I asked Swami if my soaking was a gift from him. **"Yes!"** I silently thanked Him that it wasn't coffee or tea or juice.

Since the interview, I have been hearing Baba giving me advice or instructions via my Inner Voice. It is my hope that He will continue, in spite of my not following it this time. As I wrote this in my journal, I heard Him say that He will continue so long as I follow His teachings, including gossip, watching my thoughts, dedicating actions to Him, not watching the TV or reading newspapers, etc. That is a very tall order for me, because I have been guilty of all these transgressions, regularly. I can only do my best. **But who really is the doer here if everything is God's Will?**

"God is the only 'Doer' of all acts and He is the only 'Enjoyer' of all fruits.....All acts are done by Him and all fruits go to Him. He is present everywhere and in everything as Atma. The Atma is the source of all action just as the current is the source of light. You are only instruments in the hands of God.....God acts through you. And since He performs the actions, only He is entitled to enjoy the fruits of the actions.

"I will give you an example. Take a puppet show, for instance. The puppeteer has the dolls attached to strings. He jerks and pulls the strings and makes the dolls move and dance according to his wishes. The puppets cannot move of their own accord and will. They are entirely in the hands of the puppeteer. If the show is good, the puppeteer earns credit and if the show is bad, he earns discredit. So, you see, success or failure both belong to the puppeteer. He is the 'doer' and he is the 'enjoyer'. It is the same in the case of God also. He is the Divine Puppeteer: He is the Doer and the Enjoyer. You are merely His dolls and tools." SSAV P 38

    Until my plane leaves for home, I am to stay with the Indian company's CEO and his wife, who is supposed to meet my plane, but I do not see her anywhere in the airport and she is over an hour late. Just as I was beginning to think that I should call her home, she arrived. She tells me the driver had first gone to the wrong airport and then got stuck in traffic. Their home is a large ground floor flat in a gate-secured area on the bay. A flat such as this can go for around three million US dollars, as property in Bombay is very expensive. That accounts for the high cost of hotel rooms, upon which they tack on a 20 percent surcharge.

    The area where they live reminds me of where I lived in Hawaii, with the sound of the tide coming and going, night and day, rocking you to sleep and soothing your nerves. Here it also serves to block out the traffic and other big city sounds. The constant cooling breeze also reminds me of the tradewinds in Hawaii. Here they serve a greater purpose for those living on the bay, because they blow the pollution into the city and away from their flat, so the air is easier to breathe than anywhere in Bombay. I am told there are officially 16 million people living in Bombay. There are so many people living on the streets, I wonder how they keep track. Other 'unofficial' estimates, I am told, set the number much higher at 30 million.

We had dinner at Mrs. R's mother's home tonight, where they dine nearly every night. The food is absolutely delicious - the best Indian food I have ever had! There are no hot chilis, because neither Mrs. R nor her mother can tolerate them, and neither can I.

Tonight, Mr. And Mrs. D will pick me up and take me to their home for dinner. The R's will be attending a wedding. I met the D's on my first trip to India. It was Mrs. D who escorted me around Bombay to all the gemstone houses and for other shopping. They, being Hindu, are strict vegetarians, and have been to see Swami on at least one occasion.

The Parel Miracle House

Bombay, January 5, 1995

Another wonderful dinner last night at the D's home. If this keeps up, I will regain all the pounds I worked so hard to leave behind in Puttaparthi. I truly love Indian food, without chilis of course, and vow to learn how to cook it when I get home.

It has been a wonderful day. Mrs. R and I went to the Patel's home this morning, and then we went to the home of some Baba devotees to witness the many miracles occurring there. Normally Mrs. R would not have gone with me, as she is not a devotee of Sai Baba's. Madhu asked me to invite her, and she accepted, much to my great surprise. I had no idea she would be the slightest bit interested in such things when I described where we would be going.

The first thing we noticed when we entered the Parel home was that Swami has written (remotely as He has never been to this home), the Sanskrit sign for OM everywhere in vibhuti, even on the ceilings. There is no way anybody else could make the vibhuti stick upside down on the ceiling like that. As we walked in front of a picture of Swami, two roses fell from the picture at our feet. Mrs. R and I were each given one of them. Red Kum Kum and vibhuti decorated many of the pictures of the different Hindu and other Gods around the room, including one of

Jesus, which had a cross like the crucifix in thick vibhuti under the glass.

The owner of the home told us that pairs of Padhukas (sandals) in a variety of sizes and made from different materials from solid gold to leather, had been materializing from time to time under one of the pictures of Swami. There had been a new and different pair arrive every morning for the last 21 days. One tiny pair had just arrived this morning. We were given vibhuti to eat and apply when we first arrived, and a banana as prasad. There were piles of vibhuti at the foot of every picture. As the vibhuti grows in depth on each picture, it falls to the table below to make room for the continual manifestation of vibhuti on the pictures. The altar was full of things that Baba had materialized remotely, including lingams, icons of various Gods, and crosses. I took several rolls of pictures with my camera to share with my devotee friends at home.

Madhu arranged for Mrs. R and I to be taken into the bedroom where we were shown volumes of pictures of the miracles taken over the years as they occurred in their home. Some were of Swami's footprints in vibhuti that He left as He walked around in the room. He also told us many stories of Swami's leelas, including one where he wanted to go see Swami in Puttaparthi, but he didn't have any money for the trip. He awoke the next morning to find the exact amount of Rupees on his bedside table needed to make the trip.

Another story occurred about a year before when the owner asked Swami to make an appearance in their home so he could take a picture of Swami there. The next morning they found an exposed roll of film that Baba had left on the altar. When it was developed, there were pictures of Swami in different poses around their home.

The owner showed us a two foot tall stainless steel container that Swami keeps full of the sweetest tasting vibhuti you would ever want in your mouth. It smells like Swami. He gave us each a film container full of this nectar-like vibhuti. He said that he only gives things to people when directed to do so by Swami. He showed us a picture of Swami on the altar of where a necklace of golden coins had materialized on Baba's recent birthday. Then he gave Mrs. R and I both one of the coins and some dried sandalwood paste which had materialized on another picture. He got a small piece of paper and also scraped some grains (rice, barley, etc.,) into it that were clinging to another picture of Swami on the altar and put them in a coin envelope for us to take home.

Niranjan Patel said that since Swami changed my ring by remote control, that it is very probable He will do a similar thing in our home. He advised us (Syd and I) to keep on the alert for such events. Madhu told me to put the gold coin where I keep my money or where I do my puja. It remains on my altar right under the two pound, solid sterling silver statue of Swami that the Patels gave us. She also told me to put the grains where I keep my own grains for cooking at home so that we would never be without food.

Niranjan told everyone present several stories of Swami's leelas. One was regarding a western man who became very ill while staying in a shed recently and was taken to the Super Specialty hospital where surgery needed to be performed. Just as the surgeon was painting a line on the man's stomach where he would make the incision, Swami appeared in the operating theatre and redrew the lines, and proceeded to perform the surgery Himself. He then left the surgeon to sew the man back up. This surgery was performed at the exact time that Swami was also giving interviews in the Interview Room back in the Mandir. The surgeon later confirmed this with the people who had been in the Interview Room with Swami. He also talked to Swami about it, and Swami advised that the surgeon was going to make his incision in the wrong place and the man would not have survived the delay it would have caused. It was the surgeon himself that told Niranjan of this leela.

Another story from Niranjan was that the Elections Minister of India is a devotee of Swami. Swami told him three things when he first was elected, only two of which I can recall. 1. If everything he attempted to do was right, Baba would help make it happen. 2. He would be protected from harm no matter what happened. I understood from Niranjan's story that elections results in India are often fraudulent, and Swami was encouraging the Minister and agreeing to help him keep the politicians or the elections honest. A very tall order!

Niranjan and Madhu told us they would be returning to their home in Santa Barbara on January 31st and would return to their flat in Bombay sometime before Swami's 70th birthday celebration in November. Swami had told them the year before to move back to India, so they were going to sell the California home they had lived in for twenty years and finalize their business affairs in the USA. Niranjan was going blind from the diabetes he had had since he was a young man, and their ability to travel was going to be very limited in the future.

As we were leaving, the owner and his wife took padnamaskar of Niranjan's feet. This surprised me, but I later learned that their actions were a sign of respect for one's elders in India.

We had dinner once again at Mrs. R's mother's home. Just as good as before, but this time she included a salad for me because I had shared during our last meal that what I missed most while visiting India was the green salads. So very gracious of them.

When we returned back to the R's flat, I finished packing and their driver took me to the airport late that night to catch my flight home.

Back Home Again

After my return home, I had a number of dreams in which Swami was involved, and some in which I was traveling around the world teaching people about Swami. It also seemed as though I am working out a lot of karma in my dreams now.

In one dream, we had gone to visit Sai Baba and when we arrived we did not have proper clothing to see Him in so we borrowed (without permission), some from the guest house where we were staying. We were permitted to spend the whole day with Swami. I sat next to His beloved form, ate with Him, slept with Him (others were sleeping in the same bed with us). When it got close to time to leave, Swami asked me for my plane tickets and I gave them to Him. When they were returned to me, I saw that I had been rescheduled to leave a day earlier at 0:10 a.m. from 'the first place'. I got very upset and was trying to figure out how I could change the ticket when He asked me if I was in surrender. I said "Yes". Then He said if that was so, why was I resisting the time He had chosen for me to leave. Then I realized it must have been for a good reason, as is everything that happens to me. I was so very grateful in the dream to be so close to Swami.

After that dream, I put a sign up on the wall above my altar, which is where I usually go to talk to Swami when something is bothering me. The sign read: "If you are unhappy about anything, it is because you are not surrendered!" Later, I added another sign: "Suffer or Surrender!" I have 'known' what the results of suffer or surrender means for a very long time, but there are times when I so easily slip out of that state of surrender and forget that it isn't something outside of me that is causing my unhappiness. The little note is there staring at me as a constant reminder, and a subliminal message even when I am not paying attention.

"Where a person is fully surrendered to God, Baba acts in the mode of Divine Mother, caring for and guarding that devotee, doing more for the devotee than the devotee could ever imagine to ask for. But, if a person chooses to follow ego desire, then such a person is left to work out his or her destiny. Here Baba is saying that if we surrender to God's will, happiness will be gained and nothing lost, but if our interest and our desire are turned to worldly life, we are then using individual free will and must live by it and accept the responsibility." Hislop in MBAI P 143

Another lesson about surrender came in a dream. I was having a lot of trouble with an old friend and it was causing me to be very miserable. I started praying to Swami (in the dream) for an answer on what to do to get out of this mess I had gotten myself into with this friend. The answer to my prayer came like a thundering bolt of lightening from the sky, **"SURRENDER!"** So I did and all was well - I was at peace once again in my dream.

There have been times where I actually hear Swami speaking out loud to me. The first time I ever heard His voice was here in my home in Colorado. Syd was traveling on business. We had just had a satellite dish installed as that was the only way we could receiving anything up here in the mountains on our television. I planned to watch a certain comedy movie, but not being familiar with the new complicated remote control apparatus, I somehow tuned into a pornographic film. What was going on on the screen caught my attention, but for only a moment, because Swami spoke out loud in a very firm and syncopated voice, **"Turn...that...off...now!"** It shocked me so much I dropped the remote control and it shut itself off, or maybe Swami had a hand in that too? Whoah! We had not signed up for that channel and it never showed up again on our set, so it must have been a little drama Swami arranged for my benefit.

In another dream, I was up in an airplane with Sai Baba. Later He left me alone and moved up into a spaceship with other devotees. I speculated that the reason they wanted Him with them while they orbited the earth was so there would be no problems with their safety. Later, I talked with one of the men who was on that spaceship and he was telling me he didn't spend a lot of time thinking or caring about Swami's teachings or his spiritual self, but just enjoyed being around Swami because of the good feelings he got. I told him I could not imagine being that close to Swami and not caring about wanting to make changes that would improve his life and spiritual growth. Other people on that spaceship included a lady author of books about Baba, and similar long time devotees. The dream moved into another part where I was studying and sharing Swami's teachings with others. When I awoke, I 'knew' I was supposed to get back to my seva project of putting together the book of Swami's teachings He had asked me to do. I had not touched the manuscript since weeks before we left on the trip to India.

One morning I awoke around my usual time of 4:30 and was contemplating getting up. Then my mind switched to talking to Swami about helping me to cook and eat less. I must have drifted back to sleep, because all of a sudden I felt somebody blow on my right cheek and face. Syd was traveling, so I knew it wasn't him. Then I heard Swami say out loud, **"It's time to get up!"** There He goes again, keeping me on my toes.

In still another dream, I was in Puttaparthi and witnessed Swami taking away privileges from some long time devotees because they had failed to live by His teachings and were also failing to help others when the opportunities arose. Some of the privileges He took away from them were sitting on the veranda and getting to spend a lot of time near Swami.

While in India, some friends told us about the film, "Pure Love", made in Australia. They gave me the name and address of where to locate this film, but also asked me to encourage James Redmond, (USA producer and distributer of videos about Swami), to distribute it here in the USA so that it would be easier for everyone to purchase. Upon our return home, I sent a letter and money order off to Australia, and also called James Redmond. When the video arrived, Syd and I were absolutely enthralled with it. We played it over and over again. It is the finest video of Swami giving Darshan we had ever seen, and whenever we need a lift, we pop it into the VCR. So many wonderful scenes with Swami interfacing with devotees, smiling, joking, loving. What a special treat! For the reader, James Redmond is now carrying this video, and he has also produced a similar one called "My Sweet Lord", which is equally wonderful and we view it alternately with "Pure

Love". It's truly Darshan in Absentia!

The vertigo I experienced after my interview with Swami returned shortly after I came home, this time accompanied with nausea. It was so bad I was unable to do my Hathya Yoga positions for days, because each time I would attempt a position, I would lose my balance and fall over and feel very nauseous. After struggling with it for a while, I cried out, "What's happening to me Swami?" Immediately I heard Him say, **"Call Rocky, he can help you!"**.

I had not even thought of that! Rocky is a friend of Syd's who is a long time student of Nityananda's teachings. He is not a devotee of Sai Baba, although Swami has appeared to him during his meditations and he has great respect for Sai Baba. When I told Rocky that Swami had told me to call him, he said he felt honored, as he views Sai Baba as a great master. He tuned into my body and soul, or whatever it is that he does, and told me, "You are experiencing vertigo because Sai Baba has given you siddhis - powers - and you will now be able to do things like see spiritual beings." The vertigo eventually subsided, but it still returns from time to time, perhaps as a reminder of that wonderful day with Swami in the Interview Room. Sometimes when the vertigo returns, I feel like I have left my body for a period of time and then returned abruptly and had difficulty getting back into this body, like I got in crooked or something. Then there is a moment of struggle while things straighten themselves out.

On another occasion I was driving in to town at a pretty good clip, as I was trying to get to the post office and do my grocery shopping before 10:30 a.m., which was when the inauspicious time period would begin. As I drove along, I recalled reading something Swami had said - "Start early, drive slowly, arrive safely". If this was a warning, I paid no attention to it and still did not slow down. As I left our nearly five miles of dirt roads and moved on to pavement, I heard Him say, **"No need to hurry, I am here with you and will take care of you!"** I immediately slowed down with the comforting awareness that He was there with me, taking care of me, just as He always is, even when I tend to forget.

I believe that my awareness and understanding of Swami's teachings has been elevated from this last trip. It feels as though Swami planted another seed which seems to be growing in my mind. It is not like I didn't know it already, but now I am dwelling and meditating on the fact that Baba as God resides in my heart and that is where the Voice Within speaks to me from, and always has, even though I usually hear it in my mind. And because He resides in everyone's heart, that is how He sees all and knows all, and is there waiting and ready to help if we just call upon Him. Also, with God always present, there can be no secrets.

Many years ago when I first started surrendering my life to God, I knew It was my Higher Self I was surrendering to, and I would always picture my Higher Self (as the part of God within me), as being just above my head, leading and guiding me on and arranging the future events for me in accordance with my karma. When I realized that Sai Baba was God years ago, I then started surrendering to Him. Somewhere in one of Swami's Discourses, I read that He said the physical heart is on the left side of our body, while the Spiritual Heart is on the right side. So now when I surrender or talk to Swami, my Higher Self, I focus on my Spiritual Heart.

We can't hide anything from God, not even our thoughts. The thoughts we think are extremely important, because our thoughts are in a way telling God what lessons we need to learn. Whatever any of our senses takes in, plays a large role in what our thoughts will be. Even the food we eat creates our thoughts and our thoughts create our future. That can be frightening when I think of some of the thoughts I have had in my life.

"Men's thoughts determine their destiny. Hence, men should cultivate good thoughts and eschew all bad feelings." SS October 1994 P 260

Anger used to play a ponderous role in my life; when I was much younger I was always angry about something or at someone. I can recall the first time I was made aware of what an angry person I really was. It was in 1976. One of my male colleagues seemed to feel he was superior to the rest of us because he graduated and had a doctorate from Oxford University, drove a Jaguar and lived in the finest area of town. He was also known as the resident MCP in our office, or Male Chauvinist Pig. In short, he appeared to be a social snob and a woman hater as well. One day he told me that women had no place in the work force; that they belonged in the kitchen, the bedroom or on Second Street (where the ladies of the night were found). I retorted with, "Now I know why your wife left you!". That went straight to his heart, as I had intended. He did what he could to make my life miserable after that and I came to hate that man. After that incident, whenever he would pass by my office, I would childishly send daggers to him, or worse.....

My secretary was sitting with me in my office on an occasion when I expressed my resentment toward this man and she upbraided me with, "Charlene, you are so filled with anger and hatred, and that is not healthy. You need to get it together girl or it will eat you alive!". I instantly realized she was right, but I didn't have a clue as to how to go about it. Coincidentally, that Sunday, Lori, the Minister of the Religious Science Church I attended gave a talk on anger and hatred and the devastating effects, and that we need to learn to love the anger and hatred away. She suggested we take the most unlovable person in our lives and learn how to love them. Immediately, my thoughts went to my co-worker.

Without telling anyone, I went to work on learning to love my colleague. This is when I was inspired to develop my own method of sending LOVE and focusing on loving the good in someone. It worked! It changed my entire attitude about him and consequently, his attitude about me changed as well. And we became good friends. And I have never ever hated anyone again.

Swami says that a bad thought hurts both the sender and his target. Regarding anger and hatred, Swami says:

"As long as man is filled with anger, he can have no peace. To secure peace and happiness man has to subdue anger. An angry man may become the enemy of mankind. A man filled with anger will not be able to achieve anything. He will commit many sins and will be an object of derision. He will forfeit all prosperity and lose the respect of all persons. Anger is the cause of total ruin. The first requisite for a person embarking on spiritual development is control of anger." SS May 1996 P 126

"Do not hate anyone. If you hate others, how can you expect them to love you? This is not possible. When you want everyone to love you, then you should love everyone. This is what is said in the scriptures, 'What you think, you become.' Our thoughts and actions are responsible for our good and bad." SSN Spring 1995 P 5

Syd and I have been to only one movie since we met over fourteen years ago when his daughter talked us into joining her. After a few minutes in the theater, I began to feel the vibrations of those around us as they took in the events on the screen. It felt almost like we were participating in the events. This was not a really violent movie, but it created emotions inside me that really disturbed my equanimity.

Just imagine what happens to your thoughts when you are watching a violent show on television. It is even worse when a mass of people are watching it, like in a movie theater, because now you have violence en mass being created with those thoughts, and those thoughts are creating the future. So, it is extremely wise not to observe anything violent. I have become so sensitive to violence that I can not tolerate even the slightest thought or hint of a violent act, let alone watch it on television. It actually creates a pain in my solar plexus and weakens my whole spiritual and physical being.

"The Lord can never design violence and blood-shed. Love is His instrument; non-violence is his Message. He achieves the correction of the evil-minded through education and example." BTBOS P 305

"Buddha taught that Truth, Right conduct and non-violence constituted the most sacred qualities. You consider Ahimsa (non-violence) as merely not hurting others. This is not the whole truth. Speaking too much, working too much, harping on the mistakes of others are all acts of violence (Himsa) and should be avoided. These result in the wasting of energy, which causes harm to oneself. You must observe restraints in eating, talking, sleeping, working, and all actions in daily life." SS July 1995 P 190

When I returned home from India I was the bearer of what Swami had asked of His devotees in His Birthday Discourse:

"Today, let it be anyone, whether one deems himself a devotee or not, he should give up meat eating. Why? Meat eating promotes only animal qualities. It has been well said that the food one consumes determines one's thoughts. By eating the flesh of various animals, the qualities of these animals are imbibed. How sinful is it to feed on animals, which are sustained by the same five elements as human beings! This leads to demonic tendencies, besides committing the sin of inflicting cruelty on animals. Hence, those who genuinely seek to become devotees of God have to give up non-vegetarian food. Calling themselves Sai devotees or devotees of Rama and Krishna, they fatten on chickens. How can they be deemed Sai devotees? How can God accept such a person as a devotee? Therefore, whether they are devotees in India or outside, they should give up from this instant meat eating.

"Next, there is the question of drink. The water that one drinks is life giving. It issues from the head of Siva. It is sacred. Instead of such wholesome drink, it is wrong to drink intoxicants. It makes a man forget his true nature. Alcoholic drink is utterly obnoxious. It degrades the addict. It makes him forget God. The drink addict is not conscious of what he says or does. The very sight of such a person is revolting. The drink evil has ruined innumerable families. Alcoholics have caused misery to their wives and children by wasting all their money on liquor. Of what use to the world are such derelicts?

"In addition to liquor, many are addicted to smoking tobacco. Today cigarette smoking is the cause of many diseases like asthma, lung cancer, eosinophilia and heart ailments. The evil effects of smoking can be easily demonstrated. If a whiff of cigarette smoke is blown at a handkerchief, the cloth turns red at the spot. If smoke can cause such damage to a piece of cloth, how much damage will it not do when it gets into the blood stream? It ruins one's health and shortens one's life-span. Therefore, those who aspire to become true devotees of God have to give up meat, liquor and smoking." SS December 1994 P 315

We had already given up meat eating in 1987, and I had quit smoking cigarettes on January 29th of that year also. And, we had been celibate for some time, so there was nothing left to give up but our occasional glass of wine with dinner. Syd balked at first, because he really enjoyed the wine, not for the alcohol effects, but for the taste. His complaint was that there was nothing left to give up, and he wasn't ready to become a saint yet. But he quietly acquiesced because the directive came from Swami.

When we lived in California, we used to entertain occasionally, and our liquor cabinet was full of nearly every type of alcoholic beverage you could find, which we never touched. It was still all packed in the same box that we moved it to Colorado in when we gave it away many years later. The only alcohol we ever touched was an occasional glass of fine wine at dinner. There was never any temptation to drink any of the hard liquor, and we have never had the type of people in our Colorado home who would want to drink it. It is not because we are snobs; it is because we want to retain the sanctity of our home, the whole of which is our Temple for Swami.

Several years after Swami's 1994 announcement regarding devotees giving up alcohol, meat and tobacco, we were flying home from India and seated nearby was one of the Sai Organization officials. We were very surprised to see this person order and drink a glass of wine. For a brief moment, I thought childishly, *If a Sai Organization official can drink wine, then why can't we?*

Swami says that alcohol drives the Spirit right out of the body. This makes sense because people do terrible things they would not otherwise do when sober. My first husband used to get drunk and do some pretty awful things like beat me up or rape me. He would never do something like that if he was sober because Spirit was in his body. Afterward, he would simply blame his actions on the alcohol, or say that he was drunk and didn't know what he was doing and therefore it wasn't his fault, in his view, (because Spirit wasn't in his body). Sometimes he would black out and have no recall of the brutal things he did when drunk. Swami didn't say so, but I am certain that street drugs do the very same thing. And I wouldn't be surprised if many of the pharmaceuticals do the same thing, like sleeping pills, valium, painkillers and anything else that is 'mind-altering', like the prescription drugs my son Mark takes.

Our Center Problems

When I returned from India, I learned that not a single Sai Baba Center meeting had taken place during my two month absence and the Center had virtually fallen apart. We had been having the meetings in Vincent's apartment in town because the roads to our home were sometimes difficult to travel in inclement weather. Vincent had been appointed the Center's Vice President, and was in charge of things in my absence.

The fact that Vincent had nude art work, (sketches and watercolors), in his apartment living room where we met used to bother me, because they did not fit in with Swami and our Center meetings. I told him my feelings, but he insisted they were expensive paintings he had purchased in Paris and saw no reason to take them down. When he explained it that way, it made me feel like a prude. What really bothered me was a statue he had of two pigs in a coital position, and I always tried to get to the meetings early so I could hide it before everyone else arrived. Vincent came from the San Francisco gay culture where things like that were part of the natural lifestyle. I say this because I was in a few of his friends' homes in San Francisco and witnessed it first hand. Sometimes when I would arrive early, I could feel what had obviously gone on in Vincent's apartment that day, and often wondered if anyone else felt it too.

When Vincent returned from India in 1992, he told me that he was so taken with Swami that he was going to change his lifestyle and become celibate, so he could focus on growing spiritually. Vincent was raised a Catholic, but had been a practicing Buddhist for years. After moving to Trinidad, he really attempted to change, but eventually resumed his previous lifestyle of partying and had taken several lovers. I knew he loved Swami too and I tried very hard not to be judgmental. But, I became angry with him when I found he had not conducted any Center meetings in our absence. I knew he had been ill and in the hospital for a few days, but he had also done a lot of partying before and after the illness.

I dreamed of Vincent when he was so ill:

"Dreamed of Vincent and his having AIDS and how I went inside his body to see if there was anything that could be done to fix him. I checked his bloodstream, his tummy, etc. When I came out, feeling hopeless, I knew the only thing that would help was if he could completely surrender, and only Baba could help him with that. So I prayed to Baba to help him with that before I awoke."

Nino had returned to California, so we had lost one member there. There were several older gentlemen who had been attending our Center meetings before I left on this recent trip to India, but I was told that they had resigned from the Center as well. Syd and I went to visit one of them to find out what had caused him to leave the Center. He was a former Methodist minister and frankly told us that he was not a dummy and had figured out that Vincent was a homosexual. He had read that Swami said to be very careful who you spend time with because you will become like them, and he told me he never wanted to become like Vincent.

"Like-minded people attract like-minded friends; a drunkard befriends a drunkard; a thief befriends a thief; a musician befriends a musician; a doctor befriends a doctor; and a lawyer befriends a lawyer. The noble minded people befriend only the noble minded ones. Even our noble thoughts undergo an evil change in the company of evil people. Even the creation can be changed by thoughts.....The thoughts are full of might and danger. Thoughts are not only capsules of danger, but they are capsules of immortality and nectarine sweetness as well." SSIB 1993 P 37

I told this old gentleman we would now be holding the meetings in our home, and he acquiesced to come to one meeting and see how things went. During the meeting, Vincent was seen running his hand up and down his lover's ankle and leg during the study circle. That did it for the old man. He never returned. He joined a church in town and told us he could worship Swami there just as well. After that meeting, I told Vincent that if he ever did that again, he would have to sit on the ladies side of the room during the meeting. I truly loved Vincent and saw him as a dear friend, and tried to be candid with him about the Center meetings. He seemed to take what I said personally, because he felt I was attacking the way he lived.

The other older gentleman, who was a member of the Theosophical Society, just never returned to any meetings, and would not discuss his reasons for leaving the Center. But I knew they were the same as the other man's. Another man, who was a follower of Elizabeth Claire Prophet, did not return to our meetings once they were held out here in our home, possibly because of the long drive. He never really was that interested in Swami, but loved to debate Swami's teachings, comparing them with the Bible and other teachings. He did provoke a lot of interesting study group sessions, and we missed his presence.

So now we were down to four members, Syd and I, Ruth and Vincent, and our meetings were sporadic, depending upon the weather or when either Ruth or Vincent could come to them. Syd and I continued doing our bhajans every night, substituting them for the Center meeting when nobody showed up.

I had gotten into the habit of talking to Swami a lot since my return from India, and asked Him for advice and help on even the smallest of things. One morning I asked Swami if I should advertise our Center meetings in the local newspaper again to see if any more people were interested. There were new people moving to this area all the time, mostly from California and Texas, and I thought some may have heard of Baba and be interested in attending our Center. Immediately after I asked, I heard Swami say: **"No! I will send you devotees!"**

"After the harvest when the sheaves of grains are winnowed, the wind blows away all the chaff, leaving only the grains behind. Through this process, the true devotees will remain steadfast. The wavering puppets will drift away. This is the process of winnowing." SS December 1993 P 333

Vincent's health began to decline at a rapid pace. His former lover in California, Jon, was dying of AIDS and this really bothered Vincent. Jon was Ruth's friend, and she met Vincent through Jon, and we met both of them as a result of our friendship with Ruth.

Vincent told us that just he and Jon were the only ones still alive from the group of 30 or 40 gays that he had been very close to in San Francisco. He said he felt guilty that he was still alive. Jon came to Colorado to visit Vincent after he moved here. Vincent hoped that Jon would also fall in love with the area and move here too, and spend the rest of his time on earth with Vincent.

Jon attended several of our Center meetings and Syd and I gave him some of the vibhuti Swami had given us, and some books to read. He suddenly developed pneumocystis and had to be taken to Kaiser Hospital in Denver, because he was suffering so badly and needed more care than our little community hospital could provide. He later told us that one night while in the hospital, he was in desperate pain and called out to Sai Baba to help him. Sai Baba instantly appeared and rocked him to sleep in His arms, like a baby. I cried when I heard that. Our Beloved Baba is so compassionate.

Jon's health improved enough for him to return to California. But he soon became very ill again and needed a full time attendant. Toward the end, he refused to take any more medication, and spent a lot of time semicomatose. During one of his lucid moments, Ruth got to talk to him on the telephone. She asked if he remembered who Sai Baba was, and Jon told her, "Yes, He talks to me all the time!" A month or so later, just moments before Jon left his body, he sat up and said, "It's true. We are all one!". It seems that Jon was working on his spiritual growth even through the comatose state, right up to the very last breath.

I used to be a supporter of euthanasia, but after hearing about Jon's experience, I have changed my opinion. Sometimes it is when one is suffering one's worst, that one will finally turn to God. And if one is still working on one's spiritual growth while in a comatose state, then what better argument is there in favor of sticking it out to the very end, especially if one's thoughts are turned towards God?

"The fate of man after death is molded by the thought that predominates at the moment of death. That thought is the foundation on which the next birth is built. Whoever at that time remembers Me attains My Glory, reaches Me in fact. So each Action of man, every striving of his, every spiritual discipline, should be aimed at sanctifying that fateful moment; the years of life must be devoted to the discipline that will bring up at that moment the thought of the Overself or Om." BTBOS P 15

After Jon's death, Vincent decided he wanted to fit in as much 'fun' as he could before it was his turn. So he did a lot of traveling around the world. On one trip, he went with a number of his new gay friends to Spain. He became very ill while there, and his lover had to nurse him the whole time. Vincent was extremely debilitated when he returned. At one Center meeting, he shared with us that there was nothing to eat for a vegetarian in Spain, and maybe it was the meat that he was forced to eat that had made him so ill and brought on AIDS with a vengeance.

Vincent eventually left this plane of existence six days after his birthday in August 1996. He left the bulk of his estate to his lover, and he also left his share of the equity in the little renovated adobe house he died in to Ruth for her help in taking care of him until the end.

I came upon the following quote regarding what Swami has said to some long time devotees about the purpose of Sai Baba Centers:

"We left Puttaparthi with mixed feelings. The first and most dominant one was sadness at leaving the physical presence of our Beloved Swami. The second one was a feeling of relief to get away from all of the mixed-up vibrations of the people, actually the multitudes. It reminded me again of what Swami had told us long ago when I asked Him about the 'Circus', the Sai Baba Centers, and such. He told us then, in no uncertain terms, to stay away. This was right in the beginning when we, in the West, first started to put together the Council of the Americas.

"About Centers, He said this, 'Swami has no need of Centers, they are good for some new people for satsang. This......,'He pointed at my heart, '...is Swami's real Center." Ten Steps to Kesava, by Lightstorm, p 179-180

Syd's Birthday Trip

It was an absolutely beautiful day on Syd's 65th birthday, April 21, 1995. It must have been 75 degrees and the skies were clear, just as they had been for days. Weather reports showed more of the same. So we decided to drive down to Santa Fe, New Mexico and have dinner with a friend. It was a long beautiful drive down the Interstate, which normally takes us about three and one half hours.

Syd's friend Rocky, from Texas, had brought a friend of his to visit us recently. They stayed the weekend, and his friend had invited us to come visit him in Santa Fe when we could, and he would fix dinner for us. He owned a restaurant, and we assumed we would have dinner with him there. When we called and told him we were coming to Santa Fe, he asked us to call him when we got into town. So we did, and we were surprised when he gave us directions to his home.

His home was full of ancient artifacts from India and Nepal, from large statutes of Ganesh to small poorbas from Nepal, and he proudly showed them all off to us. He served us a wonderful vegetarian meal in elegant style, starting with a grapefruit and artichoke salad, herbed bread, and a potato and eggplant curry over rice. Dessert was strawberry and custard tarts, which he made without eggs especially for us.

One of the reasons we called him was because he had expressed an interest in Sai Baba, and so we talked mostly about Swami during our visit. We became so engrossed in Swami that we didn't notice it was dark outside until it was already 9 p.m. After sharing some vibhuti with him, we quickly got in the car and started the long drive home, figuring we would arrive around 1 a.m., which was very late for us. Our normal bedtime is usually closer to 9:30 p.m..

It started to rain as we drove out of Santa Fe, and within ten minutes it turned to snow as we headed North into the mountains. A few minutes more and it turned into a full fledged blizzard, but we kept on going because there was no where to stop and no way to turn around. I was at the wheel, and soon began to realize that we were in serious trouble, because I could see nothing in front of the hood of the car. It was a total whiteout! My headlights reflected glare from the thick snow back to me and we did not have fog lights. Syd sat very intensely next to me, probably silently praying to Swami.

The white and yellow lines on the pavement had already disappeared and I was virtually driving blind. I called out to Swami to please be with us, and started chanting the Gayatri Mantra. Then I just surrendered it to Swami, and could feel Him driving the car through me. We could not see any road signs that would give us a clue as to where we were. We could only guess how far we had gone or where we were, based on the mileage shown on the dashboard.

I chanted the Gayatri Mantra while I sat behind the wheel for over three hours until I was so dry and so hoarse that I could not continue. Then Syd took over and began chanting. About every half hour or so a large truck and trailer would pass us throwing up wet snow from the pavement. The truck drivers could see the lines on the pavement because of their fog lights, so they knew where they were going. Forgetting that Swami was driving, I would try to follow in the tracks of these big trucks, but the snow and slush they threw up on the car placed a big demand on the windshield wipers. Their tire tracks filled up very quickly. I eventually would fall back, unable to keep their pace. Then Swami would resume driving through me. It seemed much easier driving in their large tracks as long as I could, because the snow was really beginning to pile up on the highway.

Eventually, I am certain even the trucks could not see the white lines because we saw no more pass us. Some of the drifts we encountered were as high as the hood of our big Mercury Station Wagon. There was no sign of snow plows in any direction and all we could do was push on with Swami's Grace. We didn't dare stop the car and park it because we could not tell where the road or shoulder was, and one of those speeding trucks might run into us before we could get out of their way. And, we could sit there and freeze to death before someone might find us if we went off the road.

There was another drama going on here - learning to trust that Swami was taking care of us, versus my 'trying' to take over and follow in the tracks of these large trucks. When I relaxed and let Swami drive through me, things went very well. On the contrary, when I took over, I became extremely tense and worried about not being able to see anything but snow and more snow.

This maddening drive went on for **five hours** before we finally reached a place where the snowfall became lighter, and we could see the road signs for the first time. We were actually nearing the Raton Pass, on the border of New Mexico and Colorado which meant we were nearly home. We had made good time - far better than we expected. I don't remember driving that fast, but then I never looked at the speedometer. I hadn't wanted to take my eyes off the road, if Swami was using them to see with. Thank You Swami! By the time we reached home, with Syd still chanting the Gayatri Mantra, we could see that it had only been snowing for a short while, as there were only a few inches on the roads.

Swami's Robe

Shortly after I returned home from India with Swami's Robe, we went shopping for a throne to place it on. The first furniture store we stopped in up in Colorado Springs had what was probably the most perfect throne for the robe, and it was absolutely beautiful, but the price was really up there. They even called it the "Throne". We looked in every new and used furniture store in that town, but found nothing close to being comparable to the first one. Syd and I talked it over and agreed that this was Swami we were buying it for, and He certainly was worth it, and the money was His anyway. So we returned to the first store and purchased this magnificent oversized, hand carved birch throne, which is about four and one half feet tall. The large seat cushion and a portion of the back are upholstered in white linen, and on the top of the back there is a hand carved fleur de lis with the hand-carved rays of the sun radiating out from it. The throne with His robe on it now sits in the corner next to our altar, and every time I walk into that area of the house, I am amazed to discover His presence there. It is like I feel someone there and turn and it is Swami in His robe on the throne. For a split second each time, I 'see' Him there with my 'Inner Eye', and it is always a surprise.

When we do bhajans every night, we sit in front of the throne and the altar, and one of our dogs, Maggie, often joins us, residing right near Swami's throne on my folded yoga mat. She often sleeps there at night too, right at Baba's Lotus Feet. There are many occasions during which she has watched Swami while we sing, and she has gotten up and sniffed where His feet would be. Sometimes she will raise up and sniff the air while watching Swami with great interest. We have seen her laying her ears back and her head down as she was obviously being petted on the head by Swami. Such a lucky girl! She joins in the vibhuti ceremony and patiently lets us apply the vibhuti to her head and body, and in her mouth.

We have often been asked by friends and visitors why we let Maggie stay in the house, while none of the other dogs get to come in. Well, we used to let them all in, but when the fourth dog, Rama, arrived on the scene, both he and Nik would lift their legs on everything in sight. They were evicted forever. Angie pesters everyone to death and won't give any quarter so long as she is indoors. Her fur is very long and thick and she would leave part of the outdoors (leaves, twigs, dirt, dust, etc.), behind each visit. Maggie is a perfect, gentle animal who never wants to do anything that would ever upset anyone. She just caves in when we correct her about something, and never repeats it. We only have to tell her 'no' once when she is inside with us, while the others just don't pay any attention to us. And they don't seem to mind that Maggie is our 'house dog', although she does spend most of the time outdoors during the day with them.

Rama is Nik's dog, or so Nik thinks. Nik brought him home one day from one of his travels. One morning several Winters ago, we caught a glimpse of a black puppy near the house. Obviously some heartless human had dumped it out here in the woods in the middle of the Winter. It was in dreadful shape and would not let us come near it.

We immediately put food out for it, but Nik would eat the food, to keep it from eating. So we hid the food down by the garden and kept Nik away from it, and later found the puppy had eaten it.

Gradually, the puppy would let us get closer and closer to it, until one day he let us touch him. We could tell he had been abused before he was dumped as he was very cautious about humans. Since day one, Nik has used this puppy, now named Rama, to exert his authority over. They have had some mean battles, and Nik has not always won them. But he does prevail as the Alpha dog and never lets Rama forget it for a minute. Sometimes he won't let Rama eat or get near the drinking water, or even near the house. It all depends on Nik's moods. He used to treat Maggie like this, but she never rebelled because Nik is her Dad, and she would just go hungry or thirsty. She became our house dog when we started feeding her inside. We can only accept all of this as their karma, and let them work it out as best as they can.

"Animals did not come for the purpose of supplying food to human beings. They came to work out their own life in the world." CWSSB P 19

We tried giving Rama away once and dropped him off at his new home on our way to catch a plane to India. He ran away from that home and found his way back here in the dead of Winter. How he managed to survive the six weeks of blizzards and freezing weather while we were gone only Swami knows. Syd thinks of Rama as Swami's dog because of that.

My dear friend Olga, called me not long after they returned from India, and shared a story of what happened with the robe Swami had given her. When she returned home, she learned that her grandmother who was very dear to her was dying. When Olga went to visit her, she felt guided to take Swami's robe along. Her grandmother was a long time Catholic, and not a devotee of Swami. However, she knew about Sai Baba because Olga had shared the stories of her trips to India over the past ten years. When Olga arrived, she stretched the robe out over her grandmother's form while she was sleeping then sat down beside her. Her Grandmother awakened and they chatted intermittently between her lapses of consciousness. Some time later, her grandmother suddenly sat up and said, "Sai Baba, You are here!", and then fell back on the bed and left her body.

Before Swami gives His robes away, the gold buttons are removed by His tailor, and presumably sewn into one of Swami's newer garments. Thus, the robe He had given me was sans buttons. Whenever we made a shopping trip up North to Colorado Springs, I would search every store we went into for the same type buttons. Finally during my travels, I found some brass buttons in a large fabric chain store that looked just like the ones on Swami's robes.

It was months later when Syd mentioned that I still had not sewn the buttons on Swami's robe and I promised I would do it soon. My grandson Ian had just returned home to Hawaii after spending his second Summer with us and I really wanted to get back to working on the book of Swami's teachings that I had to keep setting aside. I had so much to do and so little time to get it done before I was to leave for the Sai Baba Retreat in Jemez Springs in a few days. Syd had just flown off on another business trip and I was feeling very depressed. I was also stressed out because my workload doubles when Syd travels. But I had made a promise and was determined to keep it.

"A truly wise person is he who does not go back upon his promise. A real worshiper of God is the one who keeps up the word that he has uttered." DD 1987 P 137

I was frustrated and in tears after wasting hours hunting around looking for the brass buttons I had purchased. When I finally remembered to ask Swami to help me, I found the buttons almost immediately, and sat down to stitch them on the robe.

"Every rise will be followed by a fall. Elation will be followed by depression. You cannot avoid such antithesis in life. Affection that follows attachment leads to pain that follows separation. Affection and pain are two things between which man is being tossed about. In order to escape from the tossing between affection and pain, the only way is to believe in and surrender to God." SSIB 1972 P 123

The tears started to flow again as I sat there holding His blessed robe in my lap. I soon began to feel better as I stitched away, and by the time the buttons were intact, I was in a state of Bliss. The energies from His robe had completely renewed me, and I was able to tackle and complete all the jobs I had assigned myself on my impossible list of 'Things to Do'.

On another occasion, I became very ill with some kind of virus, and was praying to Swami to please help me to get well because I had so much to do and no time to be sick. I heard Him say, **"Lay down and place My robe over your body"**. So I unfolded my yoga mat and stretched out on it fully clothed, doing as Swami told me with His robe going from my neck to my ankles. I must have fallen asleep for awhile, but when I awoke, the fever had broken and this body had returned to a healthy condition. The fever and aches and pains were no longer present. Thank You Swami!

Ian's Second Visit - 1995

Our grandson Ian arrived after school was let out for Summer vacation from his home in Hawaii. This would be his second visit with us since we all moved away from Southern California, in 1990 and 1991. Ian and his mother and siblings moved back to Hawaii, and we moved to Southern Colorado. Ian turned 14 on April 10th, and had grown about a foot since his first visit to Colorado in 1992.

Ian is such a joy to have around us, and is always so helpful. At every opportunity, he asks, "Is there something I can help you with?" There is so much to be done around here, from weeding in our large organic vegetable garden to working on building our home. This year he and Syd will stain part of the exterior of the house.

I had promised Ian that we would take a driving trip of some kind so he could see more of America. When his mother was a child, I took my children on driving trips nearly every summer around the country. We managed to visit every one of the 48 states in the

Mainland by the time they were adults.

Once I made the decision to travel around, a variety of events opened up to give us things to do and places to visit on our trip. An invitation arrived from California inviting us to share in the joy of my nephew's wedding reception in July. He had joined the Mormon Church when he was younger and had just married a lovely young girl from a strong Mormon family in Idaho. Since their wedding took place in the big temple in Salt Lake City, we couldn't attend the ceremony itself because we are not Mormons. The strange thing I learned about this, was that his own Mother, my sister, was not permitted to attend their wedding because she was not Mormon either. Nor could his father. Oh, well.....

There was also scheduled a Sai Organization regional meeting in Scottsdale, Arizona, just a week before the reception. And Syd told me he had to be in San Francisco for a meeting just a day before the event in Sacramento. It was like Swami was setting up all these opportunities for us to take advantage of during our two week trip. We decided that Ian and I would drive to Sacramento, via Scottsdale and visit friends along the way. Syd would fly to San Francisco for his meeting, then fly to Sacramento where he would join up with us. Then we would all drive home, visiting more family and friends along the way.

As Ian and I were packing for the trip, we could not find the video camcorder. Syd and Ian had looked everywhere there was to look around the house for two days. In the midst of cooking dinner, I sat down at the kitchen table, and in front of Ian, I said, "Okay Swami, we are unable to find the camcorder. If it is no longer here, then we understand that somebody else must have needed it more than us, and I accept that as Your Will and I surrender it up to You. But if it is here, and if we are supposed to take in on our trip with us, then please help me to know where it is."

A few moments later, I received a vision of the camcorder in the little brown cabinet in the library. So I told Ian and Syd that Baba showed me where it was. Ian said, "Grandma, I just looked in that cabinet this morning. It's not in there."

Syd called out from another room that he had already looked in that cabinet twice, and hinted that I must have misunderstood the message from Swami. I said, "Look again!", and they both did. Of course it was there, Swami is never wrong.

This had a profound effect on Ian, because the same sort of incident had already happened two other times during this visit with us. In one of them, I was teaching Ian how to make a quilt. Ian is a very creative young man and had begged me to teach him how to construct a quilt. Quilting is really more of an artistic-engineering feat than a feminine hobby and many men make quilts too. One of the tools needed for this process had simply disappeared. Both Ian and I looked in every possible place for this small tool, but it was nowhere to be found. He watched as I closed my eyes and surrendered it up to Swami and then asked Him to help me find the tool. I immediately had a vision of it in the drawer under my sewing machine which is where it normally would have been stored. And because of that, we had both looked in that drawer, over and over and over again during our search.

Of course, when I opened the drawer, there it sat. Ian's eyes got very large, as he realized what had just happened, because we had taken that drawer literally apart before and it was not to be found. With this third confirmation of Swami helping out, Ian was really impressed. I had the feeling that Baba was arranging these little scenarios for Ian's benefit.

I took Ian shopping with me one time, years before when we all still lived in California,. When we drove into the large parking lot of a discount store, I found a parking place right up front, as usually is the case for me. I said, "Thank You Baba!".

Ian was about eight years old then, and he said, "Grandma you always thank Baba for everything. He didn't give you that parking place, it was just there.". I am sure his mother had something to do with him saying this to me.

"Yes He did, Ian - Baba is God and He takes care of all our needs for us.". Ian was not impressed then, but I feel certain that these recent experiences have had a major impact on his belief system.

Ian would join us, voluntarily, every night for our bhajan session. He sang along with us, and participated in all our Sai Center meetings as well. He had also gone with us to the Trinidad Sai Center meetings during his previous visit in 1992. I was really hoping that he would become attached to Swami in some way, or absorb His teachings because with the life Ian had at home, he needed all the help he could get. I have always tried to counsel him from a distance, and he has called me nearly every week since he moved back to Hawaii in 1991. We acquired a toll free number so he and his brother Sean could call us from anywhere, at anytime. His brother Sean was not prone to a close relationship with me, no matter what I did or how much I tried to reach out to him. He preferred to be jealous of Ian's relationship with me. I did not know how to deal with that, so I just continued to love and encourage and counsel him, as I did Ian.

Ian and I set out bright and early one morning on our adventure. The last thing Syd said to Ian was, "Make sure your grandmother stays awake!". This worried Ian so much that he refused to take a nap while I was driving. Instead, we talked and talked as I drove along. We first traveled South into New Mexico. Ian was greatly surprised to see lava surrounding the highway, as he thought it was only native to the islands. I pointed out to him that there are volcanoes everywhere in the world, and they had a large part to play in the construction of its geography.

We played a game that I used to play with my own children - make a list of every State's license plates that you see on the road until you have all 50 of them. There were so many cars on the road that Summer from everywhere, far and near that Ian got most of them before it was time to turn around and drive home. This helped him to learn the 50 states. After that, we started on the capitals of those states, using the Rand McNally maps we brought along. In short, he found that learning can be fun too. Up until that time, his grades had reflected his poor home life, but that all changed when he returned home this time.

But mostly, I talked about Swami and His teachings, which were still fresh in my mind from all the work I had been putting into the book. Ian asked questions on occasion, but usually he just listened with half an ear. We checked into the resort hotel in Scottsdale, where the regional meeting was to be held. I asked where the pool and hot tub were, because I knew Ian would enjoy them while I was busy with meetings and such. We made certain there was a pool for him to swim in at every hotel we checked into. It helped him to relax after our long days in the car. I was greatly surprised when Ian chose to go to the meetings and other events with me, instead of taking a swim. It pleased me to no end that he wanted to see what other people thought about his grandmother's Sai Baba. He was genuinely curious about our Lord.

During one of the gatherings, we were asked to share some recent stories of our experiences with Swami. I occasionally looked over to the men's side of the large room and watched as Ian listened intently to all the glory and wonder of the every day miracles of our Sai Baba, as many of the people recanted their tales. He participated in the bhajans also, as he sat alone toward the back of the room.

One session was devoted to the Sai Organization leadership answering questions that we had written on pieces of paper prior to the session. My question was: "What does Sathya Sai Baba say about eating eggs?" I was very disappointed in the answer that was given to my question. It was, "We think it is enough to ask the devotees in the USA to give up eating meat." I didn't ask them what they thought, I asked what Swami says, because I knew what the answer was, "Eggs give you doubts and confusion!", and I was hoping that everybody else would hear that answer, including those who were arranging the menus for the retreats in this Region. It was difficult for me to understand why these people did not follow Swami's teachings, unless it was out of ignorance. And I was hoping this was the opportunity to dispel that ignorance. My understanding was that if eggs gives one doubts, then how can one surrender and place their full faith and trust in Swami?

I have been told by others who eat eggs that Swami once told a devotee that she could eat eggs, so long as they were unfertilized. But nowhere have I read in all the books about Swami did He say in a discourse or otherwise that it was okay for everyone or anyone to eat eggs so long as they were unfertilized. I have also heard that He has said, "No eggs in My house!", and that is the reason no eggs are permitted on the Ashrams.

It really disturbed me that morning at a retreat put on by Baba devotees when I walked into the dining room and found there was nothing to eat but scrambled eggs and muffins with eggs in them. The retreat was held in a remote area where there was nowhere else to eat, and no other options.

In hindsight, I really used to get very upset about the eggs being served at Sai Baba events and retreats, when I really had little room to talk since I was not perfect either. I still have some bad habits too, that are probably affecting me just as much as eating the eggs affects the others. I have not yet given up watching the news and movies on television - nor have I given up reading the newspapers. Both of these habits keep me very much in the world, when I really should be focusing on going within. I know these habits are holding back my spiritual growth because they affect my dreams and thoughts, and at times make it impossible for me to get into a good space. So, I decided recently that I will no longer worry about what they serve at these functions, and will always make certain to pack something that I can eat.

When we left Sacramento, we drove down to Santa Barbara and spent a few days visiting with Niranjan and Madhu Patel. During this visit, Ian had an opportunity to see how other devotees of Sai Baba live. He joined us every night while we did bhajans in their home, and he heard many stories about Baba and His miracles. He also fell in love with Indian food and watched intently as Madhu prepared her wonderful dishes. Ian loves to cook, just as most Hawaiian men do.

Actually, Ian looks like he would fit in anywhere in India as though he were of that race, with his oriental eyes, skin and hair color.

Our trip went very well, except for one small incident. Ian and I had checked into a hotel in Sacramento just before we were to go pick Syd up at the Sacramento Airport across town. We just had time to bring in the luggage, freshen up and head for the airport. Ian's job throughout the trip was to load and unload the luggage in the car each day. We were very tired after such a long drive that day up through Central California. After we checked in, we both carried up the first load and I gave him the keys to the car to get the rest of our bags and ice chest, reminding him to make certain to put the keys in his pocket after he unlocked the door, so they did not get locked in the car. You guessed it - he locked the keys in the car! The look on his face when he returned to our room told me what had happened. He was extremely angry at himself, and threw himself down on his bed and cried.

At first I got caught up in his drama. Then I told him to just calm down and lets get quiet and then give this whole thing to Swami and see what He tells us to do. As we sat there, I remembered that we have AAA, so I got the card out of my wallet and called for help. They told me it would be several hours before they could get to me because of so many others calling for help that day. It was the fourth of July weekend and everybody was out on the roads. I began to panic then, because we needed to leave in less than an hour or we would be late meeting Syd's plane. Ian reminded me that I should sit quietly and ask Swami for help again.

Fifteen minutes later, the AAA tow truck driver called from the front desk. He was there to help us unlock the car. As he worked on the window, the driver shared with us that he was on his way to another AAA member in distress when he got the call to add us to his long list of people needing help. Something told him to stop and help us first, and he followed that inner guidance. Ian was impressed once again. Thank You Swami!!! Thank You for Your never ending Grace!!!

Vibrations

We were asked by the Sai Organization Regional Director early in the year 1995 if we were going to attend the 70th Birthday Celebration in Puttaparthi. The answer was an unequivocal "NO". After hearing of the crowds that arrive for Birthday, we had decided long ago that we never wanted to be in Puttaparthi during Birthday.

Crowds are very difficult for Syd and I. We live in a remote area, and rarely see another human being unless we drive into town on errands. When we do venture out, we try to return home within an hour. If we must make a day long trip to shop up in Colorado Springs, it usually takes both of us a day or two to recover from the static energies we have absorbed from the people we encounter. Whereas Syd has learned to block most of the energies he is surrounded with, I am like a sponge, and tend to become like those I associate with after a few minutes of absorbing their energies. I've had people tell me, "You are so much like me!". And it is true, I become like them after just a few minutes in their presence, and there are times I have seen some who have noticed a part of themselves in what I have become that they did not like and I feel their repulsion. We have had some old friends visit who we knew were not spiritual and other house guests who we thought were spiritual, but their vibrations suggested otherwise. When vibrations near me are difficult, it simply turns my life upside down. It is so challenging for me to focus on simple tasks like cooking when others are in our home. Thus, we rarely travel and have few house guests who are not strong devotees of Swami, unless it is absolutely necessary or we know it is Swami's Will.

Many people have suggested solutions for overcoming or rising above other people's vibrations, but none work for very long. I've tried putting a white light about myself and the people whose energies are difficult. I've put myself in a rubber ball, prayed for protection, and chanted the Gayatri Mantra. The Gayatri Mantra is about the only thing that really works, but it only works so long as I am focusing on and chanting it. When I am shopping in the grocery store, I must stop with the white light or the focusing and chanting in order to make a decision of which head of lettuce is best, or speak to the check out clerk.

Madhu Patel shared with me that she has had the same problem with other people's energies for a very long time. She recommended to me that we attempt to keep our time away from home at an hour or less, because it is after that when we are more subject to absorbing other people's vibrations.

"Though the body is mortal, the thoughts are immortal. The power of the thought vibrations run round the world. As the heat waves, the electrical waves and light waves radiate, the mental waves too radiate. The thought vibrations are the cause for man's joy and sorrow, health and disease, woe and weal, birth and death. Man's life becomes meaningful if he conducts himself fully aware of the power of the thought vibrations. The entire world is suffused with mental vibrations. In fact the whole world is the very manifestation of mental vibrations. Hence it is necessary to direct our thoughts on noble paths. Man's mind shines with resplendent purity if he cultivates noble thoughts, ideas and feelings. It is only in developing the purity of mind, we can ensure the purity of action. Only pure deeds can yield pure results." SSIB 1993 P 35

Even good people, including devotees of Sai Baba can have terrible vibrations, especially if they are ill, or have recently spent time reading books or watching movies with violence in them, or they have not been careful who they have associated with, or even by the food they ate in a restaurant. What we feed to any of our senses affects who and what we are. I know there have been times when I have not been fit to be around because my vibrations were affected by something or somebody.

"Nature has many mysteries in its makeup. Man is able to unravel only those that are cognizable through his five senses; he does not realize that there is a vast unknown beyond the purview of the five faulty instruments of perception that he has. For example, from every being and thing, constantly, without intermission, millions of minute particles and millions of vibrations are issuing forth. Certain substances like camphor emanate so much of these that a lump disappears in a few days. The bodies of others affect us by these emanations and we too affect them in the same way. For good or bad, we are interacting in this manner, inescapably. Naturally, the growth of the body is affected, as

well as its health and strength, by the contact or company we develop."
SSS VOL IX Chap 26 P 140

Preparing for 1995 India Trip

Never say you never want to do something, especially regarding Swami, because that is just like telling Him you have some lessons to learn by doing what you never wanted to do. Before we knew it, we were planning to go to Birthday. We had both been instructed by our Inner Voice that we were supposed to go. When we called to make reservations, we learned that the fare had been reduced down to $1,100 per round trip ticket. Amazing! We hadn't seen fares like that, especially on Delta Airlines, since our first trip to India together. We knew it had to be Swami's way of making it possible for more of His devotees to come. We already had our tickets when we learned that some flights had been chartered by devotees to go to India for the Birthday. One of our friends was on a chartered flight, and she said it was exhilarating to be singing bhajans nearly all the way to Bhagavan.

Since we agreed early in the year to make the trip, we had a long time to wait and prepare to leave. During this period, I had a number of dreams, several wherein we were granted an interview. There were also a number of dreams wherein I was being chased or threatened with harm, and in each of those dreams, I called out to Sai Baba for help and I was saved. Hopefully I was working out karma in those dreams.

In March I dreamed:
Swami granted our group an interview, and it was nearly the same group of people as the year before, with Gilly and Olga and one other. There were other small groups sitting in an outside area, like at the Ashram Post Office seating area. It was not the interview room where we went into before. When we finally got inside, Syd put his arm around Swami, on His shoulder, just like He was an old friend. I remember while waiting outside, I was thinking and plotting how I could move in a ladylike fashion and still get to sit at Swami's feet. Once we got inside, Baba sat on the floor in the middle of us, chatting with us like

we were His best friends, and everybody was close to Him, so it didn't matter where we sat.

In July, I dreamed:
We were traveling, and I went back to my hotel room and Ruth had moved in or left some of her things there - cosmetics, clothes, etc., even though she had her own room. She had also slept in the same bed with me the night before. Than Swami came into the room and laid down where she had slept, and put His head on the pillow she had used, but the pillowcase was missing. The pillow was black and gray striped ticking. Then all of Swami's close male devotees came in and were touching Him all over. I figured if they could do it, I could too, so I held His right foot, and then started to massage firmly up and down His leg. I had read that Shirdi Sai used to love having that done for Him. There was nothing illicit implied by my touch, but He pulled His leg away as if to tell me, "Don't do that", so I went back to holding His foot. When He first laid down, He said something, and I didn't hear it all, so He repeated it: "I made it rain everywhere today!" I finally left and went outside and it was raining to my left, but not on me. I encountered a lady who stopped in the rain to adjust her pantyhose. She was soaked. I was floating in the air above, untouched by the rain, still filled with bliss from holding Swami's feet.

In August, I dreamed:
I saw myself in the first row at Darshan. Swami came along and asked me, "How Many?" I said "Five, Swami!". He said "GO!" After the dream, I had the strongest feeling this will happen and I knew that it would be five people only. Even when my ego tried to be negative, and refused to believe we would get an interview, I knew it would be so. When I awoke, I knew I should not share this information about getting an interview on this trip with anyone because their egos could cancel it out."

In November, I dreamed:
Swami was busy eating and consuming our karma and digesting and eliminating it. That was how He was dealing with it, and I also knew in the dream that He started doing this about a month ago.

One morning, while sitting at my altar, I was polishing the two pound Sterling Silver statue of Swami sitting on His throne. This was given to us by the Patels during our last visit to their home. They told us that it had been blessed by Swami, and we felt very honored that they would give it to us. As I was lovingly moving the cloth over the statue, I suddenly realized I could smell Him. At first, I thought it was coming from the statue, but then found it coming from the flannel polishing cloth, which never had smelled of anything before, as it was non-chemical. I had performed this ritual hundreds of times, but it was the first time I could smell His wonderful, sweet aroma. It was the same scent that my hands smelled of right after He held them, and I knew He had once again fulfilled His promise that He would let me smell His wonderful aroma in the future.

I continued to work on the book of Swami's teachings nearly every day. Chastising myself for not asking Swami during our last trip whether He really told me to put this book together, I wrote a note to Him at my altar one morning asking if I really am supposed to put together a book for the students of His teachings, and to please give me a sign as to whether I should continue. I was still in doubt, for some strange reason. That afternoon, while I was reading, I came upon the following paragraph in "Life is a Dream, Realize It" (By Joy Thomas):

"Whatever talent a person has, should be dedicated to the service of the rest of humanity.....indeed, to all living beings. Therein lies fulfillment."

When I read the above, I remembered my note to Swami, and knew this was His answer to my inquiry. Well, I certainly was getting fulfillment, and nobody else had seen the manuscript yet, but me. I told only a very few people that I was even working on it, because Swami has said that when you share what is going on in your life with others, their thoughts, or opinions, or jealousy or sadness, etc., can affect the outcome of what you are doing.

Trip to India 1995

Puttaparthi, November 12, 1995

    We arrived in Puttaparthi by plane and Syd went to get accommodations for us while I stayed with the luggage. When he returned he told me he was unable to get an apartment for us, and we were assigned to Shed 11. We had so wanted to be able to stay inside the Ashram for the Birthday celebrations, and thus we quickly agreed that we would stay in the assigned shed and continue attempts to get an apartment.

    At the doorway to Shed 11, we could smell the toilet facilities at the other end of the building as we entered. The shed was empty, except for one English speaking couple sitting on the floor inside. They were surrounded by their belongings and two large pails of water. Everywhere I looked I saw dirt and rubbish laying around on the floor. This couple told us that if we planned to stay we should first go get some buckets for water, because this shed had no water, and when they checked with Maintenance, they learned there was no hope of getting any water. They told us we could haul water from two sheds down the way because the shed next door had no water either. My thoughts turned to visions of how we would be able to flush the toilets or take a shower.

    I went back to the toilet area and my worst fear was realized - they were of the Eastern type, just holes in the floor, and with the condition my legs are in, I would never be able to use them. Besides, there was an accumulation of filth and body waste all around the holes. This was a health hazard to be sure, because if you can smell it, it means there are airborne particles of the same matter you are smelling, which of course was full of germs. These airborne particulates are taken into your system via your nose and mouth. It was just too much for this Virgo. I knew there was no way we could stay there under those conditions. We had purposely arrived well in advance of the Birthday celebrations with the hope that we would get decent accommodations. We knew that it was all Swami's Will, and so we agreed that if Syd was able to find some other accommodations, than that too must be

Swami's Will.

Sai Towers was fully booked up, so Syd went to see if our friends the Patels were in their apartment, to find out if they had any suggestions or knew of anybody who could help us find decent accommodations. Several hours later, Syd returned to Shed 11 with a car and driver, who took us back outside the Ashram and several miles down the Main Road to an unfinished large condominium type building. Inside was a lovely two bedroom apartment, complete with a primitive kitchen, (a long counter with a sink in it and a bucket under the drain hole), and one full bath with a Western toilet, shower and basin. The only drawback was that we had to take a three-wheeler taxi back and forth to Darshan twice a day, but it was worth it for the sake of cleanliness.

Back at the Ashram, we registered as USA Delegates representing our Trinidad, Colorado Sai Center. We had been told back home that Delegates would get special privileges throughout the celebration. We assumed that meant that we would also get decent accommodations.

From my Journal:
Puttaparthi, November 15, 1998
So many people are here, and multitudes more arriving each day. The Darshan area in front of the Mandir is full to overflowing and many people are unable to make it to the inside of the Mandir grounds. Several times I found myself in a line that did not get inside. Our Beloved Swami came outside and waved to us for a short while. He filled us with so much LOVE that I burst into tears and sobs of joy. On another occasion I was left outside, He came to the wall near where I was sitting after He gave Darshan and blew us all a big kiss - soooooo very sweet of Him. More tears of joy.

Everyday, Syd is busy trying every way he can to find us an apartment in the Ashram. They tell him that only donors can stay in the apartments. Syd tells them that we have been trying to become a donor for years, but have been turned away every time we try because,

"There is nothing available, and the waiting lists are full!". Later we learn that a friend of a friend just became a "donor" this year. We ask her how she managed that and she said a friend of hers in the Sai Organization called and asked if she wanted to become a donor. When we heard that, we gave up the donor idea, realizing that it must be Swami's Will for us not to become donors.

Before we made the trip this year, Syd and I had been talking about the possibility of selling our home in Colorado and moving to Puttaparthi where he could retire and afford to live comfortably on his Social Security income. What better place to spend the rest of our lives, than at the Lotus Feet? We learned the apartment we are staying in can be purchased for around $10,000 US, and have been giving it serious consideration.

Puttaparthi, November 17, 1995

This morning, Swami gave Darshan to the music of Kitaro, who is a Japanese composer and musician. I thought I passed Kitaro on the path yesterday as I walked to Darshan. It seemed such appropriate background music for God to be giving us His Darshan. Today, I am fortunate to sit even closer to the front and on the aisle in the Poornachandra. Swami is giving discourses nearly every day. He announced that November 19th will be the first annual observance of "Ladies Day", and that only the ladies would attend the ceremony. Then He came walking down the red carpet just inches from me while giving Darshan. He looked each one of us on the aisle in the eye and gave all of us the sweetest smile and blessing. I left the auditorium not long after that because I was so full of the Love and Bliss He gave us when He passed by that I wanted to preserve it and take it with me. I found Syd at the Ganesh Gate waiting for me. He must have seen me get up and leave the program early. We are moving again this afternoon!

After many trips and meetings where nobody showed up, Syd was finally able to obtain an apartment in one of the new North Buildings for us. He was told we must share with an Indian couple from the Midwest, who are about our age. They were very lovely people, a retired engineer and his wife of many years. They insisted on sleeping on their mattresses on the floor while Syd and I occupied the only two beds in the apartment. She cooked nearly every day using our pots and dishes, as well as theirs, and occasionally we would eat with them. Syd would do the dishes, using his little Indian 'Zero B' to purify every drop of water in both the soapy and rinse water. Syd is very particular about the cleanliness of the dishes and utensils used in cooking and eating. Having managed a large water purification company, he was also very aware of what bad water can do to one.

The meals our roommate cooked were absolutely delicious. I would have cooked too, and brought the pot, hotplate and equipment with which to do it, but I knew they preferred their Indian food and would not be happy with my attempts at Western cooking. Instead, I let her use my equipment and watched her and learned more about Eastern cooking. We went shopping together and she gave me many tips. And I don't even remember her name. If she ever reads this book, please know how much we appreciated and enjoyed sharing, and knowing and learning from you and your husband. And please know that Swami took your letter the first opportunity I had to give it to Him after you left.

There are many programs and activities going on each day now. During one of them, I was able to find a place on the aisle inside the Poornachandra where I could sit comfortably and watch the music program. We had been sitting for a collective total of nine hours that day with only a short break for lunch in between. The program is outstanding with the youth performing many ancient folk dances, and popular Indian musicians playing their unusual (to us) instruments, and vocalists chanting bhajans and singing songs from antiquity. Fortunately, I had a few things to snack on with me, so I could last throughout this program. Between two of the performances, I was able to stand up for a minute for a quick stretch, but was quickly told to sit down by a seva dal. Why they don't permit us to take a good healthy stretch is beyond me. But then seva dals can only tell you what you can't do, not what you can do, and I can imagine the chaos that would occur if 30,000 people all stood up at the same time.

All of the performers are dressed in bright colorful costumes. The folk dancers are fantastic. They seem to be dancing on clog-like shoes made of thick wood, and each step they make is part of the beautiful rhythm they are creating. It is almost like tap-dancing in clogs. Sometimes their dance is accompanied by musicians, mostly acoustics and sometimes strings. I have never seen anything like it. One set of folk dancers is on roller skates, doing a dance on skates which is very similar to the cloggers' dance. Absolutely superb!

We watched as Swami materialized a beautiful pendant on a chain for one of the musicians. I am told by my neighbor that he is a very famous person in India. His lilting music is transcendental in nature, and I feel hypnotized by it. I make a mental note to find a CD of this artist's work before I leave India. According to my neighbor, his name is Pandit Shivkumar Sharma, and the instrument he is playing is a stringed instrument called the Santoor, in which he uses two wooden mallets to strike the strings. His Santoor was designed by him after years of studying and playing this instrument. As a note: A year later I found a CD album from a live performance he gave the following month in Mumbai, and Shivkumar is wearing the medallion that Swami had materialized for him at Birthday in the photo of him on the cover.

Puttaparthi, November 18, 1995

Syd said he sat next to somebody in Darshan from a Mediterranean country that he had met several years before. His friend told him that he had just had an interview with Swami in October. Baba told this man and others during the interview the following things: (1) The USA current president is not an effective president, but our next president will be very effective; (2) Seventeen heads of state will be Baba's devotees; (3) Two thirds of the people of the world will know Baba; (4) The earth will turn upside down; (5) There is a lot of political turmoil all over the world, with the assassination attempts of the Egyptian Prime Minister, and Canadian Prime Minister and the assassination of the Israeli Prime Minister; (6) After four to five years, there will be no more interviews.

This afternoon, the 'Delegates', or Officers of Sai Organization

Centers were permitted to enter the Mandir grounds early and I was able to get a seat in the second row. As Swami gave Darshan, He looked into the eyes of every single person in the first row on the way in and the second row on His way back out. When He looked into my eyes, He asked, "When did you come?". I was stunned that He would speak to me, but the lady in front of me thought He was talking to her and answered, "Yesterday, Swami!". But as He walked on, He turned and looked back at me to let me know it was me that He had addressed. Olga, who was sitting near me confirmed that as we left Darshan. My heart thrilled at the thought He would speak to me, but my ego also doubted that I was worthy of His attention.

"A word spoken in love is balm to the tired feet. You come to Prashanthi Nilayam, by road, rail or bus; you walk into the garden, exhausted and eager. I ask from the verandah, O, when did you arrive? Others may doubt, why is Baba asking this question? 'Does He not know?' Surely, He must be knowing all about him and us. Why then this query? But, you, to whom this question is put, you are elated that 'Baba spoke to me as soon as I walked in!' I seek to give you joy and so, though I know, I ask such questions. If I do not ask, but you keep quiet, you feel forlorn and frustrated, don't you? You know that I am asking you, not for the sake of the answer which I am asking you, which I am already aware of, but, for the sake of the satisfaction my words give you. So also, I may ask, 'How are you?' though I know that you are well and that is why you could come or that you are unwell and that is the very reason that has brought you to me! This is the Mayasakthi, the spirit that charms; If it speaks, if it casts its eye, if it does something, you derive pleasure thereby! It is yogamaya, which makes you happy when I accost you or talk to you or do something to you"

Ladies' Day

Puttaparthi, November 19, 1995

Ladies' Day was one of the worst days of my life, in recent memory. I have struggled with whether I should include these painful parts of my growth process, because one rarely reads about such things happening to devotees once they come under Swami's care. Most books written by devotees are full of glory and happiness and promise. But there are lessons to be learned, and they are sometimes not pretty. In the midst of lessons such as these, I was there at the Lotus Feet getting all the help and guidance and Love I needed to get me through them. What was manifesting was my karma, and what better place to work it off? This time I also learned what Group Karma was all about. As I mentioned before, when you visit Puttaparthi, it seems like you are on a fast karma track, so you better fasten your seat belts and hang on for dear life when you get off that airplane.

I was up early as usual, at 1:30 a.m., and in line by 3 a.m. with a group of about 300 USA ladies who had assembled hoping to get into the Poornachandra Auditorium as a group. We had seen groups of ladies from other countries go through this procedure every day, and that is why we have gathered together as a group early this morning. We assumed this would get us special seating also. We marched together up to the Auditorium and waited until nearly daybreak when the lines start filing in. We (USA group) watched while ladies from all the other countries were called and taken in, country by country. These country groups were standing all around us, in front and behind. We could not understand why our USA group was being ignored, as we were very visible. Finally, the seva dals said the Auditorium was full and nobody else was permitted inside and they closed the doors behind them.

When the thousands of Indian villagers behind us heard this, they became very angry and started pushing in waves of force that kept cramming us into smaller and tighter spaces in front of them and up against the building. There was an eery noise coming from the villagers which sounded like a roaring machine or a swarm of bees magnified over a loud speaker each time they pushed at us. Finally there was no more room to give and we were knocked down and trampled over until there were dozens and dozens of bodies on top of us. I was on the bottom, face down against the concrete and started praying to Swami to please help us. The weight of all those bodies on top of me crushed me flat and I was unable to get any air into my lungs. There were ladies screaming and yelling for help all around me. Mentally I called out to Swami as I fought and struggled for air. Finally,

I felt myself drifting away as I began to lose consciousness. In an instant, like the wave of bodies that came over us, the wave receded and I could see daylight again. Swami heard my prayers.

Several of the villagers carefully pulled me off the ground and were comforting me as best they could. They were fanning me and gently moved me in behind a pillar where it would be safe if the mob took over again. By now I was shedding tears and still gasping to get air into my lungs. One older Indian lady put my head on her shoulder and comforted me like I was her child. Somebody found a bottle of water and gave me a drink. When I recovered enough, I pulled out a packet of vibhuti Swami had given me the previous year and shared it with all around me. I realized at some point that this was the first morning in memory that I had forgotten to put my protective vibhuti on. I vowed at that moment to never leave home or go anywhere without putting my vibhuti on ever again. Every time I ran into those dear villager ladies who comforted and cared for me, we would acknowledge each other with love and respect.

When the seva dals obtained some semblance of order outside, they opened the doors, (which normally form the length of the wall) on both sides of the auditorium, so that even those outside could see and hear (to a degree) the ceremony that was about to take place inside. When the bhajans began, the crowd shifted some and I was able to turn around and look inside the auditorium. I could not believe my eyes. I saw that the other half of the auditorium where the men would sit was now filling up with men, not ladies, as Swami had announced. Anger swelled up inside me as I reeled at the unfairness of it all. What had just happened with that mob scene would not have happened if they had followed what Swami had said about only women being permitted to attend on Ladies Day. Swami, why aren't You doing anything about this? I was shaking all over now, and wasn't sure if it was from anger or shock. It was more like shivers, but it was too hot for me to be cold.

Knowing there was no way I could continue standing up in this crowd throughout the ceremony, I very slowly threaded and limped my way back through the scores of ladies and returned to our apartment. Syd and the Indian gentleman were having a cup of coffee and sharing Baba stories. I was still in a state of shock from nearly being crushed to death, and Syd held me while in a fit of sobs, I blurted out my story of what had just happened. My body was full of abrasians and bruises were forming from head to toe, and I ached everywhere. My punjabi was torn and filthy.

That afternoon, the USA ladies lined up once again and marched to the Auditorium. We watched as all the Oriental and European countries were taken in and then we were told it was full and to go away. When we didn't move, they brought in male seva dals waving large sticks at us to get rid of us. I got a look inside and once again there were men filing into the men's side of the Auditorium. "Some Ladies' Day, Swami", I thought.

For the first time ever, I became disappointed in my Swami. I could not believe that He would allow such a thing to happen! Doubts crept in and no matter what I tried, I could not shake that feeling of being let down. I had never before doubted His Will. I felt I had been betrayed. At this point, all I wanted to do was sit down and cry out all those emotions that were building up and tearing me down inside. But that was also impossible for me because I did not feel comfortable letting go with the men still in the room. So I went on and on about how could Swami let this happen, and how disappointed in Him I was. Finally, it was bedtime, 8:30 p.m. and just before I fell asleep, I set the alarm for 1:30 a.m.

Puttaparthi, November 20, 1995
Sleep must have done me some good, because I had calmed down to where I was able to reassess the events of the previous day. It had to be my karma, and I realized I was blessed that it happened there where Swami could save me from a probable death. As for the men taking up the seats on the men's side, when we were told only ladies would attend, I recall that Swami has said that the only true Male is God, and all else are females.

"Your own bad thoughts and actions are the cause of your misery. As you sow, so shall you reap. The seed determines the fruit. When man cherishes bad thoughts, bad results haunt him. When he has good thoughts, the results are also good. Those who do not recognize this fact go about blaming God. They lament: 'Oh God! Why are you inflicting these miseries on me? Why are you denying me peace of mind?' God is the Eternal Witness. He is the dispenser of the fruits of actions. He gives you according to your deserts. He is in no way responsible for your grief or happiness." SS August 1995 P 198

There was one thing that stuck in my craw though, regarding events of the previous day. While standing in line at 3 a.m. with the other USA ladies, we were told that the reason the ladies from all those other countries were able to get inside the Auditorium was because the Sai Organization leaders of their countries obtained special passes for them for their entire visit at Puttaparthi.

The reason we were unable to get inside was because our USA Sai Organization Leaders had done nothing. Some of the ladies approached the Leaders and they were given a note to take to the Administrative Office so that we could get in on a special pass for "One Day Only". I can only say that there were a whole lot of very unhappy USA ladies, with many threatening to start another Sai Organization. We had been told that Swami said we needed more unity in the USA Sai Organization, but this only united us in anger at the Organization.

I don't always understand why things happen the way they do in Swami's drama, but I do understand that Swami often rubs two devotees together to get the friction needed to help us with our spiritual growth. We had certainly been given a lot of food for thought and plenty of opportunity for growth.

Several years later, I found the following that Jack Hislop had said to an audience while delivering a talk:

"The question is, so many people who long for liberation and give their attention and time to that end, have debilitating diseases or all sorts of problems. Sometimes people say, before I went to see Swami I was

O.K., but now I am having nothing but trouble.

"Swami told me that it was important, if you can, to go to India to have His direct Darshan. It is not necessary, but better, because if you have His Darshan, then something happens; something in your spiritual life speeds up. Things start to go faster and, likewise, karmic crises come faster, faster, faster.

"Swami says that the true devotee says, 'yes, yes, yes' to everything. Swami, Himself, says 'I say, yes, yes, yes to everything'. The devotee should say 'yes, yes, yes' to everything, regard everything as a gift from God–sickness, pain, disease, death. No matter what it is, it is for our best. It is like medicine from the doctor. Merely because a debilitating disease strikes us, it does not mean that Swami hates, or God hates us. He is prescribing the medicine." SD P 49-50

70th Birthday, November 23, 1995

Once again, a group of about 100 USA ladies met at 3 a.m. and marched single file all the way to the Hillview Stadium gate, which was already surrounded by thousands of people by the time we arrived. We tried to maintain a line and were successful for awhile until it seemed that a million ladies arrived out of nowhere, falling in and around and in front and behind us. Our group tried holding hands so that we wouldn't be separated, but we were being pulled and pushed from every direction. We stood there at the gate waiting for over two hours to enter, and the seva dals at the gate still would not let us go inside the Stadium grounds, although the men had been ushered in earlier.

At one point, a VIP arrived for her special seating, and the seva dals made the mistake of opening the gate to let her through, thinking they were going to be able to block the crowd from entering also. As soon as that gate opened, the crowd that had gathered around us turned into a mob, pushing, shouting, ramming. Somebody behind me started singing Ganesha bhajans, and we joined in to help remove the obstacles around us, as we were spun in circles and lifted off our feet while being pushed onward. When the mob worsened with its pushing and shouting, we chanted the Gayatri Mantra over and over. I kept trying to wipe the events of Ladies' Day out of my mind, and focus on

Swami being there to usher us in an orderly manner through the gate.

Eventually, the mob ruled out and we were pushed from behind through the gate and inside, still chanting the Gayatri Mantra. I struggled to keep my balance as I was lifted entirely off my feet and being carried along with the mob. I could feel them pushing all the while from behind. For awhile, my feet became entangled in someone's sari, and when my feet did finally touch down, there were shoes and slippers everywhere. We heard rumors later that many people were injured and that there were two women and a baby who had fallen underneath that mob and were trampled to death. I met one young lady from Australia later who had been at the bottom of the crowd for awhile. Her sari had been torn from her and she was trampled, but Swami somehow saved her from serious harm. Like me, she had bruises and abrasions only. Swami has said that if anyone is lucky enough to die at His Ashram, they will realize liberation. Thus, if the stories were true, their karma was complete!

Once inside the stadium, several other USA ladies and I were able to find advantageous seats where we would have a wonderful view of everything. Before the parade began, we could see the top of Sai Geetha as she walked through the village from her stall in the Gokulum. She waited at the entrance for Swami to arrive before she led the parade. She was so majestically beautiful in all her finery. Behind her were dancers and musicians, and representatives in costumes from every country, proudly bearing their flags. The girl from the USA was dressed as the Statue of Liberty, while the President of the San Francisco Center carried our flag.

We could see bits of Swami through the crowd, glowing in His white silk gown, as His gayly decorated silver chariot draped with large pearls, moved slowly along behind the parade. He was blessing everyone with His LOVE as He was carried along. When His chariot stopped in front of us, the LOVE He was sending out was absolutely breathtaking and our hearts swelled to bursting. Tears of joy flowed again. Once Swami moved up on to the stage, the celebration really began.

We heard a noise overhead that sounded like a lawnmower. In the sky several hundred feet above us, was what looked like a bicycle with wings flying along towing a streamer bearing a message. I believe it said 'Love All, Serve All'. From this flying apparatus, paper streamers rained down upon us of varying bright colors. It was all so ethereal.

Many dignitaries from the Indian government were there for Baba's birthday to help ordain Swami's water project. Some very wealthy people from all over the world had donated millions of dollars and rupees to the Sri Sathya Sai Trust, which paid for this immense water project. Several years before, Swami had asked the Indian government to undertake this project, but it never got its act together. Swami's massive water project now provides water to numerous villages that previously had little or no access to water due to natural causes and water mismanagement by the government and others. Countless villagers and their children had suffered disfiguring diseases and death from the effects of bad water they were forced to use before Swami's project was inaugurated. There were a number of speakers preceding Swami's discourse after which prasad was distributed.

Several of us USA ladies waited until long after the ceremony was over before we attempted to return to our quarters to avoid the crowds. We wended our way through the back roads by the Puttaparthi hospital and the VIP housing where we knew the crowds would be smaller. At times we could see and hear the confusion and shouting and screaming coming from the multitudes of people as they tried to return to their accommodations via the main road. It was a replay of the morning scene, and I was very thankful to whomever it was that suggested we wait and take the back roads.

Swami had reportedly told some of the Sai Organization leaders that there were three million there for His Birthday Celebration, including five thousand thieves, who always gather wherever the 'wealthy' Westerners congregate. Later, Niranjan suggested that there were one million in body and two million in spirit attending the Birthday Celebration. It is difficult to imagine even one million bodies crammed into this tiny village in the middle of nowhere, but it happened. And the miraculous thing is that Swami fed all these souls **free** for ten days! And they were housed and bathed and ......

Syd returned to our apartment about an hour after I did and was so glad to see me home, safe and sound. He had returned from the Stadium on the Main Road through what he described as a crazy mob of people pushing anyone and anything aside that got in its way, with many people getting injured and crying and shouting everywhere. Syd told me to forget about going to the evening ceremony because of the madness of the crowds out there. I knew he was right, but I so wanted to see Swami on His Joola (swing). Thus, we stayed in where it was safe.

Not surprisingly, it was at this point that we decided we did not want to buy an apartment and move to Puttaparthi. Swami had cured us of that idea! And furthermore, we did not want to ever return. After all, we have Swami in our home. We can feel Him there and talk to Him there in our home and in our hearts; whereas here in India, He is always over there somewhere and we can barely see Him or get close to Him. And, here in India, we are subject to the abuse of those who flock around Him. Those who are close to Swami are there to learn their lessons also, and Swami uses them to help set up learning experiences for others. We know that it is all in perfect order, even though it does not feel like it when you are the one being abused.

Would we go back to India for another Birthday Celebration? If Swami calls, we will be there in 2000. We are not the same people we were in 1995.

Sending Love

In 1995, my friend and neighbor, Lynn, was diagnosed with cancer and was having a very rough time of it. She had to have surgery as they detected her lower intestines were full of the disease. She had asked me to pray for her even more intensely, because the prognosis was not good. I had given her vibhuti from the outset, which she used as instructed and it helped her to cope, but did not heal her as hoped. I also gave her several books about Sai Baba, and a copy of a bhajan tape which she had asked for.

Lynn and her husband watch over our home when we are away, and we watch over theirs. She asked if I would mind if she sat at my altar and talked to Baba, and prayed for His Grace, especially on Swami's Birthday. I assured her that was fine with me, and told her I would send her Swami's energies (LOVE),as a channel while sitting and taking His Darshan. Thus it was that every time I would think of Lynn while sitting in Darshan, or wherever, I would visualize Swami's energies entering through my heart chakra and I then sent it out through my crown chakra to Lynn, wherever she was. There was one time that I could actually feel her at the altar on Swami's Birthday, and later when we discussed it after my return, I learned my feelings were accurate.

Sending LOVE is something I have been doing for twenty years now. To send it while sitting at the Source was a new and exciting experiment. The inspiration to send LOVE first came to me during meditation in the early 70's. In those days, I began by filling my heart with LOVE, colored it pink, and felt it swell to overflowing. At that point I would send it out the top of my head through my crown chakra and on to who ever needed it, using my heartbeat as an imaginary pump to keep the flow going. I have since heard it referred to as 'pumping pink' by another Baba devotee, and I thought it was my original idea back in the 70's! It is important that you are in a pure state of mind before sending LOVE, otherwise you will send whatever you are feeling.

As a part of my daily ritual since 1976, every morning, while in the shower, I first would send this LOVE to all my family and friends, mentioning them by name, and to anyone I knew who was in distress. Then I would ask God to help me be a channel to send this LOVE to everyone with whom I come in contact with each day. Yes, even Swami was on my list - I started sending LOVE to Him when I learned He had fallen and injured His hip in 1988.

If I see a child crying in a store or restaurant or on a plane, I fill the child <u>and</u> the stressed parent(s) with LOVE. Within a short period, the child calms down and we all feel better. If I see someone with a car broken down on the road or anyone in distress, I send them LOVE. I have seen couples arguing, or a husband berating his wife, and I send them LOVE, and watch the results of my efforts. Now, whenever I learn of the terrible things going on in the world, I send LOVE to everyone there. Although I continue to send LOVE when ever it is needed, every morning, while doing my puja, I also ask Swami to fill me with His BLISS, and I send that out too. The BLISS seems to consume my whole body, whereas the LOVE fills my heart. All the while I am pumping this BLISS and LOVE, I visualize it covering the earth and everyone and everything in it.

"The foremost duty of everyone is to make the love of God flow towards all in creation. Every man lives not for his own sake but to render service to society. To forget concern for the body is the way to realize self-satisfaction. Of what use is human birth if you do not manifest unsullied love towards all beings?" (Telegu Poem recited by Baba) SS Oct 1996 P 259

".....love is the natural state and all other contrary emotions are unnatural. Therefore, when you send a wave of spontaneous love to a person, it is bound to strike some chord in him or her. When you go on showering love, it will slowly begin to cleanse and purify, and soon the undesirable traits will be weeded out and goodness will shine through.

"The ananda (bliss) that can be derived by unselfish scattering of Love is a rare elevating experience. It is a very valuable sadhana (spiritual discipline)." SSS VOL VII B Chap 38 P 260

Just recently, Syd and I were sitting in the waiting room of the automobile shop where we were having our new car serviced. I used this time to work on editing the first complete draft of this book. A very distressed man walked into the waiting room, stopped in front of me and said, "Have you ever bought a lemon?".

I smiled and asked, "What do you mean?", knowing full well what he meant, but I was stalling for time so I could think of a way to get out of this conversation without appearing rude.

He said, "The car I bought here several years ago is a lemon - I have had to replace the engine twice, the radiator, the carburetor, and now I have........". I immediately tuned him out as he gave this long list problems and started sending him LOVE, as I pretended to go back to working on my book. Syd saw what I was doing and took up the conversation with the man. I really poured the LOVE into and around him. In a minute or two, he stopped complaining, smiled, and walked out the door. Thank You Baba for this wonderful tool.

After Birthday

Puttaparthi, November 27, 1995

There was no Darshan again this morning, so I slept in, a full nine hours of sleep, after getting around four hours sleep per night. I really feel rested for the first time since we arrived.

On November 24, 25 and 26th, it was virtually impossible to get inside for Darshan. I was fortunate on the 25th to get in Line two in the afternoon and sat in row nine. That morning, and again during both Darshans on the 26th, nobody got in because a multitude of seva dals completely occupied the entire Mandir grounds for the padnamaskar they receive in exchange for being a seva dal. Madhu Patel told us that even the VIP's, of which she is one, could not get inside the Mandir grounds for Darshan on the 26th.

Thinking the seva dal tribute was over, we queued up at around 3 a.m. again. The crowds were still very thick and every time we assembled, we were crammed in against each other like sardines so there would be room for as many people as possible. Seva dals kept telling us to move closer, move closer, until there was barely room to breathe or turn or scratch an itch.

On the 26th, I watched as thousands of ladies arrived too late and were turned away. Then around 5:30 a.m. it became obvious that the seva dals were going to occupy the entire Mandir grounds again. This meant that there would be no Darshan for us once again, as the last two days Swami spent all His Darshan time giving padnamaskar to the seva dals and never came outside where we could see Him.

Frustrated from sitting so long for no apparent reason, I stood up to stretch. A young seva dal told me to sit down. I asked if she spoke English and she nodded yes. Thoroughly angered by now, with the help of my seat mates who had all been grumbling steadily and feeding each other's anger, I said, "Would you please explain to me why you have let us sit here since 3 a.m. again today without telling us that we would never be able to get inside, especially after going through the same exercise yesterday. Why didn't you seva dals tell us yesterday that this was going to continue today so we wouldn't waste time waiting in line?" Suddenly the young seva dal turned and walked away as though I were not there. I continued with, "So now you don't speak English. Well, I don't understand you either." That afternoon, they announced there would again be no Darshan for us on the morning of the 27th, saving us the trouble and the hours of waiting in queues. Normally, I would have remained passive along with everyone else. But I was not only feeling my frustration, I was absorbing the feelings of all around me, and after giving a lot of thought to my actions, I felt that Swami had used me to ventilate for everyone.

While meditating as I sat in the queue lines in the dark the following morning, I resolved to just accept everything once again as Swami's Will. Somehow I had totally slipped out of my state of surrender to Swami's Will for me. After my experiences at Birthday, I was ashamed of myself for getting upset about the seva dals taking up the whole Mandir. After all, they were doing seva, some under very unpleasant circumstances, I had learned. And many of them missed having Swami's Darshan because they were on duty. It was only fair that they should get special treatment from Swami.

We visited the Patels last night in their apartment. Like us, they said they would never return to Puttaparthi for another Birthday Celebration, or anytime there are large crowds for that matter. It is just too hard on everybody and there is so much illness going around. I brought along several surgical face masks which I usually wear on the long overseas flights. I have been wearing them full time whenever I venture outside our apartment, only taking them off when Swami walks by. The crowds are so heavy that there is a constant thick haze of dust and dirt in the air. Everybody is stopping me to ask where I got my face mask, so they can get one too. Men are hacking and spitting their sickness on the ground everywhere. When their sputum mixed with the sand becomes airborne, it is further spreading the respiratory illness nearly everybody has come down with. And most of the coughers never cover their mouth, spreading their germs to all around them. There are very long lines of some very sick people at the Allopathic, Homeopathic and Ayurvedic infirmaries.

Last night while visiting with Madhu, I told her I feel so surrounded by confusion and anger and other negative emotions, that I can not think clearly, and that I am not myself and surprised at my actions because of it. She shared that she was having the same experiences and that for the first time ever, she just wanted to leave the Ashram and not be here with Swami. I suggested to her that maybe what we are feeling is only a small part of what is going on in the world outside, and we are better off here.

Puttaparthi, November 28, 1995

Amazing, but there are no longer the extremely large crowds. This morning I got line one and am in row two awaiting Swami. I am hoping He will take the letter I have for Him. It asks Him to please take this letter if I am supposed to be writing a book about my life with Him. It also asks Him to help me to be worthy of being His devotee. At least three people in the past week alone have told me I should put all my experiences into a book. There were several others who encouraged me even before Swami's birthday. But that is another major project, and I really want to finish the book of His teachings before starting another. The feeling is very strong that these are messages from Swami that I am getting. So, if He takes the letter, then I know what I am getting is correct. He never came on our side, so was unable to offer Him my letter.

Earlier I had written another letter asking Him once again to take the letter only if I am supposed to be putting together a book of His teachings. He took the letter the first opportunity I had to give it to Him.

Our roommates left for home yesterday. We really enjoyed their company, but the tiny apartment seemed to get smaller during the last few days. I am sure it was the same for them also. Syd has had his trials with accommodations again the last two days, and I with the seva dals. Syd was told that all the people in our building must vacate it and return to the sheds by this afternoon after Darshan. There are only USA citizens in our building, and about one third of them have returned to their homes already. The people in Accommodations tell Syd they need to do maintenance on the building and that everyone has to leave so they can perform their tasks. We tried to imagine what could be so serious in a brand new building that we needed to be evacuated, but nothing came to mind. So, Syd arranged for a room for us in Sai Towers and we began the packing and moving process again.

Puttaparthi, November 29, 1995

Was in line six this morning and line eight in the afternoon. Got my first Ayurvedic massage since my arrival with Vidya yesterday, and my second today. My dear friend Hennie from Holland is back here with Swami again. She has been here for a while and we have had only a few chances to get together. This morning she sat next to me in the queues and at Darshan. She told me she had been hunting all over for us because when she went to our apartment yesterday, she found that a Chinese family was now staying in it. They must have moved in right on our heels. She told me that the whole building the USA people had been in for Birthday until yesterday morning is now occupied by Chinese devotees. Inside my head, red bells and whistles went off, but I immediately prayed to Swami to please help me to overcome the anger that was building inside me. He did! If only I could remember to turn to Swami before I get myself in a dither. This was just another test for me.

Syd got padnamaskar twice today and he is totally blissed out. Thank You Baba! Life with him will be easier now. About the time that he was receiving his padnamaskar, it came to me that if either of us has

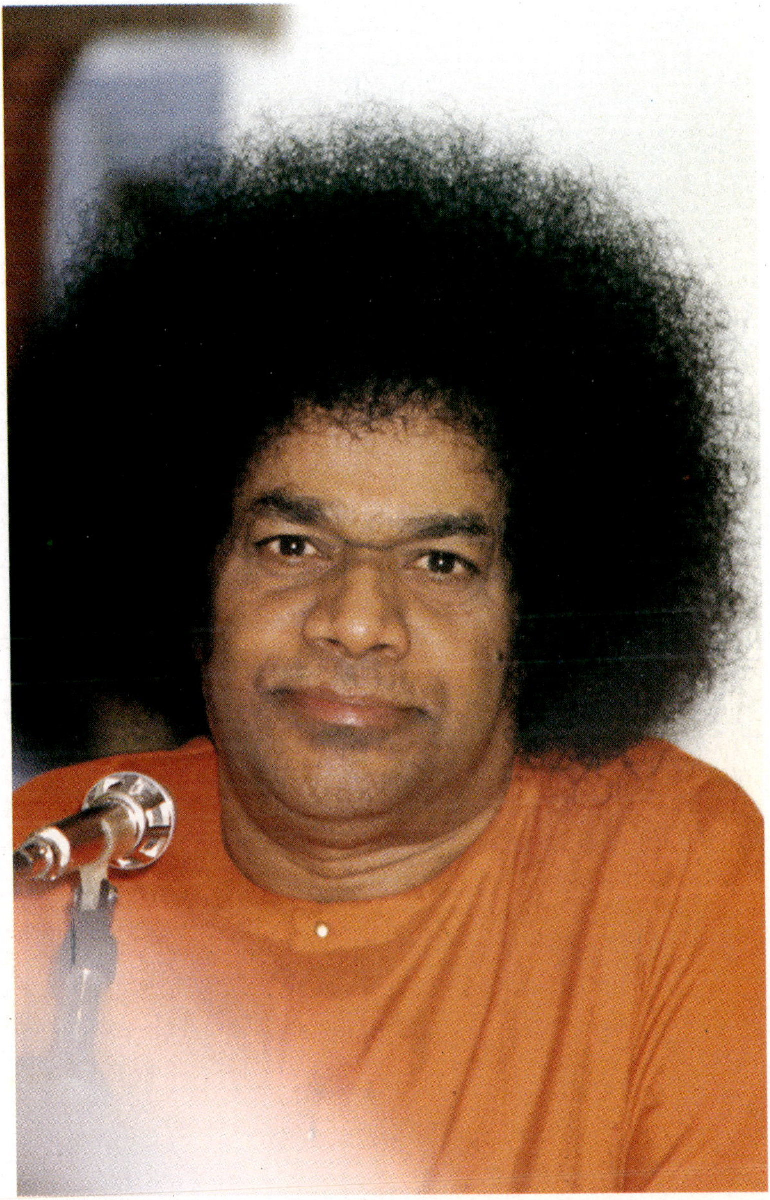

a chance to ask for an interview, we should consider whether to ask for us as a couple, or for eight as a group. Olga and Gilly are here with some people from their Center in Nevada.

This afternoon, the large 3 ft. x 4 ft. picture of Swami that we ordered has arrived and we picked it up. He is sitting on His throne looking straight into your eyes with His Hand up in the Abisheka (blessing) position. Soooooo beautiful! Syd is going to carry it to Darshan to see if Swami will sign it for us. Several days ago, an Indian held up a large photo and Swami signed it on top of Syd's head!

It's All a Test

Puttaparthi, November 30, 1995

Dreamed last night that we were all lined up to get padnamaskar from Swami and the dream seemed to repeat itself all night long. Syd is a bear today and doesn't want to talk about it. There is a thick, heavy dark cloud of anger surrounding him and it puts me on a real bummer and makes me want to chuck it all. It is so hard for me to be around him when he gets like this because what happens to him happens to me. He refuses to admit there is anything wrong and just won't talk about it. I know he is getting his share of lessons here too, but life is hard enough this year without his moods.

Puttaparthi, December 1, 1995

Dreamed we were in the queues for Darshan and going into the Mandir grounds, and some of us were painting the boards or walls red (anger?). As though this dream were a prophecy, I got angry this morning when for the fourth time the seva dals took up most of the Mandir grounds and we, the public, were shoved to the very back, many never making it in from the outside lines. I recognized some of the same seva dals that were lined up for their special padnamaskar just a few days ago. We have been told that a new shift of seva dals comes in every ten days, so the familiar faces don't belong there over and over again. They must be keeping their seva dal scarves once they have served their ten days and just keep going in time after time, taking advantage of the situation. Swami knows what they are doing,

I reassure myself. And they are only creating karma for themselves, I tell myself. But, then so am I. Please help me with this Swami!

But then the light suddenly dawns in my mind - IT IS ALL A TEST! Everything that has been happening here this year is simply a test; a test designed to teach us lessons in patience, awareness, trust, etc. And I have failed every single one of them! I got angry with the people who were in charge of doling out accommodations because they put us in that filthy shed with no water. I got angry with the seva dals for taking up all the room in the Mandir grounds over and over again. I got angry when I learned we were kicked out of the apartments so the Chinese could move in. I got angry with Syd because of his bad moods. I got angry with Swami over my nearly getting killed on Ladies Day. I got angry with Swami for my not being able to get inside and observe the Ladies Day celebration. I got angry at whoever did not listen to Swami and left all that space for the men on Ladies Day, when it was just supposed to be reserved for ladies. I got angry at all the line jumpers while waiting in those terribly long lines at the bakery and the canteen. I got angry with the ladies who knocked me over or pushed me aside when I was trying to get up or sit down in Darshan.

All this anger I did not know I had inside me - and Swami brought me here to India for His Birthday just so I could become aware of it and deal with it. I am so ashamed for failing every single test. I thought I had evolved beyond that. But then, there are few tests at home anymore, because we have very little dealings with other people, except for a few close friends, so there really has been no opportunity to deal with the anger I have apparently been carrying around.

I started serving food in the canteen yesterday and did it again at lunch today. It feels so verrrrry rewarding. Last year and the years before, I worked in the canteen cutting vegetables and thought this year I would do something different. As the people came to my position to be served, I would look each one in the eye and shoot them full of LOVE. It was sometimes amazing, because I could spot someone coming in the line who really needed a lift. When I was able to make eye contact, I would smile and send them a burst of LOVE and then watch the transformation right before my eyes. It didn't always work, because some people choose to hold on to their discomfort. Thank You Swami for this wonderful opportunity to serve You.

Puttaparthi, December 2, 1995

This morning I drew Chit #2 and sat in the third row in Darshan. Baba came along and took my November 27 letter about writing the second book at 6:58 a.m. He first came on our side and as soon as He almost reached where I was, He turned and went across to the other side. I squeaked out softly, "Swami!", and He turned around and I had to reach over the lady from Belarus in front of me, but He waited patiently and took my letter. Then at breakfast with Elizabeth, I met Joyce from Canada. She showed us her new book that is in the Ashram bookstore, "Touched by Baba". It was like another sign from Swami that I am to write the second book.

Puttaparthi, December 3, 1995

This morning I was the third person in Line one and sat in the front row on the Mandir side with Olga, Joan, Mary and Adrian. Swami came along and looked me right in the eye, but totally ignored my request: "Baba, interview for our group?" It seems we all asked the same question at the same time. I was able to take a short padnamaskar with my right hand on His right foot as He walked away. Thank You Swami!

Puttaparthi, December 6, 1995

This morning I wrote the following letter to Swami: "Beloved Swami, I desperately need Your help in dealing with this spontaneous anger I have been experiencing here, **AND** also Swami, please help me to maintain a level of consciousness at home so that I do not need or feel the need to return to Your Lotus Feet. All my love, Charlene Leslie-Chaden, Trinidad, CO USA". This letter is a result of losing it (my temper) again at the way those of us from the USA have been getting treated. None of my attempts to conquer and rise above the anger worked. I realized I needed help because I could not do it on my own.

We (USA people) have been virtually brutalized by some of the seva dals, who have purposely and roughly pushed us around, and used every manner to let us know they resent us. I was physically thrown to the ground by one seva dal shortly after our arrival, and have watched the same thing happen to others. The newspapers tell us that Clinton has broken Bush's agreement and the USA is now selling arms to Pakistan. India is furious about it and the newspapers are feeding the fury. Since Syd and I have stopped wearing our USA scarves several days ago, we have been getting better treatment. Now we are just seen as Westerners. We have noticed that many other USA people have also stopped wearing their USA scarves.

It is obvious that most of the rest of the world, represented here in Puttaparthi, has a great deal of resentment for USA citizens. I am told it is because we think we are the best and most powerful country in the world, and we think that we have the right to tell the rest of the world how to run their countries. And if they don't do as we say, we enforce our will upon them.

This afternoon I wrote another letter to Swami: "I surrender and dedicate my life to You. Please help me to serve You in the best way possible. All my love, Charlene". Baba came along and took this letter and the one written this morning from me. Thank You Swami.

Another Interview

Puttaparthi, December 7, 1995

While I was sitting in the queue line this morning, Olga came up and told me that there were now six in our group. Three ladies from our group had left for home several days before, and we had been down to the 'magical five'. Back last Summer, I had a dream about only five in our interview, and then while sitting at my altar, Swami told me we would get an interview, and that there would be five of us in the group. I understood I was not to tell anyone, because it "could change things" if I did. So when Olga told me we were now six, my heart fell, because now, we would not get our interview, or so I thought.

Shortly after 7 a.m. I was sitting way in the back crying, feeling very sorry for myself and for the rest of the USA people like us because Baba seemed to be ignoring us. None of the USA people, except a few VIP's have had interviews in the whole time we have been here. Baba had once again quickly breezed through the women's side, and I could no longer see Him. Is Swami angry with the USA for some reason I wondered as I put my head down on my knees and sank into deep sorrow?

As I sat there, I wondered why I had come to India and decided there was no need to return, not with crowds like this. I was thinking of leaving Darshan early because I couldn't see anything from where I was anyway. I sat up on one hip and looked up to try one more time to see if Baba was visible, but couldn't because He had disappeared deep into the men's section. Suddenly, as I was about to turn away, I saw Syd wave his hat and put it on his head walking to the veranda for an interview! Waving his hat and then putting it on his head was his way of letting me know for sure that it was him. It is really difficult to see who it is from the distance I was at. My heart did a flip-flop. "Oh, Sai Ram", I said and got up and collected my things and headed out for the veranda. My whole life changed in a flash and I was on my way to my Lord!

I almost did not make it past the security girl stationed not far from where I had to enter onto the veranda. She grabbed my arm and said, "Where is scarf?". I told her, "My husband!", and pointed toward the veranda. She repeated, "Where is scarf?", and I repeated, "My husband!", pointing again to Syd. I don't think she was paying any attention to what I was saying, or possibly she did not understand English. I could see Swami heading towards the veranda now, and was beginning to get worried that I was not going to get in for the interview. When she asked the same question again, I roughly jerked my body away from her tight grip, and ran toward the veranda before she could stop me. As I ran, I heard another seva dal tell her, "No scarf if husband gets interview!". Syd and I had stopped wearing our USA scarves several days before this.

I sat down in the front row opposite Syd and Gilly. Yes, it was Syd who had asked Swami for the interview. He was just bursting with bliss! When Swami came and looked at the men and women assembled for the interview, He turned to the lady sitting behind me and harshly told her "GO!", while pointing back to the crowd assembled for Darshan. There was no doubt in what He meant, because His message was given in the strongest way possible, with a look of anger on His face. The lady behind me, who I had never seen, immediately got up and left the veranda. Later, Olga told me that it was the lady she had said would be number six in our group. Now I understood how Swami's drama played out and why I was not supposed to tell anyone that just five of us would get an interview! I learned later from this lady who was sent back, that it was the third time Swami had refused to let her come in for an interview with different groups! She said she understood why He was doing this to her, but would not elaborate.

Once inside the interview room, Swami stood over me and asked, "Where is God?" I moved both my hands upwards and said, "You are God, Swami!". He said, "No, no, no! God is Everywhere, God is Everywhere!", His arms spanning outward as if to include the whole world. Then He asked me again, "Where is God?". I started waving my arms the same way Swami did and said, "God is everywhere!". Before I could even finish, Swami interrupted and said, "No, no, no! You are God! You are God! You are God!", He said, pointing His finger at me each time, and getting right in my face, looking me straight in the eye. I felt this go right to my heart chakra. When God looks you in the eye and tells you that you are God, something happens deep inside.

Then Swami asked me, "Why do you come here?". I knew instantly He was telling me that He knew what I was thinking while sitting out there in the Darshan lines, crying and feeling sorry for myself, and wondering why I even came here, when we have such wonderful access to Him at home. I answered, "For You, Swami!". Then the thought whirled in my mind, "And to get my batteries charged!", but for some reason I was not able to say the last words.

When it was our turn to go inside the "Inner Sanctum", Gilly muttered something on the way in and Baba said to him, "Smart Alec!". I giggled as I walked past Swami through the doorway. Baba repeated it, "Smart Alec!", and then He giggled playfully too.

Once inside, I sat at His Feet on one side, with Gilly, Syd and Olga to my left and Adrian on my right. Baba talked to Gilly for awhile and told him He would help him, after asking him some questions. Then He asked Syd, "How are you?".

Syd responded, "Good, I'm wonderful now Swami!".

"No, health not good." Swami heard me gasp, and He said, "Health not bad either. Head always thinking, no rest in the mind. Stomach upset, gastric kind. Sometimes not eating properly. Your wife knows. She knows. She is a good lady. A very good lady. She worries about you and always thinking about you. I know!". Swami paused for a moment, then said, "I came into your dreams. You didn't believe it. You think it was your imagination. I was there. I was in your dream."

Syd answered, "But I don't remember Swami!". But I remembered. One day several years before, when we were out for a walk with our dogs, Syd broke the silence and suddenly said, "I think I dreamed about Swami last night, but I can't remember what happened. Maybe it was just my imagination. I never dream about Him. You are the lucky one with the Baba dreams."

Swami then addressed Adrian, "How are you Sir? (Adrian is a lady) You have problems in your legs, ankles and knees; it is rheumatic kind."

Then He did some marriage counseling with Olga and Gilly, just as He had done in our previous interview. As He finished, He asked Gilly, "When are you leaving?" Gilly responded, "In January".

I jumped in and pointed at Syd, saying "December, leaving soon Swami."

Baba said to Olga and Gilly, "Too many personal things." Then to Syd and I, "I will see you privately later." He ushered us to the door and we were back into the outer interview room.

While all the conversation was going on with Olga and Gilly, I was taking padnamaskar several times and kissing Swami's Feet. Adrian bent over to kiss them too, but could not reach, so I gave her a little boost on the buns and she went face down as though somebody had forcefully pushed her. She gave me a funny look when she sat back up. Then Olga on my left tried to take padnamaskar also, but she too could not reach from her position, so I gave her a little boost too. Amazingly, she went down to the Lotus Feet just as quickly as Adrian did. Later, Olga said that when I touched her, she felt a great force pushing her down to Swami's feet, and she knew it was not my gentle push that caused it. Syd said he saw the gentle push I had given Olga and Adrian and agreed that it must have been Baba's doing.

Back in the outer room, Baba made another gold bracelet for a college student and then took him inside. After all the interviews, Baba passed out vibhuti packets to all of us, and I took another long padnamaskar while He stood next to me. Later, it all seemed like a dream that was over so quickly but all of life is a dream. There was a lot of conversation with Swami going on, but we could only collectively remember the above.

Swami made vibhuti and put some in my hand and into the hands of the other ladies. I sat there for a minute wondering if I should try to save some of it. Syd motioned for me eat it. I noticed it was white and barren of taste. Then sitting down on His chair, He asked, "Where do you come from?" I answered: "Colorado, USA". He said, "Colorado is good, very good place!" Then He looked at Gilly and said, "Where are you from?". "Las Vegas, Swami". Baba repeated, "Las Vegas", and made a face as He said something else, almost under His breath, which sounded like 'Bad Place', then shook His head, feigning disgust.

Swami called a student to the front of the room and talked to him for a few minutes. Then, within 18 inches of my eyes, He moved

His hand in a circle, and out popped a gold wrist chain and band. Then He called an Indian lady up front and also her husband. Swami materialized a gold chain with a Baba pendant and gave it to her husband to put round her neck. Swami then moved His hand again and out came a large gold watch with diamonds all about it. He told the husband to give Him that 'cheap thing from his wrist'. Swami set the new watch at 7:17 a.m. and put it on the man's wrist.

Swami asked the Nepalese man across from me to give Him his ring, asking where he got it. "In the shops in 1977, Swami.", came the reply. It looked it, all dilapidated, with the enamel worn off and the picture of Swami barely discernible. Baba passed it around to us to look at and then He blew three puffs on it and it changed into a gold ring with Swami's face on it as He held it in front of our eyes. Swami passed it around again to be sure we all saw the change.

As He talked to another young (Indian) man, Swami asked his parents what he was studying in college. They proudly replied, "Masters of Human Resources". Swami asked, "What is study, what is education?", and nobody attempted an answer. So Swami gave a mini discourse on education. Baba then motioned the three of them toward the inner interview room, but stopped them abruptly when He said to the student, "You have a girlfriend. She is outside!" A look of shock and horror came over the father's face and he turned and translated to the wife, who then looked even more devastated. Baba repeated it, and the boy put his hands over his face. Baba went a step further, "She is a school teacher!". With the shock on the parent's face, one could almost assume they had already planned a marriage for him with someone else, and this was totally unacceptable to them.

After Swami passed out vibhuti packets to one and all, He ushered us out the door of the Interview Room. Syd and I had planned to visit the Patels after Darshan that day and I had forgotten briefly after the excitement of the interview. Halfway back to our hotel room, I recalled our plans, and walked all the way back to their apartment in the round buildings. Everybody there was sick, still suffering from the viral infection that had accosted everybody. We briefly shared our interview experience with them and returned to our hotel room to rest.

Syd's Illness

Puttaparthi, December 10, 1995

A strange thing occurred this morning when I returned to our hotel room after Darshan. I had been fortunate to be in the first line this morning, and was silently pleading to Swami to come to me and make some vibhuti for Syd, or to heal him, or to please help me to know what to do for him.

Syd was very ill and he never gets sick, and to see him down like he was, really disturbed me. Swami passed me right on by, ignoring me. Syd was running a high fever and had stopped eating yesterday morning. It was not like Syd to skip a meal, or to be sick. Actually, his illness began the day after our interview. It is interesting to note that Swami told Syd about some gastric problems he had, and Syd was confused about that because he felt just fine at the time.

When I returned from Darshan, I asked Syd how he felt. He just groaned. I tried to get him to drink some water, and he only would take a few sips. I prayed again for guidance from Swami on what to do to help Syd. Then I dug through my homeopathic medicine supply and found my bottle of Echinacea/Goldenseal drops, which was about the only thing I had that might help him. I was having trouble reading what the dosage should be in our dimly lit room, so I stepped out into the hallway, held the bottle up to eye level, and tried once again to read it, this time in a better light.

An Indian man came up the stairs, took the bottle from my hands, read it and said, "I am a doctor. Do you need help?". I opened our door and pointed to Syd laying quietly in the bed with his back to the door. I knew instantly that Swami had sent this doctor in answer to my plea and I silently sent Him my very grateful thanks. Syd would never let me go find a doctor for him. His regard for doctors went downhill more than 25 years ago when he was diagnosed by a company insurance doctor as having a terminal heart condition with less than six months to live. Other doctors confirmed the diagnosis. Syd decided that if he lived or died was up to God, not the doctors and he stopped going to doctors. But, he could no longer get medical or life insurance, and this nearly cost him his position.

    The Doctor came right inside, checked Syd over, and asked him some questions. He left, saying he would be right back, and when he returned it was with some antibiotics. He told us that many people are suffering from the same thing in Puttaparthi this year - intestinal pain, fever, diarrhea, lethargy, and so on. He said if it was treated early enough, the healing process would progress quickly, whereas there are many others in the Puttaparthi hospital who waited too long to get treatment and are really suffering because of it. This kind and gentle doctor said he would return tonight after bhajans to check on Syd. When he did, we asked how much he charged, and he said that he had a clinic down the street and if we cared to make a donation, that would make him very happy. We ended up giving him Rs. 2,000, which he said would go a long way to help the village people who came to him for treatment because most had no way to pay for medicines and his services.

    The next morning, I brought some black tea, dry toast, and yogurt with honey from the restaurant up to Syd, which is what the doctor had prescribed. He felt better almost instantly after eating, and said he would go to Darshan that afternoon. Thank You Swami!!!

Puttaparthi, December 17, 1995
    We had the most wonderful car Darshan this morning down in front of the bus station. Syd is leaving in the morning for Bombay and we were buying peroxide and dewaxer at the Chemists for his ears, which were terribly plugged up from the viral infection he just had. We heard a lot of commotion behind us and turned to see what was going on. Swami was being driven down the street in His red Mercedes. We moved closer to the street to get a more advantageous position, and as the car pulled in front of us, Swami looked me right in the eyes and then behind me to where Syd stood. I have felt absolutely wonderful since

that moment. Just a chance happening. I feel so blessed!!! Thank You Swami for giving Syd Your blessings too before he leaves.

Christmas 1995

Puttaparthi, December 18, 1995

Syd left this morning for the airport. I reported to Shed 23 after Christmas Satsang to find out what I was supposed to do in the Christmas program and was told to return at 1:30 and ask for a certain man. I had signed up the day before to participate and help in the Christmas Program. Since I had already been in the Christmas Choir, I knew I did not have the energy to keep chasing back and forth to the back sheds for practice, and I signed up to help with the children in the Poornachandra. With time to spare, I had lunch and hunted up the massage lady, Vidya, for a massage tonight.

When I returned to find that 'certain man', he curtly told me my name was no longer on the list, which he said, meant that I was not needed. I said to him, "It is Swami's Will, thank you.", and started to walk away. I could tell he was surprised by my response. He seemed prepared to go on the offensive with me, just as he was doing to another lady, who was in tears when I walked up to them. I told him I was sorry he was having such a rough day. As I walked away, I heard a plane flying overhead - the one carrying my husband to Bombay. I silently sent him my LOVE.

While sitting in Darshan, a message from my Inner Voice told me that I was supposed to work on the manuscript draft for the book on Sai Baba's teachings while I am here, instead of becoming involved in the Christmas program. I had brought the manuscript along in case there was time to proofread it and otherwise work on it. Olga and Adrian had suggested that I could work with them if I wanted, as Olga was in charge of makeup for the play. I declined and spent every single spare minute after that working on the book, and made a lot of progress. With Syd gone, my time was much freer.

Puttaparthi, December 20, 1995

Met a lady from Northern Europe this morning at breakfast downstairs. She first came to Swami in 1978 and has published one book about Swami and is now writing another. She said this place has changed so much and that we can no longer find peace here. She wondered why Baba has so many 'sick' people around Him anymore. It seems like everyone is getting a lot of karmic lessons dredged up this year, with difficult encounters with staff, seva dals, aggressive 'devotees', etc. I had previously thought it was just limited to the USA devotees, until I began to hear from devotees from other countries.

Puttaparthi, December 21, 1995

Had supper last night with Shimshon and Chedva of Israel, whom we met earlier this year. We shared about how we both noticed that some of the ladies who are living on the Ashram have become progressively angry and hostile over the years, and seemed to have aged considerably in the last year or two. Nobody wants to sit near them in Darshan as their vibrations are very repelling. It seems to me they have been having some extra heavy lessons while living on the Ashram. If their lessons are anything like the ones we've been having, and theirs are happening every day, it is a wonder they have survived their stay in the Ashram this long. And we had been thinking of moving here??? Swami has sure cured us of that desire. Perhaps these ladies are all holding in a lot of stuff and are 'trapped' in this space. Swami had said several years previous that all who lived there with Him would either leave the Ashram or their bodies soon.

When Swami asked me, "Why do you come here?", I got the feeling He also meant that I no longer need to come all this way, as He will work with me at home. Chedva told me this afternoon that she is no longer affected by the energies of others. Oh, Swami, how I would love to go home with that Grace from my Lord!

Puttaparthi, December 22, 1995

One year ago today - my special interview with my Beloved Swami. This morning while sitting in the token lines (queues), the thought occurred to me that some of us, like Chedva and I are like young birds in the nest and Swami is telling us we are now ready to fly on our own, and make room for the next ones. But the thought of never again having His Darshan brings me to tears. "Please help this fledgling to fly Baba!", I pleaded silently. "I know You are in my heart, Baba, but I need Your help in remembering that too." Like Chedva said, "We need to move on and make room for all the newcomers. We are the lucky ones - we have graduated!" I don't remember getting a diploma, but I know I have had some pretty tough lessons this trip. I just hope they stick!

This evening, I must be feeling some of Syd's sorrow, because this is his last day in India. He's in Bombay and tonight he leaves for home. I am staying on through Christmas and New Years once again. Thank you so much Syd for allowing me to do this!

Puttaparthi, December 23, 1995

My thoughts as I am sitting and waiting for Swami to give Darshan this afternoon: If I am surrendered to God and God in me is the Doer of everything, and the Decider of what comes into my life, then it is only the ego that is resisting and getting upset and involved in everything going on around me. It is all just a test, and if I can just get hold of this ego and keep it from reacting, then God will stop sending people to push my buttons. And - everything that happens is already going to happen no matter what I do - it is only my reactions and thoughts that set the chain of events for the future. How can I hope to accomplish this when I keep absorbing everybody's stuff?

More thoughts: What has happened to the people I saw here last year? All of them seemed to have aged like ten to twenty years in only one year. One tall young blond lady last year was always smiling and radiating happiness. Such a sweet girl and so refreshing to see. This year, she never smiles, is filled with sorrow and seems to be waiting for the next blow to strike her. The energies here are not good, full of confusion, anger, volatility, and the village people continually push and elbow their way through the crowds knocking people out of their way at will.

Americans are not well tolerated and the newspapers continue to print negative stories of how bad the USA is. The Ashram is no longer an abode of peace. It is more like Hell this year. But wait - Didn't Swami say that He is not needed in Heaven, that He serves us best when we are in Hell? I remember hearing that Puttaparthi is His Hospital and the Ashram is the ICU (Intensive Care Unit) where all the sick people come looking for a cure, and that includes ME! But what of the new people coming - what can they gain from what is going on here? Is their experience different than mine? Will they see this as an abode of peace and fit in like I did in my first trip to Swami? Things were so peaceful and loving when we first came to Swami. Was that my illusion then?

Puttaparthi, December 24, 1995

It's Christmas Eve, and Hennie came by after Darshan at 10 a.m. and we chatted, had lunch together in the Western Canteen, sat together during choir and attended the Christmas Drama together, but we sat outside rather than within the crowds. The children were adorable in their costumes, but we were at such a distance it was difficult to understand the plot of the play.

Afterward we went to Sai Towers and had boiled vegetables and French fries in the restaurant. Hennie returned to her shed and I fell asleep early to be up and refreshed for Christmas Nagarsankirtan. Hennie is a very dear, sweet lady, and I feel so comfortable with her that I have invited her to come visit us in the USA. She said she probably would have difficulty with all the materialism, which repulses her. I told her we would probably have a lot to learn from each other.

Puttaparthi, December 25, 1995

Thousands of us Westerners gathered at the Ganesh gate with our candles to do Nagarsankirtan, in which we will sing Christmas Carols as we walk in the streets of Prasanthi Nilayam before Sunrise. Last year it seemed the carolers were only in the hundreds. Each of us has a candle signifying the flame within, which we have each set in a crudely fashioned holder to keep from burning ourselves or the person in front of us. We are cautioned to wear our hair up and our scarves tight so that none are set on fire by the person behind them. There are so many people this year that the streets will be full of us before we begin our march around and back to the Mandir grounds. It is quiet, and everyone feels the sanctity of the moment. It is such a special time and such a special way to celebrate Christmas. I wish my children and grandchildren could be here to experience this.

We marched around the Ashram and finally arrived at the gates to the Mandir. We slowly trickled in, still singing Christmas Carols. We gathered under the balcony and all the way to the back of the Mandir grounds, with some still outside, and begin to sing "Silent Night". After a few minutes, the Silver Doors above us slowly swing open and out walks Swami in His white silk robe. We burst out with "Joy to the World the Lord Has Come, Let Earth Receive Her King!".

Swami is filling us with so much LOVE this morning, moving back and forth, lifting His hands to raise our consciousness level. No wonder there are so many people here - word gets out fast when something as wonderful as this is happening.

Hennie and I find each other and we sit on through Darshan, with a perfect view of Swami sitting on His throne. We enjoy the show put on by Maynard Ferguson, the famous jazz musician, and David Bailey, the concert pianist from London. The college boys play their music also and give recitals of parts of Revelations from the Bible, and other Christian writings about Jesus.

When we arrived at the Western Canteen for lunch, we found they had opened an hour early without notice and that they had already run out of food and were closed, and I had only had a quick piece of toast for breakfast. So many people here, especially Westerners. Hennie and I wend our way through the crowds, back outside and to my hotel, where we find the dining room is full and overflowing, with another crowd waiting to get in.

I'm really feeling weak and dizzy now and remember that I have some crackers and peanut butter in my room which will hold me until I can get a meal. I share them with Hennie, and take this moment to present her with a Christmas gift, a brooch with Swami's picture under glass made by an Australian lady. Hennie shared with me that this was her first Christmas gift ever. I was shocked and did not know what to say as I saw tears of gratitude forming in her eyes. Giving Christmas gifts in America is so common and so natural that I found it difficult to believe they did not have the same customs in her home country.

Back to the Ashram and the Poornachandra for Swami's Christmas Discourse, which is preceded with many speeches by the girls who are members of the "Messengers of Sai". This seems to dominate the afternoon. These "Messengers of Sai" give an update each Christmas on the multitude of seva projects they are doing around the world. After five hours of sitting, I left early for dinner in the Canteen just in case they open early again. I'm weak, drained, and so very tired from not really eating today. The Christmas supper in the Canteen was wonderful, and I was pleased to find some of the cake Swami had blessed this morning as prasad was still available.

Puttaparthi, December 26, 1995
Was so tired last night I set the alarm incorrectly on my clock and overslept until 4 a.m.. I was busy chastising myself because of that as I rushed through getting ready for Darshan. But, with Swami's Grace, I made it to the lines in time and actually got in line six and had a good seat and a wonderful Darshan.

While sitting and waiting in the dark for daylight when Swami comes out to give Darshan, I relax and go into a meditative state. Then I tried chanting, "I am not this body, I am God", over and over, until there was only my consciousness left. Amazingly, I was able to disassociate from the body. I had to mentally separate my self from my Self, but it worked!!! What a wonderful feeling!

This afternoon in the token lines, I failed another test miserably. I am so ashamed. I had just put my cushion down and was lowering myself onto it when a heavy set Indian lady kicked it out of the way, knocked me over backwards and sat in front of me, with part of her large derriere on my feet. Anger flared inside me and I pushed her from behind, called her an animal and really raised a ruckus. And then I had all the other Indian ladies around me telling me to make room for her. *How dare they*, I thought. I was sooooooooo angry I wanted to hit her, to hurt her in some way. My body and mind were screaming with rage. What came over me?, I wondered. This is not at all like me. At home, I very rarely experience anger of any kind. But then, I never get treated like this at home either. Have I been saving it all up to come here and display it before God and everybody else? They must think I am mad!

"It is only because of lack of control of mind one gets into bad temper, which causes loss of discrimination and spells ultimate ruin. It is imperative that one should control the temper and avoid getting angry.....Anger comes from temper inside and one who yields to this bout of temper is bound to suffer. You should control anger and avoid talking or acting while in an angry mood." SS July 1994 P 179

"Do not entertain bad feelings about anyone. They do you more harm than to others. As the saying goes: 'One's own anger is one's enemy and one's peace is one's friend and kinsfolk. One's happiness is heaven and one's sorrow is hell.' (Telegu poem). Develop sacred and pure feelings." SS December 1993 P 314

It took a while to get myself under control, and when I did, I felt so ashamed. I know that I am not the only one this has been happening to as other USA ladies have complained about being shoved around and knocked down by Indians. But that doesn't make me feel any better about it. As I sat there wishing I could disappear, I remembered reading in a book recently where the author says that Swami stopped helping her when He felt she was ready to move on without Him. After what just occurred, I certainly do not feel ready for Swami to leave me to myself. Then I got upset that maybe Swami won't be there for me as He has in the past to protect and help me. I prayed over and over for the continuance of His help and guidance. Then I realized the state of mind I had gotten myself into and was finally able to surrender it all back to Him.

After Darshan and eating two coconuts plus waiting for over one hour in the bakery line, I walked past the gardens and realized I was smelling Swami in the air - Nothing smells as good as Him. "Oh, Thank You Swami!!!" I say out loud. "I Love You so much!!! I know I do not deserve this blessing from You. Please help me to control this anger."

Returning to Sai Towers, I see Shimshon and Chedva in the dining room and join them for a few minutes. As soon as I sit down, she tells me about her trial with anger this morning. It seems a little Indian boy took the balloon she had just purchased away from her as she walked down the street, saying that he wanted it. She became very angry and yelled at him, while grabbing the balloon back, "No, this is my balloon, and you can't have it, etc., etc., etc.,". Like me, she was now very angry at herself for being angry over such a trivial thing.

We shared our other trials by fire and then talked it over, trying to figure out why we were having these experiences. We agreed that perhaps the anger is coming from outside us with all these people here, or from the people handling our food, or from within, and Swami is purging us of it. Or, maybe all three.

Puttaparthi, December 27, 1995

Right now, I am so happy Swami. While in the token lines, there was a New Zealand Indian lady who came and sat on my feet in the tiny space in front of me. I did not get the least bit upset! Nor did I feel anything when five of her friends crowded in into that tiny space in front of me, pushing me back even further. Then, once inside the Darshan area, I passed the 'anger' test again of being blocked by the seva dals from going to the side closest to the men where I prefer to sit because of the longer view of Him. As soon as they opened it up again, I was able to move there. Thank You Swami for all Your help!

When Swami slowly entered the Mandir grounds with the sun shining from behind and all around Him, and through His glorious aura of hair, it was so ethereal and beautiful and full of majesty. Such a special Darshan today!

Puttaparthi, December 29, 1995

While sitting here waiting for Baba to give Darshan, I just had another realization. The things that go on here in the Ashram - the power trips, problems with accommodations, seva dals, VIP's, line jumpers, etc., Baba does not interfere with our karma in the outer world. So just as the outer world is spoiled by people, so the Abode of Peace is also. When I can learn to see it all as good, it will no longer bother me or be a part of my experience. Oh Swami, please help me with this major lesson.

Puttaparthi, December 30, 1995

Hurray! I was in Line one this morning. I have been feeling so close to Swami, and so thankful that He has not left me behind to work things out on my own. When I am up or high spiritually, I notice I usually get to sit up close to where Swami is. When I let things get to me or react badly to a test, I end up sitting way in the back. It doesn't matter, because I can feel Him just the same no matter where I am! But it is so nice to be nearer to Him where there is possible contact.

Puttaparthi, December 31, 1995

Line 27 this morning. After Darshan and bhajans, I met with a Western lady as I had promised earlier, and gave her an Astrological reading from the chart she brought with her from home. Haven't done one of these in years, but felt pushed by Swami to do so. As we talked, we shared the stories of our lives. Hers included an addiction to cocaine which ruined her career and her life. She was in desperate shape when she recently came to Swami.

The reading went well, and evolved into the subject of both of us feeling or knowing we were supposed to write books of our experiences. Swami had come to her in a dream and told her to write a book sharing her good and bad experiences, but she was extremely reluctant to reveal her painful experiences. She was telling me I should write a book showing how I went from a difficult childhood to where I am today, so other people will see there is light at the end of the tunnel. She said that people who have written books about their lives with Swami never talk about their bad times; that they only reveal their angelic sides from start to finish. I said to her, "Do you hear what you are saying to me? You are giving me the very reason that **you** should get busy and write your book.". She shuddered and said there was absolutely no way she could put those things on paper yet.

I had been extremely reluctant to give that reading, and had tried in every way I could think of to get out of it. I only acquiesced when my Voice Within let me know I was supposed to do it. It was only after talking with this Westerner, that I knew Baba put her in my path as a messenger to tell me once again that I was supposed to write this book. In my later visits to Puttaparthi since this trip, I have run into this lady and have been amazed at her transition. She told me she stayed on with Swami, because it was the only place in the whole world she really felt safe. In the beginning, she was afraid if she returned home, she would slip back into her old lifestyle. Now she just stays here to continue in her growth process. Today, she radiates Swami's Love. The change in her is so dramatic that she is like a beautiful work of art, done by the Master Artist Himself. Well Done Swami!

Puttaparthi, January 1, 1996

New Years Day! I wrote the following and faxed it home to Syd: "Happy New Year - Just received your fax after the morning Darshan and New Years celebration, and a pinch of prasad - that is what was left by the time the seva dals reached the back rows where I was. Did you receive my other faxes? You did not mention them in your fax and I want you to know that I have not forgotten you.

"Would you believe that the seva dals lined up again this morning to take padnamaskar? They took up more than half the Mandir grounds and there were soooooo many people that could not get in to see the New Years Program. Unbelievable they would let this go on during a holiday celebration. It seems to me it would have been better for everyone if their ceremony were held on the day before or after a holiday. But then, it is always Swami's Will. I was very fortunate to get inside the Mandir grounds, and once again, Maynard Ferguson and David Bailey played for us. With Maynard on his horn, and David on the piano, they played 'Five Foot Two' and other jazz pieces for Swami and us. Then the Indian musicians presented their best to Swami also. Both performances were beautiful.

"Only six more Darshans until I leave. Olga and Adrian just returned from Bangalore. They also went to Mysore and brought back some of that Amrit from the orphanage there and shared a bit with me. They had invited me to go with them, but my time was so short and I came here to spend my time with Swami, and really prefer to do nothing else. There is simply no way to describe the taste of the Amrit. It truly is the Nectar of the Gods. I saved a little for you and hope it survives the long trip home. See you soon....."

While sitting in Darshan, a lady next to me, Crystal from Chicago, shared the following from her notebook, which she had copied from another person's notebook, who had copied it from a handout, the origin of which is not clear. I am including it here because it is something I wish I had had to read before I ventured out of my room each time. Unfortunately, I needed the 'two by four' effect this trip, and I got it. With Swami helping us, we always get what we need, don't we?

Swami's Message

Use every little experience as a teaching tool. Put out of your mind any belief in chance or accident, and know that everything that happens here down to the smallest thing is an outpouring of my limitless Love and tailored especially for you. Notice the line you get and the state of your health and body, the way you feel, watch, act and look, who you meet and how. Observe especially your reactions to situations.

Just as in school, some will be teaching tools, others are testing you to show you how you are doing. See the whole atmosphere as a reflection of your Inner Being. The Mandir is your heart; I dwell in it. The Ashram is your identity and the Village is your worldly desires. In the Village you are strongly pulled outwards and away from Me. In the Ashram, you have more of a chance, but it is still very easy to become distracted. In the Mandir, (your heart), you can actually see Me from time to time, but even there it is easy to be only half present and not realize that I love to give. By my Grace, this outer show gives you the means to strengthen the contact to me in your own heart.

Make use of your time, concentrate every iota of your attention on Me. Open your self totally whenever you catch a glimpse of my gown. Be ready to accept an outpouring of my grace at anytime. What you want, ask for, and I will give you. But don't expect.

Think always of those more deserving than you and know that what you receive is an act of Grace and Love. Be open and free from fantasy and projection. Just be mine and I will be yours. This way you will find happiness and fulfillment. Remember that I am not only in Sai Baba form here, though that is central, but hidden embodied in everyone who is here. Can you find me in them or are you distracted by the outer characteristics and habits? Look deep with eyes of love and surrender your habits. Yearn for me. That is my Darshan which is also available. Honor the many examples here. Accept my grace from whatever source it comes. Be loved, blessed. Life with God is Bliss because you surrender everything to Him. Do everything for Him.
Sri Sathya Sai Baba

Puttaparthi, January 2, 1996

A lady sitting next to me in the token lines this morning tells me that Swami told her that Prashanthi Nilayam is the ICU where seriously ill devotees come to get healed. Once they are no longer seriously ill, they need to be returned to their respective homes around the world.

Puttaparthi, January 3, 1996

No matter what I have tried the past few days, keeping myself centered has been impossible. This morning I could not even surrender and was actually blaming Swami for my problems. When I came to my senses, I prayed to Swami to please help me get myself together. Then inside the Mandir Grounds where I am currently sitting, I finally realize that none of this really matters because I AM GOD. All of the rest of this is a trap set by the ego to make me think it is real so it will keep me there.

Over the years I have heard stories from other devotees about their different trips to see Swami. The first one or two trips are like they are in Heaven. Then Swami puts the heat on, and their lives seem to turn upside down. The lessons and tests are fired at them one by one. Still, they keep coming back to the Source, just as we have been doing and will continue to do as long as possible, like the moth to the flame, until we finally merge.

Soon I will be returning home where there is peace and serenity. This trip has been a trial by fire and I have had so many uncomfortable lessons, and beat myself up so much over what I let this ego get me into. I am not certain if or when I want to return. Life is much simpler at home, but do I get as much growth there as I have here? What did I accomplish this trip? Time will tell.

Home Again 1996

Once again, I had a number of dreams after returning home wherein I was traveling all around helping and teaching people about Swami's teachings, giving them vibhuti and pictures of Swami. In some of the dreams, I was visiting Swami back in India or on my way there, or at Retreats and meetings having to do with Swami. In my dreams, I was also busy processing more lessons, but nothing of the magnitude of the lessons I experienced in Puttaparthi this last trip.

Trinidad Colorado February 2, 1996

As often is the case, when I have said or done something that might have upset somebody, I go around beating myself up for letting the ego get out of control. One time, I spent nearly all day chewing myself out because I had gotten caught up in gossiping and criticizing others again, and when I am down on myself, it is nearly impossible for me to work on the book of Swami's teachings. I didn't know which was worse, the gossiping or beating myself up. It was like I had the feeling I wasn't worthy, and my vibrations were so bad that I was unable to let Swami work through me on the book when I was in that state of mind. I was already very insecure and did not feel deserving of being given such a mission. So I went to bed still angry with myself and with a prayer to Swami to help me get out of this space.

As I awakened the following morning, I heard Swami saying to me, **"Stop beating yourself up!"**. I don't know if I had been dreaming or what, but that message rang through my ears and planted itself in my conscious mind. Thank You Swami! You are the Doer and I keep forgetting that. I felt that if Swami could forgive me, than I could also. I will try harder next time not to get caught up in gossip and talking about other people. My problem is that I am into it before I become aware that I am doing something wrong. Please help me here Swami!

"The uncontrolled tongue indulges in four sins: lying, scandalizing, vain gossip and wanton fault-finding. God resides in everyone. The Lord has declared: all living beings are a part of Me. They are all a part of His Ancient Self, His Eternal Self. So every one is an embodiment of the Divine. When any person is ill-treated or harmed, it is God who is the target of that sacrilege. We declare that Truth is God and in the same breath adore falsehood. Resorting to falsehood is a demon that possesses and over-powers the weak. Indulging in unnecessary talk, talk for its own sake, is a morbid habit. It is also a waste of energy. It disperses company, for no one likes to listen to a bore. If he is tolerated for a minute, he will stick to you for days. There are others who spread rumors and gossip and spoil your peace of mind by poisoning the springs of Love. You must be engaged in developing the good in you, weeding out the bad qualities and heightening your purity and holiness. How can knowledge of the good and bad in others help you in this task? Talkative persons easily slip into scandal-mongering. Too much talk and a tongue addicted to scandal are twins; they work together and in unison.....Even when speaking the truth, one should not inflame passion, diminish enthusiasm or inflict injury: Speak the truth, speak pleasantly; if unpleasant, do not speak the Truth, as a modifying factor. Also, because it is pleasant, do not speak falsehood.

"Criticism of others is a very great sin. Criticism of others is like a great disease. It is an incurable disease. There is no medicine at all for this disease. Criticism of others is like cancer. Do not criticize, comment or make remarks about others at any time. We get into various difficulties by criticizing others. Be at a distance from criticism of others." DD 1987 P 24

Trinidad Colorado March 15, 1996

One night I dreamed we had gone to see Sai Baba and He called us in for an interview. But there was something I had to do before going in, like maybe go find Syd or something because he had not come to Darshan. So I was late getting there and when I did return, Swami ignored me completely, just like I was not there. Perhaps the lesson of this dream was that He was showing me that there should be nothing more important to me than my relationship with Him, the God within me.

Trinidad Colorado March 16, 1996

In another dream, I was walking along with some friends downtown and saw this bright orange movement out of the corner of my eye. It was Sai Baba leaving His white Mercedes and walking into an office. I said, "Look there is Sai Baba". Swami went inside and sat down on a sofa in front of a big picture window. I knew instantly what He was doing there and said, "He's buying property in Colorado!" Sure enough, when I looked up there was a real estate sign over my head. I locked outside at His car again and it was a big white Mercedes Benz. My friends kept wanting me to leave and I said, "How can you want to leave this wonderful Darshan we are getting?", and I just kept standing there feasting my eyes on Him until I awoke.

Trinidad Colorado March 28, 1996

Syd was traveling a lot after we returned home from India, and one night when I was doing bhajans alone, my dog Maggie was sleeping peacefully and gently snoring at the foot of Swami's throne. Suddenly she awoke and sat up and just stared at Swami sitting on His throne. I knew He was there with me, and it brought tears of joy. Thank You Swami!

Prayers, Life and Death

Trinidad Colorado, March 23 1996

Our neighbor Dave called after returning home from Denver to tell me that Lynn, his wife, was in very bad shape up there in the hospital. He could barely keep his voice steady. We did our best to comfort him. Since her last surgery, Lynn had developed a grapefruit sized cancer right near her liver and hipbone, and was receiving chemotherapy, but was not doing well at all. I called her in the hospital the following morning. She sounded just terrible, and I could feel a sense of hopelessness in her voice, as though she had given up.

I silently asked Swami to help me to know what to say to her, and felt He put the next words in my mouth. "Do you want to live?" She thought for a while and then she said "Yes." rather weakly. Then after a pause a stronger "Yes!", uttered forth. Then her voice picked up and gave an even stronger "Yes!". I told her I would pray to Swami for her and reminded her to keep using the vibhuti everyday.

Normally, I am not in the habit of praying for anything specific. When someone asks me to pray for them or for somebody else, I feel awkward because I am reluctant to pray for anything except Swami's grace, even a healing. When people are suffering, it is because they have lessons to learn. It is through suffering that they are more likely to surrender to God when turning to Him for solace.

"Give up; be willing to be a permanent invalid or to recover as God wills, but suspend all conclusions. Open your heart to pain, for it is God's will, wrought for your own good. It is His plan to dissolve the ego. Welcome it as a challenge. Turn inward and derive the strength to bear it and benefit by it." TEOL P 232

"To take upon Myself the sufferings of those who have surrendered to Me is My duty. I have no suffering, and you have no reason to suffer too when I do this duty of Mine. The entire give - and - take is the play of Love. It is taken over by Me in Love, so how can I suffer? Christ sacrificed His life for the sake of those who put their faith in Him. He propagated the truth that sacrifice is God." BSS Part II, P 171

I know from my own experience that when I was suffering, it was because I had a lesson to learn, and during the process of learning that lesson, I eventually realized that I needed to surrender it to God. If God had taken away the suffering without my learning the lesson first, nothing would have been accomplished. Back in the 70's we used to say: Pain is growth, and growth is pain, whenever we were suffering. It sounded cold to some at the time, but oh so true. My suffering is what got me to where I am today, and I would not trade places or my past experiences with anybody. When people are suffering, is when they are most likely to turn toward God. If things are going well, where is the incentive for them to surrender their lives to God?

"When grief overtakes you, and pain has you in its grip, the Lord does not always announce the exact sin for which that particular experience is the punishment. You are left to deduce in a general way that every experience is a lesson and every loss is a gain. You have got to learn that you bind yourself and you liberate yourself." SSS VOL II Chap 31 P 174

To ask God to end someone's suffering without them first gaining the benefits from their pain seems incongruent to me. Therefore, when I am asked to pray for someone, I will pray that Swami be with them, and grant them His blessings and His Grace. And, I ask Him to help them through their trying times and guide them to a peaceful resolution. Swami has some definite things to say about prayers:

"You should not pray to God seeking this favor or that. The reason is: no one can know what immensely precious, Divine and magnificent treasures lie in the treasure-house of Divine Grace. No one can know what God intends or desires to give to a devotee. In such a situation, by asking for trivial and petty things, man is demeaning his Divine estate. No one can understand what valuable, sacred and Divine favor God chooses to confer on a deserving devotee. Hence man should not seek from God, nor desire, nor pray for some petty trifles. More precious and desirable than anything else is God's love.

"If you wish to ask anything from God pray to Him thus! 'Oh Lord! Let me have You alone'. Once you have secured the Lord, you can get anything you want." DBB P 89

"Prayers for worldly ends do not reach God. They will reach only those deities who deal with such restricted spheres. But all prayers arising from pure love, unselfish eagerness to render service and from hearts that are all inclusive will reach God. For God is the very Embodiment of Love." SSS VOL XI P 68

"When people pray to God they should not seek any favors. You should not even pray for the curing of any illness, because the world is full of disease. You must feel that what is ailing numerous others is also ailing you. The world is full of wealth, houses and many other things. You must seek from God what is not readily available in the world. You do not have peace. You must pray for peace. Only the Divine has peace. The Divine has been described as the very embodiment of peace.....Nobody else except God can give you real peace.

"The second thing for which you must pray is happiness. Real happiness cannot be had from others. They may give momentary worldly pleasure, but only God has enduring happiness, permanent bliss. You must pray for that bliss. God alone can give it. He is the Lord of Bliss. You must pray to God for enduring peace and bliss and not for any earthly gifts."

"If you can only concentrate on the name of the Lord, all your wishes will be fulfilled. Do not ask for things. Aspire for God. That is true devotion. That is how you should live. All that you have to get is God's love. All that you have to do is Namasmarana." DD 1987 P 135

"Follow God's command fully - then prayers will be answered." SC May 1996

For several days after Dave called, I prayed to Swami for Lynn whenever I thought of her which was very often. On March 25, while sitting at my altar, I was praying intensely for her, so strongly that I started crying. After sometime, while still at the altar praying, I had a 'knowing' that I did not need to pray anymore, 'Because the decision had been made as to the outcome.', and I knew nothing more could be done on my part, and that 'What was to be would be', no matter what. Lynn continued with the chemotherapy and other treatments and experienced all the devastating side effects, with her hair falling out, nausea, etc.. She also continued with the vibhuti., and chanting "Thy Will be Done!", a bhajan I had taped for her at her request.

Trinidad, Colorado April 28, 1996
Prayers do work! Lynn's grapefruit size tumor disappeared! It was nowhere to be found when they did an MRI scan on her this morning. Thank You Swami!!! They did exploratory surgery anyway, 'just in case', to make certain it was all gone.

I didn't hear from Lynn for quite a while after her MRI scan and surgery, so I called her one day. We knew that Dave was a born again Christian and was the son of a Baptist Minister, but we thought he was tolerant of our beliefs as well. We learned he had extracted a promise from Lynn that she not get involved with Sai Baba, because Dave was afraid that they would not be together in Heaven after they died. They know that our lives totally revolve around Sai Baba, and thus she should not spend time with me, because it might rub off. She told me then, "But I know who really healed me!", meaning Sai Baba.

Their trials and suffering through the drama of Lynn's disease created a much closer bond between the two of them, and they have both become more spiritual and more reliant on the Lord in their daily life. Lynn went from suffering to surrender. Watching them now, you can tell that together with the Lord's help, they know they can overcome anything. When I speak of the Lord, I am referring to the One we all pray to, even though we all see Him differently. To me, of course, He is Sai Baba. Swami does say, "Call Me by any name and I will answer!".

Lynn is now working in the construction industry with Dave, and looks great, although she will always have a limp because they had to remove part of her hipbone. Their faith in God has since been tested over and over again, but it has remained ever so strong.

Trinidad Colorado, August 19, 1996

Our dear friend Vincent finally left his body this afternoon at 5:42 p.m., just six days after his 52nd birthday. He never suffered physically from the AIDS that ravished his body, and I believe that is due to Swami's Grace. The only suffering Vincent seemed to bear was the embarrassment of not being able to take care of his own needs toward the end. Prior to his death, Vincent arranged in advance and paid for his own funeral services and for the social gathering of his friends, family and loved ones that took place in a local restaurant after the funeral. Vincent went out in style, just as he lived.

More Baba Dreams and Leelas

Trinidad Colorado April 5, 1996

In another dream, someone was worrying about 'earth changes' and telling me all about what they anticipated to happen and also about their troubles. I said "Don't worry - Don't you know that Baba will take care of it all and I pointed up to Baba who was standing above us looking down on us.

Trinidad Colorado April 19, 1996

I dreamed that we were with Sai Baba and He had made a bunch of vibhuti and had given it to me. He told me to give everyone in the group some vibhuti at a later time to protect us, and that I would know when that time was. It was like we were viewing the world from a very large picture window and we could fast forward or reverse the scenes in time. A plane had been sprayed with fuel while sitting on the runway by vandals, (we all had been on that plane) and only a few of the people on the plane and nearby on the ground were able to get away before the fire started. We reversed the time of the scene, and I gave everyone there at the window some of the vibhuti, even some to Swami, who was there with us. I sprinkled some on everyone and put some in their mouths, Baba's also, and we were all saved from the fire on the plane. (I wonder if this dream had anything to do with the incident in the Bombay Airport in December of 1993?).

Trinidad Colorado April 24, 1996

Dreamed that I was with some people who were telling me about their problems and I told them Sai Baba would fix their problems if they would only ask Him for help, and I pointed up to Baba standing or levitating just above us. It was like as soon as I mentioned His name, He appeared above us.

This morning when I awoke I 'knew' I was supposed to start the book of 'my life before and after Swami'. So I set aside the book of Swami's teachings, and have begun the long journey through my life on paper.

Trinidad, Colorado June 1996

Have had many dreams about Swami and traveling back and forth to India and other functions related to Sai Baba. Following are some dreams of note:

Dreamed that Sai Baba said to me, **"Your marriage to Syd is for life and is not to be broken. Fix what is wrong if you don't like it!"**.

Dreamed that I was watching a movie that turned out to have a very unhappy ending. Then I heard Sai Baba say: **"We can fix that if you like. Just change your thoughts!"**.

Dreamed on a number of occasions where my life was being threatened or I was in some kind of danger, and I started chanting 'Sai Ram', over and over until I woke up. I find it very interesting that even my subconscious mind knows that calling out to Swami, or chanting Sai Ram will protect me from any danger. In several other dreams, I told people to chant Sai Ram over and over to protect them also.

Trinidad Colorado, August 30, 1996

Dreamed that Swami came to our home and told me He was going to spend a whole month here with me. We were doing different things together around the house. He told me He would help me fix all the things that needed fixing in our home. The first thing that needed to be fixed was a picture of Swami; in other words, how I saw Him as a part of my life, and I'm not certain, but I think it was the frame that needed fixing. I understood that He was going to spend the next month helping me to fix and finish and repair what needed to be fixed, finished and repaired in my home and also, what is wrong or needs fixing inside me. After a while, He was accompanying us on the piano while we sang bhajans, and He very dramatically ended a song by lifting His hands and fingers so gracefully at the end, after playing the highest note on the piano, which seemed to be a little off key. Or perhaps the white part of that highest note was broken. This was the second thing we found wrong. Then He told me to go get the glue along with what we needed to fix the first thing we found wrong. I told Baba that what I needed was upstairs and as I started to go toward the stairs, He smiled such a beautiful warm smile at me, and I smiled back and then fell at His feet in ecstacy, and said, "Thank You so very much for helping me fix what is wrong, Swami." He nudged me on the side and said, **"Yes, Yes, go on now child!"**, and the dream ended.

Our home was only partially finished before this dream, and no work had been done on it for several years now. Thus I had been more than a little disturbed because it did not appear that it would ever get finished the way we were going. I walked around with 'pretend blinders' on for six years and was tired of looking at plywood kitchen counters, cement and plywood floors, unfinished staircases and walls, etc.. My studio was still the storage place for all the building materials and assorted junk so I had been unable to unpack or work with my clay. I was also unable to work on the house anymore. In cutting and hanging the drywall and working on many other projects the first two years, I over stressed the muscles and nerves, injuring my right arm, so I am very limited to what I can do. Syd has been extremely busy with his work and has not had the time or inclination to get back to work on the house.

So, Swami gave me this wonderful dream, which was prophetic in a way, because within a short period of time, a man, spiritual in nature, who was living temporarily in Trinidad needed to make some extra cash. He was a General Contractor by trade, with experience on every phase of building a house. And, his birthday was November 23, the same as our Beloved Lord. We worked out a deal and he began finishing our home, little by little, as we had the money to keep him going. Thank You Swami!!!

Trinidad Colorado, September 20, 1996

Tonight while doing bhajans, our dog Maggie was watching Swami on His throne for a very long time, and would occasionally wag her tail and lay her ears back in the submissive position, as though He were talking to her. At one point, I felt that Swami must have leaned over and was petting her because of the movements she was making. She walked over and sniffed His robe and His feet (or where they would be if we could see Him). Whenever anybody comes to the house, she sniffs them all over just like she did Swami tonight. Thank You Swami for letting us know You are here with us.

Trinidad Colorado, October 7, 1996

Dreamed that I went to India to see Swami and I was in a building in or near the Puttaparthi Ashram and I saw my Aunt Gladys, who seemed to be some kind of authority figure there. She went in the back room and I told Syd, "That's my Aunt Gladys, my stepfather's sister!". I followed her into the room and there seated at a long table was my Aunt Mary and Gladys' daughter, my cousin Janet. They were all dressed in white. I told them I was surprised to see them there as I had been coming to see Sai Baba for a long time and had not run into them before. There was also a baby in the dream and I believe it was my son Robbie. All of these people have been dead for a long time, including my baby Robbie who died in 1966 at two months old of SIDS (Sudden Infant Death Syndrome). To know that they are with Swami there at the Ashram meant a great deal to me. Thank You Swami for showing me this.

Trinidad Colorado, December 21, 1996

While struggling to get Chet's (a long time friend of Syd), quilt finished one evening so I could get it in the mail to him before Christmas, I realized I had made a mistake that would take hours to correct, and I swore out loud, "Sh__!". Immediately, across the room from me, a bright light flashed twice from Baba's robe around the tummy area. It illuminated that whole end of the room. Thank You Swami for letting me know You are here with me.

Trinidad Colorado, January 12, 1997

Tonight while doing bhajans, I saw Maggie looking toward the doorway, as she has done before. She was staring intently and I knew there was something there that she could see and we couldn't. I closed my eyes and immediately could see them - there were three beings, very tall, dressed in ancient garb. The color of their garments was white. One was an Angel with wings and a long white gown; one felt like an evolved being who shined and radiated love and purity and was dressed in a toga like wrap with gold braid; and the third one had tightly curled yellow blond hair with a toga like garment, with a brown leather strapped vest and a sword. Together, they were radiating such beautiful energy and enjoying Swami's Darshan and the bhajans, as they stood there facing Swami's throne. I know they have been here before because I have felt them, but I had never tried to 'see' them until tonight. And Maggie lets us know when they are here because she stares at them in the doorway, aware and alert.

Trinidad Colorado, January 19, 1997

Dreamed that we were getting ready to go to India to see Sai Baba, but we had to wait for certain things to come in first and they just trickled in. Supplies? Money?

Sanjeevini Healing System

Every time we travel to Puttaparthi, I purchase every book about Swami that I have not seen before, plus a multitude of other books to bring home to friends and others who are new to Swami. We come home from every trip to India with all of our luggage bulging with books and usually have to pay for overweight baggage.

I normally carry a book to read and my journal with me to every Darshan so that I can read or write or just meditate, whichever feels right, while waiting for Swami to come out. One of the new books I purchased and read during my recent trip was 'Ten Steps to Kesava', by Lightstorm. Towards the end of the book they mentioned the new healing system that Swami had given to the world, but they did not say where or how one could learn about it. So I filed this information in the back of my mind, hoping to hear or read of it again.

One day at lunch in the Western Canteen, my dear friend Hennie told me that there was a lady next to her in the shed who was learning how to use a new healing system that Swami had given to the world, and that she (Hennie) was going to attend a class given by a Homeopathic doctor who lives on the Ashram. When she told me where his apartment was, I realized it was the homeopathic doctor who had treated me (and thousands of others) at no cost for the respiratory problems I had experienced during Birthday. Most of these illnesses were caused by all the dirt and germs being kicked up in the air by the multitude of bodies moving about. I wondered if those little sugar pills he gave to me was part of this new healing system. Hennie and I agreed to meet just before the open class began and we would arrive together.

There were a dozen or more people in attendance, from China, Japan, Europe, Australia, and the USA. The doctor explained to us that Sai Sanjeevini is a spiritual vibration healing process - it is God's Energy given to us to serve mankind. He told us it is a gift from God to mankind, and nothing can equal it. Therefore, doctors and all other healers must remember that the real healer is God, and that they need to keep their egos in check. Sanjeevini means: One which is God - the power to provide - even bring back the dead - used by Lord Rama.

It turned out to be a very simple system wherein there are a number of different cards, one for each body part, and one card for each type of a variety of different diseases and maladies. One simply places the medium (pills, etc.), on the applicable cards and chants the name of God, or the Gayatri, or just any other mantra like 'Sai Ram'. We were told we could use any ingestible or topical medium to transfer this spiritual vibration into, such as water, banana, soup, pills, vibhuti, depending upon the need of the patient. There are many other possibilities with this healing system, such as purifying water, distance healing, charging your vitamins, purifying your medications from potential harmful effects, removing blockages, and so on.

The doctor shared with us that a lady who had cancer had an interview with Swami the previous day and told Swami about her problem. Baba said "I will take care of you". When she asked Swami if she should continue with the Sanjeevini medicine the homeopathic doctor had given her, Swami said, "Yes, this is very important medicine." The doctor also told us about an Italian lady who had been diagnosed back in her country with renal failure. She prayed to Swami, flew to India, and He put this homeopathic doctor in her path, who prepared the Sanjeevini pills for her. She returned home, still taking the pills, and her doctors' reports there showed that she was healed. She came back for Birthday and shared her healing with this homeopathic doctor.

Before I left Puttaparthi, I purchased the Sanjeevini book outside the Ashram and some homeopathic sugar pills. Then I charged up a supply of pills using the above process and the Gayatri Mantra on all the cards I could think of for myself and began taking them. Every time I thought about it, I would pop one of the tiny sugar pills under my tongue while on my way home, which included a few days in Bombay staying again with Mr. And Mrs. R again.

I had been home about a week when Syd mentioned that he

noticed I had not been napping or sleeping in, and that I did not seem to have any jet lag like he had and that he was still experiencing. When I stopped and thought about it, he was right! Usually it takes us nearly a month to recover from the effects of a long trip like that, and this time I was full of energy and going about life just as if I had never left home. I knew it had to be the Sanjeevini pills!

Several months later, our five year old dog Maggie, began to experience some serious problems with her hips and hind legs. As it got progressively worse, she would cry every time she tried to get up or move about. It went from bad to terrible overnight. It was Sunday night and the Vet could not see her until in the morning, so I charged up some vibhuti using the Sanjeevini method and rubbed it all over her, and put some in her mouth as well. She lay there patiently and let us do it, even though it seemed our touch was painful to her. We told her that if she was not any better the next morning, we were going to take her to see 'Doc'. Our six pets know 'Doc' very well, because he has spayed or neutered all of them, and cared for them when they have encountered porcupines, rattlesnakes, coyote packs and mountain lions. We also board our animals with 'Doc' when we go away for only a few days.

The next morning, Maggie seemed to have recovered from whatever had been paining her. She was bouncing around and eating again. But, just in case, we took her to see 'Doc' anyway. He anaesthetized her and checked her over thoroughly, and x-rayed her, and found nothing wrong. We could only attribute her change in health to Swami and the Sanjeevini. She has been fine ever since.

The next time we were in Puttaparthi, I went to the doctor's apartment, but he was no longer living on the Ashram. What I was told was that all of the so-called healers, including rolfers, chiropractors, Reiki practitioners, etc., had been told to leave the Ashram because some were misrepresenting Swami.

1996 Jemez Springs Retreat

Jemez Spring New Mexiso, September 6, 1996
    Ruth and I left early Friday morning for the Sai Baba retreat in the mountains in New Mexico on the Labor Day Weekend. We stopped in Taos for lunch and a brief bit of browsing and shopping in the two bookstores near the restaurant. Then on to the Buddhist Resort in Jemez Springs where the retreat is held.

    These retreats are always so difficult for me at first because I am unable to sleep the first night with all the confusion of the people I am sharing the bunk room with. I actually live in a retreat already, and this is like coming to the big city for me, because my roommates are bringing all the energies from the city along with them. In spite of ear plugs and Rescue Remedy and other homeopathic relaxants, silent chanting and prayers to Swami, I am unable to relax and shake their energies. My body is rigid from the tension in the room, and no matter what I try, I can not sleep the first night. Whereas, at home, I am always asleep within seconds of my head touching the pillow. Tomorrow night, it will be better as people mellow out, and the following night, our last night here, I will probably get a full night's sleep.

    The reason I keep coming to the retreats is because of the wonderful satsang and the bhajans, the speakers and group meditations, and the morning rituals, including the Omkar, Suprabhatam and Nagarsankirtan. I really love being with Baba devotees in this type of setting, because we can talk freely about Swami, and I thoroughly enjoy listening to other devotees sharing their stories about Baba. These are the only social events I go to anymore.

    It seems that Swami has brought me here this year to learn more lessons about myself and my ego. He has used my subconscious mind to point out to me every time this ego has sought recognition, which it did every chance it had. I awoke the second morning with Swami's voice still echoing in my mind, making me aware of all the negative thoughts I have had. He told me to listen more to the guidance He is giving me from the Voice Within. I am left with the impression from this dream that Swami's messages can't get through because I am always filling my mind with stuff and things, like watching the news and movies on television and talking on the phone about worldly things.

Back to the Book

When I returned from India, I started putting every ounce of my energy in to finishing the book of Swami's teachings. If I was ever going to write the book about my life before and after Swami, I knew I had to finish this big one first. Working on the book of teachings really has been an interesting process, because at one point I had over 1,100 full sized pages. But Swami pared it down here and there, as pages of text would disappear from the hard drive of my computer, never to be found or retrieved

Finally, I considered it finished and asked Swami what its title should be, so I could create a title page. From my Inner Voice, I later heard, **"A COMPENDIUM OF THE TEACHINGS OF SATHYA SAI BABA"**. I then called Jon Roof, our Regional Director, who had written the book "Pathways to God", and asked him about the process of getting the book published and distributed by the Sai Organization. He told me there was a committee of three that would have to approve it before it could be accepted by the Sai Organization, but that if I sent it to Leela Press, and they accepted it for publishing, it would probably be accepted by the Organization without further adieu.

So, I called Jack Sher of Leela Press and told him about my manuscript. He asked me to send him the book on floppy disks, which I did. I also included some printed parts of the book for a quick look-see. He called me sometime later and told me he thought I had done a good job, but that they, (he and Dr. Goldstein and others on the committee), had been focusing all their energies and resources on putting together all of Swami's teachings on CD-Rom. He indicated (without actually saying so) that my book would therefore be unnecessary.

Among the many reasons I used to try to convince him this

book had a purpose, I attempted to explain that the Compendium was designed to be used in study circles or other places where one would not be sitting with a computer in front of them. But the decision had already been made by them.

When I hung up, I felt like I had been dropped on my head. I went immediately to my altar and just simply surrendered it to Swami. I felt His peace and grace descend upon me as it often has when I turn to Him during troubled times. It was His now, and I wasn't going to worry about it anymore. As I sat there, I told Him, "It is Your book, Swami. You told me to put it together. If you want it to get published, please tell me what to do!". After I sat there quietly for a few minutes, I heard Him say, **"Publish in India!"**. Well, I had never thought of that, and it seemed so logical! But we were not planning to return to India for several years, mostly because of our experiences at Birthday.

Swami had something else in mind, because some months later, Syd got a call from the firm he consults for in India, telling him they needed him there the following week. Syd asked me if I wanted to go, but I declined because he would only be in India for a week, which meant he would not be able to see Swami, and I would only have a few days in Puttaparthi.

Several days later, Syd was sitting in his meditation area, when he heard Swami say, **"Take wife!"**. He shared this experience with me, and I told him I would sleep on it, as I do with any other important decision. As I think back, I can't believe I did not just jump on it and say I would go with him. Since the moment Syd learned he would be going to India, I had been working feverishly to get the Compendium manuscript in order for Syd to try to get some bids from publishers in India, if he could find the time. After being turned down by Leela Press, I found other teachings that needed to be included in the book so I had been adding to the manuscript again, and it was no longer in shape to submit to a publisher.

I awoke the following morning knowing that I should go to India with Syd. I now had only three days to get everything ready for us to travel, and I worked at it night and day, i.e., paying bills ahead, rearranging tickets, arranging for a neighbor to watch over the house and our plants, make sure the kennels had room for the dogs and cats, laundry, ironing, packing, etc.. And all the while, I was busy trying to get the manuscript finished and ready for publishing, in two sets of both printed pages and floppy disks.

Syd was busy getting his own paperwork done to take with him for his meetings in India and was unable to help. But, once I made the decision to go, everything started falling into place, and I miraculously found the energy I needed to get everything done. Syd's work required him to extend his stay in India to over three weeks, thank You Swami, so that he could spend some time in the middle of his trip with Swami too.

1997 India Trip

As usual, we spent the night in a hotel in Colorado Springs before our flight took off the next morning. This way we would be certain to make the flight, rather than take a chance of missing it if there was a problem during the long drive in bad weather from Trinidad. After we checked into our hotel, we had dinner at our favorite restaurant, India Gardens. When we told him where we were going, the owner, Mr. Singh, a Sikh, asked us many questions about Sai Baba - How do you worship? Do you consider yourself Hindus? Have you had interviews with Sai Baba? Then he told us of his American friends in Florida who were devotees of Sai Baba, and the many miracles in their lives.

During the first leg of our flight from Colorado Springs to Cincinnati, Syd pointed out that he smelled something overhead and asked me if I could smell it too. I did. It was electrical smoke, like wires were burning or something similar - like the flight that went down in the Florida Everglades, I recalled. Immediately, I said, "Oh Swami, we need your help here", and started chanting the Gayatri Mantra while Syd got the Flight Attendant. By the time she finally arrived, it was gone. Thank You, Swami! Swami has said that if you have problems while you are traveling, if you chant the Gayatri Mantra, He will come to the rescue. There was once a plane that crashed near Bangalore that had some of Baba's devotees on it. When Swami was asked why He did not go to the rescue of His devotees, He said that if only one of them had chanted the Gayatri Mantra, He would have saved them all.

The second leg of our flight to Frankfurt is delayed for hours because every single plane at the Cincinnati airport is covered with ice and has to be de-iced immediately before take off. Our plane is nearly last in the line to be de-iced. But, Swami always has a reason for delays, doesn't He?

While we were sitting in the Business Class Lounge, one of the ladies who works there asked us where we were traveling to. When she heard India, she asked us if we had heard of a man called Sai Baba. Then she told us the story of a man who had just been through there the week before who was returning from India. He showed her a beautiful and unusual ring and told her that Sai Baba had materialized it for him. I took this opportunity to show her my ring and tell her the story about how it was changed by remote control. She had many questions about Sai Baba and India. Then as we were sharing other 'Baba Stories' with her, another lady who worked there joined in to listen and asked even more questions. Before we left, I gave them each a bookmark with some of Swami's sayings on them plus some vibhuti. It was all I had with me to give.

We arrived in Bombay and checked into our hotel around 3 a.m. After we rested, Syd was picked up by car at 9:30 a.m. on Saturday. I was fortunate to get a massage in the hotel, which helped work out the muscle spasms and tightness that happens when one sits for two days in airports and airplanes.

We visited with Madhu and Niranjan Patel for three hours. Niranjan is not well, and because of his diabetic condition, has had steady and continuous pain in his eyes for many months. We can see that he is very debilitated and suffering tremendous pain. He is considering having an operation to remove the eyeballs that are causing the pain. But, he perks up as he begins telling us the latest 'Baba Stories'.

Regarding getting the COMPENDIUM published, Niranjan advised that I contact Mr. Narasimhan at the Ashram, who is the editor of the monthly Ashram magazine, Sananthana Sarathi. He also gave us the name and address of one of the publishers of the Ashram books, and told us that if they publish it, it will be almost certain it will get into the Ashram bookstore.

While awaiting my plane to Puttaparthi in the boarding section of the Bombay Airport, a tall good looking young man walked up to me and asked if I was going to Puttaparthi. He looked relieved when I told him "Yes!" and sat down beside me, telling me his name was Ron from the UK. Ron said he had just been ripped off in front of the airport by a man pretending to be a cop. The thief had taken a large part of his cash intended for his trip to Puttaparthi. When he realized he had been taken, he reported it to the policeman in the little cubbyhole station outside the airport. I told him not to worry, because Sai Baba would take care of it for him, just as He takes care of all people who are in transit to see Him. Ron wasn't sure about that. This was his first trip to India, and seeing Sai Baba was a side trip for him after visiting friends in Delhi.

As we were talking, several policemen came up and asked Ron some questions. Then I watched as the officers gave him back his money. They told him they had found the crook and retrieved his money. Ron was totally blown away. He had heard horror stories about India and never expected to see his money again. I assured him it was only Swami's grace that he had just experienced, and sometimes Swami revealed His Divinity to people in such a way.

When we arrived at the Puttaparthi Airport, Ron helped me with my luggage, bless his heart! There are no porters there and one must be responsible for one's own baggage. I found a taxi for us and we dropped Ron at the Ashram gate. Then I was delivered to Sai Towers Hotel, checking into Room 302, the top floor and a long walk up for me.

Went to Darshan at 3 p.m. and just walked right in. Everyone was already seated, and I got a very decent seat behind them, not too far back. When Swami came out, I burst into tears of joy at the sight of Him. It happens to me every time I first see His glorious form when I return. As the tears streamed down my face, I heard a little girl nearby ask her mother, "Mommy, why is that lady crying?". "Hush", her mother said. Later, I found Vidya at her apartment and arranged for her to come to my hotel room to give me a massage that night.

Sai Towers now has telephones in their rooms, so I called Syd at the President Hotel in Bombay to tell him all is well here, and I shared the story of Ron and the police. Syd had been watching the scenario from the large window on the floor above us in the Bombay Airport. I filled in the blanks for him. After talking to Syd, I had some boiled vegetables in the vegetarian restaurant downstairs, had my massage, and slept until 3 a.m..

Puttparthi, February 1997

First morning at Darshan and I was in line 4 and got to sit in the first row on the side where Swami first comes in, if He comes early. But His routine has changed again and now I understand why I was easily able to get a seat in the first row! In the afternoon, I got line 2 and sat in row 2. When Swami came out, I offered Him my manuscript to sign and He turned and walked away, so that all I got was 'Back Darshan'! I cried with joy like a baby, because when He looked me in the eye, I knew He knew I was there. I did not actually carry the entire 770 page manuscript to Darshan, because I could barely lift it. I met a lady from California when I first arrived who gave me a wonderful suggestion and I took her advice. All I carried in to Darshan was the first 30 or 40 pages of the manuscript in a glycine envelope.

Served lunch in the Western Canteen and bought two extra roasted sweet potatoes for supper in my room tonight so I won't have to leave my room to eat. Had two coconuts after the afternoon Darshan. They are so full of healing qualities. I really wish there were some way we could have these at home.

I renewed our two subscriptions for the Sananthani Sarathi and found out how to contact Mr. Narasimhan, its editor. As instructed, I went to his apartment after bhajans, and he was just leaving. He told me to walk with him, and then to come back to his apartment at 2:30 and he would meet with me. I walked along with him and we talked briefly. He was not very encouraging and told me there are other books like mine already published. I knew that my meeting with him would be very important and I also knew that I would possibly miss Darshan. My feeling is, "Don't miss this appointment.", even if you must give up Darshan.

I arrived promptly at his apartment at 2:30. He was sleeping, and his wife awakened him. He asked why I was there and I told him Niranjan Patel advised me to see him. He asked how Niranjan was doing, and said that Niranjan and the publisher he had suggested are very good people. Then I showed him the manuscript.

He browsed through the Compendium manuscript for awhile, than said, "Fantastic!". "Fantastic, simply fantastic!", he repeated over and over as he looked at page after page. Mr. Narasimhan noted that many of the quotes were current and taken from the Sananthana Sarati, the magazine for which he is the editor. He asked whether we could afford to publish the book and I told him we were in the process of getting bids in Bombay and Bangalore, and maybe from Sai Towers, who had recently begun the publishing business. Mr. Narasimhan shared with me that Sai Towers was in the process of publishing his autobiography, "Bapu to Baba", which he was going to present to Swami as part of the ceremony on Mahashivaratri, on March 7th. Then he gave me some other advice and wished me well.

Wednesday February 19, 1997

A very busy day - awoke at 3:30 a.m. Feeling very high spiritually today. Was in line one again and sat in the first row facing the back of the bookstore. While running to get my space on the floor, I lost my chain with the rudruksha bead, the Ganesha pendant and the OM sign. The chain broke, but I kept going so that I could get a spot in the first row. I put my cushion down and went back to search for my chain. The head Security lady gave it to me after I described it to her. I returned to find that there were now three cushions where my cushion once was. Undaunted, Swami's will is accepted. There was still a tiny space for me.

Line one again this afternoon - I could barely contain myself while waiting for Swami, and when He finally came out, my heart pounded rapidly. He went first to the dignitary across from me, who I later learned was the wife of Japan's Prime Minister. Back Darshan once again. He completely ignored my manuscript which I held up for Him as He passed by. I had the feeling I was being used as an example to show how even though He ignored me, I never lost faith or got upset or anything. Its like I knew this and that He will sign it someday. And, after He passed by, I KNEW something BIG was going to happen. I felt that He planted that seed thought in my mind. Thank You Baba!

February 20, 1997

Had breakfast with Ron from the UK and Stan from Australia in the Sai Towers' restaurant. Stan tells us he is going to be the one to give Faye away in her and David Bailey's wedding ceremony in the UK this Summer. His wife is home right now, as we speak, making Faye's wedding gown. He has known Faye for a very long time.

Ron announced, "It's Christmas today!". He is so happy that he is moving to a hotel today after a few days in the sheds where he bunked near Stan. Some red ants had attacked his ankles while he slept and their bites have become infected. The doctor at the Puttaparthi Hospital advised him to leave the sheds and find a hotel room outside.

After I rested, I went upstairs to see Rajendran. He is the Publishing Manager for Sai Towers that Padmanabhan, owner of Sai Towers told me I should see about getting a quote for publishing the book. Rajendran will let me know in several hours how much it will cost to publish the Compendium.

And, once again this afternoon, I got Back Darshan. I've been beating myself up all afternoon for being naughty. I should not have talked (gossiped) about that crazy lady who says she and Swami walk together when He gives Darshan and they teach together, etc. It is really none of my business what she believes. Her vibrations were extremely bad and I got away from her as soon as I could, but some of her rubbed off on me. Before this incident, I was feeling so smug - thinking how realized I am now and having few challenges. But Baba took care of my inflated ego, once again. "Thank You Swami! Thank You for pointing out my weaknesses so I can work on them while I am here with You to help me."

Puttaparthi, February 21, 1997

This morning I was in line 10 and sat behind the VIP section in about the 15th row, but a seva dal moved me up to the 6th row. Thank You Swami.

Puttaparthi, February 22, 1997

This afternoon it is amazing, but I am in Row one once again after being in Token Line one. I wonder what the odds on this are with the many thousands of people here. Swami came along and lifted both of His hands up, as He often does when He is lifting up the energies and/or our consciousness. Well, this time, He lifted me right off my cushion. I am totally blissed out. He filled us with so much of His LOVE I am dizzy. When I am at home, I use these times to recall from my memory, and can actually recapture the same feeling, over and over. What a blessing He gives us!

In the afternoon, I am in the third row sitting next to Dahlia from Israel. She is a good friend of Shimshon and Chedva and will say hello to them for us. As we sat waiting for Swami to come out, she told me she decided that she would have an interview today, and by golly, her group got one. Amazing! I am very happy for her.

Puttaparthi February 23, 1997

Full Moon in 3 degrees of Virgo today. Was in the last line this morning and with Swami giving the seva dals their padnamaskar, we had a long Darshan. Then as Swami left, He turned and waved goodbye to us. I cried and cried with tears of joy at the LOVE He filled us with when He did that.

Had lunch with Ron and Stan at Sai Towers and a couple whose names I don't remember. They have been traveling around India for some time. We all got along nicely until I mentioned in a conversation we were having about the Dali Lama that I was present at a conference where he was eating a hamburger and how I lost my esteem for him at that point. When the couple asked why I lost respect, I told them what Swami says about eating meat. I also told them what happens when you eat a fish, or any other animal for that matter. Their next incarnation is as a human being, and that they are not ready to be human beings yet because they have not learned the lessons they need to learn as they evolve up through the evolutionary chain; and that Swami says this is the reason there are so many cruel and animalistic people in the world.

I also shared with them that Swami says, "We are what we eat and if we eat animal, we think and act like an animal, and we are an animal.". The couple abruptly left after that. Ron and Stan had a good laugh and then explained why. They told me that the couple had been written up in an Indian newspaper. The article they are proudly passing around about their trek through India told how they were on their way to McDonald's in Delhi for a hamburger. I felt very strongly that Swami was using me as a messenger to impart His teachings to them. I probably would not have gone as far as I did about eating meat if they had not asked questions.

The Interview and The Compendium

When I learned our row got line one, my first thought was, "Ok Swami - Have You given me line one so You can ignore me again?". This afternoon at 4 p.m., when Swami walked towards me, He looked me right in the eye and an eternity passed in that moment of eye contact. After the eye contact, He turned and walked to the other side, and quietly said to me, **"Wait for husband!"**. Wow! Frankly, I don't know whether I heard Him say it out loud or if it came through my Inner Voice, but I absolutely did hear it. Now I understand what is going on. Oh Swami, You are so wonderful! Now I can relax and just enjoy being here.

Puttaparthi February 23, 1997

Was in Line three this morning and there are soooooo many students that there is no chance to get close. But, still the tears of joy come after Swami passes by. I sat next to a lady from Tennessee - she tells me there is a letter going around saying that Baba says no interviews for USA groups. Is this a test, Swami?

While I was in the queue lines, a Russian lady sitting next to me was reading a Russian newspaper. There were two full pages devoted to Swami with His picture set in the middle of one of the pages. And we never even see an article about Swami in our USA papers. I know it is Swami's Will and that so long as our society in the USA is so materialistic, my fellow citizens will never want to read or hear about Swami, nor will they be ready for His teachings.

Went late to this afternoon Darshan - it is getting hotter every day - too hot for me to sit that long - was already overheated when I got in the token lines. Syd arrived this afternoon - gave him a big hug in the street as he got out of his taxi. He really looked good, but tired. Now he can rest. Syd had stopped in Bangalore and met with the publisher there, who will have a quote ready in a few days to publish the Compendium.

Puttapathi February 24, 1997

Was in Row 4 in the morning and Swami never walked down our side again. "Love My Uncertainty", He says. I was in the last row called this afternoon. I could really feel Swami after He first came out and went inside to "work" in the Interview Room before Darshan. He was sending out love with all caps, **"LOVE"**. Very uplifting and worth sitting in this heat waiting for it.

Puttaparthi February 25, 1997

Line 14 this morning, Line 12 this afternoon. Got a good Darshan both times. A bunch of Dignitaries complete with military guards arrived for the afternoon Darshan. An Indian lady tells me one of them is a Minister in the Indian Government. I saw Swami make vibhuti for them and put it in their hands. Then I watched as one of them looked at the vibhuti, and after Swami was gone, he wiped it off his hand on the side of his trousers.

Puttaparthi February 26, 1997

Line three this afternoon and got to sit in the second row facing the bookstore - a very advantageous place. It is so hot and a European lady is trying to crowd into my space. The lady next to me tells her there is no room for her. She starts whimpering and moaning and crying like a child who is not going to give up until she gets her way. We ignore her efforts, but she continues trying to move up and squeeze in between us.

When Swami passes by, the ladies on this side of the grounds all turn and shift their positions to the right so they will be able see Swami while He is off to the right in the men's section, then they turn and shift one more time to the right as He goes up on the veranda. When we start to turn the first time, this European lady gets her revenge and quickly moves back up against me so that I am now crowded into a tiny space and I cannot turn with the rest of the ladies. She is taller than I am and there is no way I can see beyond her, and she knows it. I recognize this lady now - she did the same thing to me several years ago. First come the feet between the lady on my right and me. Then come the knees, and then when you are not paying any attention to her, she quickly scoots the rest of her body in between us, pushing us both aside at the same time. I let her move in beside me that time, but that didn't stop her from moaning and crying - she started the same thing with the ladies in front of us, trying to wedge herself in between them. What a way to go through life, I thought!

Later, as I am sitting there nearly facing away from the veranda, I twist my head around and I can see a piece of Swami's robe standing outside the Interview Room with His hand on the door. I somehow manage to raise up on one hip and look around to see if everyone has gone in yet. As I sat back down, I thought I saw Syd's hat dangling next to Swami. So I push myself up on one haunch and look again. Sure enough - it is Syd! I cried out, "My husband!". I don't know how I managed to stand up from that tiny space, but I did and I ran as fast as I could. The security seva dal sitting behind me told me to take the short cut to the veranda, rather than run all the way around behind the women. The crowd of ladies applauded. Apparently, they had been watching the drama of Syd and Swami both looking for me in the crowd, and there I was, just 20 feet in front of them.

Swami opened the door and let the both of us in. I stood with my back to the wall, trying to catch my breath and shake off the horrible feeling that I came within a second of missing this interview. My heart quakes even as I write this at the thought of missing out on what happened next. Swami walked in and looked at me and said firmly, "Sit down!". I slid with my back down the wall to the floor into a sitting position, still in shock. I realized I had left my cushion and book and bag where I had been sitting, but I didn't care about that. I had the portion of the manuscript with me and I made it in time, and that is all that was important.

Syd told me later that Swami was telling him to go back because I had not come to the veranda, and He would call us again tomorrow for an interview. This of course was all Swami's leela because Swami was standing there holding Syd's hand. Syd could not leave the veranda so long as Swami was holding his hand, and Swami was not letting go, and Syd wasn't about to pull his hand out of Swami's hand either. Baba had already sent back a large group of Italians while Syd was standing there, because there were too many of them. He told them He would call them again tomorrow, but He never called them again while we were still there. Swami's tomorrows and laters and soons mean something entirely different to Him than they do to us.

As I gazed around the interview room, I saw two Italian ladies, about six or seven Italian men, two Indian families and a single Indian man, besides Syd and myself. Swami moved about the ladies side of the room, making and distributing vibhuti into our hands.

Baba sat on His chair and called an Indian man up to Him and asked for his ring. Swami held it up and pointed out how dark the metal had gotten, then He blew on it three times and it changed into bright gold again. Baba told us that the ring became dark because of bad use. The man he gave the ring to looked like he didn't know whether to be happy or hide his face after Swami's comment.

Next, Swami addressed an older woman in the back and acknowledged that her health was not good. He materialized a white lingam for her and instructed her to pour water over it and take one teaspoon of that water each morning and night and it would heal her.

Then Swami materialized a beautiful diamond watch for another man. And then out of thin air came a beautiful etched silver container with a Ganesh Idol on top. He passed it to an Italian lady for her to admire, and she opened it and showed it to those around her. It was empty. Swami then asked her to return it to Him. He tapped the cover three times and then opened it Himself to show us that it was now filled with His sweet smelling vibhuti, which actually smelled like Him. As He handed the container back to the lady, He told her its contents would heal her. She melted in tears.

Swami took in each family and group for separate interviews. An older Indian lady had trouble getting up from the floor to go into the Inner Room and had to be helped up by her children. Swami turned to us and said, "Too fat!", as He made a round motion with His hands and giggled. We all laughed at His playfulness.

He gave robes to each of the Italian ladies, and turned to me and asked me if I would like one of His robes too. I answered, "Oh Swami thank You, but You gave me one already in 1994!" This was a big mistake, as I will elucidate later in the book.

He then asked me in front of everybody, "What do you want?".

As I held up my hands, I answered, "Only You Swami!". This answer was not planned because I never really expected the question, it was just spontaneous. When they heard Swami ask me what I wanted, two of the Italian men asked Swami for a ring and something else, simultaneously. Swami turned to them and said, "Jealous?".

Swami asked one of the Italian boys, "Where is wife?". The boy looked astonished. Swami said, "Girlfriend?", and indicated this was not right. Swami made a large diamond ring for him. Swami turned to the Italian boy's mother and said, "Very happy!"

Swami then asked me if I had been inside yet and I said, "No!".

He pointed to the door of the Inner Room for me to go inside, and I said, "Husband too?".

"Yes, Yes." Once inside, He asked me twice, "How are you Sir? How are you Sir?".

I answered "Just wonderful now, with You!". Then He asked Syd the same question. I have been told by others that when Swami addresses you as Sir, whether you are man or woman, He is telling you that you will be liberated in this lifetime. This is understakable if God is the only male. Of course, this could be just another one of those rumors that makes its way around.

Swami looked at Syd and said, "Health not good, don't worry, mind is good, but always busy. Not bad."

When we first sat down, Swami took my right hand and placed it on His left knee, and held it with His left hand. I put my left hand on His left foot and held it there completing the circuit and felt the energy flow from Him through me. Swami also took Syd's left hand and placed it on His right knee, holding it with His right hand. This felt like it went on for a long time as we sat there in silence and He was just staring into our eyes. There seemed to be some inner communication going on between us. Then, He massaged the tops of both our hands continually as He spoke to us. Syd and I sat there in silence, totally blissed out and immersed in Swami's LOVE. Then He looked at our wedding rings, looked at us, and said to us, "This is your marriage!". We both understood that He was blessing our marriage. This was the ultimate moment of all and there are truly no words to adequately describe it.

He turned again to Syd and said, "Your health not good, Don't worry. What kind of work do you do?"

Syd responded, "I'm a consultant."

Swami continued, "Your mind is good, but always busy. You work part time, sometimes the money is there, sometimes short. Don't worry, I will take care. You worry about money. (When) you need money, don't worry, I will take care. You work very hard, and work is not always good. Sometimes you have plenty and sometimes you run short. But what are you to do - everyone needs money to survive. You don't always like the work you have to do. You should not worry. No need to worry. I bless you! I have blessed you and will take care of you." (When Swami talked about Syd's work, I had the feeling He meant the *type* of work Syd has to do is not always good and that Swami would find a new way to provide an income.).

Swami held Syd's hand and looked at his wedding ring, which was on his middle finger because it had split at the joint and was now too large to fit on the ring finger. He asked Syd, "What do you want?".

Syd said, "Only You Swami!".

Swami asked me, "What do you want?" again.

I simply answered, "You!", and held my hands up to Him.

He looked at my rings and said, "This is not a Baba ring, this is a bazaar ring."

I responded in disbelief, "But You changed it Swa....."

He said, "Yes, Yes, I will make you a real Baba ring". Then He asked me several times, "What do you have for Me?". I realized He was looking over at the manuscript I had set down beside me. There was a little turmoil going on in my mind over this situation, because if I was going to hand Him the manuscript, I would have to take my hand out of His to pick it up, and I never wanted to let go. At that point I could care less about the manuscript. Then, feeling Swami's insistence, I knew that was what I had to do, so I picked it up and handed it to Him.

Syd said to Swami, "This is a book of Your teachings, Swami.".

"Yes, Yes, Yes, Very good." Swami said as He took and held the manuscript in His lap with His hands on the top and the bottom of it. When I handed it to Him, I put the Dedication Page on top. He said, "Very good book!". Then He looked through it for a few minutes, read aloud the dedication page and the quote at the bottom. With His right hand, He blessed it three times, each time saying, "I Bless, I Bless, I Bless this book! Very happy, Very happy!."

Again He looked at me and asked, "What do you want?".

I asked Him, "Would you sign the manuscript?".

He answered, "Yes, Yes, Very happy, Very happy", and started to reach for His pen on the table beside His chair. I quickly grabbed the only one I had, a hotel pen, and handed it to Him. I wanted the pen as a memento and had to think quickly. He signed the Dedication page, "With Blessings and Love, Sri Sathya Sai", and then read to us what He had written. He then asked me the title.

"A Compendium of the Teachings of Sathya Sai Baba", I replied.

Again He said, "Very happy!". Then He handed the manuscript back to me and put His hand on top of my head and on top of Syd's head and blessed us both, saying, "I bless You too (two)! Very happy! Very happy!"

Swami than said to me, "You want spirituality, and you worry about your spiritual progress. Don't worry, I will help. Sometimes the mind goes this way, sometimes that way", He said as He made motions with His hands back and forth. "I will help!". "You worry about your husband. You worry about your family all the time and what will happen to them. Don't worry! They are Mine, not yours, and I am taking care of them. No need to worry!"

He asked us, "When are you going home?"

We both answered. I said, "Syd on the third and I leave on the 7th".

As He got up to usher us back into the Interview Room, I said, "Oh Swami, I love You so much!".

He turned, looked me in the eye and said so sweetly, "I love you too!".

Back inside the Interview Room, Swami immediately materialized a three diamond ring set in gold and said something to me about each stone representing something. Syd said he saw a flash of light in the air under Swami's hand, just as the ring appeared in mid air. Swami pretended to struggle as He attempted to put this new ring over the silver bust ring, and when that didn't work, He pretended to attempt to put it on my other fingers as well on the right hand. I finally understood that He wanted me to remove the silver 'bazaar' ring, and He immediately slid the new diamond ring onto the index finger of my right hand, which I am told is my power finger.

As He put the ring on my finger, He said some words in Sanskrit, three I think, but they were quickly erased from my mind as though He willed that to happen. I caught the last word, I think, and I believe it was Mukti, meaning Liberation. I didn't think to ask Him to repeat what He had said, and Syd had not heard any of it. He told me later Swami was speaking too softly for anyone but me to hear Him.

Swami passed out packets of vibhuti to everyone, and when He came along beside me, He slapped me on the left side of my head with His right hand which was full of vibhuti packets, and then gave me a childlike, sweet, devilish smile. I believe this was meant to be the 'two by four effect'. I knew He was knocking some sense or whatever into my head.

On my way out the door, as I passed Swami, He looked down at my hand and said to me, "Four rings.". Those two words echoed in my mind as I tried to figure out what Swami meant. It was only after we arrived home that I understood what He was imparting to me. He wanted me to remove the Silver bust ring, which would leave "Four rings" on my two hands. I really resisted giving up the Silver ring because it was such a beautiful rendition of Swami and I had grown very attached to it since He changed it. Was He telling me when He said, "That is not a Baba ring, that is a bazaar ring", that I only imagined that He changed it? Were all those other people who 'witnessed' the ring change three times in the same illusion? Only Swami knows.

After we returned home, I asked Swami what should I do with the 'Bazaar ring'. He promptly answered through my 'Inner Voice', **"Give to husband!"**. It would not fit any of Syd's fingers, so he put the ring on his mini-altar where he communes with Swami.

In the Bangalore Airport, while waiting in the line to pay for extra weight on my luggage, I noticed a ring exactly like mine on an Indian man in front of me in line. I asked him if it was a gift from Swami and he nodded in the affirmative. It was on his index finger of the right hand also. We held our rings up next to each other and they were identical in size as well. The clerk began taking care of him and I was unable to ask anything further.

On my subsequent trip to India, I noticed a lot of rings like the one Swami made for me, but wasn't always able to ask the circumstances of how or what Swami said when He gave it to them. One young lady told me that Swami had made her three diamond ring for her when He married her to her fiancé. When He put it on her finger, a lady in the back said she had heard that those were not real diamonds. Swami quickly responded, "These are more than one hundred percent real diamonds and you can not find them anything like them anywhere else in this world!".

Another lady told me that a diamond fell out of her three diamond ring and she was told later by Swami that the part of her work it represented was finished.

A friend of a lady who has the same ring told Syd how the lady went into a jewelry shop to have the ring appraised out of curiosity. As she reached to take the ring off her finger, she found it no longer there. She searched all over inside and outside the shop, but it was nowhere to be found. On her next trip to see Sai Baba, Swami let her sweat for awhile, but just before she was to leave Puttaparthi, Swami came up to her during Darshan and re-materialized the ring on the spot and gave it back to her. All He said to her was, "The ring has no value!".

In an exchange over the Internet with a male devotee in Australia, he shared his story of the three diamond ring Swami materialized for him. His friends had told him it was a guna ring, representing the attributes of the three gunas, Satwic, Thamasic and Rajasic. A friend of his suggested that he should have the diamonds set more permanently, as they can and do come out. Later, when his wrist watch stopped overnight, he found a jeweler to get it repaired. Remembering the ring, he asked the jeweler, who specialized in gemstones, if he could make the diamonds more secure. The jeweler took the ring and began to examine it with his eyeglass. The devotee became very upset because his purpose was not to have it examined. The jeweler looked at him and asked where he got the ring. The devotee told him it had been a gift.

The jeweler said, "The setting is very odd - nothing seems to be holding the stones in place, no usual claws, clamps or glue. The stones are cut as they used to be done, ages ago - is it an old ring? You called these diamonds - they are not diamonds, but they are not zirconia either. I've never seen stones like these. I don't know what they are. The cut and setting is just like ancient times." The jeweler then asked if the devotee would leave the ring because he wanted a Master Jeweler he knew to see it because it was so unusual. The devotee declined, took his ring and quickly departed.

Publishing the Compendium

I am certain that Swami said other things to us in that Inner Room, but it was so dreamlike that it was difficult to keep a grip on all the things that happened. It was the following day before Syd and I could sit down and put our memories of this wonderful experience on paper. We returned to the hotel immediately after the interview and ran into Pad (Padmanabhan, owner of Sai Towers). Syd told him that Swami had signed and blessed the Compendium in the interview we just had, and that Swami had said it was a "Very Good Book!".

Syd and I had already discussed which of the publishing houses we should go with to publish the Compendium, and we had both checked with our 'Inner Voices' to determine if we were making the correct choice. The choice we made was obviously the best for a number of reasons. Neither one of us thought to ask Swami during the interview if we had made the correct choice. Certainly Swami would not tell me to **"Publish in India!"**, and then have us choose a publisher who charges nearly three times what we ended up paying to publish the Compendium.

At that point, we told Pad that we would contract with Sai Towers as the Co-Publisher, and that we would pay for the publishing and shipping of the printed books to Puttaparthi, with a supply to be shipped to Colorado. Syd prepared a contract that, among other stipulations, would give Sai Towers a portion of the price of each book sold, and the remainder would be set aside in a trust fund to pay for and perpetuate the next printing of the book. Sai Towers would be responsible for distributing the Compendium everywhere in the world except in the USA, where I would be distributing them. My Inner Voice, who I know to be Swami was telling me that I should continue my seva project by distributing the Compendiums.

Sai Towers' bid for getting the Compendium printed was about one third of what the publisher in Bangalore had quoted, and half what the Bombay printer wanted. We still do not understand why this is the case, especially since Pad promised and delivered to us a much higher quality book than the others could provide. Also, the Bangalore and Bombay publishers told us it would be at least two months, maybe more, before we would even have a proof copy in our hands, whereas we had printed and bound copies of the Compendium in our hands within five days from Sai Towers!

After the interview, I set to work immediately at one of Sai Towers' computers upstairs, repaginating and realigning the pages of text so that it could go to press. Their word processor software was different then the USA version that I used, and it kept rearranging everything and turning words into symbols. Eventually we decided it was more feasible to send the manuscript in (laser jet) printed form, rather than on disk to the printers in Delhi.

Sai Towers has a 'state of the art' publishing house on their top floor, with all new and modern equipment, and a fully trained staff to operate it. Pad had his artist do the graphics and help us design the cover on his computer, while Pad's editor did the writeup for the back cover. I chose a deep blue fading to a lighter blue which would surround the photo of Swami we had yet to choose. After I went through a multitude of photographs of Swami, Pad produced one that he said would be perfect, because it showed Swami in a "teacher-like mode". I took Pad's experienced advice. He used to be Swami's personal photographer and had an eye for things like that. It is Pad's photograph of Swami in front of the Mandir that sits over our piano in which the golden helix surrounding Swami appeared in a photo of that photograph.

Finally the manuscript and instructions were sent off on Friday night, and they reached the printer in Delhi on Monday morning. At four o' clock in the morning, five days later on March 7th, just as I was about to return to the Ashram for the ongoing Mahashivaratri celebration, Pad presented me with a copy of the Compendium from the stack of them on his desk. He pointed out that the printer had made a mistake and the cover turned out to be in shades of violet, rather than the blues I had chosen. There were several other things that were not as ordered, but to me the book looked better than what I had chosen for it. I told Pad, "It is all Swami's Will isn't it!", and carried the five pound book off to Darshan. As I walked with the Compendium held close to my heart, I could actually feel the LOVE in the book, as though Swami and the printer had filled it with LOVE.

While sitting and listening to the students singing bhajans that early Mahashivaratri morning, an old Indian lady sitting next to me reached over and touched the cover of the book and then touched her eyes, as though Swami was in the book. Then she smiled at me and patted me on the leg. She felt the same thing I had! To this day, people tell me they can feel Swami's LOVE radiating from the Compendium, even from the second and third printings. Thank You Swami!

When I talked to Syd later, I learned that he had received 27 copies of the Compendium in his hotel room in Bombay on Thursday, March 6th, just four days after it left Bangalore for Delhi! Syd said that he had taken one copy out of the box, put it on a table and sat there for an hour or so, looking at it, and thinking that it was Baba's miracle. We had ordered copies of the book to be delivered there so we could carry them home. Syd spent nearly one full day hunting up a heavy duty suitcase to pack some of these books in. it didn't survive the trip, but the books did.

While in Puttaparthi, I called the author of the Sai Sanjeevini book in Delhi and requested that a dozen copies of her book be shipped to Syd at his hotel room in Bombay. They arrived the day before the Compendiums did. I had checked at the little shop where I had purchased this Sanjeevini book in 1995 nearly every day while we were in Puttaparthi, and they kept telling me that they were expecting a shipment to come in soon. They never did arrive, and I had promised a lady in Colorado that I would do my best to bring a supply home for her. She had been at my workshop in Northern Colorado where I shared and taught the concept and principles of Sai Sanjeevini, and she wanted to start putting on her own workshops.

Puttaparthi March 3, 1997

Syd left this morning for Mumbai (Bombay). When I returned to my hotel room after eating lunch in the Western Canteen, I was nearly hit by a large van speeding down the street. As I quickly dodged to get out of its way, I came within inches of being hit by a motor scooter. The traffic and crowds were really heavy now, and unlike in the USA, it is the pedestrian's responsibility to stay out of the way. And somewhere along the way, I was christened by a bird on my sleeve. Thank You Swami! Later, Vidya, my massage lady, told me she saw me nearly get hit both times and she said, "You are very blessed by Swami, Madam. That scooter stop very fast." She's right, the scooter stopped instantly and it is a wonder its driver wasn't thrown over the handlebars. The driver looked as surprised as I was at how quickly he stopped. Thank You Swami.

Vidya gave me a recipe for an Ayurvedic topical potion to take the poisons out of my body:
> Mix one teaspoon of Turmeric and one teaspoon of ground Neem leaf. Make a powder and mix with one half cup water. Cook ten minutes then let it cool. Mix in some oil (coconut or sesame or mixture of both) and spread it over the affected area of your body. Let it sit for one hour and then bathe it.

Puttaparthi March 4, 1997

This morning I again got line one and sat in the first row facing the Poornachandra Auditorium where Swami's apartment is. He came to near where I was, facing me, then turned abruptly. I had the feeling He saw the letter I was trying to hand Him, and He was telling me that if I had wanted to ask Him for this, I should have done it during the interview when He asked me what I wanted.

In the afternoon, I am in token line three and find a seat in the second row facing the bookstore. I wasn't going to go early to Darshan, but I felt Swami telling me to, so I went. Swami never came down the center aisle; just the side to the Interview Room and later only to the men's side.

Puttaparthi March 5, 1997
In row five this morning facing the Mandir, Swami came along and His eyes passed over mine for a quick second. Thank You for this Blessing, Swami!

Spent all my spare time putting together an article for the new Sai Towers magazine, Spiritual Impressions. Was going to write about our interview and Swami blessing the Compendium, but as I began, I knew Swami wanted me to write about one of the times He saved my life.

This afternoon, I sat next to two lovely ladies from South Africa who saw us get the interview and asked about it and wanted to see my new ring.

Puttaparthi March 6, 1997
This morning everybody is in a foul mood, and there is one lady sitting next to me who smells very foul. Phew! The energies are extremely heavy and the crowds have increased tremendously. Its very difficult to move about. Almost like just before birthday in 1995. Tomorrow is Mahashivaratri. The seva dals are pushing people to the limit with their constant orders and won't let anybody pass the word back in the token lines as to which line we are in. An Indian lady in front of me is in a terrible mood and made a big deal of pushing my foot away when I accidentally touched her, and then later she physically pushed me out of the way so she could get past me in the mob scene as we entered the Mandir. Thank You Swami - I did not react.

I found Barbara of Australia last night in a dither - she needed to change her plane reservations and Suleman was not there to help. I took her to his office and had his people call him, but it was too late and there was no time for him to get the tickets to change them for her. Later she called Singapore Airlines on her own and made her own reservations. Barbara will share my taxi to Bangalore when I leave tomorrow morning. Was so happy to see her get an interview with her group this afternoon. She had been praying to Swami to put His right hand on her head and bless her, and He did at the end of the interview. She was absolutely blissed out. This was her first trip to India and to see Swami. Barbara is the minister of a small church in a rural part of Australia.

Puttaparthi March 7, 1997

Today is Mahashivaratri. A mob scene again this morning. The pre-queue lines were extremely long for Darshan. Finally entered the queue area, and we are line ten. Once inside, I have a good view of Swami's chair. The Mandir area is gayly decorated with flags, pennants, umbrellas, garlands - all bright and colorful. After being squashed into the tiniest possible space this morning in the queue lines, I was able to sit comfortably inside the Mandir grounds. The college boys' singing was exquisite - they sang what must have been old folk songs. Then they led bhajans. Most of the bhajans are familiar to me, a pleasant surprise!

Swami instructed the boys and seva dals to pass out prasad. We waited and waited, but none ever made it up to the back where we were. The seva dals kept going back to the same areas after reloading their containers and passing them out to the same people, and some were leaving the area with both hands full of prasad. I said to one Indian lady with a large handful, "Tsk, tsk, you took so many and there are so many of us who got none!" She pretended she didn't hear me, but her eyes told me a different story. As I look back, this was my karma, because of that time I took an extra laddu to take home to Syd.

Before Swami had the boys and seva dals pass out the prasad, I was beginning to feel very weak and lightheaded from not eating and I knew the prasad would bring me back to life. I had forgotten to pack a snack in my little shoulder bag. Without food when I need it, the effects of hypoglycemia set in and I become dizzy, disoriented and find it difficult to keep my balance or think clearly. This is what happened when I came up on all these ladies with their handfuls of prasad and I shot my mouth off. As we were trying to leave the Mandir, it was another mob scene with the villagers pushing and roaring, just like on Ladies Day 1995, and I started chanting the Gayatri, and continued chanting all the way to the hotel. By the time I arrived, I was soaking wet with perspiration and so very weak and wobbly, and I could not think clearly. I ordered some yogurt with honey, dry toast and black tea in the Sai Towers restaurant, and was fine after a few bites.

As I sat eating, one of the clerks pointed out to me that the first copy of the Compendium was being sold to a tall Indian gentleman at the book table near the front door. On this display table, outside their bookstore, were the new books Sai Towers had just published, including copies of 'Bapu to Baba', by Mr. Narasiham, editor of Sananthana Sarathi.

Two hours later, I was on my way to Bangalore with Barbara. We had lunch at the buffet table in the Holiday Inn. I had heard tales of their wonderful buffet of Indian vegetarian food, and I was not disappointed. We ate until we were stuffed. Barbara had never before eaten Indian food and she fell in love with it. Afterwards, our driver took her to the bus station, as she was heading off on another adventure. Her plan was to take the bus to a mountain, whose long Indian name I can not recall, climb up the mountain and spend the night of the new moon (Mahashivaratri) there. She had been told it was the most auspicious time of the year to do this. After I was certain she made it safely onto the bus, I did a little shopping then had the driver take me to the Rama Hotel where I could sit in the restaurant and read and rest until it was time to go to the airport to catch a plane and reunite with Syd in Mumbai.

As I sat in the Rama Hotel Restaurant sipping my cold coffee with ice cream, I reflected on the vast difference between this trip and our 1995 trip for Birthday Celebration when I had so many trials by fire.

The challenges were certainly fewer this time, and my reactions were far better than last trip.

Back Home 1997

Once again, upon returning home, I had many dreams of traveling all over speaking to and teaching people about Swami and His teachings. I don't know why these dreams keep happening to me when I return from India, but I would like to think that Swami has filled me with something that is worthy of being shared with others and He is using me as His vehicle. Only He knows! I have prayed daily since finding Swami to help and let me be of service to Him and my fellow human beings.

In one dream, we were sitting at Swami's feet and He was giving us an interview. I was at His feet and on the right side of me were several other ladies. Swami put His hand on my head to bless me, and then He gave me something. Later, I remember saying, "I never thought we would get another interview!"

In another dream, I was describing to someone about how Sai Baba materialized my ring. They did not believe me, and Swami suddenly appeared in the dream and showed the person how He did it. It was a much longer dream and after it ended, I was trying to recall it in my sleep during another dream in which I was traveling around India with two other women. We took a plane to a remote area and they fed us a wonderful meal on the plane.

Syd had to start traveling shortly after we returned home, and there was little time in his busy schedule to make the 100 mile trip up North to Pueblo with me to obtain my business license. Normally, we make the trips up North together because it is not unusual for bad weather to creep up on one out here, which can make travel hazardous. One day when the weather was sure to be good, I felt Swami urging me and I made the long drive by myself. The shipment of 270 copies of the Compendiums from India was due to arrive any day and I wanted to have everything ready so that I could legally distribute the books and collect sales tax on any sales in Colorado. I had received a very strong message from Swami that this was to continue to be my seva project, and there could be no room for profit in the sales price. After figuring up what it cost to publish and airfreight these 770 page, five pound books, and other expenses involved in getting them to the USA, it came to around $16.95 per book.

After asking Swami what name I should give to this new business, my Inner Voice came through with JAI SAI RAM, which roughly translates to Victory to the Lord! I felt kind of funny using a sanskrit name, especially here in Southern Colorado, heart of rednecks, coal miners and cattle country. Numerologically, JAI SAI RAM added up to nine, a spiritual number and Swami's number, and it all felt right, so I went with it. The clerk who took my application asked what it meant and I told him. He didn't bat an eye, but he didn't say anything either.

Once I had my temporary business license, I stopped at a nearby cafeteria and had some vegetables for lunch, then drove the 100 miles home, singing bhajans most of the way. That night and the next day, I felt fear all around me; fear because Syd was away on business in California and I was alone, fear at what might be in our shop downstairs in the dark, fear at what might have entered our home while I was out of town yesterday. Somebody's fear must have been in the food I ate. I had silently offered the food to Swami for blessing, but did not sing the Food Prayer because I was in a public place. Perhaps my offering was not sincere? Since we gave up eating meat so many years ago, I rarely ever experience fear about anything, especially with having the knowledge that Swami is always taking care of us. This fear was very real and I prayed over and over for Swami to be with me. After a few days, it disappeared entirely. Perhaps that is how long it took the food or the effects of it to pass through me.

"The Bhagavad Gita refers to purity in three aspects: The vessel, the process of cooking and the cook - all need to be pure and clean. It is very important that the cook should be a pure person. He should not only be clean and pure outwardly, but inwardly as well. That is why we say the food prayer, 'Brahmarpanam, Brahmahavir', we offer all the food to God.

"Since ancient times food was offered to God and so it became prasad. Then we can ensure the purity of the food which becomes transformed. Nowadays, the husband and wife are fighting at the dining table. The reason is that the impurities of the cook causes all these disturbances. The cook cooks for a salary. The housewife cooks with purity. It was the same in the royal families also. The queen alone should serve the members and not the servant. As is the feeling, so is the reaction. If the family is secure and happy the society is happy; if society is happy then the entire state is happy. So it should begin with the individual."
Kodaikanal Discourse, Apr 19, 1996

The Customs Officer in Colorado Springs called and informed me that our shipment of Compendiums finally arrived from India. He told me I would need a Customs Agent to help me prepare the paperwork and tell me what else I needed to do to get them out of customs. I asked him if he knew of any agents, and he faxed me a list of about 15 agents, both in Denver and in Colorado Springs.

Not having any idea which was the best, I asked Swami to help me make the right choice (as I always do with everything), and dialed one of the numbers. It was a lady in Colorado Springs. The first words out of her mouth, even before I could explain why I was calling, were, "You are calling about the Bibles, aren't you?". Now how did she know that? The Customs Officer had inspected the large, heavy boxes from India, an unusual shipment for them, and opened one of the books. He read some of Swami's spiritual teachings and labeled them "Bibles", which was the best word he could come up with for spiritual books. Each shipment since then has been labeled "Bibles and Testaments" by the Customs Officers, and by my Customs Agent, who purchased one of the Compendiums from me.

Because I live in virtually the middle of nowhere, I wondered how I was ever going to reach enough people to get the word out about the Compendium. Swami had given me this project, so I surrendered it entirely to Him and waited for His guidance. Several people came forward and shared their mailing lists with me, which was a beginning.

At Birthday Celebration in India in 1995, I had talked to several people who were online and they told me about SaiNet, a group of devotees from around the world who communicated their ideas and news about Swami with each other. We had just gotten online for the Internet before we left on this recent unplanned trip to India, and I met someone in Northern Colorado while I was putting on a Sai Sanjeevini workshop, who helped me get on SaiNet when we returned.

Meanwhile, I scouted around for somebody to put together a website for me, and found a young man who worked for the Internet server we used. I later learned it was his first attempt at creating a website, and it became a real learning process for both of us. At the time, there were so many things you could not do, like simply having a choice of fonts. But, eventually, a very simple website was established which basically duplicated the flyer I had put together. I once again approached Sai Net, this time to the Sai Discussion group, to get the word out via my website. Orders trickled in, and with each Compendium I put in the mail, I included a flyer that could be passed along. Then one day, somebody on SaiNet downloaded a copy of a news article from The Hindu, a large newspaper in India, giving a very favorable review of the Compendium. Word got out even more, and I quickly ran out of Compendiums. Coincidentally, Sai Towers had also run out and we had a second printing done and another shipment to Colorado from India.

Another significant dream - I was at a Sai Baba retreat in New Mexico and was talking with a lady about the Compendium. She said there was another lady who wanted a copy of the Compendium but she was dead. We all discussed how we could get a book to a dead person. I went out and sat in my car to contemplate how this might work and Swami suddenly appeared out of nowhere and said, **"If she wants MY BOOK, give it to her. Don't worry about how she will pay for it - the money will come!"** I went back inside where everyone was waiting for me and told them that Swami had appeared to me in person and I repeated what He said about giving the dead lady a copy of the Compendium, and that He referred to the Compendium as His book!

Several days after the dream, I knew who the dead lady was that Swami wanted me to give a copy of His Book to and I mailed it to her. She was among what Swami calls the 'walking dead', as she had been 'dead' in spirit for some time. The Compendium helped to reawaken her and get her back working her way along the path again. I was extremely gratified when Swami called the Compendium His Book. I had 'known' that all along, but to me this was proof positive that the Compendium was His book and I could share this dream with other people.

"Complete faith is most essential if you want to experience Divinity. There should not be an iota of doubt. One living without faith in the Divine is like a lifeless corpse." SS July 1994 P 177

In another dream, there was a disk which had something to do with Sai Baba. On this disk were written four or five words. The bottom words were Surrender and Play. I believe that Serve and Work were the two words on the top. This was a gift to me from an unknown source.

In checking our accumulation of frequent flyer miles we discovered that we had some that needed to be used soon or we would lose them. So, we arranged another trip to India for mid September through October and up to November 11th. I wanted to be there for my birthday in September and for our wedding anniversary, October 4th, and we preferred to avoid the crowds this time. Our friends, Olga and Gilly were arranging to go at the same time.

Once again, Swami had something else in mind. In early August, Syd learned that the CEO of the Indian company he consults for was going to be in the USA in October and November, and wanted Syd to travel around the country with him to a variety of meetings for three weeks. This trip was right in the middle of our planned India trip. There was nothing else to do but postpone our trip until after the first of the year. We chose February and March, so that we would be there again for Mahashivaratri, which we know is a very special time to be with Swami because His Energies are at their greatest then.

Mother's Death

In the midst of marketing the Compendium, we had what could be called a family crisis occur. On the night of April 29th, I had the following dream:

I dreamed that everything I did was being watched over by this very mean and nasty woman. She criticized everything I was doing and judged me very harshly. No matter what I did, it was not good enough, according to her. I resented it in the dream and felt that I was always being judged unfairly. I did not recognize this woman.

I awoke feeling like I had been beaten up all night long. That afternoon, I got a telephone call from my youngest sister Colleen. She said simply without emotion, "Mom died!". My two sisters have had little or nothing to do with our Mother for the last few years. I had not spoken to my Mother for over twelve years. Colleen explained to me that Mother's roommate heard a noise in Mother's room during the night, around 1:30 to 2:00 a.m., but thought it was my Mother's dog who stays in her room. My 76 year old Mother had gotten up and had apparently had a cerebral hemorrhage caused by or as a result of her high blood pressure. She had fallen to the floor in her bathroom while attempting to take some medicine. There was a gadget around her wrist that she could have pushed a button on and called for medical help. Because she had not pushed the button, they said she must have gone very quickly.

After Colleen's phone call, I realized that it was my Mother who had been the mean and vicious woman in my dream earlier that morning.

I experienced no emotion over hearing of her death. If anything, I felt shock and surprise. We all thought Mother would live forever. Her father was over 100 when he left us. But that night after Colleen called, I was unable to sleep. I kept feeling my Mother there with me trying to communicate her hate and anger to me. Every time I would fall asleep, I could feel her mentally shaking me back to an awakened state and then she would begin her onslaught of hate and anger again. I called out to Swami to please come and take her, but for some reason, He did not intervene and this went on all night. I chanted the Gayatri Mantra over and over, but still it did not repel her. Finally around dawn, she left me. I was ragged, drained and exhausted. It occurred to me the following day that if I had just sent her LOVE, she would have left me much sooner. But I don't think I was in a space where I could do that, even if I had thought of it.

Syd and I flew back to California for the funeral and memorial services. My Mother had been married five times, in which she was divorced once and widowed four times. But she was buried next to her second husband, my step-father, the father of my step-brother Patrick, and my two step-sisters, Patricia and Colleen, and the only father I really ever knew because he was the one who was there when I was a child. They had been married forty years when he died.

I did not mourn the loss of my Mother. I did mourn the loss of the mother I never had, the mother who should have loved me and comforted me and held me and taken care of me. As I went through this grieving process, I realized I do have a Mother like that living in India in Puttaparthi who is known as Sathya Sai Baba, my Mother/Father/God! And He had just told me during our recent interview that they (my family) are not mine; that they are His, and I should not worry about them because He is taking care of them.

The lack of a loving mother used to really bother me when I was young, because it does terrible things to one's self esteem. If your own mother can't love you than how can anybody else love you? You must be a pretty terrible person if your own mother can not love you. And how can you love yourself or anybody else? When I would read of a mother loving her child, or I would see how my friends interacted with their mothers, or I would see a movie showing a mother's love for her child, I could not relate to that feeling, because I had never experienced it. Years later, I remember reading somewhere that Swami said that if a child does not have its mother's love, than the child will never know how to love. After reading that, I got very angry and depressed and I cried out to Swami that it was not fair because I had done nothing to be denied the love of my mother. I begged and pleaded with Him to help me to learn how to love. I still pray daily for Him to teach me how to LOVE, and I know He has slowly been moving me into that space.

Somewhere in the Bible, it says the sins of the fathers will be passed on to the sons. This apparently is true for mothers and daughters also. My Mother's mother was a cold woman, and my great grandmother even colder, based on the stories my grandfather told me of his mother-in-law. And, I was probably just as cold as a mother to my children. But, I was never mean and cruel like my own Mother, although I was a strict disciplinarian. I had been hurt enough by my Mother that there was no way I would inflict the same on my children. In fact, I used my Mother as an example of how not to be.

My way of dealing with raising my children was to work and keep busy night and day because I did not know how to cope otherwise. Some of that busy-ness was time spent with my children, teaching them to read and cook and survive, helping with homework, making their clothes, traveling, camping, etc. It was the only way I knew how to love. I did the best I could, as I am sure my own Mother did, and her mother before her, etc.. The bottom line is - What happens to us is a result of our own doing - our karmic debt that must be paid!

My siblings had spent most of their free time (they all have careers), before and after the funeral going through our Mother's possessions, and she had a lot of them. She was a collector and never threw anything away. They hauled load after load to the dump, saving what, in their opinion, could be sold at a garage sale. I knew my Mother would just die all over again if she were there to witness that, and I felt sad about it for her. During the four days that Syd and I were there, we helped where we could. I found my Mother's Bible and learned that she had been involved in several churches toward the end. In her Bible, I could tell by her notations and written comments that she had finally begun to work on her spiritual growth and was making progress. My heart swelled in joy for her at this find! I took her Bible home with me in memory of the Mother I never had.

Her roommate was a lady about ten years younger than me whom Mother had taken in when she was down and out and had no place else to go. Mother treated Marlene like her own daughter and gave her the love and companionship that her own daughters never knew. I was very happy to hear about this also, and told Marlene so.

When Mother's Will was read, it showed that she had been true to her word. She had written me, her oldest child, out of her will. She had threatened to do that when I refused to give her my home phone number twelve years previously. I did not want her calling and talking with Syd in an attempt to break up our relationship as she had done in other relationships of mine in the past. She had my office number, so there was no problem with her being able to contact me if she wanted to. Her last words to me were, "If you don't give me your home phone number then I will write you out of my will!". I answered with, "You know what you can do with your money Mother!". My three siblings, Patrick, Patricia and Colleen had a meeting, unbeknownst to me and agreed that they should divide Mother's estate into four equal parts, to include me. Their generosity overwhelmed me. After the estate was settled the following Winter, with my share, I put a healthy down payment on a badly needed four wheel drive, as our other two cars were already ten and eleven years old, and experiencing frequent problems.

While in California, I tried to bring up the subject of Sai Baba once again to my siblings. My brother listened intently, and asked a few questions. I gave him and his wife a copy of the Compendium, just in case they ever really wanted to know about Swami. When I shared the story of how Swami materialized the ring for me, my brother said, "Now I would have trouble with accepting that.". We were then interrupted by one of his children and never returned to the subject. My sisters and their husbands were not interested, so I dropped the subject quickly after briefly mentioning Sai Baba and our trip to India.

Several months after Mother's death, I dreamed that someone or something was sitting on my chest trying to choke the life out of me and I awoke struggling and fighting for breath and for my life. It looked like a gargoyle and I knew it had something to do with my Mother.

Hennie

Hennie and I met in 1993 at Puttaparthi in the Ladies Shed during her first trip to see Swami. We quickly became friends and have kept in touch ever since by letter and by telephone. Hennie lives in Holland and we share several interests, the most important of which is Sai Baba. She became another dear friend and I invited Hennie to come visit the USA and spend some time with us. I told her we could have a great time traveling around the country. She and her housemate in Holland have a caravan (motorhome) and travel around Europe nearly every summer. Hennie has been all over the world and speaks five languages fluently.

Hennie took me up on my offer and spent a large part of the Summer with us in 1997. She arrived with only a single backpack as her luggage. I don't know how she managed to fit everything in the backpack that she would need for several months here, but she did. We had such a great time together. Syd was very busy traveling on business, and Hennie helped me out considerably with the chores in the garden and the house. When Syd travels, my workload doubles and triples sometimes, keeping everything going.

This was Hennie's first trip to the United States and I wanted to show her as much of it as possible. But we didn't really have a lot of time to travel with Syd being gone most of the time. Hennie was amazed at how far apart the cities and towns are in Colorado and elsewhere in the Southwest, and how barren the areas in between can be. She shared with me that the longest distance across her country, the Netherlands, was about 200 miles, and that there isn't a centimeter that has remained untouched by humans. I pictured the distance between my home and Denver - 200 miles, and that seems incredibly small for a country.

We did manage to fit in a two week driving trip, which began with the Sai Baba Retreat at Jemez Springs in New Mexico. Prior to the Retreat, one of the retreat organizers called and asked me to bring a supply of the Compendiums, because there were a lot of people wanting to buy them. They bought every book that I had with me, and would have bought more if I had them.

Just before we set out on our driving vacation, Syd had taken the station wagon in to be serviced, and a few days after he picked it up, it started making a funny roaring noise in the back. I pointed the noise out to Syd, but after checking it over, he determined it was nothing serious. So off we went on our journey.

Hennie thoroughly enjoyed the Retreat. There were four other people there who were originally from Holland, and had migrated to the USA. It was like old home week for Hennie. The Retreat was a wonderful experience, and we both had a great time, as I usually do, in spite of being unable to sleep the first two nights. This Retreat gave Hennie an opportunity to visit with and meet other USA devotees besides myself. Coincidentally, Hennie was also unable to sleep those first two nights at the Retreat, after spending a month in our home.

After we left Jemez Springs, we drove on through New Mexico and into Arizona. Hennie had always wanted to visit and experience Sedona because she had seen the beautiful red rock country in so many advertisements. Sedona has changed significantly since I first visited it when I still lived in Alaska. It is very commercial now and the energies have dramatically changed too, but there are still some beautiful places there worthy of a visit.

We spent three days in the Sedona area, visiting the different red rock formations and vortexes. From there we headed North to the Grand Canyon, another dream of hers to visit, and then through the Hopi Indian Reservation. We drove on to Four Corners (the only place in the USA where four states meet at one point), but never stopped to experience the area because of the outrageous entry fees. Hennie is very frugal, and could not believe people would charge or pay that much to look at something like a point where four states meet. Frankly, I couldn't either. Heading home, we drove across the southern part of Colorado, which included the highest mountain highway pass in the USA. We stopped everywhere along the way to take in ancient Indian

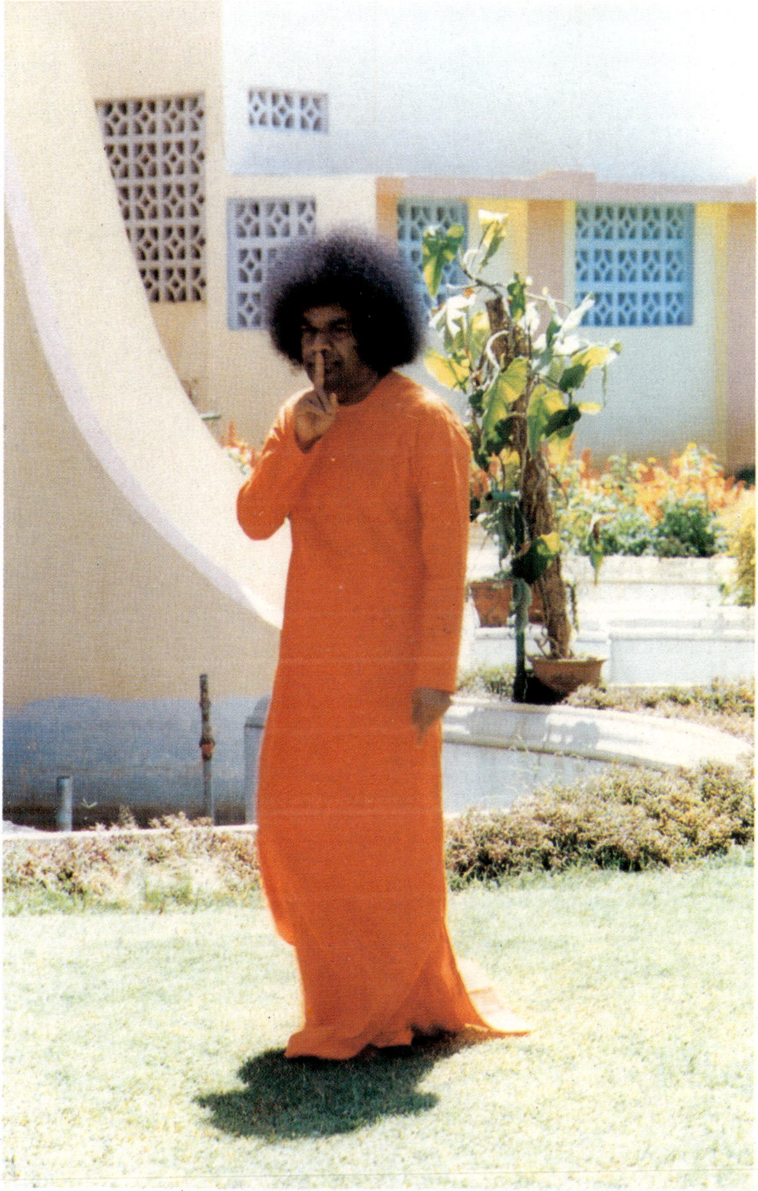

villages, historical sights and monuments, museums, and other special places.

Having Hennie here was very good for me. Whenever I would get upset about something or other, Hennie would be there to remind me that everything is just 'Passing Clouds', as Swami has said many times. It helped me to get right back on the right track. And I would do the same for her when she would have her moments, which were few and far between. She was a wonderful house guest, and was always there helping.

We have a large collection of videos about Swami and of people at retreats speaking about their experiences with Swami, most of which were filmed and produced by James Redmond. Every night that we were home, we would pop one in the VCR and get high on Baba. This was very good for me, as before Hennie visited us, most evenings I would entertain myself by turning on the television and watching a comedy or light drama movie. Hennie, who has a lovely singing voice, joined us for bhajans every night also.

We put Hennie on a plane for home at the end of September. Shortly after her return home, she repacked and flew off to the Lotus Feet for four months, which would end her "One year vacation the way it began". Her presence was sorely missed for weeks after she left. Some people just leave a big dent in your life after they visit, and she was one of them. We had gotten so used to having her here and she fit in so well. Syd and I agreed that she could come and stay as long as she wanted. She plans to return for another, longer, visit in the year 2000, Swami willing.

After Hennie departed, Syd took the car Hennie and I traveled in to a different shop to have it serviced, and they told him the rear end was totally shot because all the fluid had leaked out, and it was a wonder the car made it to the shop. Thank You Swami for giving Hennie and I a safe journey.

A similar thing happened to Joy and I when we went to the

Jemez Springs Retreat the year before. As we were loading up the car to make the long drive home, somebody pointed out they heard a hissing noise coming from one of my tires. The nearest station was many miles away, and I said a little prayer to Swami to help us to make it that far. I made a mental note to have it checked, and then totally forgot about it in the melee of saying goodbye to everyone.

Eight hours and hundreds of miles later, after dropping Joy off at her house, I drove home. As I got out of the car, I heard a hissing noise and there was my tire going flat as a pancake. Swami had kept it full of air until I returned safely home where Syd could help me with it. Thank You Swami! You take such good care of us!

Some more Baba dreams:
Dreamed that my husband, my sole support died and I was left with nothing and was wondering how I would support myself as I had not worked in years. Immediately, I knew that my real support was Swami and all I needed to do was pray to Him, and once I did, I relaxed because I knew everything would be okay.

Dreamed about Swami in three parts:
1. A lady was up on a stage like area and she was very uncomfortable about it. So Sai Baba put her in some kind of white wrapping, and sat her in His very large throne, which dwarfed her. She seemed to still be uncomfortable and looked so small on His throne. This dream came shortly after I was the guest speaker at Sai Baba's Birthday Celebration in Denver on His birthday. I know the lady was me and the day before the dream my ego came through during a telephone conversation after which I cried and begged Swami to PLEASE help me with this ego, over and over.

2. We were in a train station in India on our way to see Swami and the ticket agent said, "So many people going to see Him - I guess I should go too!". I had the feeling he was hoping we would encourage him to visit, so I started telling him some Baba stories from our own experience to help convince him to go.

3. Syd and I were sitting side by side watching the television and suddenly Sai Baba appeared in our home sitting across from us. Syd didn't see Him at first, so I elbowed him with my right elbow and told him what Sai Baba had telepathically told me: **"Look at Baba. You**

should not be watching TV when He is here with you! (Which of course He always is!)". There was more to the dream but it was like this is all Swami wants me to remember because it is so important. The look on Baba's face was so very loving to both of us. (This dream came on the heels of me watching a movie one evening and Syd getting upset and saying that he was forced to listen to it while he ate dinner. Not wanting to argue, I kept quiet and did not speak my thoughts, which were: "I'm forced to listen to the TV every morning because you are watching it when I come downstairs for breakfast!").

1998 Trip to India

At last the day arrived for us to leave for India. Upon our arrival in Mumbai in the early morning of February 9th, we rested, then visited our friends the Patels. Niranjan looks so much better this year, a year after his surgery, although he seems physically weakened since our last visit.

Mumbai, February 10, 1998

Before we left for India, I arranged an appointment with the Shuka Nadi Palm Leaf Reader in Mumbai. I know my life is entirely in Swami's hands, and I never really wonder or worry about my future anymore. I have no need to know, but this has not always been the case. I used to visit different psychics and clairvoyants all the time before and shortly after I found Sai Baba. In my quest to learn what the future held for me, I was actually looking for hope that things would get better down the line than what I was currently experiencing. But with Swami taking such good care of us, I just don't feel the need to know what is coming anymore. I'd rather sit back and see what Swami has in store for me. After hearing from so many people about the details of their palm leaf readings, curiosity got the best of me and off I went for the reading.

As I first entered his little office I could smell an Indian curry dish in the air, and it made the saliva form. I love home cooked Indian food. The reader, an old gentlemen, poked his head around the corner and asked me to take a seat, telling me he would be with me in a minute. Finally, out he came. He began by asking a few questions and told me he had read for thousands of Sai Baba devotees, including Phyllis Krystal, Rita Bruce and others. Then he took a small ruler and quickly measured the palm of my hand at different angles.

When I called the reader from the USA to make an appointment, I had given him my birthdate at his request. I was told to prepare a list of questions for him to answer before I left the USA, but I could not think of anything I really wanted or felt I needed to know. As he began my reading, he reached under the little table counter that separated us and pulled out a palm leaf from the shelf underneath. I had the feeling it was the only palm leaf he had, meaning he used the same one for everybody. I could be wrong - he may well have previously pulled the one out of a supply in the back room corresponding to my birthday to have it ready before my appointment. But then, why did he go to the trouble of measuring my hand? Was that not part of determining which palm leaf was for me? Over the years, I have met many psychics, tarot and palm readers, channelers, clairvoyants and other readers, including the ones who came into my bookstore in California years before. I learned very quickly that there are many phonies and incompetents out there trying to make a buck off of people looking for something good in their future. And I have known some of the rare few who truly were accurate with their predictions.

The reader proceeded to tell me things that would happen to me based on when I am a certain age. When asked, I learned that he uses the Indian age, which starts a child at birth as one year old. He said that money would always be in hand when I needed it, that Baba will come in my dreams and call me to India. And that Swami will come in my dream after one year from now and arrange for us to move to a different location.

He told me I would write seven books, that I would get an interview when I am 60-61 and then all my problems will be solved. He said I would get another interview at 68, which was ten years from then, and during that interview Swami would make a ring for me with His picture on it. He will come in my dreams and help and guide me. My health will then be good.

At 63-64 years of age, I will do seva for Swami and begin Kundalini Yoga, and Baba will give me healing powers. At 65-67, I will be successful in all things and will have nice health. When I am 69-70 Swami will give me a home in India.

When I am 71-72 years old, he said I will find peace of mind and will be able to go into a silent trance. At age 73-75 all my desires will be fulfilled and Swami will always be with me, heart and soul, blessing and watching over me. At 76-78 years of age, all my chakras will be opened, my third eye will be open and I will be able to see past lives, this one and the future one.

At 78, he told me I will move into Swami's Ashram until my life ends. He said that my last seven lives were spiritual and that my most recent incarnation was as an Englishwoman, who was a preacher and a devotee of Shirdi Sai Baba; that I had escaped to India via steamboat and was with Shirdi Sai until my death, wanting liberation. He said I will die at the age of 82, and will be reincarnated as a man in India and will live out my life with Prema Sai Baba. During that life, all my karma will be finished and I will get liberation. He offered that I have had many lives in India, Tibet, Japan and Egypt.

All of these things are believable, but for some reason, I was not convinced he was really reading my palm leaf. He only looked at it once that I was aware of during the hour that he talked to me. He could not tell me whether I would get an interview on this trip. When asked, he told me that earth changes, meaning the axial shift, would occur in 2002, but we (Syd and I), would remain unaffected by them. Only time will tell whether my Rs.1,000 was well spent. It sounded to me more like he was reading my Jyotish chart, not my palm leaf. And I would be very interested to hear from others if any of the events in their readings from this reader came to pass.

Mumbai, February 11, 1998

Last night we dined with the Board of Directors and their wives of the publicly owned company Syd consults for at an exclusive club - the Bombay Gymkhana Club. There were thirty or more at this large dinner party which began at 8 p.m., with cocktails. Syd and I sipped fruit juice until the buffet style dinner began. The food was exceptional, most of which was vegetarian, and we ate our fill. We were not aware until after we arrived that the dinner was in honor of Syd's recent achievement. Syd had helped to negotiate and acquire a settlement of millions of dollars for the company. Syd was their hero tonight!

I have attended dinners similar to this each time we have

traveled to India, but none before where everybody wanted to know about Sai Baba. They knew about the Compendium, and all of the ladies and some of the men wanted to hear about our experiences with Sai Baba. And where could they get a copy of the book? Actually, we had given a copy of the Compendium to the President of the company the previous year and he had installed it in the company's library, so I referred them there, and to Sai Towers in Puttaparthi. It was a wonderful time being able to talk about Swami to these people, because at these occasions in the past, it was always about small talk, which I am no longer capable of maintaining for long. My life revolves around Swami, and He is all I really care to talk about.

Mumbai, February 12, 1998

Today we leave for Puttaparthi. I awoke feeling separated from Him - the first time in a very long time. Perhaps it had to do with all that talking last night and the vibrations I probably absorbed. Jet lag really has a hold on us this time. We missed connecting with Hennie - she was to be traveling through Mumbai yesterday and today. Her plane leaves for home today.

Puttaparthi, February 12, 1998

The people who registered us and the ones in the Accommodations Office are so very nice this year. We were greeted as though we were long lost friends, with questions about our well-being. There had been rumors that Swami had replaced some of the old Ashram Staff, and it must be true. We first were assigned a room on the third floor, but soon found it unsuitable because of the smoke pouring in from the burning rubbish outside. The toilet had also come loose from the flooring and was unsafe to sit on, for fear of tipping over. So after one night, Syd went back to Accommodations and acquired a lovely ground floor apartment across the way in the same North apartment building, where the smoke did not reach if we kept the front door closed.

Puttaparthi, February 13, 1998

When I found myself in the first row the afternoon of our first full day in the Ashram, I wrote the following letter to Swami: "My Beloved

Lord, I've brought You another manuscript. It is about my life before and after You came into it. Please help me to know how to revise and finish it and give it Your Blessings. And if You would sign the manuscript, I would very much appreciate it.....All my love, Charlene"

Swami came along, looked me in the eye briefly and took my and Kathy's letters. He really gave me a long look as I said, "Sai Ram Swami!", (A dumb thing to say, I thought later. One time when He took my letter several years before, I said to Him, "God Bless You!". Even dumber, isn't it?). Then I spontaneously whispered, "I Love YOU!", while still looking Him in the eye. He asked, "From where did you come?". I softly replied, "Colorado". I'm waiting for Him to ask, "How many!", which is the usual question following the first one, and was surprised that He just kept on going.

A short while later, as He moved over into the men's side, I whacked myself upside the head as I realized what He meant when He said, "From where did you come?". I knew the correct answer should have been, "From You Swami!". So at that very moment, I prayed for Him to give me another chance to give Him the right answer. And every time I thought of this event, I repeated the prayer. When I told Syd about Swami's question, he laughed at me because I was so upset with myself.

Puttaparthi February 14, 1998

Was in Token Line one again this morning! Sat in the front row facing away from the Mandir. Swami came along and just as He came near us, He turned and gave us "Back Darshan".

After Orientation, we walked outside to Sai Towers and arranged to bring twelve copies of the recent second printing of the Compendium back to our room. I had done the revised manuscript in a narrow typeface to accommodate all the new additions to the book, while adding only a few more pages.

On the way back to our apartment in the Ashram, we ran into Chedva, our dear friend from Israel, and I gave her a copy of the Compendium. She was thrilled, and asked me to sign it. This is always awkward for me. Whenever I am asked to autograph or sign the book, I first make certain they understand that it is not my book, and that I did not write it. I was merely Swami's very fortunate instrument in compiling the words that He has written and spoken. I have done my very best to keep my ego out of the Compendium, but Swami is constantly sending people and situations to test it for me. Isn't Life just one big classroom?

Puttaparthi, February 15, 1998

Line 12 this morning, sitting way in the back because today is the day Seva Dals take their padnamaskar, which means Swami will be visible to us for a long time. Tears of joy are pouring down my cheeks - I am so verrrrrrryyyyy happy to be here! Now that I have gotten over being upset about the Seva Dals taking up so much room in the Mandir Grounds for their padnamaskar, I can realize the wonderful benefits of it - longer Darshan, and Swami seems to be pumping more LOVE than usual. Before, I could not feel it because the old ego and my anger was in the way of it.

Line 11 this afternoon. After Darshan, we went to our room to rest and awoke to bhajans outside our window at 8:30 p.m.. Too late to do anything about supper except eat the cake we purchased at the bakery and go back to sleep. Still jet lagging.

Interview 1998

Puttaparthi, February 16, 1998

Line 11 again this morning. So surprised to find so many people here this time of the year. This morning Oscar died. Oscar is the name we have given to the large electric water heater device that we stick in our bucket of water each morning to heat the water for bathing. We purchased it years ago in Whitefield. It died right in the middle of my bath while heating more water for Syd's bath, and blew out the lights at 3:30 a.m.. So we had to go back outside the Ashram after Darshan and buy another one, as this one was irreparable.

I served lunch in the Western Canteen again, ate, rested a few minutes and back to Darshan. It is very hot today, almost too hot for me.

Am in Line 1 again this afternoon. Swami came along and I held up my manuscript and asked for an interview. He looked me in the eye and said that magic word, "GO!". I didn't move quickly enough for Him and He repeated, "GO......GO!", while making a motion with His hand toward the veranda. I was up and gone in a split second after that. Once upon the veranda, I stepped out to the edge and waved the manuscript in the air, trying to get Syd's attention on the men's side. There are so many people here, I wondered if he was close enough to see me. Syd is near sighted - he can't even see me from three aisles away in the supermarket. Syd is not forthcoming. I say a prayer to Swami to help Syd see me standing here waving the manuscript back and forth. Swami is approaching the veranda now and I begin to wave with great fervor. Finally, I see Syd pop up out of the middle of the crowd and wave his hat at me to see if it is really me up there. I move my arms as if to say, "Come on!". Whew!! Another close call, as Syd arrived just seconds before Swami.

Swami ushers us into the Interview Room and makes vibhuti for all the ladies. I eat half and offer the rest to Syd. He shakes his head no and indicates it's for me! I have a strong feeling from within that I am to share it with him, so I persist and motion to him to go ahead. Finally, He takes the vibhuti and eats it. An older Indian man is staring at me with a look that says he is classifying me as impudent. Oh well.....

Swami sat down in His chair and immediately says to Syd, "From where did you come?" (Hey Swami, I'm the one you were supposed to pose that question to!). Syd gives Swami the answer I had prepared, "From You Swami!". Swami looks at Syd as if he has lost it or something. Then He looked at me and asked me the same question, "From where did you come?".

I responded with, "From You Swami!".

Swami rapidly shot back, "Copycat!". Everyone laughed, including Swami. Then He said to me, "From Me? From everywhere.".

Swami then turned His attention to Syd and asked him, "What do you want?".

Syd replied honestly, "Just You Swami!". Swami then reached out His hand for Syd's hand. He looked at Syd's wedding ring, which was now back on his ring finger, the third finger, left hand. (Last year when Swami looked at that ring, it was on his middle finger. Just before we left for India, I purchased a clasp that joined the ring back together so it would fit and stay on Syd's wedding ring finger. He had been wearing it on his middle finger last year for fear of losing it again.)

As Swami fondled Syd's wedding ring, He asked, "What is that?"

Syd replied, "My Wedding Ring, Swami".

I showed Him mine and He said, "Yes, Yes." Then Swami moved His hand in that now familiar way, and a sparkling object formed right underneath His hand in mid air. Swami grabbed it out of the air and put it on Syd's wedding ring finger, right over the wedding ring. "Perfect fit!", He said.

Syd just melted and said, "Oh Thank You Swami!", and laid his head in Swami's lap, which he does not remember doing. Swami patted him on the back and Syd took padnamaskar and then returned to his position on the floor.

It is a beautiful solid gold ring with a large rectangular shaped piece on top of a band. There is an upraised gold ॐ (OM) symbol on the rectangular piece which is surrounded by etchings so exquisitely cut that one would think it is diamonds until one gets a closer look.

Swami looked at me and said, "Now how many wives does he have?". I knew Swami was telling me that He had just married Syd to

God.

But, I played along and gave Syd a pretend look of betrayal, then back to Swami and said, "But he is a good husband Swami!".

"Then why do you fight with him?"

"But Swami, we never fight!".

"Yes you do!".

"No, Swami we don't!"

"Yes you do!".

"But Swami we don't fight!".

"Yes you do!".

I could see that this was never going to end until I relented. So I said, as I held up my finger and thumb with a tiny space between them, "Well maybe just a little bit!".

"Seeeeeeeeee!", He said, and everybody roared with laughter. Truthfully, we never really have had a fight. On the rare occasions when one of us becomes out of sorts or angry, one of us goes to our private space until everything has cooled off. Then we discuss it calmly later, if it still seems to be important to either one of us.

Swami then said to us, "Husband.....Has Been.....His Band!". I knew Swami was telling us that this ring was a reward for Syd's and my celibacy.

Swami than asked me, "What do you want?", and I responded, "Only You, my Lord!".

At that point, Swami stood up and said, "Very happy, very

happy. Go inside!".

Once inside the Inner Room, Swami asked Syd again, "What do you want?". Syd replied, "Just You Swami!".

"What do you do?"

"I'm a consultant."

"Where do you come from?"

"Colorado USA Swami!".

"Colorado very good!

Swami turned to me and asked, "What do you want?". Again I replied, "Only You Swami!" (This answer was not something I prepared for - it just came out spontaneously because I don't really 'want' anything, and because I have never yet been prepared when Swami has asked me this question.)

Swami got right up in my face and said, "I am always with you, You always have Me around you, I am in you, around you and about you, Always!".

"Wow!" That went deep down inside me and whenever I recall it, I can feel Swami right there in my heart chakra, just to the right side of my physical heart. Since He said that, I find it much easier to communicate with Him by focusing on Him in my Heart, rather than Him in India, or Him in the picture, or Him in His robe on the throne next to my altar, as I always used to do. Thank You Swami!!!

Swami then asked for the manuscript I brought with me. "What is this?"

"It is a book about my life before and after You, Swami."

"What is it called?"

"Well Swami, I have some titles that have come to me and am having trouble choosing the right one - 'My Beloved Lord', or 'Your Life is My Message', or.....

Swami interrupted and said, "'Your Life is Your Message', call it 'Your Life is Your Message'. It is not finished and has some patches that need fixing and needs more balance. You (will) know what they are. Fix it and bring it back next time.", He said as He handed the partial manuscript back to me.

When Swami told me that I knew what needed fixing, I really did not know, but I realized He was planting the seed idea in my mind with that statement. Before leaving home, I had reached a point where I was concerned about how to go forward, and had many questions whether I was even on the right track to begin with. It got to the point where I wondered if I was supposed to be writing this book. Now I had my confirmation of that.

Syd then asked, "Swami can I ask you a question?". Swami nodded approval. "Swami, in 1995 during our interview, You said my health was not good. Then last year in our interview, You said my health was not good.". I know Syd asked this question for my sake, because I am the one who worries about his health and well being.

"How is your health now?"

"That is what I was going to ask You Swami. I feel fine."

Swami replied, "Health is okay." Swami then put His hand on Syd's head and the other on Syd's shoulder, and said, "I bless you with long life and good health and happiness!". Syd melted under the touch and the glory of such a declaration. But he quickly revived, and said to Baba:

"Swami, her health has been bad this last year.

Swami looked at me as though He was looking inside me and said, "Health is not bad. There is no disease. These things are because of adjustments. She is adjusting to changes in the body." He looked me in the eye and said, "Be with nature. Love nature. Be with nature. Pains are not rheumatism, just changes in nature." He then rubbed His mid-section and said, "Not because of a bad condition. It will pass. I will make you a diamond.....I will give you a ring.....in a longer interview before you leave. Must go now - trouble outside." We could hear some rather loud voices back in the Interview Room.

Back outside, the old Indian man and his wife that Swami had taken in first were fighting with each other. The old man had been sitting next to Syd and had been scowling and radiating anger since he first entered the room. (He is also the one who did not approve of my giving Swami's vibhuti to Syd.). If anything, he appeared even worse when we returned to the Interview Room. Swami sat back down in His chair and started talking to the lady next to me, but the old Indian lady interrupted Swami each time, and kept interrupting, with "Swami, Swami, Swami, Swami, Swami", and each time she said it louder than the time before. Swami abruptly got up and ushered us all out the door. The troubled Indian couple ignored Swami's message to leave and stayed behind, and I never looked back to see whether Swami told them to leave or not.

Later, I could have kicked myself all over the place, because just as Swami was saying He would make me a diamond, I interrupted and said, "But Swami - You already did", as I held out my hand to show Him. I did the same thing when He wanted to give me a second robe. When I shared this part of the interview with our friends back in Bombay, the Patels, Niranjan scolded me and said I should never ever deny Swami the joy of giving me something. He reminded me that I had done it twice now. Then he made an analogy: "What if Swami came along and told you to go for an interview? Would you tell Him, 'But Swami, You already gave me an interview!'?". This made perfect sense and I knew I really did blow it this time. Thank you Niranjan for your wise advice.

More Life on the Ashram

Puttaparthi, February 17, 1998

Was in Token line 14 this morning and was back in about Row 13 inside. I can still see Swami most of the time He is giving Darshan from this position.

Worked in the canteen again. This time I am assigned to serving and making various teas and hot water, so there is little chance for eye contact because I am so busy keeping the cups full.

It happened again this afternoon - just as I was squatting to sit down on my cushion, an Indian lady, not a villager, pushed me over, just as I reached that vulnerable position. When I got up, she was sitting in the place where I had placed my cushion. I lost it - "What kind of animal are you? You are an animal!!! I was absolutely furious. We were only in the token lines, so her actions did not make any sense to me at all. If we were inside vying for a good position to see Swami, I could have understood. This was just plain meanness on her part! What kind of karma do I have anyway?

A Westerner near by told me to calm down as my anger would affect our line draw. It took me awhile, but I did return to my center. Before I could let go and surrender it all, I wanted to crack the Indian lady over the head with my fan, among other retaliations that crept into my thoughts. Once we got inside, I ended up next to a young girl who is very ill with some kind of respiratory virus and fever. On the other side of me was the Indian lady who had helped draw the anger out of me. Oh Swami, You are certainly giving me plenty of opportunities to observe my anger in action. How many times must I endure these tests before I am finally unaffected? Please help me Swami!

Puttaparthi, February 18, 1998

Oh Swami, You are still working on me, aren't You? This morning in Darshan, I was busy lost in thought while writing a letter to You, and apparently did not hear a lady with a seva dal scarf telling me to move over and make more room. She finally pushed me and then

I realized it was me she had been talking to. I moved over into an even more cramped position, and she sat herself and her friend down next to me and then later removed her seva-dal scarf! When I realized she had abused her power for personal gain, I began to feel the anger rise up in me again. This time I was able to recover quickly, and did not say anything to them. Then I brushed it off to karma, and went back to my letter.

The letter I was writing was asking Swami's advice whether I should give (donate) a copy of the computer disks of the Compendium to a devotee who wants to put it on a CD-Rom for resale. I asked Swami in the letter to take the letter if He approves of the CD-Rom this person is putting together and if it should include the Compendium in it. Afterward, I carried that letter to nearly every Darshan day after day until the last few days. On occasion, I would forget the letter and I would get in a good line. But, Swami never even came near me so long as I was trying to offer that letter to Him. After I stopped carrying it to Darshan, I was able to get a good seat again.

Puttaparthi February 20, 1998
Forgot the CD-Rom letter this afternoon and got in line 2. There are two ladies who want the lady next to me and me to move over so they can squeeze in between us. They are crazy - we are already squeezed together. Some people will try anything to get closer to Swami. The lady next to me says "No Way!". I just ignore them. Teri from the Denver Center is leaving tomorrow and they are in the first row across from me. I pray to Swami to bless them with an interview if possible. He did! How wonderful for them! I started to applaud with joy for them, but luckily came to my senses before the first clap. Teri and Jill have been faithfully meeting before each Darshan and chanting the Gayatri and praying together. Teri's younger brother has just passed away unexpectedly, and she really wants to talk to Swami about it. I am so happy for them.

Puttaparthi, February 21, 1998
This morning while waiting for Swami to come out, I watched

as the monkeys across the way, one by one crawl out of the Temple Archway that Swami's car drives through. They are all hanging out watching the Darshan area, probably waiting along with us for Swami's Darshan. The sun is about to rise and all is beautiful here this morning.

I arrived early and had lunch alone in the new Punjabi Canteen - wonderful Northern Indian food - not hot at all, a variety of dishes to select from. Delicious! I noticed Chedva when I went to put my tray and dishes away and visited with her briefly, while she finished her meal. As she got up to leave, I saw Teri and Jill and joined them to find out how their interview went. They said that basically, their interview was short, like Baba had a lunch date or something. Swami told Jill she would be writing a book in the future.

Puttaparthi, February 26, 1998

This morning in Darshan, just as Swami was walking into the Interview Room, I felt Him walking into my heart. I know He designed this imaginary event for me. Perhaps it was symbolic, but He felt very real in my heart and after several days passed, I realized that He only comes out to give Darshan. I can communicate with Him in my heart and no longer need to think of Him anywhere else. Thank You Swami!!!

Puttaparthi, March 1, 1998

The heat has become unbearable, and the power is off more than it is on. After Darshan, we collapse in our Ashram apartment on the bed soaking wet with perspiration, with the fan slowly moving overhead trying to cool down. Most of the time the power goes off in the hottest part of the afternoon, and it has been impossible to cool down. Syd is suffering too. We talk it over and he makes a trip to Sai Towers to see what is available. He returned with wonderful news - he was able to get us an air conditioned room at Sai Towers and we moved this afternoon. Thank You Swami!!!

Several months before we left for India on this trip, I was sitting quietly at my altar when I was struck with a sudden inspiration, which I believe was planted there by Swami. The idea was that there are so many other books published and distributed by Sai Towers, like the Compendium, that are not available in the USA, and that somebody needs to make those books available. We had been bringing home hundreds of books on every trip for people who could not make the trip themselves.

Many of the Sai Towers books, like the Compendium, have been blessed and/or signed by Swami. I was already distributing the Compendium, so it seemed to fall into the natural course of events that distribution of the rest of the books be my project also. When Swami signs and blesses a book or tape, then it tells me that He is saying that it has value and should be shared with the world. I talked it over with Syd and he thought it would be a great seva project for me and agreed that I should look into it.

But, with so many other things going on in my life, I completely forgot about it until one day while I was walking out of the Mandir after Swami had given Darshan. What came to me was a very strong feeling that I should get started on this right away.

Rumors had it that Swami was leaving for Brindavan soon which meant I had to do something quickly. We had already had our interview with Swami, and it did not look hopeful that we would get another interview so I could ask for His approval. I was no longer getting in the afternoon token lines because of the heat so there was no way I could ask Swami for an interview. Syd was not having luck getting close to where Swami walks so he could ask for one. The intolerable heat had become unbearable for me. I would arrive for Darshan just before Swami came out, go directly to the seva dal passing out water, get a glassful and pour it over my head to cool myself down. The seva dals laughed at this crazy American. The next glassful went inside.

I wrote Swami the following letter while sitting in Line 2 in Darshan, where I could easily hand it to Him: "My Beloved Lord, if there is anything wrong with my being the mail order distributor in the USA for Sai Towers, please tell me now by taking this letter because I would never want to do anything that would separate me form Your Grace or.....". Twice in different Darshans, Swami could have taken my letter, but He totally ignored it.

Just to make certain there was no mistake about this, and since I was unable to ask Him personally, I prayed to Swami and asked Him if it was Him guiding me to do this. I asked Him if I should get involved in this and become a distributor of His books. The answer I got from my Inner Voice was very strong **"Yes!"**. So, I said to Swami, "If it is the right thing for me to do, then let it be. If it is going to do anything that will cause me to get in trouble with You, then please do not let it happen, because I would never want to do anything that would negatively affect my relationship with You in any way." In short, I did everything I could think of to make certain that I was doing the right thing by approaching Sai Towers to distribute their books about Sai Baba in the USA. It felt right in every way and after asking this of Swami, there were no doubts left in my mind that to continue onward was the thing to do. I had learned to trust that Inner Voice and Inner Feeling, but with a venture like this, I did not want to take any chances.

I discussed it with Syd again and it felt right to him also. We walked over to Sai Towers to talk to Pad, the owner, about my proposal. He had just returned from Australia where he had been setting up his new shop in the Sydney Ritz Carleton. I presented my idea to him and we discussed how it might work. He told me that I may have problems with the Sai Organization. I told him that I had considered that, but that I knew in my heart it was what I was 'supposed to do'. When I shared with him that I had owned a bookstore in California and managed another in Hawaii, I could see in his eyes that it was all he needed to hear. After discussing and coming to an agreement on terms and conditions with Pad, Syd wrote up a formal agreement the following day, and I was in business. We signed the contract on March 2, 1998 at 5:50 p.m., IST. I later learned that these same books and other items are also being distributed by Sai Organizations in other countries around the world, so I was not exactly doing something new.

After I returned home from India, I got some very strong Inner messages from Swami that this was to be a seva project, and that there must be no profit involved, just as with the Compendium. So I structured the prices of each item based on my wholesale costs, the air freight, customs and other estimated expenses like printing and mailing the catalog. Syd and I agreed that we would donate the cost of equipment, labor, storage and related expenses.

This project has not been without its challenges. But, the beautiful thing about this seva activity is that it has put me in touch with so many wonderful devotees of Swami around the USA. With calls and orders coming in every day and people sharing their Baba stories, I no longer feel isolated out here in the middle of nowhere, and I get to have satsang every day! I have received hundreds of calls and notes and faxes and e-mails from people thanking me for providing this service to them, and only three from people who were not in favor of it. Many people have sent me names and addresses for my mailing list, and many others have called for a catalog. The word is getting out, and I am so very grateful to all who have helped make this seva project possible and successful. Baba did say He would send me devotees, He just did not say how.

Brindavan 1998

Bangalore, March 5, 1998
Baba came along this morning and gave me 'Back Darshan', refusing my CD-Rom letter again, just as He came near enough to take it. I assume that the answer is I am not to participate in the CD-Rom project.

After Darshan, we ate, packed and took a long, hot drive from Puttaparthi to Bangalore, following Swami and His entourage until they turned off to Brindavan. Most of the time we were the fourth car behind Swami. Whenever we would come to a village, Swami's car would slow down or stop. It was marvelous to see the joy on the faces of the villagers immediately after Swami had given them Darshan. The natives were just blissed out, some in tears of joy at seeing their Lord.

Brindavan, March 6, 1998

Line one this morning, so I sat in the front row of the third block. The first two blocks are full of VIP's. Swami went right around us.

When Syd was able to negotiate that settlement agreement for the Company in Bombay, one of the officials for the other side asked Syd if he ever came to Bangalore. This led to a conversation about Sai Baba and the man insisted that if we ever were in Bangalore that he and his wife would love to have us to their home for dinner. Syd called him from Bombay and had pre-arranged for that dinner tonight. There was another young man there who Syd had previously met and who had been a student of Swami's and was being married next week, through family arrangements, to a lovely young girl. He wanted to drive us to Darshan the following morning and sit with Syd. His hope was to be able to present Swami with a Wedding Invitation to get his wedding blessed, which is to take place next week. I presented him with a copy of the Compendium as a wedding gift. He was ecstatic with joy over the gift and asked me to sign it.

We had a lovely Indian vegetarian dinner and spent hours talking about our experiences with Swami. The wife of the older gentleman said she occasionally went to Darshan on the weekends when Swami was in town and would love to have a copy of the book too. We made arrangements so that we could meet after Darshan and I could also give her a copy of the Compendium.

March 7, 1998

The young man from dinner last night picked us up very early this morning for the long drive to the Ashram. When Swami came along, He blessed the young man's Wedding Invitation. Overjoyed with all of this, he later shared with us on the drive back to our hotel the reason getting Swami's blessing was so important to him. His family had previously arranged a marriage for him to another young lady, a devotee of Baba, and he had taken off to America to work, because he felt he was not ready yet for marriage. That first young lady became one of Swami's security seva dals, which I understand is a position for life. His concern was whether Swami was angry with him for not marrying the first girl chosen to be his bride. Now that he had Swami's blessing, he could move forward into his new life.

Brindavan, March 8, 1998

Line two yesterday morning and in the back during the afternoon. Swami has been so very good to me this trip. My legs have been giving me problems the past few years, and before we left on our trip this year, I prayed to Swami for help in being able to sit in the lines and rows comfortably. Nearly every Darshan, I have been blessed to have a place to stretch my legs to keep the circulation moving so they won't go to sleep. Thank You Swami!!!

Brindavan, March 9, 1998

Wrote a letter to Swami this morning - "We are leaving tomorrow and we are hoping You will give us the 'long interview' you promised when you cut our first interview so short....". As Swami was giving Darshan, He maneuvered away from where I was sitting, so He did not take the letter.

Just as Swami got up to leave and was walking across the stage this morning towards His exit door, He looked at me, and I heard Him say in my Inner Voice: **"Take My message home: Love what you see; Love what you do; Love who you are."** Thank You Swami - what a wonderful message! A tall order for this lady, and I will do my best to put it into practice!

In the afternoon, I am sitting in the front row facing the door where Swami comes in. Just before He opened the door, I could see Him through the peephole. When the door opened, there were deer and other wild animals standing there watching Him. After the beautiful bhajans, and while Swami walked on the stage past me to the door, He looked me directly in the eye, and whatever was in that look caused me to burst into tears. He had done it to me again - blissed me out.

Brindavan, March 10, 1998

Dreamed last night that someone said to me: "Look, there is Swami!". I looked and saw a variety of different scenes with Swami in them - landscapes with Him in a Garden; riding a bicycle; talking to people in a group as part of the group; standing on a hillside; etc.

When I awoke, I knew this dream was for Ellen from Hawaii, whom I recently met in Darshan. She is an artist and does landscapes of the beautiful scenery there on the Big Island, my former home, and where my grandchildren and daughter still reside. Ellen is here for three months with Swami and has been painting pictures of Swami from various photographs of Him. Ellen has let me take my pick of the paintings, and I am very grateful. I promised to mail her a copy of the Compendium when I return home, as I have already given away the twelve we collected at Sai Towers before we left. I have shared with her that I will be doing a mail order catalog of Sai Towers' books, and suggested that she put together a brochure of her paintings that I can mail out with the catalog and see what happens. She asked Swami on the Inner and felt she received an affirmative response. I suggested that she paint Swami into scenery like in the landscapes in my dream.

Ellen lived in Kona at the same time I did back in the late 70's and early 80's, but we never met. She also moved to San Diego about the same time that I did, and first learned of Sai Baba at the 'Introduction to Sai Baba' meeting in my bookstore. What a wonderful coincidence Swami! She remarried and returned to beautiful Kona and started up a Sai Center there.

Syd and I had lunch today at the Le Meridian, which was the Holiday Inn just three days ago when we took Ellen to lunch there. The place must have been sold. It is a beautiful hotel. Today we have a different waiter - he asked us right off if we are Christians. We told him we were here to see Sai Baba. That launched him into a hate campaign, wherein he told us that Baba works in Black Magic and only draws westerners for their money. After assuring Him that Swami is as pure as snow and we have never been asked for a cent, I realized we should not even be talking to him because he is never going to believe a word we say. He has been programmed by his church and his energy and anger is very draining and it is affecting the food we are eating. He had a negative answer for everything, and was not making sense at all, even though he may have thought he was. After wondering why his boss did not do anything about him standing there at our table harassing us all that time, I silently prayed to Baba to take this man away from our table so we could eat in peace. Swami says that we should never talk to non-devotees about Him because of what it does to you, and I have learned a big lesson here. Thank You Swami!!!

".....to engage in individual private conversations with those who have no faith will just result in argument and discussion and will be a waste of time." CWSSB P 99

"God is understood only by the one who loves Him. The one who truly loves God is understood only by Him. Others cannot fully understand such a one. So, do not discuss matters relating to the love of God with others who have no devotion. If you do, your own devotion will be drained and diminished." TOSSSB P 39

"If anyone speaks to you and is obviously misinformed concerning his subject try to accept the true meaning behind his words and do not argue with him. Be sweet and kind." TOSSSB P 40

At our last Darshan this afternoon, I am sitting in the 'Leaving Line', (this line only happens in Brindavan, never in Puttaparthi to my knowledge), and I can see that Swami is heading directly toward me. He is going to give us the long interview that He promised! Oh thank You Swami! Just before He crosses from the men's section to where I am sitting, He looks to His left and sees Isaac Tigrett sitting there on the corner with a younger man. Swami looked at me, and then at Isaac Tigrett and then back and forth again, and chose Mr. Tigrett. My heart didn't even skip a beat, because I knew it was something that was meant to be. Oh, well.....

Upon our arrival at the Bangalore airport, we were welcomed

by swarms of mosquitoes. They were so thick everywhere in the airport that it was hopeless to escape them. I had this same experience the last time I took the late flight from Bangalore to Bombay. Even the airplane is full of mosquitoes and people are complaining and swatting at them, but nothing is being done about it. Once the plane takes off, the mosquitoes disappear - I wonder if they have their own seatbelts? It is only on the last flight of the day to Bombay that this happens. I must make note of that.....

Home Again 1998

Before we left for India, Syd and I had an appointment with an Ayurvedic physician in Albuquerque, New Mexico. When he checked my blood pressure it was 165 over 110. He prescribed Ayurvedic medication for the high blood pressure. I have had this problem for as long as I can remember - the first time I was diagnosed with it was when my first child was born in 1957. I had only taken allopathic medicine for it the last eight years, but the medicine had its side effects, and I discontinued it last year. Syd was given medication for the sinus problems he had been having.

After we returned home from India, I checked my blood pressure and it was down to 135 over 90. It was NORMAL for the first time in my adult life without allopathic medicine. I am aware that everything that happens is Swami's Will, but I am uncertain whether it was Swami's Will, or His Will that the Ayurvedic doctor's medicine stabilized my blood pressure. Maybe my change in diet helped. Perhaps it was all the above. I had only taken the Ayurvedic medicine sporadically because of the time constraints and my poor memory in India. When I went back to Albuquerque for my return appointment the first of April, the doctor was overjoyed to see such success so quickly. My blood pressure was 130 over 87 when he checked it! He knew I had been to see Swami, and he knew who Swami was because he had been to see Him also the year before.

Truthfully, after being home for several more months, the blood pressure rose again, but not to the level it used to be. This probably has to do with the fact that after I resumed my usual habits of television, newspapers, talking on the phone, coffee (one to two cups per day), and diet, the blood pressure returned to the appropriate level. In other words, while I was with Swami and for a while after our return, my blood pressure was normal, and if I want to keep it that way, I must give up the bad habits.

Once again after returning from India, I had many dreams of traveling around and helping other people, teaching them about Sai Baba and His teachings. Some of the people this time were famous movie stars. I also had a lot of dreams giving me messages that my ego was out of control again.

In one of my dreams, it was my first day at the Ashram. Sai Baba came along and told me to "Go!". I got up to the veranda and saw my Mother there waiting for an interview. What's going on here Swami, I thought. When I had gotten up to go, I heard someone gasp behind me, but I did not turn around. While up on the veranda, I turned and saw that it had been my dear friend, MJ. She stood up as if she were coming to join me on the veranda, and I was very surprised because I never dreamed she would be there, while I wasn't the least bit surprised (in the dream) that my Mother would be there. MJ is a very dear old friend, who is spiritual, but has never been the least bit interested in Sai Baba, although I used to do my best to change that. I awoke before the interview began.

Shortly after our return, I was working at the computer on the new JAI SAI RAM catalog and I suddenly had a blinding pain in my left temple. The pressure was so intense I could not think clearly, and if I could have, I would have gone to or called out to Syd for help. My Inner Voice told me he could not help me anyway, and I would just have to suffer through this. The blinding pain could be somewhat related to a strong electrical shock. I don't know how long it lasted, maybe and hour or so, but after taking two Tylenol, it very slowly subsided. When I turned the light switch off in the bathroom afterward, sparks flew all over the place and I got a terrible shock from it. Maybe this body is full of electricity, perhaps from so many hours at the computer? Swami, what is happening to me? I was unable to put a conscious thought together or talk clearly or construct a complete sentence the rest of the night. I was not much better the following morning, but it eventually subsided as the day wore on.

Not long after the above event, I dreamed that someone was giving me a healing massage while I was in bed sleeping and it ended with these two hands over my eyes like someone giving me a Reiki healing. I could actually feel the healing energy just pouring out into my eyes. When I awoke, I had the feeling it was Sai Baba. Thank You Swami - You are always taking such good care of me, and I feel I have done so little to deserve it.

In June, I dreamed that Swami was here in our home, and I was taking movies of Him with our camcorder to prove it to others because I knew they would not otherwise believe me. Swami and I were astral traveling around our home and ended up in the master bedroom. When I looked down, there was Swami sitting in the middle of the bed with Syd asleep on one side and I was asleep on the other. Swami had His hands on our heads, and He was joyfully smiling at me and posing for me as I video taped the whole scene. Then Swami wrote or called or told me somehow that He would meet me tomorrow somewhere else. Then a friend called and needed my help and I was trying to figure out how I could be with Swami and help her too. At that point the phone rang in the dream, and it was Swami - He told me not to worry, that He would be with me all day anyway.

Also dreamed that Syd and I were walking together in the Ashram, and suddenly, there stood Swami, all alone outside the Poornachandra Auditorium on the ladies side. He looked me right in the eye and gave me that loving smile of His. We walked up to Him and I sank to my knees and said, "I love You so much, Swami!"

Ian's Visit - Summer of 1998

Our grandson Ian, who lives in Hawaii is seventeen now and

getting ready for his senior year in high school. Ian wanted to come visit us again this year, and we arranged to use some frequent flyer miles to bring him over for the Summer. He has told us that our home is the only place where he has found peace and quiet, which is what he yearns for at home in Hawaii. Ian has three younger siblings in his mother's home and two younger brothers at his father's home. None of the children are well disciplined and he has to go to the library to find peace where he can get his homework done.

There is something going on with the younger generation in the lack of discipline of their children. In my own daughter's case, her children run wild and do whatever they please because they are not disciplined. Perhaps this is my fault, because I was a strict disciplinarian with her when she was a child and she really resented it. But, now she has a 15 year old boy who is totally out of control and refuses to listen to any authority, be it teachers, police, judges or his mother. He was recently sentenced to one year in detention for everything from stealing cars to doing drugs. To me, discipline is love; it is showing your children you care enough about them to want them to behave and become good citizens, and to respect other people's rights. Swami has a lot to say about discipline:

"Generally, I speak sweetly, but on this matter of discipline, I will not grant any concessions.....I will insist on strict obedience. I shall not reduce the rigor to suit your level, for that will only ruin you. I pay attention to your ultimate good." SSS Vol 2, P 186

"A sense of discipline must be cultivated right from childhood. Discipline cannot be learned from the pages of books. It is only through constant practice that discipline gets strengthened." GA P 167

"Today the parents give unlimited freedom to their children which is highly disastrous. If the children are not controlled at the tender age, they can never be controlled." SSIB 1993 P 109

On Ian's second day here in Colorado, we were driving into town to get mail and groceries. When we pulled up at a stop sign, Ian noticed a car off to the side that was in trouble. It had gotten stuck on a divider when the driver attempted to make a U turn, and needed a hefty push to get over it. Ian jumped out of the car and ran over to help the out of state driver. If someone needs help, Ian is there to rescue them. Ian had really matured since his last trip and he continued to demonstrate his helpfulness, both with us and anybody else who seemed to need help.

Ian is an excellent athlete, and his favorite sport is basketball. Back at home Ian is the Captain of the school's basketball team and is an All-Star player, as well as the winner of the Most Valuable Player award every year. We took Ian to the community center in Trinidad regularly, where they had basketball games going nearly every day, and anybody could play. The locals here recognized what a value Ian would be on their high school team and they did everything they could to encourage him to stay on and finish his senior year in Trinidad.

We told Ian it was fine with us if he wanted to stay in Colorado, but we suggested he ask Baba what he should do. To our surprise, he did ask Baba what he should do, in the quiet of his room that evening. A short while later, he said he heard Baba say out loud - **"Return home and finish what you started!"**. Ian was totally blown away when he heard Swami's voice speaking to him. He told us he didn't know what it was he needed to finish, but said he would return home, as Baba had instructed him to do.

Then, the night before we were to take Ian to Colorado Springs to catch his plane home, unbeknownst to us, before he went to bed, he asked Baba to be with him and help him after he returned home to Hawaii. He awoke in the middle of the night to find Baba standing there - right next to his bed. Swami was looking down at him with a loving smile. Ian started to tell me what Baba said to him, but then stopped, as if he remembered he was supposed to keep it to himself. Ian swears he was not asleep and dreaming - that this actually happened. **He was so impressed, that he now believes like us - that Swami is God!** And he tells all his friends that Baba is God when they inquire who that is in the pictures in his room.

When Ian returned home, he moved in with his Dad and

Stepmother, instead of returning to his mother's place, which is probably Baba's doing. It is certainly a more stable lifestyle there. And we can tell that Baba is helping him - he sounds so well-balanced and happy when he calls us every week. Ian has brought his Grade Point Average up from a 3.4 in his junior year to a 3.8 in his senior year. He is looking for academic scholarships, while his basketball coach is trying to get him an athletic scholarship. Some college and university scouts came to check Ian out recently, and they were very impressed with his ability to maneuver on the court. But, they said he needed to grow a few more inches, if he was going to be able to compete with other students. Ian says he has surrendered it to Baba and will go with whatever is His will for him.

Ian has told us that he is doing his very best to eat vegetarian food now that he is back home, but it is not always possible because there are times that he has no alternative but to eat what is served at home and school.

Christmas 1998

It's another quiet Christmas for us this year. We are having our friends, Joy and her fiancé David over for dinner - they requested that I make roasted eggplant fajitas with black beans and corn, and have a Feliz Navidad! We did the mock seitan turkey, (vegetarian wheat meat), with dressing and all the trimmings at Thanksgiving, so this change will be nice. After dinner, we watched Sai Baba videos all afternoon and into the night, the same as we did on Thanksgiving Day.

We don't have a tree up this year, but I did put up our outside lights which span the length of the house on our upper and lower decks. We have very little traffic out here in the middle of nowhere, but some of our neighbors have children, and they love to see the lights when driving home at night. So do we on the rare occasion we come home after dark.

I have been extremely busy since last month, since we decided to return to India and made our reservations to leave January 30, 1999, (Swami willing). We will be going with our dear friends, Kathy and Howard, who live up in Northern Colorado. It is their first time to see Swami and it was their suggestion that we go in February. Early last Summer, we planned and made reservations to travel with them to India on the first of January, but by Summer's end, we all 'knew' we were not supposed to travel then. So, we canceled our reservations, and agreed that next Fall would be a better time to travel. But, as often happens, Swami had something else in mind.

One morning in early November, I awoke with the 'awareness' that we would be getting ready to go to India soon. I asked Syd, "Is there any reason that the company you consult for will want you to be coming to India in the near future?". He answered in the negative. Kathy called me two days later, and said some of their good friends had just returned from India. They visited their own guru, not Sai Baba. In talking with Kathy and Howard, their friends encouraged them to make the trip to see Sai Baba as soon as possible, while they still can. After sleeping on it, Kathy called us and said they had decided to go in February to see Baba, and would we be interested in traveling with them. The seed had already been planted here by Baba, and we made reservations and purchased our tickets almost immediately.

While in India in February and March of 1998, Swami looked at my partially finished manuscript (of this book), gave me the title (YOUR LIFE IS YOUR MESSAGE), and told me to fix it and bring it back to Him. Well, this whole year has been busy with house guests, starting up and taking care of the new book distribution business, and so much else, and I had not gotten back to the manuscript. At Summer's end, I assumed I would have until the Fall of 1999 to get the book finished so it continued to sit. And there was a whole lot of work to be done on it. But the biggest concern is, that it is possible that this may be our last trip to India, with the World going the way it is.

So, I have been working day and night on the manuscript ever since we made the reservations, arising between three and four in the morning every day to get an early start before the energies of this part of the world filter into my consciousness. For me, writing can become a struggle when energies around me are not good or a phone call from a negative person comes in, because I absorb these energies and it reflects in what I write. It can take me hours to shake it off and recover so I can write again from a positive space. Sometimes I have to wait until the following day to resume time at the computer.

This morning, while doing Puja at my altar, I was thinking about Christmas and how many who celebrate this holiday have sent cards wishing their friends and others peace and a 'Happy New Year"! Many people around the world are praying for peace as the turmoil of war, and the escalation of famine, drought, flooding, genocide, cannibalism, hate crimes etc., is taking its toll on our planet. I chanted the "Loka Samastha, Sukhino Bhavantu!", as I do regularly, at least twice each day. This time, I also prayed out loud for Swami to bring an end to the pain and suffering that is going on all over the world, and to hurry and "Usher in the Golden Age", as He has promised He will do.

It suddenly occurred to me, or perhaps He planted the seed thought in my mind, that I have to do more than just pray for peace. We all have to do our part. I realized that this Virgo mind has been helping to create the turmoil, rather than helping to bring in peace and the Golden Age. The mind is constantly analyzing and judging everyone and everything going on around me.

"When you pronounce another person as vicious or bad, you are making a pronouncement on your own wickedness or vice. Your own impurity casts suspicion on him. No one can judge another, for when another is judged, you are yourself condemned." SSS Vol VII P 461

"You must cultivate love towards everyone, regardless of what they are like or what they do. You have no right to judge whether a person is good or bad, or whether an action of his is good or bad. Leave the judgement to God. He is the only Judge of persons, things and actions. What you have to do is to offer love to others. However hateful or unendearing a person may be, you must show love, affection, understanding, tolerance, sympathy, charity and compassion." SSAV P 29

I have tried not watching the news on the television, but I have not stopped. In the past, I have tried to not get caught up in gossiping with friends and others who call, but the next time the phone rings, I am right back into it without realizing it. I have tried to keep my thoughts focused on Swami and to see everything around me as good, but this mind is constantly running away from the good, looking for something to analyze or criticize. I have tried not to read the newspapers, but this inquisitive mind weakens and becomes curious about what is going on in the world.

"Man's mind is so peculiarly constituted that he puts faith in newspapers and bizarre rumors.....This is because the newspapers cater to his senses, to his craze for sensationalism and curiosity about other men and their affairs. Man's sense of values is so degraded that he does not revere the Gita as much as he values and scans the pages of the daily newspaper. This is to be attributed to sheer ignorance and perversity or pitiable fate. People lend their ears and mortgage their brains to wicked and vicious men, reveling in sin. They get the admirers they deserve, the following that fouls the air as much as they.

"The fear and anxiety that infect humanity today are the results of this degradation of values, this ignorance of what is of significance and what is not, this want of faith in what the elders and sages have handed down as the wisdom of the ages. People prefer what is pleasing to what is beneficial. The patient is dictating to the doctor and insisting on the medicine he likes to swallow, the regimen he feels will keep him happy." SSS VOL V Chap 13 P 70

During the six years I went to college nights and worked days, I never watched the television or read the newspapers, and I never missed either. I was more concerned with keeping my family intact and my 4.0 grade point average. Years later, when I moved to Hawaii, I never watched television or read the newspapers during the four years I lived there, and I never missed them. I was more concerned with my spiritual growth and sticking to the 'path'. I remember one time I was in the Kona airport in Hawaii and the television was on. It showed that Ronald Reagan had just won the election as President of the United States. I didn't even know he was running for office! And I used to be deep into politics when I worked for Reagan (indirectly in two of his cabinet offices), back in Sacramento. Life was so much simpler for me when my thoughts were not influenced by television and newspapers!

Facing Death

Since we moved to Colorado in 1990, I have had trouble breathing and it got increasingly worse as each year passed by. I wrote it off to the high altitude, 6700 feet, because whenever I have returned to sea level in California or Hawaii or India, the problems seemed to dissipate, and almost go away. Over the years, my ability to breathe has gotten progressively worse, and other symptoms have crept in, such as my feet have slowly become numb and my knees and legs go weak whenever I have to climb the stairs or go up hill during our walks. My physical energy level has dropped to where most housework tasks are very energy consuming.

We had a house guest, a Baba devotee, visit us for Thanksgiving week in 1998. She is in the medical profession and used to be a pulmonary clinician. After going for walks and climbing the stairs with her, she recognized the symptoms I was experiencing as serious and suggested I see a doctor before it became irreversible. She explained that the numb feet and weak legs are symptomatic of not getting enough oxygen. After asking me more questions about symptoms, she suggested that I might have emphysema, and probably need to go on oxygen at night. That got my attention - frankly, she scared the H___ out of me! I know that emphysema is a death sentence - my stepmother, whose birthday was the day after mine, was a heavy smoker most her life and she succumbed to emphysema at about my age. And I was a heavy smoker for many years.

After our house guest left, I struggled with this news and for weeks afterward, I resisted calling the doctor she recommended. As several of my friends have reminded me, Swami did tell me nearly a year ago that this body had no disease. So what was there to worry about? I had stopped going to allopathic doctors years ago for a variety of reasons, and we haven't had medical insurance since 1986, except for Syd's Medicare for the past year. We have had no real need for insurance. Syd had a few things that grew on his face that had to be removed but other than that, we have had no medical bills to speak of.

For years I have considered Swami as my doctor, and I put my total faith and trust in Him to take care of me. And He has. Syd feels the same way. I have a sign that hangs over my altar quoting Swami, "Whenever your faith meets My Love, there is a cure.". But, I wondered whether He sent this lady into my life as a messenger that I needed to see a doctor. I have heard of Him doing this for other people.

What kept running through my mind was that if I do have this dreaded disease, I will probably only have a few years left, if that much. In the area where I live, there are so many old men running around with portable oxygen attached to them because of the coal dust from the mines they worked in. I have watched them suffer and die off. Whenever I encounter one of them in the grocery store I move away from them as quickly as possible because their energies are so draining.

All kinds of thoughts played and replayed through my mind. I wondered whether we should move to a lower elevation where I could possibly gain more time in this body. I have so much to do; how am I ever going to get it done before..... After watching my sisters going through my Mother's things, I vowed then that I needed to downsize my collection of 'things and stuff', so that nobody will have to go through them. I haven't gotten rid of anything yet. No need to buy anything more for myself. I'll be fine and just make do with what I have until..... Must teach Syd how to cook some basic meals, and use the laundry facilities, etc., so he will be able to cope after..... I realized that I really had no other unfulfilled desires, like traveling or visiting old friends, just things that needed to be taken care of before I could leave with a clean slate.

But what really bothered me the most was, **will I be able to achieve liberation before I leave this body**? Do I have enough time left? I have squandered all these years satisfying the desires of this mind (by reading newspapers and watching the television and talking on the phone), that distracted me and held me back from my goal, when I should have been working more on my spiritual growth and applying Swami's teachings, and most importantly, focusing on the fact that I AM GOD!

We have a television in the kitchen and usually watch the news while we are eating, which I know is the worst thing we can do. The spin (lies) that the politicians and news reporters are feeding the public fed my anger; the moral state of the people of this Nation and its leaders, and the unjust things going on in the world would upset me; etc., and I was constantly out of balance. I eventually realized that watching the television was an addiction, and I found it very difficult to stay away from it.

It took me a long time to realize that if Syd put the TV on in the morning as he usually did when he first came downstairs, and I watched it during breakfast, then I felt compelled at lunch and again at night to turn it on and watch it, even when I was preparing our meals. It was the same feeling I used to get when my subconscious signaled for another cigarette - I was getting the same signal from my subconscious to turn on the television. I know there were days when our television was on for six to eight hours or more, and I was now the one putting it on early in the morning to catch the news.

Perhaps there is a subliminal programming going on behind or in that screen. It's the only thing that makes sense. Why else would I feel compelled to keep turning the television on? And why do people seem to get hypnotized by watching the screen? Syd teases me that I think everything is a diabolical plot. But, I have used subliminal programming tapes in the past, and can testify that they do work. I know that there was a law passed many years ago making the use of subliminal programming on the television illegal. I don't think our legislators would pass such a law if it was not possible to program us subliminally. But, is anybody monitoring what is being broadcast?

Every year when we go to India, I am away from the television and newspapers while in the Ashram. I have come home from India with no desire to watch television or read the newspaper. I've made promises to myself that I would avoid the television and newspapers and gossiping and criticizing, and all my other bad habits. I know how harmful these practices are. And if I am going to get liberated before I leave this planet, I have got to give these habits up now. Swami has a lot to say about them:

"When words referring to worldly situations have such a transforming effect on the mind of man, words conveying spiritual and elevated meaning will certainly help in cleansing and correcting the mind of man. When we fill the air with harshness, we become harsh in nature. When we fill the atmosphere with hatred we too, perforce to breathe the air, and are hated in turn. When we saturate the air with sounds of reverence, humility, love, courage, self-confidence and tolerance, we benefit from those qualities ourselves. The heart is the film and the mind is the lens; turn the lens towards the world and worldly pictures will fall on the heart. Turn it towards God, and it will transmit pictures of the Divine." SSS VOL X Chap 14 P 71

"We should not indulge in discussions which will arouse our emotions, excitement or disturb the mental peace while we are taking food. Mental agitation is responsible for ill health. We should also avoid viewing TV, videos, etc. while eating, as they cause mental disturbances." SSN Summer 1994 P 3

"Where it ennobles men, it is television, otherwise it is 'tele-visham' (tele-poison)." BSS Part I P 66

"When the foot is injured as a result of an accident, it will soon heal, but when the tongue causes injury the wound may fester for life. The tongue is liable for four major errors; uttering falsehood, causing scandals, finding fault with others and too much talking. The bond of brotherhood will be closer if people speak less and with kind words." TOSSSB P 120

"Criticism of others is a very great sin. Criticism of others is like a great disease. It is an incurable disease. There is no medicine at all for this disease. Criticism of others is like cancer. Do not criticize, comment or make remarks about others at any time. We get into various difficulties by criticizing others. Be at a distance from criticism of others." DD 1987 P 24

But these promises to change my ways when I returned from

India were invariably short lived and I was always right back into it. Now, with possibly so little time left I have finally found the strength of purpose, and I made a vow on Christmas Day to myself and to Swami while sitting at my altar to give these practices up. For about ten days after making the vow, I played what we call 'Baba videos' instead of tuning into the news whenever I got the urge to turn on the TV. I also watched them in the evenings and got high on Swami.

I have slipped a few times in gossiping before I could catch myself while talking on the phone, but with Swami's help, I know I am going to rise above this nasty habit this time. I have not watched any more news casts or movies, nor do I want to know what is going on in the world. I will just sit here and continue to send everyone and everything LOVE when I think of the outer world. It's easy enough to do without all the static energies from the television and news from the outside world. I know that it will be much easier to control the other bad habits, such as judging, criticizing and gossiping without the constant negative influence of the TV.

When I made this vow, it was like when I quit smoking the last time; I knew it would be my last cigarette. And so, I also know the changes I have just made in my life will be permanent. At least for as long as my life lasts. With these negative influences out of the way, I can focus on Swami, my seva projects and getting my house and affairs in order.

When I wrote the above, I honestly believed there was a strong possibility I would not be around for long. But Swami wasn't through with me yet. One night, I started choking on some food, and it felt like my air passage closed up, even after the piece of food had been dislodged. I could not get enough air into my lungs that night to allow me to sleep. I lay there gasping for air all night long. So the next morning I called the doctor's office to make an appointment. They were able to fit me in the following week, thanks to the lady who visited us at Thanksgiving - she used to work with them and when I mentioned her name, they went all out to help me.

The night before we made the four hour drive to Denver to see the doctor, I sat at my altar and cried my eyes and my heart out to Swami. In the end, I totally released it and surrendered it all up to Him. "I accept whatever happens tomorrow as Your Will, Swami." I was barely able to put my feelings into words before I felt a total peace descend upon me. This was the first peace I had felt since I got the news on Thanksgiving Day in November. Then, from out of nowhere, the following words came out of me, "But, if I have a choice Swami, I would prefer to live another twenty or thirty years in this life so I can get liberated and not have to come back again.". I heard Him say, **"Then it is done!".** At that point I knew He was in full charge and was going to take care of me, and it no longer mattered whether I lived or died.

I spent the day being tested and X-rayed. Afterward, Syd and I met with the doctor to learn the test results. He asked me a lot of questions and then showed us the X-rays. My lung capacity has shrunk by twenty to thirty percent because my chest cavity has shrunk. Why? Three bouts with pneumonia as a child scarred my lungs forever, combined with one karmic punch to my sternum from an ex-husband (a former golden gloves boxer) more than 25 years ago. His punch pushed the sternum inward, and left little room for my lungs, so they shrunk over time. It was the only time he ever struck me - he was angry because I left him.

The best news of all was that I do not have emphysema! And what I have can be dealt with. And even better than that, I know that this was all Swami's design to get me to give up all those terrible habits that have been holding me back in my spiritual growth. Now all I have to do is keep my vow.

Isn't Swami WONDERFUL?

Swami and My Family

When Swami told me that I should not worry about my family because they are His, not mine, and He is taking care of them, it relieved a major burden of anguish from my heart and mind. Prior to that, I knew that they were in His hands, because I placed them there every day, but the problems did not go away. After Swami told me this, I wondered if maybe His ears had grown tired of my thousands of prayers to help my children and grandchildren.

Since then, my son Mark has given up the street drugs that were interfering with his medications, and he has returned to being the loving son of so many years ago. He is volunteering at the VA hospital now to help others like himself. I am so relieved and very grateful to Swami that Mark's days of drugs and violent behavior have become a thing of the past.

Ian has come a long way on the path, in spite of all the handicaps he has had in his short lifetime. His childhood challenges have been similar to mine, and I am so grateful that Swami has helped him to develop spiritually and rise above them so early in life. Ian has shared with me that he knows his challenges have enabled him to become what he is today, and just the awareness of that will help him continue onward and upward. We have watched him grow from a very vulnerable five year old to a very stable and mature young man of 17 with great leadership abilities, and who is so wise in so many ways. His peers look up to him and admire and emulate him. When he visited us this past Summer, everybody who met Ian observed and told us that there is something very special about this young man. Another work of art by the Master Artist Himself!

Ian's mother has come a long way also. She called me yesterday and shared with me that every night, she has been reading and studying Swami's teachings in the Compendium I sent to her in 1997. She said that she starts reading the book after her two daughters go to bed, and finds that she is sometimes still deeply engrossed in the book at two o'clock in the morning. She told me that she is sharing her new found understanding of Baba's teachings with her friends, and that the previous night she was explaining to her boyfriend what Baba says about 'Monkey Mind', the one that always used to get her into trouble.

Cyndi has given up a lot of her old friends, after finally realizing that they were only using her and helping to drag her farther downhill. She has virtually stopped drinking and has given up all hard drugs, and I am very proud of her. The man that she has been dating for the past few months is a vegetarian, and she has given up red meat, with intentions of eliminating the rest of the meat from her and her children's diet.

"When Tukaram was asked how man can keep the monkey-mind from running after sensuous pleasures, he replied to the enquirer. 'Let the monkey run; you keep quiet where you are; do not let the body go along with the monkey-mind.' Tell the mind, 'I shall not give you the body as your servant'." SS August 1988 Back Cover

"There is a saying, 'Tell me your company, and I will tell you what you are'. The way to discriminate is to watch a person's conduct. Do not have too much of friendship. It is highly dangerous. Because he may be friend today but an enemy tomorrow. Have less associations." Kodaikanal Discourse, Apr 9, 1996

And, I would be remiss if I did not mention the transformation that has taken place in Syd, my husband and partner in life. To watch him grow along with me has been a remarkable experience. I have seen the difficulties and challenges in so many marriages wherein one of the partners wants nothing to do with Sai Baba and His teachings. Thus, I am extremely grateful to Swami for bringing Syd into my life. He is a wonderful husband, and we get along marvelously. I am so very grateful that He brought us to Him together and we have moved along the path side by side with His Divine Grace and Help.

"Marriage is a sacred bond and it is a promise you are making to each other because the wife is half husband and the husband is half of the wife. Half plus half is not two but one. Selflessness is God. The self which is selfless is God. To feel 'mine' and 'thine' is ego. Ego is very harmful. It is to kill the ego that two souls are brought together. They can learn to adjust to one another and forget their egos.

"Marriage means your life, a whole lifetime together, not just a few days or a few weeks, or a few years.....Marriage is a training ground for fostering transensual love. Life is like a ring. The ring is the heart;

when that is given, the gift is the heart itself. That is the sacred bond.

"Today there is the tendency of separation, not coming together. Life is full of troubles and challenges. We should not separate ourselves because of these but rather face them together. Now when trouble comes, even if it is small, it separates us. That should not be the tendency, one should give one's heart to another." GA P 140-143

The changes that Sai Baba facilitates in people truly are His greatest miracles. And I am so very grateful to You Swami!

Goals

After reviewing my life and putting it down on paper, I can see that I have come a long way on the path, but I have not really progressed as far spiritually as I hoped I would. Since I have virtually eliminated those self-destructive habits, I look forward to our next trip to India to see what tests Swami has in store for me this time. In the month since I last watched television, I feel a major shift in my thoughts - I am definitely much more at peace, and can now observe things from a tranquil space. It is truly amazing how quickly this change within me has transpired. It can only be Swami's Grace. Now, with the absence of the influence of television and newspapers it should be easier to eliminate the other bad habits, such as judging. During one of our interviews, Swami told me He would help me with my spiritual growth, and He has probably been waiting for me to do my part before He would or could really help me.

Twenty four years before Syd came into my life, I developed a long list of goals. When all these goals were achieved, I wondered where all the happiness and contentment was that I was supposed to feel once I had everything I had hoped and planned and worked for. Instead, I felt rudderless! This was when I experienced the realization that there is no true happiness in stuff and things, and so at 33 years old, I began my search on the spiritual path in earnest. But, I did not know what I was really searching for. I just knew that where I was, was not where I wanted to be. I knew there was something missing in my life, but I didn't have a clue as to what it was.

After a few years of searching in all the wrong places and finding only pain and agony, I started surrendering my life and everyone and everything in it to God. I don't know where I came upon the idea of putting my life in God's Hands and surrendering to Him, but it was when I was at my very lowest point in life and there was nowhere else to turn. I was deeply depressed, suicidal, and had hit bottom. It was such a relief to give everything, including my future, my troubles, as well as the good in my life to God and not have to worry about anything anymore! In time, I realized that God was providing me with far better than I ever could have hoped for, or thought to ask for before surrendering to Him.

When Syd and I first met nearly 15 years ago, he asked me during our first date, "What are your goals in life?". I had not thought of goals in a long time. After a few minutes, I truthfully responded with, "I want to become the best person I can be.". I was uncertain whether he would understand or how he would react to the truth that mine was not a conventional goal. At the time I was on the path searching for enlightenment, whatever that was.

Syd came into my life in 1984, we learned about Sai Baba in 1986, and the following year, He called us to India. Once I began studying His teachings, I realized that my goal of enlightenment was limited. So, I reset my ultimate goal to liberation from the wheel of life and death, and merging with Swami. Perhaps this is limited also, but it is where I am at right now. I know there are different views on what enlightenment is. To me, it means 'being enlightened as to the meaning and purpose of life'; whereas, liberation means 'being liberated from all desires'. And merging with Swami is what happens once I am liberated and leave this body.

With Swami's teachings, and His help, I know I have made great strides along the path that I never would have achieved without Him in my life. With Swami's guidance, I have found and understand the purpose for life. With Swami's help, I have learned how to forgive. With Swami's help, I am learning how to LOVE. I have been able to recognize and know that everything that happens is His Will. And this has helped me to look at everyone and everything in my life as part of the Divine plan to help us all move closer to my goal. But, I want more.

The primary goal I am working on right now is to recognize and LOVE God in everyone and everything, and ultimately to experience being ONE with everyone and everything. I want to look at anyone and know that they are God and that I am God, and interact with them from that space. I have been praying to Swami for years asking for Him to help me eliminate my perception of duality. There are times when I can actually feel this "ONENESS" and disappear into it. There are times that I 'KNOW' that I am God. But I want this awareness on a permanent basis in my daily life. Now that I have removed the harmful practices that have been holding me back, with Swami's help, I know that I will be able to move more quickly to the goal.

"Life is a journey from the position I to the position WE, from the singular to the plural, from the imprisoned one to the liberated One, who is seen in the Many.....This is the teaching contained in the ancient texts and scriptures. But, these have been forgotten ever since the minds of the people of this land were won over by Western civilization. When this happened, the goal of life became the amassing of money and not the awareness of the Self." BTBOS P 242

One thing I want to emphasize to the reader is that if you surrender your life to Sai Baba **and** put His teachings into practice, He will always take care of your needs, material or otherwise. He will render all the help needed to move you quickly along the path. He is just waiting for you to make the first move.

"Once the ego or body consciousness is surrendered, there is no bar to one's realization. It is the body consciousness that stands in the way and makes you forget God." SS October 1994 P 271

"One surrenders to oneself. Recognition that the Atma is oneself is surrender. Surrender really means the realization that all is God, that there is nobody who surrenders, that there is nothing to be surrendered, nor is there anyone to accept a surrender. All is God. There is only God.....'Surrender' is world language. To correctly describe it, language of the divine is needed. There is no adequate word in the English language, therefore the use of 'surrender' goes on." CWSSB P 93

"The Lord rushes towards the Bhaktha (devotee) faster than the Bhaktha rushes towards Him. If you take one step towards Him, He takes a hundred steps towards you! He will be more than a mother or father. He will foster you from within, as He has saved and fostered so many saints who have placed faith in Him." SSS VOL III Chap 12 P 63

Swami takes extraordinary care of us and we never want for anything. Whenever there is a need, He fills it for us. Sometimes the need is to help me get back on track, so He sends somebody, a messenger, or someone to push my buttons to let me know I still have a lot of work to do and a long way to go. But He is always there, helping and guiding me all the way home.

"Life is a pilgrimage, where man drags his feet along the rough and thorny road. With the Name of God on his lips, he will have no thirst; with the Form of God in his heart, he will feel no exhaustion. The company of the holy will inspire him to travel in hope and faith. The assurance that God is within call, that He is ever near, will lend strength to his limbs and courage to his eye.

"Remember that with every step, you are nearing God, and God too, when you take one step towards Him, takes a hundred toward you. There is no stopping place in this pilgrimage; it is one continuous journey, through day and night; through valley and desert; through tears and smiles, through death and birth, through tomb and womb. When the road ends, and the Goal is gained, the pilgrim finds that he has traveled only from himself to himself, that the way was long and lonesome, but the God that led him unto it was all the while in him, around him, and beside him! He himself was always Divine. His yearning to merge in God was but the sea calling to the Ocean! Man loves, because He is Love! He craves for melody and harmony, because He is melody and harmony. He seeks Joy, for He is Joy. He thirsts for God, for he is composed of God, and he cannot exist without Him." SSS Vol VIII Ch 1 P 3

"Prepare yourselves for a celibate and spiritual discipline from the age of 50; the five senses have to be mastered, by the time five decades of your life are over. The conclusion of six decades means that you have conquered the six foes of man: lust, anger, greed, attachment, pride and hate. When you are seventy, you must have become ready to merge with the seven sages, the seven seas and the seven colors of the solar ray; that is to say, you must be far, far above mundane desires and ideals, and as near the point of mergence as possible, through sadhana. Eighty must see you in line with the Deities that preside over the eight cardinal points, more or less Divine, in attributes and characteristics. Ninety takes you, or rather should take you to the realm of the nine planets, into the realm of the super. When man reaches the hundred mark, living out the ten decades, he must have mastered the ten senses, the five senses of action and the five senses of knowledge and become Wisdom incarnate, with no trace of action or the consequence thereof or the desire for it. He and the Absolute are One and indivisible!" SSS Vol VII B, Chap 28 P 203

Bear all and do nothing
Hear all and say nothing
Give all and take nothing
Serve all and be nothing.
Sathya Sai Baba

Bibliography

BSS	Baba - Sathya Sai
BTBOS	Baba the Breath of Sai
BV	Bhagavatha Vahini
CWSSB	Conversations with Sathya Sai Baba, John Hislop
DBB	Discourses by Bhagavan Sri Sathya Sai Baba
DBG	Discourses on Bhagavad Gita
DD	Discourses of Sathya Sai Baba, November 19-24, 1987, & Sankirtanam and Discourses during Navaratri Festival October 1988
DG	Divine Glory
Dhyanavahini	Dhyanavahini
DM	Divine Memories, Diana Baskin
FFWG	Face to Face with God, V.I.K. Sarin
FG	Finding God
GIC	Guide to Indian Culture and Spirituality
GA	Golden Age
GV	Gita Vahini
JV	Jnanavahini
JTG	Journey to God, Parts I, II, III, IV, J. Jagadeesan
LIAD	Life is a Dream, Realize It, Joy Thomas
LG	Loving God, N. Kasturi
LMSL	Let Me Sow Love, Doris May Gibson
MBAI	My Baba and I, John Hislop
PremaV	Prema Vahini
Sai Satcharita	Sai Satcharita, N.V. Gunaji
Sai Vandana	Sai Vandana
Sandeha Nivarini	Sandeha Nivarini
SBA	Sai Baba.....Avatar
Spirit & the Mind	Spirit & the Mind, Sam Sandweiss
SRBM	Summer Roses on the Blue Mountains
SS	Sananathana Sarathi
SSAL	Sathya Sai, the Avatar of Love
SSAV	Sathya Sai's Amrita Varshini
SSIB	Summer Showers in Brindavan
SC	Summer Course May 1996 Brindavan
SD	Seeking Divinity
SSN	Sathya Sai Newsletter
SSS	Sathya Sai Speaks
SSSun	Sathyam Shivam Sundaram
SSV	Sathya Sai Vahini

TEOL	The Embodiment of Love
Ten Steps to Kesava	Ten Steps to Kesava, Lightstorm
TOAR	Temple of All Religions (15th Chapter of Garuda Purana)
TOSSSB	Teachings of Sri Sathya Sai Baba
VD	Vision of the Divine, Rita Bruce
VV	Vidya Vahini

SAI TOWERS PUBLISHING
Publications List

TITLE	AUTHOR	PRICE
01. 70 QS & AS. ON PRACTICAL SPIRITUALITY AND SATHYA SAI	O. P. Vidyakar	Rs. 90
02. A COMPENDIUM OF THE TEACHINGS OF SATHYA SAI BABA (4th Ed)	Charlene Leslie-Chadan	Rs. 600
03. "ALEX" THE DOLPHIN	Lightstrom	Rs. 90
04. A JOURNEY TO LOVE (4th Ed.)	David Bailey	Rs. 180
05. A JOURNEY TO LOVE BOOK II Love & Marriage	David Bailey	Rs. 200
06. A JOURNEY TO LOVE (Spanish)	David Bailey	Rs. 375
07. A JOURNEY TO LOVE (Telugu)	David Bailey	Rs. 60
08. ANOTHER JOURNEY TO LOVE	Faye Bailey	Rs. 200
09. ASHES, ASHES WE ALL FALL DOWN	Gloria St. John	Rs. 80
10. A STORY OF INDIA AND PATAL BHUVANESWAR	Jennifer Warren	Rs. 60
11. AT THE FEET OF SAI	R. Lowenberg	Rs. 120
12. A TRYST WITH DIVINITY – In Africa	Swapna Raghu	Rs. 115
13. BAPU TO BABA	V. K. Narasimhan	Rs. 120
14. BUDO-KA - True Spiritual Warriors	Deena Naidu	Rs. 200
15. CRICKET FOR LOVE	Sai Towers	Rs. 250
16. CUTTING THE TIES THAT BIND	Phyllis Krystal	Rs. 110
17. CUTTING THE TIES THAT BIND Symbol Cards	Phyllis Krystal	Rs. 140
18. CUTTING THE TIES THAT BIND - Posters	Phyllis Krystal	Rs. 600
19. CUTTING MORE TIES THAT BIND	Phyllis Krystal	Rs. 120
20. CUTTING THE TIES THAT BIND-Work Book	Phyllis Krystal	Rs. 140
21. DA PUTTAPARTHIA PATAL BHUVANESHWAR (Italian)	Sandra Percy	Rs. 150
22. DEATHING (Indian Edition)	Anya Foos-Graber	Rs. 225
23. DISCOVERING MARTIAL ARTS	Deena Naidu	Rs. 265
24. EDUCATION IN HUMAN VALUES (3 Vols.)	June Auton	Rs. 750
25. FACE TO FACE WITH GOD	V. I. K. Sarin	Rs. 150
26. GLIMPSES OF THE DIVINE	Birgitte Rodriguez	Rs. 150
27. GLORY OF SAI PADHUKAS	Sai Towers	Rs. 100
28. GOD AND HIS GOSPEL	Dr. M. N. Rao	Rs. 120
29. GOD LIVES IN INDIA	R. K. Karanjia	Rs. 75
30. GOD DESCENDS ON EARTH	Sanjay Kant	Rs. 75
31. GOOD CHANCES (2nd Reprint)	Howard Levin	Rs. 120
32. HEART TO HEART (2nd Reprint)	Howard Levin	Rs. 120
33. HOLY MISSION DIVINE VISION	Sai Usha	Rs. 80
34. I AM I	Ratan Lal	Rs. 90
35. IN QUEST OF GOD	P. P. Arya	Rs. 120
36. JOURNEY OF GRACE	Cynthia Harris	Rs. 140

TITLE	AUTHOR	PRICE
37. KNOW THYSELF (2nd Revised Ed.)	Gerard T. Satvic	Rs. 200
38. LET ME SOW LOVE	Doris May Gibson	Rs. 120
39. LETTERS FROM A GRANDFATHER	S. K. Bose	Rs. 180
40. MESSAGES (Japanese)	Dr. M. N. Rao	Rs. 150
41. MESSAGES FROM MY DEAREST FRIEND SAI BABA	Elvie Bailey	Rs. 130
42. MIRACLES ARE MY VISITING CARDS	Erlendur Haraldsson	Rs. 180
43. MOHANA BALA SAI (Children's Book)	Sai Mira	Rs. 120
44. MUKTI THE LION FINDS HIMSELF	Regina Suritsch	Rs. 85
45. ONENESS OF DIVINITY	Ratan Lal	Rs. 100
46. PATH OF THE PILGRIM	Richard Selby	Rs. 120
47. PRASANTHI GUIDE (Revised & Updated Ed.)	R. Padmanaban	Rs. 100
48. SAI BABA AND NARA NARAYANA GUFA ASHRAM, Part III	Swami Maheswaranand	Rs. 30
49. SAI BABA GITA	Al Drucker	Rs. 200
50. SAI BABA & SAI YOGA	Indra Devi	Rs. 125
51. SAI BABA'S SONG BIRD	Lightstorm	Rs. 80
52. SAI BABA: THE ETERNAL COMPANION	B. P. Misra	Rs. 100
53. SAI HUMOUR	Peggy Mason, et. al.	Rs. 90
54. SAI NAAMAAVALI	Jagat Narain Tripathi	Rs. 90
55. SATHYA SAI'S AMRITA VARSHINI	Sudha Aditya	Rs. 75
56. SATHYA SAI'S ANUGRAHA VARSHINI	Sudha Aditya	Rs. 90
57. SAI SANDESH	Sai Usha	Rs. 50
58. SAI'S STORY	Shaila Hattiangadi	Rs. 75
59. SATVIC FOOD & HEALTH (2nd Revised Ed.)	Gerard T. Satvic	Rs. 45
60. SATVIC STORIES	Benjamin Kurzweil	Rs. 40
61. SELF REALISATION	Al Drucker	Rs. 50
62. SOURCE OF THE DREAM	Robert Priddy	Rs. 200
63. SPIRITUAL IMPRESSIONS A Bi-monthly Magazine	Sai Towers	Rs. 100
64. SPRINKLES OF GOLDEN DUST	Jeannette Caruth	Rs. 65
65. SRI SATHYA SAI BABA AND WONDERS OF HIS LOVE	John Elliott	Rs. 90
66. SRI SATHYA SAI CHALEESA	B. P. Mishra	Rs. 25
67. SRI SATHYA SAI BABA PRAYER BOOK	Sai Towers	Rs. 10
68. SRI SATHYA SAI BABA YOUNG ADULTS PROGRAMME	L. A. Ramdath	Rs. 80
69. STUDY CIRCLES FOR DIVINITY	Ross Woodward & Ron Farmer	Rs. 390
70. TEN STEPS TO KESAVA	Lightstorm	Rs. 150
71. THE ARMOUR OF SRI SATHYA SAI	O. P. Vidyakar	Rs. 10
72. THE DIVINE LEELAS OF BHAGAWAN SRI SATHYA SAI BABA	Nagamani Purnaiya	Rs. 100
73. THE GRACE OF SAI	R. Lowenberg	Rs. 120
74. THE HEART OF SAI	R. Lowenberg	Rs. 130
75. THE OMNIPRESENCE OF SAI	R. Lowenberg	Rs. 120

TITLE	AUTHOR	PRICE
76. THE PROPHECY	Barbara Gardner	Rs. 120
77. THE THOUSAND SONGS OF LORD VISHNU	Jeannette Caruth	Rs. 15
78. TOWARDS A BETTER LIFE Word Images from Sai Teachings (10 cards)		Rs. 50
79. WAITING FOR BABA	V. Ramnath	Rs. 95
80. WHO IS BABA?	Margaret Tottle-Smith	Rs. 60
81. YOU ARE GOD	Dr. M. N. Rao	Rs. 170
82. YOUR LIFE IS YOUR MESSAGE	Charlene Leslie Chaden	Rs. 225

SAI TOWERS PUBLISHING
Forthcoming Publications...

01. A COMPENDIUM OF SAI BHAJANS — R. Padmanaban
02. DIRECTORY OF MASTERS, SAINTS AND ASHRAMS IN INDIA — R. Padmanaban
03. FOUNTAIN OF LOVE
    An Overview of Sathya Sai Water Supply Project — R. Padmanaban
04. IN SEARCH OF A MIRACLE — Dr. Teri O' Brien
05. KRISHNAMURTHI AND THE FOURTH WAY — Evan Gram
06. LOVE IS MY FORM VOL. I The Advent
    Pictorial Biography of Sri Sathya Sai Baba — R. Padmanaban
07. ONE SOUL'S JOURNEY — Leni Matlin
08. VOICE OF THE AVATAR —
    Compilation of Yearwise Volumes of Discourses of Bhagawan Sri Sathya Sai Baba

NOTE: The above mentioned prices are liable to change without any prior notice.